Contemporary African Linguistics

Editors: Akinbiyi Akinlabi, Laura J. Downing

In this series:

1. Payne, Doris L., Sara Pacchiarotti & Mokaya Bosire (eds.). Diversity in African languages: Selected papers from the 46th Annual Conference on African Linguistics.

2. Persohn, Bastian. The verb in Nyakyusa: A focus on tense, aspect and modality.

3. Kandybowicz, Jason, Travis Major & Harold Torrence (eds.). African linguistics on the prairie: Selected papers from the 45th Annual Conference on African Linguistics.

4. Clem, Emily, Peter Jenks & Hannah Sande (eds.). Theory and description in African Linguistics: Selected papers from the 47th Annual Conference on African Linguistics.

5. Lotven, Samson, Silvina Bongiovanni, Phillip Weirich, Robert Botne & Samuel Gyasi Obeng (eds.). African linguistics across the disciplines: Selected papers from the 48th Annual Conference on African Linguistics.

ISSN: 2511-7726

African linguistics across the disciplines

Selected papers from the 48th Annual Conference on African Linguistics

Edited by

Samson Lotven

Silvina Bongiovanni

Phillip Weirich

Robert Botne

Samuel Gyasi Obeng

language
science
press

Lotven, Samson, Silvina Bongiovanni, Phillip Weirich, Robert Botne & Samuel Gyasi Obeng (ed.). 2019. *African linguistics across the disciplines: Selected papers from the 48th Annual Conference on African Linguistics* (Contemporary African Linguistics 5). Berlin: Language Science Press.

ISBN: 978-3-96110-212-9 (Digital)
        978-3-96110-213-6 (Hardcover)

ISSN: 2511-7726
DOI:10.5281/zenodo.3520612
Source code available from www.github.com/langsci/226
Collaborative reading: paperhive.org/documents/remote?type=langsci&id=226

Cover and concept of design: Ulrike Harbort
Typesetting: Felix Kopecky, Kenneth Steimel, Sebastian Nordhoff
Proofreading: Ahmet Bilal Özdemir, Alena Witzlack, Alexis Pierrard, Amir Ghorbanpour, Andreas Hölzl, Evans Gesure, Jeroen van de Weijer, Keith Allan, Lotta Aunio, Rosey Billington, Sreekar Raghotham, Teresa Proto, Valentin Vydrin, Yvonne Treis
Fonts: Libertinus, Libertinus Math, Arimo, DejaVu Sans Mono
Typesetting software: XƎLATEX

Language Science Press
Unter den Linden 6
10099 Berlin, Germany
langsci-press.org

Storage and cataloguing done by FU Berlin

Freie Universität Berlin

Contents

Contents

Chapter 1

Syllable structure and loanword adaptation in Fròʔò

Yranahan Traoré

Caroline Féry
University of Frankfurt

This article examines the syllable structure in Fròʔò, a dialect of Tagbana spoken in Côte d'Ivoire. In our analysis, the underlying syllable structure in Fròʔò is limited to C(C)V and V. Other surface syllable shapes, such as CVC, are the result of synchronic morphophonological processes. These processes include the formation of surface complex onsets through vowel deletion, the simplification of underlying complex onsets through liquid deletion, and the merger of bisyllabic CVCV sequences into monosyllables (CVC and CV). Evidence of these phonological process can also be found in loanwords, where syllable repairs take place.

1 Introduction

This article studies the syllable structure in Fròʔò (Tagbana), a Senoufo (Gur) language of Côte d'Ivoire (see Clamens 1952, Manessy 1962, Herault & Mlanhoro 1973, Miehe 2012, Miehe et al. 2012) and the effects that syllabic restrictions have on loanword adaptation. §2 introduces the underlying syllable structure and the basic phonotactic rules of Fròʔò. §3 discusses three resyllabification processes. First, two kinds of vowel deletion are introduced: one leading to coda emergence, and another one leading to complex onsets. The second resyllabification process is liquid deletion leading to onset simplification. §4 examines the process of merging two monosyllabic morphemes into a single syllable. §5 focuses on the way phonotactic restrictions influence loanword adaptations. §6 summarises and concludes.

Yranahan Traoré & Caroline Féry. 2019. Syllable structure and loanword adaptation in Fròʔò. In Samson Lotven, Silvina Bongiovanni, Phillip Weirich, Robert Botne & Samuel Gyasi Obeng (eds.), *African linguistics across the disciplines: Selected papers from the 48th Annual Conference on African Linguistics*, 1–28. Berlin: Language Science Press. DOI:10.5281/zenodo.3520563

Before turning to syllable structure, let us briefly introduce the phonemic inventory of Frò?ò, its lexical and grammatical tones and the nominal class system. The consonants are shown in Table 1. There are 22 consonants, 10 of which are stops and two are voiceless fricatives, but there is no voiced fricative. The 10 stops are divided into voiceless and voiced ones with five places of articulation: labial, alveolar, palatal, velar and labio-velar. Two laryngeal obstruents are present as well: [?] and [h]. Additionally, there are six sonorants, four of which are nasals. The remaining sonorants are two glides, [j] and [w], and two liquids, [l] and [r]. The Frò?ò consonant system is close to that of other Gur languages, although some differences emerge as well. For instance, voiced fricatives have been shown to exist in other Gur languages.

Table 1: Frò?ò consonants

		labial	alveolar	palatal	velar	labio–velar	glottal
Plosive	voiceless	p	t	c	k	kp	?
	voiced	b	d	ɟ	g	gb	
Fricative		f	s				h
Nasal		m	n	ɲ	ŋ		
Glide				j		w	
Lateral			l				
Rhotic			r				

Frò?ò has seven oral vowels that can be long in some environments, in particular before a heteromorphemic [r] or [l]. All vowels have nasal correspondents, except for the mid [+ATR] ones, [e] and [o], that are never nasalized; thus all in all the language shows 12 vowels, as shown in Figures 1 and 2. In this article, IPA is used (Frò?ò has no written system).

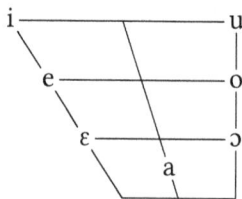

Figure 1: Short vowels

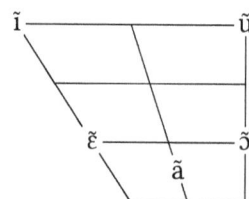

Figure 2: Nasal vowels

Fròʔò has three level tones, high (H), mid (M) and low (L). There are no contour tones. The syllable is the tone bearing unit (TBU) and every syllable in every word carries its own tone, regardless of the category and the length of the word. In other words, all vowels in the language bear one of these three tones. Some examples of (near-) minimal pairs appear in (1).[1]

Table 2: Tonal minimal pairs

H	M	L
hǔ-mǔ7 'oil'	hṵ̄-mṻ7 'worship'	hṵ́-mṵ́7 'the drink'
pà̰1 'monitor lizard	pā̰ 'to come'	
fà̰1 'bamboo tree	fā̰ 'to build'	
	jīō5 'house'	jíó 'to carry'
	kɔ̄lɔ̄ 'to cough'	kɔ́-lɔ́ 'monkey-CM1'
fìɛ̀:rɛ̀6 'the sham'	pɛ́:rɛ́ 'to sell'	

Tones play a large role in the grammatical domain, as exemplified in (1), where a change in grammatical tone signifies a change in tense/aspect/mood of the utterance.

(1)   Tonal changes due to aspect changes

    a. kí   mằ   glá̰
        PRO.OBJ PRO-2SG please
        'It will please you'

    b. kí   mǎ̰   glá̰
        PRO.OBJ PRO-2SG like
        'Did it please you?'

    c. kī   mā̰   glà̰
        PRO.OBJ PRO-2SG like
        'Make it please you!'

Combinations of tones in the nominal domain reveal the existence of floating tones in part of the vocabulary, compare (2a) with (2b). The high tone on the verb *síɔ* in (2b) is the result of a floating tone on the noun (marked with a superscript H) that spreads up to the verb.[2]

---

[1] Every noun belongs to a nominal class, see below. In the examples in Table 2, the numbers "7" and "1" indicate that the nouns belong to class 7 or class 1. The word *kɔ́-lɔ́* 'monkey' consists of a lexical root and a class marker of class 1.

[2] Thanks to Annie Rialland for working this out with us.

(2) Floating tones

    a. àtò:lò   + sī̄ɔ   → àtò:lò sī̄ɔ
       spoon-CM2   to buy
       'to buy a spoon'

    b. àblò?ò^H + sī̄ɔ   → àblò?ò síɔ́
       peanut-CM5   to buy
       'to buy a peanut'

Nouns are the result of a sequence of a lexical root and an overt or a covert class marker (CM). Table 3 provides an overview of the nominal classes in Frò?ò (see Traoré and Féry, unpublished, for nouns and nominal classes). Every noun belongs to one of seven nominal classes, which are classified according to the phonological form of their class marker and/or associated functional morphemes, i.e., the morphemes in an agreement relation with the head noun (see Corbett 1991). Six of the classes form gender pairs of singular and plural, but the nouns in class 7 are mass nouns or nouns denoting properties. This class has no corresponding plural. When the CM is covert, we do not indicate it as a CM in the gloss. The lexical root is written with its class instead, e.g., *pà̰1* 'monitor lizard' and *wótìɔ̀1* 'python'.

2 Underlying syllable structure and phonotactics

Two underling syllable structures are present in Frò?ò: the first type of syllable consists only of a nucleus (V or [n]), and the second type consists of an onset + nucleus, see (3). In the latter case, the onset can be simple or complex, consisting of maximally two consonants, thus (C)CV.

(3) Frò?ò underlying syllable structures

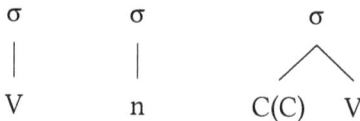

    σ   σ   σ

    | | ∧

    V   n   C(C) V

2.1 V syllable: Nucleus only

As far as syllables consisting of only a nucleus are concerned, only [a] can start a word as illustrated in (4), see Herault & Mlanhoro (1973) for the same observation for Tákpɛ̃́r, another dialect of Tagbana; [a] can be oral or nasal.[3]

---

[3]The only exception is the interjection *è.hé* 'yes, ok'.

Table 3: Overview of the nominal classes of Frò?ò and their class markers

Class markers (CM)	Examples of nouns of each class	
Class 1 (sg. of gender 1) several CM, including ∅	hō–lō elephant–CM1	wótìɔ̀1 python
Class 2 (pl. of gender 1) CM: [-hele], [-bele], -lV	hō–bēlē elephants–CM2	wótìɔ̀–hélé pythons–CM2
Class 3 (sg. of gender 2) CM: [-lV]	lā:–lā belly–CM3	kpē–lē knife–CM3
Class 4 (pl. of gender 2) CM: [-?VlV, -gele]	lā–?ālā bellies–CM4	kpē–gēlē knives–CM4
Class 5 (sg. of gender 3) CM: [-gV]/[-ŋV]/[-?V] or ∅	jē–gē month–CM5	āfɔ̃–ŋɔ̃̀ newthing–CM5
Class 6 (pl. of gender 3) CM: [-rV]	jē:–rē months–CM6	āfɔ̃:–rɔ̃̀ newthings–CM6
Class 7 (sg. of gender 4) CM: [-mV]	ɲū̃–mū̃ water–CM7	wē–bē foliage–CM7

(4)   [a]/[ã] in word-initial position

    a. ā.jlē-?è
        mirror-CM5
        'mirror'

    b. ā.wrē-?ē
        something itchy-CM5
        'something itchy'

    c. à.plè3
        'shade'

    d. ã̄.gùl
        'traditional dance'

    e. ã̄.gō-lò
        mount-CM3
        'mount'

Word-medially, all vowels can be a nucleus, see two examples in (5), each of which contains a CM consisting only of a vowel.

(5)   Vowel at hiatus position

    a. pì-ɔ̀
        child-CM1
        'child'

    b. kā.fū-ō
        sweat-CM5
        'sweat'

Word-initially, before all vowels other than [a], [h] or another consonant is needed; see (6) for words starting with [h]. In loanwords starting with a vowel, [h] is inserted word-initially, see §5.

(6) [h] initial words

    a. hē:rē
       'to press'

    b. hɔʔɔ
       'to cook'

    c. hòʔó
       'to stoop'

    d. hę́
       'where'

    e. hí-ʔí
       feather-CM5
       'feather'

    f. hú-ʔú
       thorn-CM5
       'thorn'

Syllables consisting of a nasal only are the subject of §2.4

2.2 CV syllable: onset + nucleus

All consonants can occupy the word-initial onset position except for the glottal stop [ʔ] and [r], both of which do not occur in this position. In (7), monosyllabic words are used for illustration.

(7)

a. pū̃1 'dog'	h. gū̃1 'tortoise'	o. nũ̀1 'ox'
b. bā7 'this'	i. kpē 'to take'	p. ɲĩ 'to fill'
c. tō1 'father'	j. gbò1 'gnat'	q. ŋā̃ 'this one'
d. dí: 'so, that'	k. fā̃ 'to build'	r. jō 'to say'
e. cá̃ 'to fall'	l. sē̃ 'produce'	s. wī 'him'
f. jè 'to wake up'	m. hę́ 'where'	
g. kā 'to break'	n. mì̃ 'I, me'	

Vowel lengthening is triggered by a following liquid, [r] or [l], as shown in (8). Liquids at the beginning of word final syllables often are the initial consonant of a class marker, but not always. The examples in (8) have a heteromorphemic liquid, except for (8f), in which the last syllable is part of the lexical root.

(8)   a.   lō:-rō
           mango-CM6
           'mangoes'

      b.   kā:-lā
           problem-CM3'
           'problem'

      c.   pì:-rì
           tam-tam-CM6
           'tam-tams'

      d.   pū̃:-lū̃
           dog-CM2
           'dogs'

      e.   pì:-lì
           child-CM2
           'children'

      f.   jà:.ràl
           'lion'

Not all vowels lengthen before a liquid, as shown in (9). This happens when the vowel follows [?]. In this case, it is deleted or pronounced as a short and weak vowel (see §3.2 for vowel deletion). Thus, the sequence [?VrV] blocks lengthening of the vowel following [r].

(9)   a.   fĩ?ĩ.rí
           'to frighten'

      b.   hí?ĩ.rí
           'to shiver'

      c.   ɲɔ́?ɔ́.rɔ́
           'to move'

      d.   hù?ù.rú
           'to spin'

2.3 CCV syllables: complex onset + nucleus

Consonant clusters in the onset are quite common in Frò?ò. They are mostly regulated by the sonority sequencing principle, which states that the sonority of segments rises toward the nucleus of a syllable and lowers away from it (see for example Clements 1990 for this principle). Stops are the least sonorous segments and low vowels the most sonorous ones, as illustrated in (10).

(10)   Sonority hierarchy
       Stops Fricatives Nasals Liquids Glides High vowels Low vowels
       ———→

In Frò?ò, the maximum number of consonants in the onset is two. Nearly all consonants, except for [s], [h], [r] and the glottal stop [?], can be followed by

[l] and [r]; even the glides [w] and [j] can form complex onsets with a liquid, in violation of the sonority principle, since glides are more sonorous than liquids. There is a restriction against a sequence of two coronals if the second one is the lateral, thus [tl], [dl], [nl] and [rl] do not occur as complex initial onsets.

Table 4 lists all possible word-initial complex onsets.

Table 4: Complex onsets

	p	b	t	d	c	ɟ	k	g	kp	gb	f	s	h	ʔ	m	n	ɲ	ŋ	w	j
m	-	-	-	-	-	-	+	+	-	-	-	-	-	-	-	-	-	-	-	-
l	+	+	-	-	+	+	+	+	+	+	+	-	+	-	+	-	+	+	+	+
r	+	+	+	+	+	+	+	+	+	+	+	+	-	+	+	+	+	+	+	+

Words initial complex onsets are illustrated in (11).

(11)   Complex word-initial onsets

    i. [pl]: **plɔ̀.ʔɔ̀**
        bamboo-CM5
        'bamboo'

    ii. [pr]: **prò6**
         'chip'

    iii. [bl]: **blɔ̄**
          'plowed'

    iv. [br]: **bré.ʔé**
         'to boil'

    v. [tr]: **trá.ʔá**
        'to stick up'

    vi. [dr]: **drè.ʔè**
        shift-CM5
        'shirt'

    vii. [cl]: **clɛ̄.mṹ**
         woman-CM7
         'womanhood'

    viii. [cr]: **crɛ̄.ʔɛ̄**
          'to expand'

    ix. [ɟl]: **ɟlì.ʔí**
        'wise'

    x. [ɟr]: **ɟrè.ʔɛ́**
        'to fly'

    xi. [kl]: **klã̄.ʔã̀**
        seat-CM5
        'seat'

    xii. [kr]: **krɔ.ʔɔ**
        car-CM5
        'car'

    xiii. [km]: **kmɔ́**
        'to beat'

    xiv. [gm]: **gmɔ́**
        'beaten'

    xv. [gl]: **glɛ̄.ʔè**
        tamis-CM5
        'tamise'

    xvi. [gr]: **grã̀**
        'dirty'

xvii. [kpl]: **kplɛ̀.ʔɛ̀**
former-CM5
'former'

xviii. [kpr]: **kprā.ʔā**
sugar cane-CM5
'sugar cane'

xix. [gbl]: **gblɛ̀ːr**
'beginning'

xx. [gbr]: **gbrɛ̀.ʔɛ̀**
'unripe'

xxi. [fl]: **flì.ʔì**
furuncle-CM5
'furuncle'

xxii. [fr]: **frɔ̄.ʔɔ̄**
'to scrub'

xxiii. [sr]: **srɛ́.ʔɛ́**
prayer-CM5
'prayer'

xxiv. [hl]: **hlā̃-ʔā̃**
leg-CM5
'leg'

xxv. [hr]: **hrō6**
meal
'meals'

xxvi. [ml]: **mlā̃-ʔā̃**
fight-CM5
'fight'

xxvii. [mr]: **mrũ̀.ʔũ̀**
corosol-CM5
'corosol'

xxviii. [nr]: **nrɛ̀**
root-CM6
'roots'

xxix. [ɲl] **ɲlɔ́.ʔɔ́**
'to write'

xxx. [ɲr]: **ɲrā́.ʔā́**
'to hook'

xxxi. [ŋl]: **ŋlɔ́-ʔɔ́**
dream-CM5
'dream'

xxxii. [ŋr]: **ŋrɔ̄.ʔɔ̄**
'to push'

xxxiii. [wl]: **wlɛ̀-ʔɛ̀**
day-CM5

xxxiv. [wr]: **wrē.ʔē**
'short'

xxxv. [jl]: **jlɛ̄.mɛ̄**
clean-CM7
'cleanliness'

xxxvi. [jr]: **jrā.ʔā**
thing-CM5
'thing'

Only [k] and [g] can form an initial complex onset with [m], but the segment clusters [km] and [gm] are only attested in a few words. Herault & Mlanhoro (1973) analyze them as the nasal counterparts of [kp] and [gb] when the following vowel is nasal, see examples in (12). In other words, in their analysis [km] and [gm] are allophones of underlying /kp/ and /gb/. An alternative explanation is that the vowel following [km] and [gm] is subject to nasal harmony. That explains why the following vowel is always nasal. In fact, [kp] and [gb] can be followed by a nasal vowel, and this distributional fact speaks against the allophonic nature of [km] and [gm], see the examples in (12). Word-medial complex onsets are listed in (14).

(12) a. **kmɔ́**
        'to hit'

      b. **kmã̄-ʔã̄**
        'nice'

      c. **kmɔ́.ʔɔ́-lɔ̄**
        fireplace-CM3
        'fireplace'

      d. lā.**gmã̄**.mũ̌
        belly-kind-CM7
        'kindness'

(13) a. kpɛ̃́-mũ̌
        daylight-CM7
        'daylight'

      b. kpã̌dà:-là
        funeral   yard-CM3
        'funeral yard'

      c. lāgbã̄-mũ̌
        anger-CM7
        'anger'

(14) Word-medial complex onsets
      i. [pl]: tī.**pl**ɔ̄-ʔɔ̄
          ground-CM5
          'ground'

      ii. [pr]: tì.**pr**ì-ʔì
          fresh-CM5
          'freshness'

      iii. [bl]: à.**bl**ò-ʔò
          peanut-CM5
          'peanut'

      iv. [br]: à.**br**à.ʔà
          'to bargain'

      v. [tr]: kpà.**tr**ō-ʔō
          whip-CM5
          'whip'

      vi. [dr]: kā.fĩ̄.n.**dr**ī-ʔī
          umbilical cord-CM5
          'umbilical cord'

      vii. [cl]: kā.**cl**ē-ʔē
          bone-CM5
          'bone'

      viii. [ɟl]: n.**ɟl**é.ʔè
          wall-CM5
          'wall'

      ix. [ɟr]: kɔ.**ɟr**é.lɛ́
          mangoose-CM3
          'mangoose'

      x. [kl]: tì.**kl**ɔ̀.ʔɔ̀
          'long'

      xi. [kr]: kā.**kr**ā.ʔ
          junk-CM5
          'junk'

      xii. [km]: a.**km**ɔ̄:-rɔ̀
          strike-CM6
          'the strikes'

      xiii. [gm]: la.**gm**ã̄-m(ũ̀)
          belly-kind-CM7
          'kindness'

      xiv. [gl]: hã̄.**gl**ā.ʔà
          bow-CM5
          'bow'

xv. [gr]: bà.grà-ʔà
hoe-CM5
'hoe'

xvi. [gbl]: ká̰.gblò-ʔò
cudgel-CM5
'cudgel'

xvii. [gbr] ā.gbrē.ʔē
unripe-CM5
'unripe'

xviii. [fl]: tū.flɛ̄-ʔɛ̄
wind-CM5
'wind'

xix. [fr]: kā.frɛ.ʔɛ
'to apologize'

xx. [ml]: nà̰.mā̰.ʔà̰
'name of person'

xxi. [mr]: kámrɔ̀-ʔɔ̃
agouti-CM5
'agouti'

xxii. [ŋl]: mṵ́.ŋà̰-ʔà̰
ember-CM5
'ember'

xxiii. [ɲl]: a.ɲlē-ʔē
mirror-CM5
'mirror'

xxiv. [ɲr]: ā.ɲrɔ̃-ŋɔ̃
en-CM5
'pen'

xxv. [hr]: kā.hrē-ʔè
cashew-apple-CM5
'cashew-apple'

xxvi. [wl]: kū.wlɛ̀.ʔɛ̀
'before yesterday'

xxvii. [wr]: ā.wrē-ʔē
something itchy-CM5
'something itchy'

2.4 Syllabic nasals

As mentioned above, Fròʔò has tautosyllabic complex onsets involving the nasals [n], [m], [ɲ] and [ŋ], which can be followed by liquids, except for [nl] which has been shown above to be excluded on other grounds. These clusters obey the sonority sequencing principle. Some additional examples appear in (15).

(15) Nasal-liquid onsets
a. [ml]: mlā̰-ʔā̰   b. [mr]: mrṵ̀-ʔṵ̀   c. [nr]: nrɛ̀6
   war-CM5   corosol-CM5   'root'
   'war'   'corosol'

In other cases, a nasal consonant precedes a less sonorous segment. In this case, the nasal makes a syllable on its own: syllables in Fròʔò may consist of a nasal consonant and nothing else. There is no prenasalized obstruent in Fròʔò. These syllables only appear in word-initial position. These nasals are followed by a stop (or an affricate) in the next syllable's onset, see (16) for examples.

(16)   Word-initial syllabic nasal consonants

a.	ń.klō	c.	ń.cɛ	e.	ŋ́.glɛ́ɜ
	'name of person'		'name of person'		pestle
					'pestle'
b.	ń.dā(hā)	d.	n̄.ɟlē-ʔē	f.	m̀.bìɔ
	'name of person'		wall-CM5		'ship'
			'wall'		

The structure of a nasal syllable followed by another syllable is shown in (17). It is also relevant when the second syllable has a complex onset, like in *n.klō* 'name of person'.

(17)   Syllabic nasal

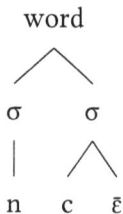

word

σ   σ

n   c   ɛ̄

When the stop following the nasal is voiced, the initial syllabic nasal assimilates to the articulator of the following stop. Before bilabial [b], the nasal is labial [m]; before [d] and [ɟ], it is coronal [n]; and before the voiced dorsal [g] and labio-dorsal [gb], it is dorsal [ŋ]. Table 5 shows the possible combinations between nasals and voiced stops word initially.

Table 5: Syllabic nasal + voiced stop

	b	d	ɟ	g	gb
m	+	–	–	–	–
n	–	+	+	–	–
ŋ	–	–	–	+	+

The feature filling process in Figure 3 assumes that the nasal consonant [N] is underlyingly unspecified for its place of articulation and that it acquires an articulator from the following stop. However, it could also be the case that the articulator of the nasal is specified as [coronal] and that it loses its coronality as a result of spreading of the articulator node.

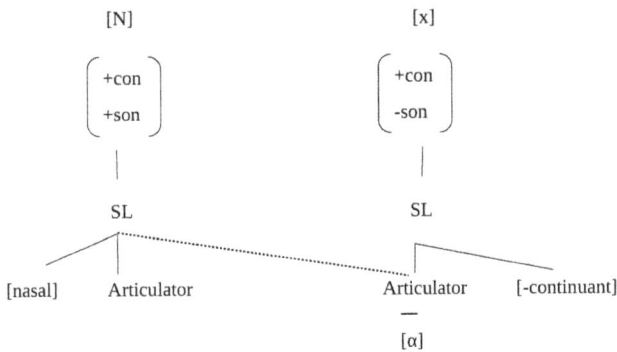

Figure 3: Consonant cluster with a nasal, where [x] stands for any plosive segment

3 Resyllabification

In some cases, the underlying syllable structures that were described in §2 are subject to modification. This section deals with the following resyllabification processes: vowel deletion of the second vowel in a sequence of two vowels in two adjacent syllables, leading to CVC syllables (§3.1); vowel deletion of the first vowel in two adjacent syllables leading to CCV syllables (§3.2); and liquid deletion, a process of onset simplification (§3.3).[4] Furthermore, Fròʔò also has a morphophonological process: two monosyllabic function words are fused into a single syllable, see §4.

3.1 Vowel deletion leading to CVC syllables

If some conditions are met, when two morphemes come together, the last vowel of the first morpheme or word deletes, and a coda is created. We refrain from calling the process "vowel syncope", since that would imply that it is an unstressed vowel that is deleted. However, there is no evidence whatever for stress in Fròʔò. Vowel deletion in Fròʔò touches all vowels equally.[5]

(18) Coda creation through vowel deletion
      CV.CV → CVC

---

[4]Vowel deletion and liquid deletion have also been documented for Syer, another Gur language, see Dombrowsky-Hahn (2015).

[5]High vowels are not deleted more easily than mid or low vowels, as is the case in the neighboring Bamana, Colloquial Bambara (see Green et al. 2014).

The result of vowel deletion appears in the third column of the examples in (19), showing a sequence of two nouns, or of a noun (or a verb) and an article or a class morpheme.

(19) Vowel deletion in the second syllable

tī.cē:.rē	+	fɔ́.lɔ́	→	tī.cē:r-fɔ́-lɔ́
'madness'		'owner-CM1'		'mad person-CM1'

tī-ʔī	+	kà	→	tīʔ-kà
'tree-CM5'		IND.ART.		'a tree'

fɛ́:.ré	+	mṹ	→	fɛ́:r-mṹ
'happy person'		CM7		'happiness-CM7'

tá.ʔá	+	IV	→	táʔ-lã́
'to walk'		CM3		'walk-CM3'

klò.ʔó	+	IV	→	klòʔ-ló
'to roll'		CM3		'fact of rolling-CM3'

pɛ́:.ré	+	IV	→	pɛ́:r-lɛ́
'to sell'		CM3		'sale-CM3'

In (20), the vowel deletion process takes place three times.

(20) kà-ʔà   + fɔ́.lɔ́   + krɔ̀ʔɔ̀   + ka   →
'village-CM5' 'chief-CM1' 'car-CM5' IND.ART.
kàʔ-fɔ́l-krɔ̀ʔ-kà
'chief of village's car'

The application of vowel deletion and subsequent coda creation are subject to three restrictions. First, the deleted vowel is identical to the preceding one. This happens when a CM is added to a lexical root, in which case it is the result of vowel harmony. The CMs are of the form CV with a specified C, dependent on the class of the noun, and an unspecified V, which is a total copy of the last vowel of the root.

In case the final vowel is prespecified and is thus not the result of vowel harmony, the final vowel cannot delete. The words in (21) are lexical roots that do not take an overt CM. Moreover, the second vowel is not identical to the first one.

(21) a. jù.gò5   b. dà̰..gò1   c. nṵ̀..bú.ó1   d. wó.tì.ɔ̀1
          'head'   'sheet'   'friend'   'python'

The second restriction is that only consonants that start a CM can become
the coda of a syllable. As a result, the sonorants [m, l, r, ŋ], the voiced stops [b]
and [g], and the glottal stop can appear in a coda after vowel deletion. All other
consonants cannot.[6]

Third, vowel deletion is blocked at the end of a sentence, see the examples in
(22). In both cases, the last vowel would delete in the sentence-internal position,
but fails to do so in sentence-final position. The words ending in a consonant in
these examples have lost their final vowel, which is always a copy of the preceding vowel.

(22) a. kàjíó:-rdā   wō   lá   dɛ? pé   nã́   tí hó?ó
          camps-CM6 REL.PRO PRO.1PL ASP show PRO.3PL to PRO.3PL burn

          'The camps that we showed to them have burned'

      b. tī-?   gā   kí   tō   nã̀dò-?   nã̀ kí   nɪ́
          tree-CM5 REL.PRO PRO.3SG fall down yam-CM5 on PRO.3SG AUX

          kpà̰   gbã̄ -ŋã̄
          big-CM5

          'The tree that has fallen down on yam is big.'

3.2 Vowel deletion leading to CCV syllables

In (23), vowel deletion applies in the first syllable of a lexical root. In such a case,
the deleted vowel is not that of a CM, but that of the root. However, it is again
identical to the following vowel. The first example (23a) shows a lexical root
plus a class marker playing the role of a nominalizer suffix. The second example
(23b) shows a derived noun plus an additional class marker playing the role of
a derivational suffix. It is conspicuous that this second vowel deletion concerns
lexical root vowels. In Frò?ò, as in other West African languages, some vowels
may be called "weak" and are subject to deletion in the right context (see Sande
2017 for similar effects in Guébié, a Kru language). Weak vowels contrast with
"strong" vowels that never delete.

---

[6] Green et al. (2014) show that in Bamana, syncope results in high sonority codas, but low sonority ones are excluded. This is not always the case in Frò?ò, although high sonority codas are
more frequent.

(23) Vowel deletion in the first syllable

wé.lé	+	?V	→	wlé-?é
'to look'		CM5		'look-CM5'
				'the look'

cɛ̃-lɛ̃	+	mũ̀	→	clɛ̃-mũ̀
'woman-CM1'		CM7		'woman-CM7'
				'womanhood'

3.3 Liquid deletion

Another resyllabification process in Frò?ò involves liquid deletion in the second position of a complex onset. The syllable structure is simplified as shown in (24): only the less sonorous first consonant C is preserved.

(24) Liquid deletion

ClV / CrV → CV

Liquid deletion takes place in the first morpheme in a sequence of two adjacent morphemes, the examples in (25) show lexical roots plus CM. In this case, liquid deletion is restricted to identical vowels separated by a CM starting with [r], as illustrated.

(25) Vowel deletion in lexical roots plus CM

a.	drɛ̃̀	+	CM6	→	dɛ̃̀:- rɛ̃̀
	bee				'bees'

b.	kàbrɛ̀	+	CM6	→	kàbɛ̀:-rɛ̀
	grasshopper				'grasshoppers'

c.	krà	+	CM6	→	kà:-rà
	file				'files'

Another context in which liquid deletion applies is a sequence of a noun and an adjective, see (26). These words are compounds consisting in two lexical roots, a nominal one and an adjectival one. The class marker is not always there, but if it is required, it is located at the end of the compound. Note that in (26a) neither *plɔ̀* nor *plè* requires a CM in isolation, and the resulting compound has no CM. The same holds for other compounds in (26). The vowels do not need to be identical. The first consonant of the adjectives is sometimes voiced. It is not clear what triggers voicing.

(26) Liquid deletion in compounds

    a.   plɔ̀   +   plè   →   **pɔ̀** -blè
        bamboo   small   'small bamboo'

    b.   krɔ̀   +   plè   →   **kɔ̀** -plè
        car   small   'small car'

    c.   hlā̃   +   klɔ̄   →   **hā̃** -glɔ̄
        leg   long   'long leg'

    d.   kámrɔ̀̃   +   kpɔ̄   →   kámɔ̀̃-gbɔ̀-ʔɔ̀
        agouti   big   'big agouti-CM5'

    e.   kāhrē   +   kē:rè   →   kāhē-gērè
        cashew   field   'field of cashew'

    f.   klō   +   kpɔ̄   →   **kō**-gbɔ̄-ʔɔ̄
        road   big   'big road-CM5'

    g.   kā.clē   +   kpɔ̄   →   kā.**cē**-gbɔ̄-ʔɔ̄
        bone   big   'big bone-CM5'

Liquid deletion also takes place if the compound is preceded by yet another lexical root, see examples in (27).

(27) Liquid deletion in nominal compounds

    a.   pìɔ   +   **pɔ-blè**   →   pìɔ.pɔ.blé
        child   small bamboo   'child's small bamboo'

    b.   tō   +   **kɔ̄.plè**   →   tō.kɔ.plè
        father   small car   'father's small car'

Liquid deletion in monosyllabic nouns without a CM is not possible. The words in (28) illustrate that in such a case, the liquid is not deleted.

(28) No liquid deletion in monosyllabic nouns

    a. klò1   + plè   → klò-plè (*kò-plè)
        country   small   'small country'

    b. klɛ̃3   + plè   → klɛ̃-plé
        post   small   'small post'

    c. krò5   + plè   → krò-plè
        rubber   small   'small rubber'

    d. plò   + plè   → plò-plè-ʔélé[7]
        plants   small   'small plants-CM4'

Liquid deletion takes place in words with a non-high vowel. A liquid preceded by a high vowel, [i] or [u], as in (29), cannot be deleted.

(29) No liquid deletion before a high vowel

    a. frù-ʔù frù:-rù   b. klù-ʔù klù:-rù   c. flì-ʔì flì :-rì
        mat-CM5 mat-CM6   way-CM5 way-CM6   spot-CM5 spot-CM6
        'mat'   'mats'   'way' 'ways'   'spot' 'spots'

Liquid deletion does not happen in verbs. In all examples, liquid deletion takes place in the first element of a compound. The second compound does not lose its liquid.

(30) No liquid deletion in the second element of compounds

    a. pìò + plò   → pìò.**plò**-ʔò *(pìò.**pò**-ʔò)
        child bamboo
        'child's bamboo'
    b. tō   + krɔ → tō.krò-ʔò
        father car
        'father's car'

4 Merging process in Fròʔò

Merging (or portmanteau building) denotes the process of making one word out of two. In Fròʔò, two independent monosyllabic function morphemes are merged

---

[7]The last noun (28d) *plò* does not have a singular equivalent.

into a single syllable, for instance two pronouns, or an auxiliary and a pronoun. The pronouns may have different functions in the sentence: subject and one or two objects for instance. There are two ways of achieving merging in Fròʔò, the first of which is fusion, resulting in a CV syllable, and the second of which is resyllabification with vowel deletion and consequent coda creation (CVC), of the same type described in §3.1

4.1 Merging as fusion

In the fusion process, only one syllable is formed out of two: the onset of the first word is preserved and the resulting vowel has features from all remaining segments. First examples appear in (31). In these fused morphemes, two mono-syllabic pronouns on the left are pronounced in one syllable, as shown to the right of the arrows. In all cases, the onset of the first pronoun is kept: these are, respectively, [k], [t], [l], [m], [w] and [p]. The fused segment is always [u] and is the result of fusing [i] from the first pronoun and [wí] from the second pronoun. In all examples, all words have a high tone, and unsurprisingly the fused morpheme also has a high tone.

(31) Fusion of two pronouns

    a. kí   wí   ɲǎ → **kú** ɲǎ
        PRO1.3SG PRO3.3SG see
        'it has seen him'

    b. tí   wí   ɲǎ → **tú** ɲǎ
        PRO1.3PL PRO3.3SG see
        'they have seen him'

    c. lí   wí   ɲǎ → **lú** ɲǎ
        PRO2.3SG PRO3.3SG see
        'it has seen him'

    d. mĩ́   wí   ɲǎ → **mṹ**ɲǎ
        PRO.1SG PRO3.3SG see
        'I have seen him'

    e. wí   wí   ɲǎ → **wṹ**ɲǎ
        PRO3.3SG PRO3.3SG see
        'he has seen him'

    f. pí   wí   ɲǎ → **pú** ɲǎ
        PRO4.3SG PRO3.3SG see
        'they have seen him'

Yranahan Traoré & Caroline Féry

The features involved in the fusion process are illustrated in (32) and (33). The features of the resulting vowel are a compromise between the features of the original vowels and [w], the initial consonant of the second pronoun. Since both vowels are [+high], this feature is kept. The feature [labial] of [w] is translated into vocalic [round] and [round] in Fròʔò only appears on back vowels. For this reason, [i] becomes [u] in the fused version.

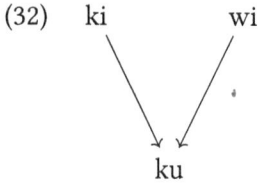

(32)   ki   wi

       ku

(33)   Features of the fused segments [i], [w] and [i]

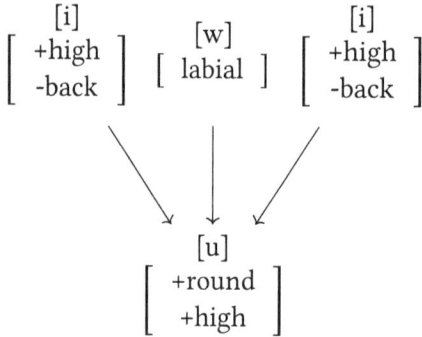

$$
\begin{bmatrix} +\text{high} \\ -\text{back} \end{bmatrix} \quad [\ \text{labial}\ ] \quad \begin{bmatrix} +\text{high} \\ -\text{back} \end{bmatrix}
$$

[i]   [w]   [i]

[u]
$$
\begin{bmatrix} +\text{round} \\ +\text{high} \end{bmatrix}
$$

However, the fused vowel is not always [u]. In (34), it is [ɔ], the result of fusing [ã] and [i]. Notice that [o] cannot be nasalized and [ɔ̃] is used instead.

(34)   mã́   wí   ɲà̰ → mɔ̃́ ɲ à̰
       PRO.2SG PRO3.3SG see
       'you have seen him'

In this case, a compromise is needed between [low] from [ã] and [+high] from [i]. The result is the mid back vowel [ɔ̃], a round nasal segment by default. Nasality of the first word is preserved, and height is a compromise. As before [round] is derived from the labiality of the glide [w].

20

(35)   Features of the fused segments [a], [w] and [i]

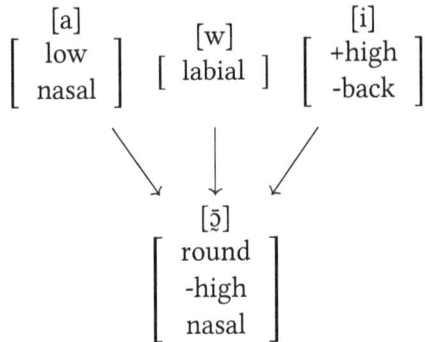

$$
\begin{bmatrix} \text{low} \\ \text{nasal} \end{bmatrix} \quad [\text{labial}] \quad \begin{bmatrix} +\text{high} \\ -\text{back} \end{bmatrix}
$$

[a]   [w]   [i]

$$
\begin{bmatrix} \text{round} \\ -\text{high} \\ \text{nasal} \end{bmatrix}
$$

[ɔ̃]

Further examples of fused morphemes appear in (36).

(36)   a.   pé   wí   ɲà̰ → pó ɲà̰
            PRO3.3PL PRO3.3SG see
            'they have seen him'

       b.   ké   wí   ɲà̰ → kó ɲà̰
            PRO3.3SG PRO3.3SG see
            'they have seen him'

In (37), two monosyllabic pronouns *pé* 'they' and *wí* 'him, her' are fused. The fusion segments are [é] from the first pronoun and [wí] the second pronoun and the result of the fusion is [ó], again a back vowel in order to keep the feature [labial] from [w].

(37)   Features of the fused segments [é], [w] and [í]

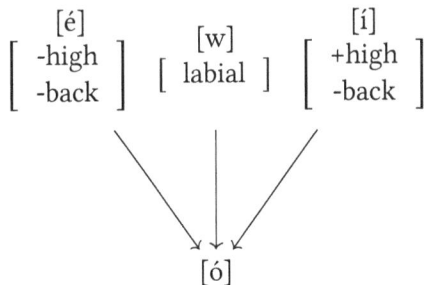

$$
\begin{bmatrix} -\text{high} \\ -\text{back} \end{bmatrix} \quad [\text{labial}] \quad \begin{bmatrix} +\text{high} \\ -\text{back} \end{bmatrix}
$$

[é]   [w]   [í]

[ó]

4.2 Merging as resyllabification with vowel deletion

Fusion of the kind illustrated in §4.1 is not always a possible outcome. In the following examples, it is still the case that two monosyllabic function words are fused into one, and the result is thus a portmanteau word in each case, but the process is different: the onset of the second morpheme becomes the coda of the syllable made by the first morpheme. The examples in (38) show how the lateral [l] of the object pronoun *lí* becomes the coda of the syllable of the first pronoun. A similar process of vowel deletion was already illustrated in §3.1 An important difference is now that the deleted vowel does not need to be identical to the preceding one, see (38f).

(38) Fusion of two pronouns leading to a syllable with coda: CV + CV → CVC

    a. kī   lí   ɲǎ → kíl ɲǎ
       PRO1.3SG PRO3.3SG see
       'it has seen hit'

    b. tī   lí   ɲǎ → tíl ɲǎ
       PRO1.3PL PRO3.3SG see
       'they have seen hit'

    c. lī   lí   ɲǎ → líl ɲǎ
       PRO2.3SG PRO3.3SG see
       'it has seen hit'

    d. wī   lí   ɲǎ → wíl ɲǎ
       PRO3.3SG PRO3.3SG see
       'he has seen him'

    e. kē   lí   ɲǎ → kél ɲǎ
       PRO2.3PL PRO3.3SG see
       'they have seen him'

    f. pē   lí   ɲǎ → pél ɲǎ
       PRO3.3PL PRO3.3SG see
       'they have seen him'

5 Loanwords

Loanwords are a good place to verify the generalizations obtained for constraining the syllable structure of a language. They validate syllable structural processes in Frɔʔɔ that have been discussed in the previous sections of this article.

Loanword phonologies have received much attention in the last decades, see for instance Itô & Mester (1995), Peperkamp & Dupoux (2003) and others. They shape the phonological structure of new words entering the language and impose native phonotactic and segmental constraints on them. Speakers of a language confronted with the task of articulating foreign words adjust the phonological shape of these words to render them more native. This implies that the segments of foreign words need to be adapted to the native phonemic inventory in case they are not there from the start. Moreover, and this is what we are primarily interested in here, the constraints on the syllable structure of the borrowing language needs to be respected. Silverman (1992) made a distinction between two adaptation tasks: at the "perceptual level", the acoustic input, or the acoustic image that the speaker has of the foreign word, is interpreted as a string of native segments. At the "operative level", all segments are assigned licit positions in the syllables. However, the two levels are not always clearly separated from each other. An illicit consonant in the coda for instance can be accommodated in (at least) two ways: either it is replaced by a licit consonant that may happen to be similar to the original one. An illicit consonant in the coda for instance can be accommodated. For example, it could be replaced by a licit consonant that may happen to be similar to the original one, the syllable structure could be repaired by adding a vowel so that the illicit coda is adapted as the onset of a new syllable, or the coda could be deleted altogether. Consider first the examples in (39) showing how French words starting with [r] are adapted in Frò?ò.

(39) Loanwords: French → Frò?ò
    a. i. radio [ʁadio] → [ā.rā.jíó] 'radio'
       ii. rateau [ʁato] → [à.rà.tō]/[hrā.tō] 'rake'
    b. i. robot [ʁobo] → [hò.rò.bó]/[hrō.bō] 'robot'
       ii. regarder [ʁəgaʁde] → [hē.rē.gā.dé]/[hrē.gā.de] 'to look'
       iii. Rémis [ʁemi] → [hē.rē.mî]/[hrē.mî] 'name'
    c. i. route [ʁut] → [hrú.tì] 'road'

When the word starts with [ʁ] in French, its equivalent [r] is disallowed word-initially in Frò?ò. Three repair options are available, as shown in (40) and (41). If [a] is the first vowel of the first syllable, this vowel is copied and added word-initially, see (40a). If the vowel is not [a], the vowel is also copied and added word-initially, but in this case, [h] is also added, before the vowel, as in (40b). Alternatively, only [hr] is realized, the vowel is not copied, see (40c).

(40) Repair processes for words with a word-initial [r]
    a. ʁa → a.ra (ā.rā.jíó)
    b. rV → hV.rV (hò.rò.bó)
    c. rV → hrV (hrú.tì)

Word-internal coda [ʁ] is repaired in at least two ways, as shown in (41). It can elide, like in the words in (41a). Alternatively, it becomes the onset of a syllable containing an epenthetic vowel identical to the preceding one, see in (41b).

(41)   Word-internal coda [r] repairs

    a.   [ʁ] is deleted word-finally:

        i.   corde [kɔʁd(ə)] → [kɔ́ː.dì] 'rope'

        ii.   porte [pɔʁt(ə)] → [pɔ́ː.tì] 'door'

        iii.   écorce [ekɔʁs(ə)] → [hè.kɔ́ː.sì] 'peel'

    b.   Word-internal vowel epenthesis: [ʁ] becomes an onset:

        i.   carcasse [kaʁkas] → [kà.rà.ká.sì] 'carcass'

        ii.   calme [kalm(ə)] → [ká.lá.mũ̀] 'calm'

It was shown above that word final codas with a low sonority are not allowed in Frɔ̀ʔɔ̀. In adapting words from French containing such codas, an epenthetic vowel is added word finally, as shown in (42). The epenthetic vowel is a high vowel alternating between [i] and [u]. [i] is preferred after front vowels and [u] after back vowels.

(42)   Epenthesis of [i] or [u]

    a.   i.   Yvette [ivɛt] → [hí.vétì] 'name'

        ii.   Frãk [fʁãk] → [frã́.kì] 'name'

        iii.   hirondelle [iʁɔdɛl] → [hì.rɔ̃́.dé.lì] 'swallow'

        iv.   aigle [ɛgl(ə)] → [hé.glì] 'eagle'

        v.   maître [mɛtʁ(ə)] → [métrì] 'teacher'

    b.   i.   robe [ʁɔb] → [hɔ́.rɔ́.bù] 'dress'

        ii.   rose [ʁoz] → [hó.ró.(z)sù] 'rose'

In sum, the syllable restrictions shown in §2 lead to a tendency of transforming vowel initial loanwords from French into Frɔ̀ʔɔ̀ words by adding an initial [h]. An initial [r] is repaired in diferent ways. Moreover, syllables with a disallowed coda in Frɔ̀ʔɔ̀ are adapted into the language with an epenthetic final vowel.

Loanwords are also frequently adapted from Bambara, a neighboring Manding language.[8] Two nouns from Bambara can combine and lead to a single word

---

[8] The Manding people come from West Africa. They are known by different names such as Bambaras in Mali, Dioulas in Côte d'Ivoire and Burkina Faso, and Malinkés in Guinea, Senegal and Gambia.

in Frò?ò, see examples in (43). The monomorphemic words of Bambara are reinterpreted in Frò?ò as consisting of a lexical root plus a CM. When they combine to form a compound, the second syllable of each word is deleted, and a CM5 is added. The onset of the CM5 is an epenthetic glottal stop.

(43)   Bambara → Frò?ò
    a. ně.ŋɛ̌ + dà.gá → ně.dá-?á
       'iron' 'pot'   iron pot-CM5
       'iron pot'
    b. kǔ.ŋǔ + tí.gí   → kǔ.dì-?ì
       'head' 'owner'   person.in.charge-CM5
       'person in charge'

In (44a) the second syllable of the Bambara noun has a disallowed coda which is deleted in the adaptation process. The example (44b) shows vowel deletion in the first syllable: a trisyllabic noun becomes disyllabic and the second syllable is now a CM. It is class 1 because it is a loanword, and loanwords often are of class 1.

(44)   a. bà.ràn.dá → bà.rā1
       'banana' banana
    b. sā.rā.kā → srā.?ā
       'aumône' aumône.CM1

Other loanwords from Bambara are not modified in Frò?ò.

(45)   sɛ́.bɛ́
    'book'

(46)   bè.sé
    'machete'

As to the question of the phonological theory of loanword adaptations vs. repairs as phonetically-based perceptual adaptations, it may well be the case they are both justified in their assumptions, but that they apply to different cases. The perceptual analysis (Peperkamp & Dupoux 2003) makes sense for speakers who are largely monolingual and do not have any plasticity in the use of several languages. Its defenders take for instance allophony between [r] and [l] in Japanese and Korean to be an explanation of loanword adaptation in terms of phonetic deafness, leading speakers to recode nonnative sounds as native ones during perception. This allophony is part of the core native phonology of Japanese (Itô & Mester 1995). The phonological perspective assumes that the phonological forms of loanwords are computed by the phonological grammar of the borrowing language, leading to massive repairs and restructuring.

However, Frò?ò speakers are confronted with a multitude of languages on a daily basis. They are surrounded by other Tagbana dialects, Manding, Baolé, Nouchi, French in at least two varieties (standard and popular) and often more, all languages with different phonological systems. It can be plausibly assumed that their perception is finely tuned. The perceptual view makes the implausible assumption that the speakers literally hear an entire syllable *hé* at the beginning of *regarder*. Rather, pronouncing this word in Frò?ò forces speakers to adapt to the phonotactic pattern of their own language.

A final question that is too often ignored is how we measure similarity between the original word in the source language and the loanword. In Frò?ò, the number of syllables only plays a subordinate role (we saw that deletion of segments is a frequent process, changing the number of syllables), and the segmental configuration of the syllables is also very important. This paper has only scratched the surface of what is to be discovered in Frò?ò.

6 Conclusion

This short paper investigated the intricate syllable structure conditions found in Frò?ò, a dialect of Tagbana. First, the phonotactic conditions regulating the very simple underlying syllable structure were examined. Two syllable structures are allowed in Frò?ò: syllables containing only a vowel or a nasal (nucleus-only syllables), and syllables with an onset (CV or CCV syllables). Word-initially, [a] is the only vowel that can appear in a V syllable, all other vowels need an onset consonant. All consonants can appear word-initially except for [r] and [?]. We suspect that [r] is associated to two syllabic positions and thus needs a preceding segment to satisfy its double association, see Fanselow et al. (In preparation) for detail. As for the glottal stop, it is an epenthetic consonant inserted between two identical vowels. In a second step, the conditions of resyllabification were discussed. Here we showed that three processes are active that cause both more complex and simplified syllables: first, vowel deletion that engenders syllables with a coda, second vowel deletion that engenders syllables with a complex onset, and third, liquid deletion leading to simpler onsets. Next, the process of merging two monosyllabic function words was the subject of §4. It was shown there that if the onset of the second function words is the glide [w], fusion can take place. Fusion is the process of making only one syllable out of two monosyllabic function words. The initial consonant of the first word is left unchanged, and the resulting vowel is a compromise between the features of the remaining segments. If fusion is not possible because of incompatible features, the vowel of the second word is deleted and the result of merging is a syllable with a coda. In the last section, loanwords were addressed. It was shown there that the syllable structure of loanwords is adapted to the syllable's constraints that have been described in the preceding sections of the paper.

Abbreviations

AUX	Auxiliary
CM	Class Marker
OBJ	Object
PL	Plural
PRO	Pronoun
REL.PRO	Relative Pronoun
SG	Singular

Acknowledgements

Our heartfelt thanks go to the organizers of the 48th ACAL conference in Bloomington, Indiana, and to two anonymous reviewers. We also thank Beata Moskal for many useful comments and for checking our English. This research was funded by the Graduate School "Nominal Modification" (DFG 2016) located in Frankfurt, Germany.

References

Clamens, R. P. 1952. Essai de grammaire senufo tabwana. *Bulletin de l'Institut francophone de l'Afrique Noire* 4(XIV). 1402–1465.

Clements, George N. 1990. The status of register in intonation theory: Comments on the papers by Ladd and by Inkelas and Leben. In *Papers in labratory phonology: Between the grammar and physics of speech*, vol. 1, 58–71.

Corbett, Greville G. 1991. *Gender*. Cambridge: Cambridge University Press.

Dombrowsky-Hahn, Klaudia. 2015. A grammar of Syer (Western Karaboro, Senufo). *Köln: Rüdiger Köppe*.

Fanselow, Gisbert, Caroline Féry & Yranahan Traoré. In preparation. *Object position in Tagbana*. University of Potsdam & University of Frankfurt.

Green, Christopher R., Stuart Davis, Boubacar Diakite & Karen Baertsch. 2014. On the role of margin phonotactics in Colloquial Bamana complex syllables. *Natural Language & Linguistic Theory* 32(2). 499–536.

Herault, G. & J. Mlanhoro. 1973. Le tàkpér (tagbana de Niakaramandougou): esquisse phonologique et corpus lexical. In *Annales de l'université d'abidjan, série H: linguistique*, vol. 6, 133–178.

Itô, Junko & Armin Mester. 1995. Japanese phonology. In John Goldsmith (ed.), *Quantificational topics: A scopal treatment of exceptional wide scope phenomena*, vol. 107-185, 817–838. Oxford: Blackwell.

Manessy, Gabriel. 1962. *Observations sur la classification nominale dans les langues négro-africaines du Soudan et de la Guinée*. Vol. 57 (Bulletin de la Société de Linguistique de Paris). C. Klincksieck.

Miehe, Gudrun. 2012. Tagbana (tagwana). In Gudrun Miehe, Brigitte Reineke & Kerstin Winkelmann (eds.), *Noun class systems in Gur languages*, vol. 9. Köln: R. Köppe.

Miehe, Gudrun, Brigitte Reineke & Kerstin Winkelmann (eds.). 2012. *Noun class systems in Gur languages*. Vol. 9. Köln: R. Köppe.

Peperkamp, Sharon & Emmanuel Dupoux. 2003. Reinterpreting loanword adaptations: the role of perception. In *Proceedings of the 15th international congress of phonetic sciences*, vol. 367, 370.

Sande, Hannah L. 2017. *Distributing morphologically conditioned phonology: three case studies from Guébie*. University of California at Berkeley dissertation.

Silverman, Daniel. 1992. Multiple scansions in loanword phonology: Evidence from Cantonese. *Phonology* 9. 298–328. DOI:10.1017/S0952675700001627

Chapter 2

Variable word-final vowel deletion and reduction in Gurmancema: A maximum entropy model

Maggie Baird

Dartmouth College

Gurmancema (Gur, Burkina Faso) displays an overall dispreference for word-final tense vowels phrase-medially. On the surface, there is vowel reduction and vowel deletion, which vary both across and within phonological contexts. This work will provide an overview of the complex data patterns and describe a weighted constraint approach to the data patterns using a Maximum Entropy Harmonic Grammar. Weighted constraints are preferred to ranked constraints due to variability in the data and to account for cases of constraint ganging, including superadditivity.

1 Introduction

Gurmancema (ISO 639-3: gux), also known as Gulmancema, Gourmanchema, or Gourmanché, is a Gur language spoken in Burkina Faso, Togo, Benin, and Niger. It has approximately 1 million speakers across this region (Simons & Fennig 2017). Primarily a spoken language, there is much dialectal variation across speakers in different villages and areas. Gurmancema is an SVO language with three tones (H, M, L).

Gurmancema has a five vowel system /a, e, i, o, u/. In this paper, I take these five phonemic vowels to be [+tense] and the allophone [ə] to be [–tense].[1] /aː, iː, uː/ are phonemic in Gurmancema and contrast with /a, i, u/. There are conflicting

---

[1]The feature [tense] is used for convenience to distinguish peripheral vowels from the central vowel [ə] and is not meant to make theoretical claims about the [tense] status of these vowels. The markedness constraints IDENT[tense] has a weight of 0 in the model and does not change the analysis.

Maggie Baird. 2019. Variable word-final vowel deletion and reduction in Gurmancema: A maximum entropy model. In Samson Lotven, Silvina Bongiovanni, Phillip Weirich, Robert Botne & Samuel Gyasi Obeng (eds.), *African linguistics across the disciplines: Selected papers from the 48th Annual Conference on African Linguistics*, 29–46. Berlin: Language Science Press. DOI:10.5281/zenodo.3520567

accounts of whether the long vowels /eː, oː/ are also phonemic.[2] There is also debate over which diphthongs are phonemic in the language. My analysis only makes reference to short, word-final monophthongs, so I remain agnostic.

Table 1 shows the consonant inventory of Gurmancema for the dialect of study in this paper. See §4 for more information about the dialect in question.

Table 1: Consonant Inventory of Gurmancema

	Labial	Alveolar	Palatal	Velar	Labiolvelar	Glottal
Stop	p, b	t, d	c, ɟ	k, g	k͡p, g͡b	
Fricative	f	s				h
Nasal	m	n	ɲ	ŋ	ŋ͡m	
Liquid		l				
Tap		ɾ				
Glide	w		j			

§2 of this paper describes the complex data patterns in question in this study. In §3, I will discuss previous work in Gurmancema and on similar patterns of vowel deletion. §4 describes the data collection and analysis process. §5 presents a constraint-based analysis of a few illustrative phonological environments. In §6, I will summarize my findings.

2 Data presentation

In Gurmancema, word-final vowels in verbs and nouns are often deleted or reduced to [ə] in phrase-medial position. The surface representation of these vowels depends on many factors, including the sound that follows them. For example, in cases of vowel hiatus, the word-final vowel of the first word is always deleted, shown in (1):

(1) /súnd-i   à=bób=à/   [súnd àbóbà]
    forget-ASP CL.PL=jug=CL.PL
    'forgets jugs'

The behavior of the word-final vowel also depends on the sound that precedes it. For example, the vowels /a, i, o/ all reduce to [ə] when preceded by an obstruent, shown in (2):

---

[2] For grammars containing phoneme inventories and justifications, see Chantoux (1968) and Naba (1994).

(2) a. /kì=bé=ga   pwá/   [kìbégə pwá]
         CL.SG=child=CL.SG hit

         'child hits'

     b. /ti=k͡pén=dì   pwá/   [tik͡pendə̀ pwá]
         CL.SG=sauce=CL.SG hit

         'sauce hits'

     c. /o=ŋumb=o   pwá/   [oŋumbə pwá]
         CL.SG=donkey=CL.SG hit

         'donkey hits'

As can be seen, many factors come together to influence the surface representation of underlying vowels, not just what sound precedes or follows the vowel. Different vowels behave differently in the same context. /i/ reduces to [ə] when preceded by an approximant (3a), but /a/ will surface as [a] in the same immediate phonological environment (3b).

(3) a. /da=lì   pwá/   [dalə̀ pwá]
         friend=CL.SG hit

         'friend hits'

     b. /a=bé=la   pwá/   [abéla pwá]
         CL.PL=child=CL.PL hit

         'children hit'

To complicate matters, certain patterns in Gurmancema are categorical, while others are variable. In (2), I showed that /a, i, o/ categorically reduce to [ə] when preceded by obstruents, but the vowel /u/ shows a variable pattern. The percentages and token counts are from the sample included in this paper, which consists of data elicited from one speaker.

(4) a. /bú=tí=bu   k͡pá/   [bútíbu k͡pá] (67%, $n = 3$)
         CL.SG=tree=CL.SG kill   [bútíbə k͡pá] (33%, $n = 3$)

         'tree kills'

     b. /kú=dá=gu   k͡pá/   [kúdágu k͡pá] (67%, $n = 3$)
         CL.SG=wood=CL.SG kill   [kúdágə k͡pá] (33%, $n = 3$)

         'wood kills'

As these examples show, this is a case of token variation, where the same word can be pronounced differently on different occasions with no change in meaning.

Word-final vowels preceded by the bilabial nasal also show a variable pattern, which is not only predictable by the CV combination, but also takes into account the first consonant of the next word. When the next word begins with a bilabial consonant, the vowel varies between reduction and deletion, but when the consonant has a different place of articulation, the vowel is much more likely to reduce.

(5) a. /mí=ɟe=má   pwá/   [míɟem pwá] (67%, *n* = 6)
         CL.SG=food=CL.SG hit   [míɟemə́ pwá] (33%, *n* = 6)

     'food hits'

     b. /mí=ɟe=má   k͡pá/   [míɟemə́ k͡pá] (88%, *n* = 32)
         CL.SG=food=CL.SG kill   [míɟem k͡pá] (12%, *n* = 32)

     'food kills'

(6) lays out the general data patterns presented above:

(6) V + # + V   deletion of the first vowel
     Obstruent + /a, i, o/ + # + C   reduction of the vowel
     Obstruent + /u/ + # + C   variation between reduction and deletion
     Non-nasal sonorant + /i/ + # + C   reduction of the vowel
     Non-nasal sonorant + /a/ + # + C   no reduction or deletion
     /m/ + /a, i, o/ + # + Non-Bilabial C   reduction of the vowel
     /m/ + /a, i, o/ + # + Bilabial C   variation between deletion and reduction

There are several environments which are not included in this analysis. /e/-final words are morphologically distinct and involve a different set of constraints than is presented below. Other environments, such as non-nasal sonorant + /o, u/, and /m/ + /u/ are missing due to a lack of data.

In this paper, I will walk through a constraint-based analysis that models all of these patterns and also accounts for the variation. Vowel reduction and deletion have been noted in the literature on Gurmancema, but never fully analyzed including variation. The model incorporates 13 constraints and necessitates supper-additivity (Albright et al. 2008; Green & Davis 2014) to account for the patterns in the most economical way.

3 Previous work

In the literature on Gurmancema, there is not a complete account of vowel deletion and variation. Naba (1994) notes that three authors have touched on issues of reduced vowels from a phonotactic perspective, but they all have different analyses. He says that too little attention has been paid to elision, apocope, and assimilation and that the description and analysis of these phenomena are very important for tonal and morphological reasons.

The only work focusing specifically on vowel deletion and reduction is Rialland (1980; 2001). She labels the process "vowel punctuation and deletion", arguing that there are weak and strong forms of words. Strong forms occur at the ends of phrases, where word-final vowels are maintained. In weak position, or phrase-medially, she argues that vowels are deleted and an epenthetic [i] is inserted to prevent illicit consonant clusters. She argues that these processes do not affect monosyllabic words. In Rialland (2001), she elaborates that monosyllabic words are slightly lengthened. Her paper does not attempt a constraint-based analysis – I will argue that these frameworks are better suited to representing the data than rule-based phonology.

Across Niger-Congo languages, vowel elision is also common as a repair for vowel hiatus. Across word boundaries, the first vowel is always deleted (Casali 1997), which holds true for Gurmancema. Although this is one aspect of the vowel-deletion process in Gurmancema, vowels do not only delete in hiatus contexts in Gurmancema, as can be seen in the examples in (5). There is no process analagous to the word-final vowel reduction in Gurmancema that I could find in the Niger-Congo literature.

4 Data collection and analysis

All of the data in this paper are based on the speech of a 37-year-old female speaker from the village of Mahadaga, currently living in France. All data were elicited in summer 2016. I designed an elicitation plan with the aim of obtaining every possible CV#C combination in the language across Subject-Verb and Verb-Object boundaries. I also elicited data in other syntactic conditions, such as relative clauses and Adjective-Noun pairings, but this paper will focus solely on the Subject-Verb and Verb-Object interfaces. There were restrictions on phonemic distribution, however, as Gurmancema has multiple noun classes, marked by proclitics and enclitics. Nouns only begin and end with certain sounds, with a few exceptions. I created an elicitation plan that included 26 nouns used as subjects, with 25 different CV endings. I elicited 20 transitive verbs and 4 intransitive verbs with each of the subjects. Verbs had to vary with both the initial consonant and the final CV, and I attempted to include as many environments as possible at both edges.

This study aims to provide a phonological analysis grounded in acoustic phonetics rather than perception. The informing data were not field notes, but rather the database of acoustic measurements. I tagged every word-final vowel (*n* = 3855) in my Gurmancema sample for important values: the vowel (a, e, i, o, u), the preceding phoneme, the following phoneme, the role in the sentence (S, V, O), the surface form (maintained, reduced, deleted), whether it was followed by a pause, the length of the vowel in seconds (3 decimal points), and F1, F2, and F3. All phonetic measurements were made in Praat (Boersma & Weenick 1996) by hand. Given the large number of attributes I was tracking, I did not find a script that I thought would be more efficient than taking measurements by hand. I took formant measurements at the middle of the vowel in the most stable portion of the formants. There is a possibility for human error and measurement variation, but taking formant measurements by hand allowed me to evaluate any problematic data points individually. Formant measurements were taken for a total of 3855 vowels, including diphthongs (*n* = 200) and phrase-final vowels (*n* = 1297), which were not included in the final analysis. Phrase-final vowels were not included as the reduction and deletion processes do not apply at the end of phrases. I also did not analyze any pre-pausal data from slow speech. The goal of this study was to model naturalistic speech and not have any confounding effects from pauses.

I used formant measurements to determine whether a vowel was maintained or reduced. I took a sample of canonically maintained vowels and took mutually exclusive ranges in F1 and F2 to determine whether the more ambiguous cases were maintained or reduced. The results of my phonetic analysis show that there is one central reduced vowel [ə], which can be seen in Figure 1. Although schwa does seem to overlap with the vowels /o/ and /u/, none of the cases where [ə] is that far back and high are underlyingly /o/ and /u/. These are cases of reduced /i/ and /a/.

Throughout the analysis, the term "prevocalic consonant" refers to the consonant that is in penultimate position of the given word (i.e. the onset of the final syllable). The term "following consonant" refers to the first consonant of the following word.

For example, in the phrase /kìbéga pwá/ 'child hits', the prevocalic consonant is /g/ and the following consonant is 'p'.

In general, there are three surface forms for vowels. If a vowel surfaces the same in the output and the input, I will refer to it as "maintained." If a vowel surfaces as [ə], I will refer to it as "reduced." If a vowel is deleted, I refer to it as "deleted."

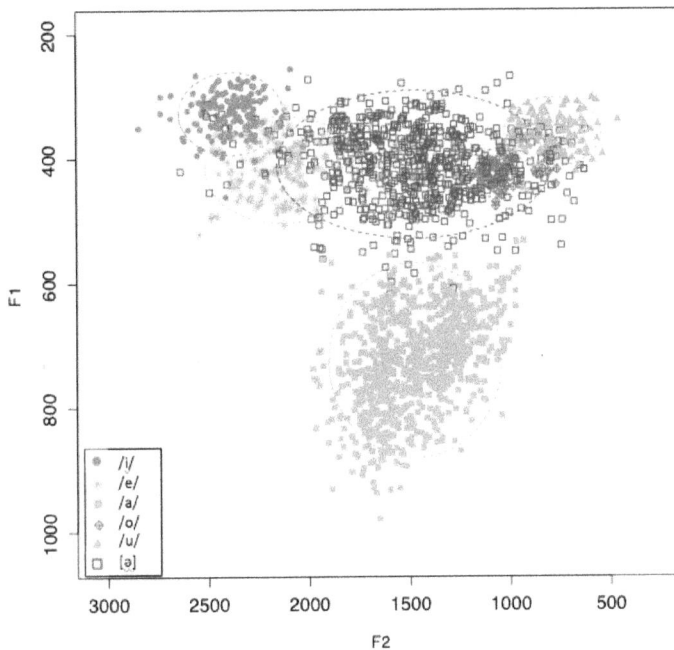

Figure 1: Plot of maintained vowels and schwa in Gurmancema. Note: Ellipses mark standard deviations from the mean formant values of each vowel.

5 Constraint-based analysis

In this section, I will explain the model I used to analyze the data.

5.1 Maximum Entropy Harmonic Grammar

Due to the complex and variable nature of the process, these data are well-suited to a constraint-based analysis. A major component of the complexity in the Gurmancema data is the free variation, which necessitates a stochastic constraint-based model. In this paper, I use Maximum Entropy Harmonic Grammar (MaxEnt), which captures patterns of variation (Goldwater & Johnson 2003; Hayes & Wilson 2008).

In MaxEnt, each candidate receives as score, which is calculated the same way as Harmony in traditional Harmonic Grammar (HG), by summing the weights of violations incurred. The calculation of the score h(x) is as follows:

(7) $h(x) = \sum_{i=1}^{N} w_i C_i(x)$

w_i is the weight of the *i*th constraint, $C_i(x)$ is the number of times x violates the *i*th constraint, and the sum is the summation over all constraints in the model.

The MaxEnt grammar tool (Wilson et al. 2008) optimizes all of the constraints and assigns each of them weights that can most closely match the observed probabilities of each candidate. Essentially, the probability of any given candidate is calculated from its score in comparison to the scores of all the candidates. For example, if each of two candidates have a score of 1, they will have a probability each of 0.5, so they will each be selected 50% of the time by speakers as they are equally well-formed.

The probability $P(x)$ is calculated as follows based on all the possible forms in Ω:

(8) $\quad P(x) = \dfrac{\exp(-h(x))}{Z}$, where $Z = \sum_{y \in \Omega} \exp(-h(y))$

The base of the natural logarithm e is raised to the negative of the score, and the probability is calculated over all possible forms.

5.2 Fitting the model

I split my data into unique CV#C combinations, and entered each with its observed probabilities into the learner. The model input consists of a set of constraints, an underlying form, and several (usually 2–6) plausible output candidates, each with observed probability computed from my phonetic analysis. In total, I entered 364 unique tableaux into the MaxEnt Grammar Tool, with standard settings. The model generates weights for each of the constraints that yield the probabilities closest to the observed probabilities. In total, the model required 13 constraints to model the patterns observed in the data.

5.3 Initial constraints

In this section, I will present the initial constraints that are the minimum set to account for the simplest data patterns. As I go through the different patterns in more detail, I will describe and add any other necessary constraints. A full list of constraints and their final weights can be found in §5.8.

Other models for reduction and deletion often attribute vowel reduction and deletion to prosodic motivators. In Gurmancema, it is the word-final position that is targeted for reduction and deletion regardless of tone or stress (which does not appear to be a salient prosodic feature of the language). For this reason, the constraint I am using to explain this pattern is simply a markedness constraint targeting word-final tense vowels in the language. All data in this paper are phrase-medial, so each constraint is assumed to be phrase-bounded.

The overall dispreference for word-final tense vowels is captured by the markedness constraint NoFINALTENSEVOWEL:

(9)   NoFINALTENSEVOWEL (*[+tns]#): Assign a violation for every word-final tense vowel

The repairs triggered to satisfy *[+tns]#, either by reducing a word-final vowel or deleting it, come with faithfulness violations. By reducing a vowel from any of the phonemic vowels to [ə], the vowel changes the feature [+tense] to [−tense]. This change violates the IDENT(tense) constraint, which penalizes changes in the feature [tense] from the input to the output. In the final model, however, this constraint did not ever influence a winning candidate, so it is omitted from the rest of the paper.

Reducing a vowel changes other features, so reduction is penalized through more specific constraints, described in (10).

(10)   a.   IDENT-IO(LOW) (IDENT(lo)): Assign a violation for every segment that does not surface with the same value for [low] in the input and the output.

        b.   IDENT-IO [LABIAL] (IDENT(lab)): Assign a violation for every segment that does not surface with the same value for [labial] in the input and output.

        c.   IDENT-IO [HIGH] (IDENT(hi)): Assign a violation for every segment that does not surface with the same value for [high] in the input and the output.

IDENT(lo) penalizes /a/ when it raises to [ə], but does not target any other underlying vowels. IDENT(hi) penalizes /i/ and /u/ when they lower to [ə], and IDENT(lab) penalizes /u/ and /o/ when they reduce. As described in (2), these vowels behave differently in the same surrounding contexts, which is why three different IDENT constraints are necessary rather than the general IDENT(tense) constraint.

The faithfulness that penalizes vowel deletion is MAX(V), described below:

(11)   MAXIMIZE(VOWEL) (MAX(V)): Assign a violation for every vowel in the input that does not surface in the output.

Constraints that interact with subsets of the data more specifically will be presented in the following sections.

5.4 Vowel hiatus resolution

Gurmancema has a vowel hiatus resolution process similar to other Niger-Congo languages (Casali 1997). The markedness constraint that motivates the hiatus resolution is as follows:

(12)   (*V.V): Assign a violation for every sequence of vowels across a syllable boundary.

Vowel hiatus in Gurmancema is always resolved by deleting the first vowel, or the word-final vowel. A tableau showing an example is shown in Table 2.

Table 2: Tableau for /di#a/ with sample phrase 'forgets jugs', $n = 10$

	p			*V.V	*[+tns]#	MAX (V)	IDENT (hi)
/súndi àbóbà/	obs	pred	score	9.34	6.14	3.62	2.99
a. [súndi àbóbà]	0	~0	15.44	1	1	0	0
b. [súndə àbóbà]	0	~0	12.63	1	0	0	1
c. [súnd àbóbà]	1	~1	3.62	0	0	1	0

In the tableau in Table 2, candidate (a) has a vowel sequence and a word-final tense vowel, so it violates *V.V and [+tns]#, incurring a score of 9.34+6.14, totaling 15.44. Candidate (b) violates *V.V and IDENT(hi), incurring a score of 9.34 + 2.99, totaling 12.63. Candidate (c) only violates MAX(V), incurring a score of 3.62. This is the lowest score by a significant amount, so the model predicts candidate (c) will surface approximately 100% of the time, which is what was observed. Vowel hiatus resolution is entirely regular and predictable in Gurmancema, with the word-final vowel always being deleted.

5.5 Prevocalic obstruents

Consonant clusters beginning with obstruents are highly marked in Gurmancema, leading to a preference for reduction over deletion when word-final vowels are preceded by an obstruent. In other words, word-final vowels are dispreferred, but when deletion would lead to an illicit consonant cluster, reduction is the preferred fix. The vowels /a, i, o/ reduce when preceded by an obstruent over 90% of the time. The vowel /e/ is not addressed in this paper, as in the dataset it is always part of root material, which behaves differently from affixal/clitic material. The vowel /u/, however, shows variation when preceded by an obstruent. To start to account for this data, a new constraint is needed, penalizing consonant clusters beginning with obstruents. This is not a general *CC constraint, because not all consonant clusters are equally marked in Gurmancema (see 2).

(13)   *[−sonorant][+consonantal] (*TC): Assign a violation for every [−sonorant][+consonantal] consonant cluster in the output.

Table 3 shows an example of reduction of a vowel following an obstruent. The tableau shows observed data for all /Ta#C/, meaning all environments of an obstruent followed by /a/ followed by a consonant.

Table 3: Tableau for /Ta#C/ with sample phrase 'child loses', n = 88

/kìbéga bìáni/	p			*[+tns]#	*TC	Max (V)	Ident (lo)
	obs	pred	score	6.14	4.55	3.62	3.52
a. [kìbéga bìáni]	0.05	~0.07	6.14	1	0	0	0
b. [kìbégə bìáni]	0.91	~0.92	3.52	0	0	0	1
c. [kìbég bìáni]	0.04	~0.01	8.17	0	1	1	0

Word-final /i/ and /o/ behave very similarly to word-final /a/ when preceded by an obstruent, but /u/ behaves slightly differently. Reducing /u/ violates both Ident(hi) as well as Ident(round), so the reduced candidate has more penalties than the other word-final vowels. This leads to a case of ganging, where the violation of two lower constraints is strong enough to overpower one stronger constraint, leading to variation. While violating either Ident(high) or Ident(labial) produces patterns similar to those seen in Table 2, violating both means almost double the penalty for that candidate, making reduction a significantly worse choice for /u/ than the other vowels. The ganging and variation is illustrated in Table 4.

Table 4: Tableau for /Tu#C/ with sample phrase 'tree wants', n = 141

/bútíbu bwà/	p			*[+tns]#	*TC	Max (V)	Ident(lab)	Ident(hi)
	obs	pred	score	6.14	4.55	3.62	3.62	2.99
a. [bútíbu bwà]	0.69	~0.57	6.14	1	0	0	0	0
b. [bútíbə bwà]	0.31	~0.35	6.61	0	0	0	1	1
c. [bútíb bwà]	0	~0.08	8.17	0	1	1	0	0

The model is very accurate in predicting the distribution for maintenance (a) and reduction (b), but the predictions are slightly off, leading to an over-prediction of deletion (c), which was not observed. This is a result of the model being more general. The goal of this analysis was to account for the data with the simplest set of phonological constraints rather than overfitting the model by tailoring constraints to small subsets of data. *TC does not have a higher weight due to the few exceptional cases where TC consonant clusters occur as a result of deletion. MAX(V), the only other constraint violated by (c), does not have a higher weight due to cases of vowel deletion elsewhere in the data.

5.6 Prevocalic approximants

Prevocalic approximants behave similarly to prevocalic obstruents overall due to a similar markedness constraint on consonant clusters beginning with approximants, parallel to (13).

(14)   *[+approximant][+consonantal] (*RC): Assign a violation for every consonant cluster beginning with an approximant.

The reason we need two constraints *TC and *RC rather than a general *CC constraint is because consonant clusters beginning with nasals are permissible in Gurmancema. This markedness constraint leads to reduction, as with the constraint *TC.

There were no cases of word-final /e/, /u/, or /o/ preceded by an approximant. Word-final /a/ preceded by approximants behaves differently from /i/, however, always surfacing as a maintained [a]. The vowel /a/ reduces in other cases, such as after obstruents (see Table 2), so this is not a result of constraints preventing /a/ from reducing. There is nothing morphologically unique about the words that exhibit this pattern, and it is very consistent. To account for this pattern, a new solution is necessary. The first ingredient in the solution is the following constraint:

(15)   *[+approximant][−tense] (*R[ə]): Assign a violation for every approximant in the output followed by a [−tense] vowel

From a data perspective, it is clear that this pattern refers to both the input and the output, where having a reduced vowel after an approximant is marked, but worse when the vowel derives from /a/ as opposed to /i/. The candidate where an approximant is followed by /a/ and the /a/ reduces violates IDENT[low] as well as *R[ə]. However, the violation of these two constraints is not strong enough to predict the correct forms. Both would need low weights to allow reduction in other environments, and their combined penalty is not enough to prevent /a/ from reducing. Thus, *R[ə] and IDENT(lo) on their own motivate variation across the language in cases where there should not be any. In other words, ganging alone is not sufficient to make the correct predictions.

The only way to add more weight to this combination is to use constraint conjunction, where a candidate incurs a violation if and only if it violates each of two constraints included in the conjunction. The conjoined constraint has a separate weight that is added to a candidate's Harmony. It may seem that Harmonic Grammar relieves the need for conjoined constraints, but this is not always the case. Superadditivity, the conjoining of constraints in a weighted model, was developed to capture cases not easily captured by simple additive constraints (Albright et al. 2008; Green & Davis 2014). Smolensky (2006) argues that superadditivity in an HG context is necessary for local violations across a specific domain. In the case of Gurmancema, the constraints both refer to the onset and nucleus of one syllable. The pattern in these data was highly specific and very regular, so the learner needs more specific grammatical tools to model it correctly, but with constraint conjunction, this is possible with ingredients already in the model.

The addition of the conjoined constraint *R[ə] & IDENT(lo) correctly predicts the data distribution. Although many superadditive models only use superadditivity for conjoining markedness constraints (Albright et al. 2008), there is also precedent for using faithfulness constraints in a superadditive manner (Green & Davis 2014). Nevertheless, there is some debate about whether markedness and faithfulness constraints can be conjoined (Moreton & Smolensky 2002). Conjoined constraints are intended only to be used for patterns in local domains. According to Moreton & Smolensky (2002), as the domain of markedness is the output while faithfulness necessarily refers to the input, it is not clear whether such conjunctions can be truly considered local. In this case, the only way to represent the data was to conjoin a faithfulness and a markedness constraint (*R[ə] & IDENT(lo)).

Tableaux showing the different behaviors of /a/ and /i/ preceded by /ɾ/ are shown in Tables 5 and 6.

Without the use of superadditivity, the model predicts variation in this environment which showed categorical behavior. An example tableau is shown in Table 7.

This set of constraints still captures general patterns, but as it predicts variation where there is none, it does not satisfactorily capture the data.

Table 5: Tableau for /Ri#C/ with sample phrase 'hair covers', n = 192

	p			*R[ə]& IDENT(lo)	*[+tns]#	*RC	MAX (V)	IDENT (hi)	*R[ə]#
/tìyúri ŋóagéni/	obs	pred	score	8.13	6.14	6.04	3.62	2.99	0
a. [tìyúri ŋóagéni]	0.05	~0.04	6.14	0	1	0	0	0	0
b. [tìyúrə ŋóagéni]	0.91	~0.96	2.99	0	0	0	0	1	1
c. [tìyúr ŋóagéni]	0.04	~0	9.66	0	0	1	1	0	0

Table 6: Tableau for /Ra#C/ with sample phrase 'children sell', n = 160

	p			*R[ə] & IDENT(lo)	*[+tns#]	*RC	MAX(V)	IDENT (lo)	*R[ə]
/abéla kúari/	obs	pred	score	8.13	6.14	6.04	3.62	3.52	0
a. [abéla kúari]	1	~0.97	6.14	0	1	0	0	0	0
b. [abélə kúari]	0	~0	11.65	1	0	0	0	1	1
c. [abél kúari]	0	~0.03	9.66	0	0	1	1	0	0

5.7 Prevocalic nasals

When /m/ is in penultimate position, it typically triggers reduction in the final vowel. This is counter-intuitive, as there is no markedness constraint against consonant clusters beginning with nasals. Consonant clusters beginning with nasals are in fact common in Gurmancema, occurring both within words and across word boundaries. Gurmancema, however, has strong nasal place assimilation, meaning consonant clusters with different places of articulation are highly marked. The markedness constraint is described in (16).

(16) *[+nasal, +$a$place][−$a$place] (NASALASSIMILATION): Assign a violation for every consonant cluster beginning with a nasal where the second consonant has a different place than the nasal.

Table 7: Tableau for /Ra#C/ with sample phrase 'children sell', n = 160 without superadditivity

	p			*RC	*[+TNS#]	IDENT (lo)	*R[ə]	MAX(V)
/abéla kúari/	obs	pred	score	9.83	9.64	7.84	3.37	3.33
a. [abéla kúari]	1	~0.81	9.64	0	1	0	0	0
b. [abélə kúari]	0	~0.17	11.21	0	0	1	1	0
c. [abél kúari]	0	~0.02	13.16	1	0	0	0	1

NASALASSIMILATION prevents the consonant clusters with mismatched place but IDENT(lab) prevents /m/ from assimilating to the following consonant. In the context of final vowel deletion, this situation leads to a strong preference for vowel reduction to avoid creating such a mismatched cluster. In the cases where the vowel after /m/ does delete, however, the nasal retains its bilabial place due to IDENT(lab). This does result in cases where there is no nasal place assimilation, which is rare in Gurmancema, but predicted correctly with the constraints in this model. A tableau illustrating all the constraints for prevocalic /m/ is presented in Table 8.

Table 8: Tableau for /mi#C/ with sample phrase 'elephants eat', $n = 44$

	p			*[+tns]#	MAX(V)	IDENT(lab)	IDENT(hi)	NASAL ASSIMILATION
/ilúomì dá/	obs	pred	score	6.14	3.62	3.62	2.99	2.55
a. [ilúomì dá]	0.07	~0.04	6.14	1	0	0	0	0
b. [ilúomə̀ dá]	0.91	~0.91	2.99	0	0	0	1	0
c. [ilúom dá]	0.02	~0.04	6.17	0	1	0	0	1
d. [ilúon dá]	0	~0.01	7.24	0	1	1	0	0

In cases where the next consonant is also bilabial, the vowel is more likely to delete because it only violates MAX(V), rather than MAX(V) as well as either NASALASSIMILATION or IDENT(lab).

Table 9: Tableau for /ma#C/ with sample phrase 'food hits', $n = 6$

	p			*[+tns]#	MAX(V)	IDENT(lab)	IDENT(low)	NASAL ASSIMILATION
/míɟemá pwá/	obs	pred	score	6.14	3.62	3.52	2.99	2.55
a. [míɟemá pwá]	0	~0.04	6.14	1	0	0	0	0
b. [míɟemə̀ pwá]	0.33	~0.50	3.52	0	0	0	1	0
c. [míɟem pwá]	0.67	~0.46	3.62	0	1	0	0	1

While there may be greater deviation between observed and predicted probabilities in this case, the sample size for this environment was considerably smaller than for other environments modeled, given its specificity.

5.8 List of constraints

In the preceding subsections, I have presented tableaux with only the relevant constraints. In order to understand the complete analysis, (17) provides a full list of constraints and their weights, in order from highest to lowest weights.

(17) *V.V   9.34
      IDENT(lo) & *R[ə]   8.13
      *[+tns]#   6.14
      *RC   6.04
      DEP(C)   5.79
      *TC   4.55
      IDENT(lab)   3.62
      MAX(V)   3.62
      IDENT(lo)   3.52
      IDENT(hi)   2.99
      NASALASSIMILATION   2.55
      IDENT(tns)   0
      *R[ə]   0

6 Conclusion

This paper provides the first full account of word-final vowel reduction and deletion in Gurmancema in a constraint-based model. These data are very complex and have been largely left unanalyzed in the limited literature on this language. Unlike in other cases of vowel reduction and deletion, the patterns are not entirely motivated by stress patterns or vowel hiatus resolution. These data can only be represented by looking at a number of phonological factors.

A Harmonic Grammar model was necessary to account for cases of constraint ganging, and a MaxEnt version of HG was used to predict the variation found in certain parts of the data. The model necessitated the addition of superadditive conjoined constraints to represent highly specific yet regular patterns. These superadditive constraints included conjoined Faithfulness and Markedness constraints as opposed to simply conjoined Markedness constraints. Although this goes against traditional theories of conjoined constraints, these constraints were motivated by the complexity of the data. It was also more natural to conjoin preexisting constraints rather than invent new and highly specific constraints to account for the data.

This model accounts for the purely categorical patterns in Gurmancema, such as vowel hiatus resolution, as well as variable patterns. This paper does not include a full representation of all the complexity in Gurmancema, however. There is much room for future work in Gurmancema. In particular, the interaction of this process with tone and syntax remain.

Acknowledgements

I would like to thank the editors of this volume as well as two anonymous reviewers for their feedback. I would also like to thank Laura McPherson and James Stanford for their feedback throughout this paper. Thank you to my consultant Lamoudi Labesse, as well as Marc Sepama and the students in Linguistics 35. I am extremely grateful for the financial support of the Stamps Family Charitable Foundation through the Dartmouth Center for the Advancement of Learning, without which this work would not have been possible.

Abbreviations

All glosses used are standard from the Leipzig glossing conventions. The marker CL is a noun class marker. All nouns in Gurmancema have a pro- and enclitic that mark noun class. These are not further analyzed morphologically here.

References

Albright, Adam, Giorgi Magri & Jennifer Michael. 2008. Modeling doubly marked lags with a split additive model. In Enkeleida Kapia (ed.), *BUCLD 32: proceedings of the 32nd annual Boston University Conference on Language Development*, 36–47.

Boersma, Paul & David Weenick. 1996. *Praat: Doing phonetics by computer [Computer Program] Version 6.0.37*. University of Amsterdam. Amsterdam.

Casali, Roderick. 1997. Vowel elision in hiatus contexts: Which vowel goes? *Language* 73(3). 493–533.

Chantoux, Alphonse. 1968. *Grammaire Gourmantché*. Dakar: Institut Fundamental D'Afrique Noire.

Goldwater, Sharon & Mark Johnson. 2003. Learning OT constraint rankings using a maximum entropy model. In Jennifer Spenader, Anders Eriksson & Östen Dahl (eds.), *Proceedings of the Stockholm Workshop on Variation within Optimality Theory*, 111–120.

Green, Christopher R. & Stuart Davis. 2014. Superadditivity and limitations on syllable complexity in Bambara words. In Ashley Farris-Trimble & Jessica Barlow (eds.), *Perspectives on phonological theory and development, in honor of Daniel A. Dinnsen*, 223–247. Amsterdam, Philadelphia: John Benjamins.

Hayes, Bruce & Colin Wilson. 2008. A maximum entropy model of phonotactics and phonotactic learning. *Linguistic Inquiry* 39. 379–440.

Moreton, Elliott & Paul Smolensky. 2002. Typological consequences of local constraint conjunction. In Lina Mikkelsen & Christopher Potts (eds.), *Proceedings of the 21st West Coast Conference on Formal Linguistics*, 306–319. Cascadilla Press, Santa Cruz.

Naba, Jean-Claude. 1994. *Le Gulmancema-Essai de systématisation: phonologie, tonologie, morphophonologie.* Cologne: R. Köppe.

Rialland, Annie. 1980. Marques de ponctuation et d'intégration dans l'énoncé en Gurma. *Bulletin de la Société de Linguistique de Paris* LXXV. 415–432.

Rialland, Annie. 2001. Une "punctuation voacalique" en Gulmacema (langue Gurma) et les consequences de sa perte dans une langue proche: Le Moba. In R Nicolaï (ed.), *Leçons d'Afrique: filiation, ruptures et reconstitution des langue,* 91–102. Peeters.

Simons, Gary F. & Charles D. Fennig (eds.). 2017. *Ethnologue: Languages of the world.* Twentieth edition. Dallas, Texas: SIL International. http://www.ethnologue.com.

Smolensky, Paul. 2006. Optimality in phonology II: Harmonic completeness, local conjunction, and feature domain markedness. In Paul Smolensky & Géraldine Legendre (eds.), *The harmonic mind: From neural computation to optimality-theoretic grammar,* vol. 2, 27–160. Cambridge: MIT Press.

Wilson, Colin, Bruce Hayes & Benjamin George. 2008. Maxent grammar tool. Software package.

Chapter 3

Toward a better understanding of speech-language disorders in African countries: The case of speech sound disorders in Cameroon

Aurélie Takam

Department of African Languages and Linguistics, University of Yaoundé 1
Department of French studies, York University

Child speech and language disorders are not well known in many African countries. The aim of this study was to analyze speech sound disorders in Cameroon in order to encourage the rehabilitation of language disorders in general in the public health system. From a sample of 1127 children, 6% of children presented with speech sound disorders including speech delays, articulation and phonological disorders. Boys were more affected than girls. Complex syllables and fricatives sounds were the most impaired while omission and substitution were the most frequent errors.

1 Introduction

Language disorders are not well known in many sub-Saharan countries. Our review of the literature indicates only a few African countries such as Togo, Nigeria, Kenya and South Africa, where studies have been carried out to describe the actual situation of these disorders (e.g. Van der Linde et al. 2016; Topouzkhanian & Mijiyawa 2013). This paper aims to contribute toward this effort of better understanding language disorders in African countries given their considerable impact on primary education. Language disorders are impairments that affect the human language faculty and appear through one or many linguistic components of the spoken and written language. It is now well known that children with one or more of these impairments are at risk for limited social achievement.

Aurélie Takam. 2019. Toward a better understanding of speech-language disorders in African countries: The case of speech sound disorders in Cameroon. In Samson Lotven, Silvina Bongiovanni, Phillip Weirich, Robert Botne & Samuel Gyasi Obeng (eds.), *African linguistics across the disciplines: Selected papers from the 48th Annual Conference on African Linguistics*, 47–69. Berlin: Language Science Press. DOI:10.5281/zenodo.3520569

Speech sound disorder (SSD) and literacy difficulties (i.e. reading and spelling problems) are the most frequent language disorders among children (Ruscello et al. 1991). Our study specifically concerns the first category which are difficulties in producing or using speech sounds, very often the consonants, without organic alteration (such as hearing loss or cleft palate). The general objective of this study is to analyze these disorders in Cameroon in order to encourage the rehabilitation of language disorders in the public health system. In fact, in Cameroon as in many Sub-Saharan countries, children are not screened neither referred for assessment of speech and language disorders during their third or fourth year as it is usual in Nord American countries for example. In what follows, we present the profile and prevalence of SSD in order to shed light on their main characteristics.

1.1 Profile and classification of SSD

Examples to illustrate some speech sound errors are given in Table 1.

Table 1: Speech sound errors

French word	Illustration	Error types
viande	[vjãd] → [bãd]	substitution
couscous	[kuskus] → [tutu]	substitution; omission
chaise	[ʃɛz] → [ʃɛ]	omission
table	[tabl] → [tab]	omission
chocolat	[ʃokola] → [kokola]	consonant harmony

The generic terminology for these disorders varies in the literature, but in this study, we use the term "speech sound disorder" (SSD) to include articulation disorders, phonological delays and phonological disorders. Articulation disorders are phonetic in nature. For example, a child can systematically replace a sound with another regardless of the syllabic context (see examples 1 and 2 above) while another may systematically omit it (as in example 2). These types of systematic errors indicate a phonetic difficulty to perform the movement required to produce a sound (Fox & Dodd 2001). Another child may exhibit phonological errors that are specific to younger children. Here, a child may assimilate or omit a sound in a specific context and correctly produce it in another (as in examples 3, 4 and 5 above). The persistence of these types of errors above the expected age results in phonological delay. Thus a delay of at least six months is significant for this purpose (Dodd 2013). However, when phonological errors are different from phonological processes (normal errors in phonological development), they are considered as atypical phonological errors and can be consistent or inconsistent depending on whether the same error pops up often or occasionally (Dodd 2013). Finally, a child may exhibit a systematic error on a sound and assimilate another sound, thus showing an overlap between articulation and phonological problems. Therefore, we use the term SSD to include both articulation and phonological problems and the likely overlap between them.

1.2 Prevalence of SSD

There is a lack of consensus on the prevalence rate of SSD from one study to another, ranging between 23% and 2% from our literature review McKinnon et al. (2007); Shriberg et al. (1999); Fombonne & Vermeersh (1997); Beitchman et al. (1986); Enderby & Philipp (1986); Kirkpatrick & Ward (1984); Silva et al. (1984); Silva (1980); Peckham (1973); Stevenson & Richman (1976); Morley (1972); Hull et al. (1971), Chevrie,. This inconsistency could be explained by the diversity of social factors (different countries: USA, Australia, Canada, France, Great Britain) as well as differences in methodological approaches (cross-sectional or longitudinal study, random or non-random sampling, one or several age groups). However, there seems to be a decrease in the rate of prevalence with age, these speech disorders being more frequent in younger preschool-aged children compared to school-aged ones (Morley 1972). This rate decrease can be explained by the fact that preschool children have not yet acquired the complete phonology of their language and tend to master the use of speech sounds between the ages of six and seven years for languages such as French (e.g. Rvachew et al. 2013). Similarly, since some speech disorders are phonological delays, they may evolve and some children can catch up without speech intervention and perform well in formal tests (e.g.Bishop & Edmundson 1987). However, it is worth noting that this apparent catch up may be illusory as some children often have residual phonological processing impairments (e.g. Stothard et al. 1998). Furthermore, all studies have higher prevalence rates for boys than girls (e.g. Shriberg et al. 1999). Finally, regarding the impact of socioeconomic status (SES) on the prevalence of articulatory disorders, McKinnon et al. (2007) conducted a study with 10425 students in Australia and found no difference between SES groups. In conclusion, the main variables to be studied for the prevalence of SSD are the status of the spoken language, age and gender.

2 Context

2.1 Sociolinguistic description

Like many sub-Saharan countries, Cameroon is a multilingual country where children are exposed to at least two languages in their environment. Generally, bilinguals are categorized according to several factors but the main ones in this study are the age and order of exposure to both languages and the social status of the two languages. Therefore, we limited our attention to early bilingual Cameroonian children who speak Ghɔmálá' and French and who live in one of the following sociolinguistic contexts: either a dominant French milieu (urban area) or a dominant Ghɔmálá' milieu (rural area). However, whatever the region, French is the main language used at school in Cameroon and children are enrolled in the nursery school system from age three. This diglossic categorization of languages is a general feature of the sociolinguistic context in Cameroon, where the Administrative Atlas of National Languages (Breton & Fohtung 1991) lists 248 languages. In addition to this diversity, French and English are the two official languages. Based on the national distribution of official languages there are officially two linguistic communities: the French-speaking community (covering eight of the 10 regions) and the English-speaking community (covering the two remaining regions). Only the French-speaking community was covered in this study.

Generally, the social status of French varies between urban and rural areas. Because urban areas are multilingual, French is the dominant language and it is acquired from an early age. This is the case in Bafoussam, the urban area investigated, where children acquire French as first language with the presence of Ghɔmálá', the major local language spoken, and other minority languages. Compared to urban areas, rural areas provide a more homogeneous sociolinguistic environment where children are exposed both to the local language and French, and their contact with French intensifies with start of kindergarten at age three. Here, the local language is the main instrument of communication especially in the family environment and French is primarily used outside the home, especially by young people. Therefore in rural areas, the use of the local language is socially dominant although French is dominant at school and for public services. This is the case of Bandjoun, the rural area investigated in this study, where Ghɔmálá' and French are spoken and where the child's contact with French intensifies with entry into kindergarten.

2.2 Ghɔmálá' and French

Ghɔmálá' and French are the main languages spoken in the Mifi, Kounghi-Khi and Hauts Plateaux administrative divisions in the western region of Cameroon (Breton & Fohtung 1991). Compared to French, Ghɔmálá' is a tone language with three simple and two complex tones (see Nissim (1981) for a detailed description of Ghɔmálá' phonology). Classified as a Bamiléké language (one of the Bantu languages) only spoken in Cameroon (Dieu & Renaud 1983), Ghɔmálá' is comprised of 18 dialectal varieties with mutual comprehension. However, the variety of Bandjoun (Ghɔmálá' jo) is used as the standard reference (Domche & Hatfield 1991). Thus, this study covers speakers of this variety. Regarding French, children are exposed both to standard French (FS) mainly at school and through television and radio, and to the variety of Cameroonian French (FC) spoken in the western region of Cameroon. Besides, the French pronunciation to which the child is exposed varies according to the education level of the speakers. The elite with a high education level makes greater use of FS, while uneducated or less educated parents speak more in the local FC (Biloa 2004). This means that children are exposed to both varieties of French.

Ghɔmálá' and French share many consonants. The consonant system of FC is based on FS phonology, comprising stops and fricatives, labial /p, b, m, f, v/, apical /t, d, n, s, z, l/, palatal /ʃ, ʒ, ɲ/, velar /k, g/, uvular /ʁ/ and glides /w, ɥ, j/. The majority of these consonants are oral against only three nasal /m, n, ɲ/. However, due to language contact, the FC may also include the nasal velar /ŋ/, the glottal fricative /h/ and the glottal stop /ʔ/ (see Biloa (2004) for a detailed description of FC). In addition to these phonemes, Ghɔmálá' also has the affricated consonants /pf, bv, ts, dz, tʃ, dʒ/ and the velar fricative /ɣ/ (Mba & Domche 1995). However the uvular /ʁ/ is underrepresented in Ghɔmálá' (Mba & Domche 1995). For this reason, and as reported by Biloa (2004), some Ghɔmálá' speakers of French may exhibit one or more of the following interference signs: in the coda position, /ʁ/ may be omitted (resulting in vowel lengthening or shortening), replaced by a glottal or a velar stop (e.g. [aʁʒã] 'money' pronounced [aːã], [agʒã] or [aʔʒã]), or simply replaced by the apical [r]; in syllable initial, /ʁ/ may be replaced by the apical [r] or the lateral [l]; finally in the consonant group, /ʁ/ may be omitted. Adding to this variation in the use of the uvular /ʁ/, the phonological interference between French and Ghɔmálá' also appears through a tendency to articulate the mute *e* in syllable final (e.g. [tablə] instead of [tabl] 'table'). There may be other interference processes but the ones listed here are the most frequent characteristics of the local "accent".

Finally, the distribution of consonants in the syllable structure shows some similarities and differences between French and Ghɔmálá'. In Ghɔmálá' all the consonants can appear in initial position except for the glottal stop /ʔ/, but only the stops /p, m, k, ŋ, ʔ/ can appear in final position. However in French, all the consonants, including the palatal glide /j/, appear in both positions but the labial glides /ɥ/ and /w/ don't appear in final. Concerning the structure of consonant groups, in Ghɔmálá' they only appear in initial position and can have from two (CC) to four (CCCC) consonants. CC structure can be nasal + stop (e.g. /ŋkáp/ 'money') or stops + /h/ (e.g. /phə/ 'bag'), and CCC and CCCC structures are made of (nasal+) nasal+stop+glide (e.g. /ŋkwə/ 'foot'; /mŋkwə/ 'feet'), nasal+stop+ /h/ (e.g. /mphə/ 'bags') or nasal+nasal+stop (e.g. /mntăp/ 'shoes') where the first nasal may be the plural morpheme /m-/. These structures are completely different from French where consonant groups may appear in initial and final syllable positions, and be composed of two (CC) and even three (CCC) consonants. French CC are formed of fricative+stop (e.g. /staʒ/ 'traineeship'), stop or fricative + liquid or glide (e.g. /tʁɛ̃/ 'train'; /bwa/ 'wood'; /tabl/ 'table'), while CCC structure may be composed of liquid +stop+liquid (e.g. /aʁbʁ/ 'tree') or stop+liquid+glide (e.g. /plɥi/ 'rain').

3 The study

3.1 Objectives

Using a clinical linguistic approach, the general objective of this study is to analyze SSD among a population of Cameroonian bilingual children. Specifically, the study aims to assess the prevalence of these disorders in preschool- and school-aged children and to describe their profile based on these age groups; that is, from 4–8 years old, in order to develop an intervention strategy. Besides, we also considered the fact that, generally, four-year-old children already have a good knowledge of the consonant system of their language (e.g., MacLeod et al. 2011). However, as Cameroonian children are often exposed to two or more languages, it is necessary to distinguish normal developing children from children with SSD. Based on the literature about the differences between bilingual and monolingual language acquisition, we have developed a procedure accordingly, as there is still no normative language data for the population under study. Even though the analysis of French consonant acquisition reveals that children living in a French dominant area master their consonant system around the age of six Rvachew et al. (2013), researchers often point out the difference in the developmental trend of bilinguals compared to monolinguals, and the impact of the interaction between languages in bilingual language acquisition Paradis et al. (2011). Therefore in this study, we limited the analysis to the consonants that are common to the languages spoken – French and Ghɔmálá' – in order to avoid all variations related to language dominance in the child's environment. We also considered that some errors may be due to that environment.

3.2 Method

3.3 Participants

This study is based on a sample of 1127 bilingual French-Ghɔmálá' children aged 4–8 years, who attended eight schools (five elementary schools and three kindergartens) with French as the only language of instruction (see §2.1 above for details). At the time of the investigation these children had been attending school for at least one year. The constitution of this sample was determined by the schools that were chosen according to their location, size and accessibility. As it appears in Table 2, this sample includes 54% of children living in the rural areas of Bandjoun, a Ghɔmálá'-dominant locality, and 46% in the urban areas of Bafoussam, a French-dominant locality. There were 49% girls and 51% boys. The distribution of these children by age was as follows: four-year-olds = 10% (117 children), five-year olds = 22% (254 children), six-year olds = 25% (279 children), seven-year olds = 20% (221 children) and eight-year olds = 23% (256 children).

Table 2: Description of the sample based on school level, gender and socio-linguistic context (*N* = 1127 children)

	School level			Gender		Sociolinguistic context		
	Maternelle[a]	SIL[b]	CP[c]	girls	boys	rural	urban	Total
N	136	518	473	553	574	606	521	1127
%	12	46	42	49	51	54	46	100

[a](kindergarten)
[b](grade 1)
[c](grade 2)

3.4 Procedure

To assess the children's speech-sound performance, we followed the recommendations of speech-language therapists regarding the combination of informal and formal procedures so as to have a sample of connected speech, to elicit a set of single-word productions by picture- or object-naming and to assess sound production in a repetition test. We therefore used a procedure based on the one proposed by Maurin-Cherou (1993) for French-speaking children. In so doing, we were able to generally evaluate each child's speech comprehension as well. Data collection took place over two school years, one school year per area, and was realized by the author of this paper who speaks Ghɔmálá' and French as first languages, in collaboration with a linguist specialized in applied linguistics who verified the API transcription, and an ORL specialist who performed the medical exam. Schools were also selected based on their location, size and geographic accessibility. Subsequently, administrative formalities were completed in order to obtain the necessary authorizations to have access to the selected schools (which report to the education department) on the one hand and the classrooms (which are the responsibility of school principals) on the other hand. There were four steps in the data collection process: the teachers' training workshop, the preliminary screening, the language and speech assessment, and the ORL exam.

Teachers' training workshop: After classifying the children by age groups, their classes and teachers were then identified. Then an information session and a training workshop were organized with the teachers of the selected classes about the preliminary identification of children at risk of developing speech-language disorders. For this preliminary screening, we explained the following criteria to the teachers:

1. The child who speaks poorly (errors in the pronunciation of sounds, syllables, words and sentence)
2. The child whose language expression is difficult to understand
3. The child who has difficulty hearing and/or understanding
4. The child who understands after several repetitions
5. the child who is agitated or violent in class or out of class
6. the child who is taciturn and doesn't speak in class or out of class

We were assisted by a speech-language therapist for the preparation of this workshop.

Preliminary screening: After the training, teachers were given three months to draw up a list of children who met at least one of these criteria. The children identified were then assessed on their language use and speech production. This procedure had the merit of having the screening done on the basis of what is accepted as normal to the local population. A total of 100 children were listed by the teachers.

Oral language assessment: This assessment was conducted in an informal setting while establishing contact with the child before the formal assessment of speech sound production. First, the child was asked to talk about his/her usual activities and/or to tell a short story. The connected speech sampling was done in Ghɔmálá' and French (see the Appendix for the list of some Ghɔmálá' words used by the children). We then conducted a short vocabulary comprehension test following Maurin-Cherou's protocol using some items randomly chosen from the picture-naming test. The child had to show the image of the spoken word among four choices. All the children passed this test. This assessment took about 15 minutes and the connected speech was recorded using an audio tape recorder.

Speech sound assessment: Each child was evaluated during one session using two speech tests administered by the author of this paper: a picture-naming test and a word repetition test all in French. The child was first asked to name each picture of the naming test. Then s/he was asked to repeat a list of words chosen based on the sounds and syllabic structures that were difficult in the first test. The assessment lasted between 40 and 45 minutes and it was also recorded.

- **The picture-naming test** consisted of producing 64 words prompted by colour pictures depicting well-known objects chosen from the local environment (see the Appendix for the list of the 64 words). For some words, we used the object itself (e.g., for the word "grain" we used a sample of mixed grains of rice, corn and beans). The test assessed consonants common to Ghɔmálá' and French but French was mainly used as the language of assessment given its dominant status at school. However, an eight-year-old girl and a four-year-old boy said a few words in Ghɔmálá', in which case s/he had to repeat after the examiner. Each consonant appeared in different syllable positions except for the fricative [v]. The glides [w] and [j] mainly appeared in the consonant group. Other structures evaluated consisted of consonant+liquid, and the syllabic structures V, VC, CV, CVC. The children were able to name all the images as they reflected realities of their daily lives.

- **The repetition test** assessed the impaired consonants in different positions. The child had to repeat the word clearly articulated by the examiner.

Oto-Rhino-Laryngology (or ORL) exam: Only children identified as having SSD benefited from an ORL exam. The exams were conducted by a specialist in each of the target schools to evaluate the anatomical and physiological auditory system as well as the oral and respiratory system. Given that none of the screened children had organic disorders that could affect speech sound production (e.g. Hearing loss), in this study we present only the results of the speech sound assessment.

3.5 Data analysis

The identification of SSD was based on the analysis of consonants and syllabic structures from the connected speech sampled, the naming picture test and the repetition test. Each child's production was collected using an individual form and recorded using an audio recorder. At the end of each day, for each child, data collected by the author of this paper were transcribed using the IPA and verified by an applied linguist. Speech disorders were identified by analyzing the child's pronunciation based on expectations given his/her age. This was based on the consonant acquisition of 127 four-to-five-year-old French-speaking Cameroonian children living in a multilingual environment (Takam Unpublished). Generally, the results of this preliminary study showed no significant difference between the age groups (four-year-olds and five-year-olds): at least 90% of the children were able to accurately produce the consonants [p, b, m, n, ɲ, j, f, s, v, k, d, ʒ, ʁ, w, z], around 80% the fricative [ʃ] and only 60% the lateral [l]. In the current study, errors were analyzed to determine the phonological processes classified as substitution, assimilation, omission, addition or metathesis as presented in the theoretical framework summarized in Table 3.

3.6 Result

3.6.1 Prevalence rate

Following the preliminary screening, 100 children were listed as presenting at least one of the criteria. At the end of the assessment, 32 children were excluded from this sample because they did not present any of the speech errors above (see

Table 3: Classification of speech errors by structure (sound and syllable)

Structure	Error	Phonological process leading to the...
Sound	Substitution	replacement of a difficult sound by another causing a change in point or mode of articulation
	Distortion	rough articulation producing a false noise
	Assimilation	replacement of a sound which becomes like a nearby sound (sounds harmony)
	Metathesis	position change of one or more sounds in the word
Syllable	Omission	erasing of a sound
	Addition	vocalic or consonantal addition
	Metathesis	position change of one or more sounds in the word

Table 3). Finally, 68 children presented with SSD in the form of phonetic disorders, phonological delays or phonological disorders, which represents a prevalence rate of about 6% of the 1127 children in the population studied. Tables 4 and 5 present this prevalence by gender, sociolinguistic context, school level and age group. There was a significant difference in prevalence rates by gender with 4.5% of girls compared to 7.5% of boys [$\chi^2 = (1, N = 1127) = 4.38, p = 0.03$] and a ratio of 3.2. The prevalence rates by school level were also significantly different between kindergarten (8.8%) and grade 1 pupils (7.5%) on the one hand, and grade 2 pupils (3.6%) on the other [$\chi^2 = (2, N = 1127) = 8.88, p = 0.01$]. However, the percentage by age [$\chi^2 = (4, N = 1127) = 1.04, p = 0.90$] and by sociolinguistic context [$\chi^2 = (1, N = 1127) = 0.37, p = 0.54$] were not significantly different.

3.6.2 Speech sound profile

On a segmental level, the analysis by age group showed some differences in the percentage accuracy of individual consonants as presented in Table 6. There was a considerable decrease in the number of highly impaired consonants with age, but less variation in the consonants mode of articulation as they appear to be al-

Table 4: Prevalence rate by gender, sociolinguistic context and school level. *N* = general population; *n* = children with speech disorders; Mat = kindergarten (4–5 years); SIL = grade 1 (5–6 years); CP = grade 2 (6–8 years)

	Gender		Sociolinguistic context		School level			Total
	Girls	Boys	Rural	Urban	Mat	SIL	CP	
N	553	574	606	521	136	518	473	1127
n	25	43	39	29	12	39	17	68
%	4.5	7.5	6.4	5.6	8.8	7.5	3.6	6.0

Table 5: Prevalence rate by age groups

	4 years	5 years	6 years	7 years	8 years
N	117	254	279	221	256
n	8	16	19	11	14
%	6.8	6.3	6.8	5.0	5.4

most fricatives. Generally, the sounds [l, ʁ] were impaired in all age groups while, on the contrary, the nasals [m, n] and the voiceless bilabial [p] were well used. Three categories of impaired consonants emerged following the classification of Shriberg & Kwiatkowski (1994)[1]. Consonants [s, ʃ, z, l, ʁ] were the most impaired with more than 30% of the children concerned, followed by the velars [k, g] with 10–30% of children, and finally the sounds [v, ɲ, f, j, w, ɥ, b, t, d, ʒ] which were impaired for less than 10% of the children.

As far as syllable structures were concerned (see Table 7), the CVC structure was the most impaired in all age groups with a frequency of about 97%. Interestingly, all eight-year-olds altered this structure against 87% of four-year-olds. On the other hand, the use of the consonant groups was much more laborious for four-to-five-year-olds.

---

[1]Shriberg & Kwiatkowski (1994) distinguished three categories of consonants: the *early-8* [m, b, j, n, w, d, p, h] with 100–80 percentage of correct production, the *middle-8* [t, ŋ, k, g, f, v, ʧ, ʤ] with 70–30%, and the *late-8* [ʃ, θ, s, z, ð, l, r, ʒ], with less than 20% frequency of correct use.

Table 6: Impaired consonants by age group. Not impaired: 0% of the children; Low frequency: consonants impaired for less than 10% of the children; Medium frequency: for 10–30%; High frequency: for more than 30%

Age groups	Not impaired	Low	Medium	Highly
4 years (*n* = 8)	p, m, n, ɲ, ɥ	n/a	j, v, d, w, f, t, b, k	ʒ, g, s, z, ʃ, l, ʁ
5 years (*n* = 16)	p, m, n, v, j	ʒ, ɲ, d, w, f, t	ɥ, g, k, b, s	z, ʃ, l, ʁ
6 years (*n* = 19)	p, m, n, ʒ, v, b, ɲ, d	w, f, v, t	ɥ, g, k, ʃ	l, s, z, ʁ
7 years (*n* = 11)	p, m, n, ɲ, v, f, b	ɥ, k, ʒ	j, w, t, g, d, s, z	ʃ, l, ʁ
8 years (*n* = 14)	p, m, n, w, ʒ, ɥ	v, b, ɲ, f, j, t, d	g, k	s, ʃ, z, l, ʁ
4–8 years (*n* = 68)	p, m, n	ɲ, v, f, ɥ, ʒ, j, w, b, t, d	g, k	s, ʃ, z, l, ʁ

Table 7: Impaired syllable structures by age group

	4 years	5 years	6 years	7 years	8 years	4–8 years
n	8	16	19	11	14	68
CV	6.2	31.2	36.8	27.3	28.6	32.3
VC	75.0	37.5	57.9	27.3	35.7	52.9
CC	75.0	68.7	31.6	36.4	35.7	52.9
CVC	87.5	93.7	94.7	90.9	100	97.0

Finally, omission and substitution were the most prevalent error forms as shown in Table 8. The Chi-square analysis of the percentage of children by age groups for each error reveals no significant difference. However, for distortion errors, the z-test with adjustment of the values according to the Bonferroni method indicated significant higher prevalence rates for four-year-olds (88%) and six-year-olds (80%) compared to the three other age groups: five-year-olds (44%); seven-year-olds (64%) and eight-year-olds (50%). (1) to (5) below show detailed evaluations of these types of errors.

Table 8: Frequency of speech sound errors by age (N=68 children, 4–8 years)

Errors	n	%	$\chi^2(4, N = 68)$	p
Omission	68	100	5.26	0.26
Substitution	61	89.7	4.36	0.36
Distortion	43	63.2	7.12	0.10
Addition	32	44.1	5.69	0.22
Assimilation	22	32.4	4.28	0.37

Beginning with forms of omission, all the children revealed at least one of the following: syllable initial and final consonant omission, omission of an entire syllable, simplification of consonant groups and complex syllabic structures (see (1) below for examples). Final consonant omission was the most frequent form regardless of age (approximately 93% of the children), followed by the simplification of consonant groups (about 65% of the children) and the omission of syllable initial consonants (about 43% of the children).

(1) Omission errors
      a. syllable final consonant omission
          (ardoise) [aʁ-dwaz] > [a-dwaz] → VC > V
          (couscous) [kuskus] > [ku-kus] → CVC > CV
      b. syllable initial consonant omission
          (parapluie) [pa-ʁa-plɥi] > [pa:-plɥi] → CV>V:
          (arachide) [a-ʁa-ʃid] > [a:-ʃid] → CV>V:
      c. simplification of consonants group
          (crayon) [kʁe-jɔ̃] > [ki-jɔ̃] → CCV > CV
          (table) [tabl] > [tab] → CVCC > CVC

d. syllable omission
    (nourriture) [nu-ʁi-tyʁ] > [nu:-ty:] → CV
    (télévision) [te-le-**vi**-zjɔ̃] > [te-le-sjɔ̃] → CV

e. simplification of complex syllable structures
    (arbre) [a:ʁbʁ] > [a:b] → VCCC > VC
    (parapluie) [pa-ʁa-plɥi] > [pa-ha-ply] → CCCV > CCV

Substitution errors appeared as a systematic or an inconsistent replacement of a consonant leading to a variety of errors such as fronting, backing, stopping, gliding and devoicing (see (2) below). In general, the substitution of [ʃ, ʒ] to [s, z] was the most frequent with a 68% prevalence rate, followed by backing, gliding and fronting errors with a 40–60% prevalence rate. Apart from devoicing (15% of the children) the other forms listed had prevalence rates less than 10%.

(2) Substitution errors
    a. fronting
        (couscous) [kuskus] > [tutu] → [k] > [t]
        (chat) [ʃa] > [sa] → [ʃ] > [s]

    b. substitution of [l] to [j]
        (crayon) [kʁejɔ̃] > [kʁelɔ̃] → [j] > [l]
        (bouteille) [butɛj] > [butɛl] → [j] > [l]

    c. backing:
        (tasse) [tas] > [kas] → [t] > [k]
        (train) [tʁɛ̃] > [kʁɛ̃] → [t] > [k]

    d. substitution of [ʃ,ʒ] to [s,z]:
        (tasse) [tas] > [taʃ] → [s] > [ʃ]
        (maison) [mɛzɔ] > [mɛʒɔ] → [z] > [ʒ]

    e. stopping:
        (savon) [savɔ̃] > [tavɔ̃]] → [s] > [t]
        (carte) [kaʁt] > [kaktə] → [ʁ] > [k]

    f. substitution of [l] to [ʁ]
        (robe) [ʁɔb] > [lɔb] → [ʁ] > [l]
        (orange) [oʁɑ̃ʒ] > [olɑ̃ʒ] → [ʁ] > [l]

    g. gliding:
        (fleur) [fløʁ] > [fwøʁ] → [l] > [w]
        (ballon) [balɔ̃] > [bajɔ̃] → [l] > [j]

    h. substitution of vowel to glide
        (parapluie) [paʁaplɥi] > [palaply] → [ɥ]> [y]

Aurélie Takam

i. Devoicing:
(doigt) [dwa] >[twa] → [d]> [t]

Regarding the errors classified as distortions, about 63% of the children glottalized /ʁ/ and only 12% of them also distorted the apical /t/ and the velar /k/ in syllable initial. It is worth recalling that in this study, distortion errors were neither a substitution nor an assimilation but an approximate production of a segment. Based on Table 3 above, the Chi-square analysis revealed no significant difference by age group $[\chi^2 = (4, N = 68) = 7.12, p = 0.10]$. However, the z-test with adjustment of the values according to the Bonferroni method indicated higher prevalence rates for four-year-olds (88%) and six-year-olds (80%) compared to the three other age groups: five-year-olds (44%); seven-year-olds (64%) and eight-year-olds (50%). (3) below shows examples of distortion errors observed.

(3)   Forms of distortion errors
    a. Distortion of [t]:
       (pantalon) [pãtalɔ̃] > [pãtʰalɔ̃] → [t] > [tʰ]
       (voiture) [vwatyʁ] > [vwatʰy] → [t] > [tʰ]
    b. Distortion of [k]:
       (car) [kaʁ] > [kʰa] → [k] > [kʰ]
       (crayon) [kʁejɔ̃] > [kʰejɔ̃] → [k] > [kʰ]
    c. Distortion of [ʁ]:
       (radio) [ʁadjo] > [hadjo] → [ʁ] > [h]
       (robe) [ʁɔb] > [hɔb] → [ʁ] > [h]

Sound addition errors were present in about 44% of the children. One form was the simplification of a complex syllable structure by adding an epenthetic vowel. It concerned about 15% to 37% of children between the ages of 6–8 years. The other form, the most prevalent, was the adding of a consonant at the beginning of words with vocalic attack. It affected all age groups. (4) below illustrates these forms of errors.

(4)   Addition errors
    a. Vocalic addition (epenthesis)
       (fleur) [fløʁ] > [fə-løː] → CCVC > CV+CV
       (brosse) [bʁos] > [bə-los] → CCVC > CV+CVC
    b. Consonant addition
       (ardoise) [aʁ-dwaz] > [naʁ-dwaz] → VC > CVC
       (hache) [aʃ] > [ʁaʃ] → VC > CVC

Finally, assimilation errors appeared as regressive or progressive consonant harmony and consonant devoicing as shown in (5) below. About 32% of children presented one or more of these errors without any significant difference between groups. Regressive assimilation of /ʃ/ and devoicing errors were the main forms observed.

(5) Assimilation errors
   a. Progressive assimilation
       (pantalon) [pãtalɔ̃] > [pãpalɔ̃] → [t] > [p]
   b. Regressive assimilation
       (chemise) [ʃəmiz] > [səmiz] → [ʃ] > [s]
       (chapeau) [ʃapo] > [papo] → [ʃ] > [p]
       (fourchette) [fuʁʃɛt] > [fuʁsɛt] → [ʃ] > [s]
       (chocolat) [ʃokola] > [kokola] → [ʃ] > [k]
       (arachide) [aʁaʃid] > [aʁatid] → [ʃ] > [t]
   c. Devoicing
       (gâteau) [gato] > [kato] → [g] > [k]
       (table) [tabl] > [tap] → [b] > [p]

3.6.3 Discussion

This study was aimed at assessing SSD from a representative quasi-random sample of 1127 bilingual Cameroonian children aged four to eight years and living in two Ghɔmálá'-French environments (rural and urban). The prevalence rate of 6% obtained in this study is comparable to the rate of 7.8% obtained by Fombonne & Vermeersh (1997) among French children between four and 16 years of age. In general, Kirkpatrick & Ward (1984) place this prevalence between 4% and 6%. These studies indicated a higher prevalence for boys compared to girls as was also the case in the present study. This difference is not yet explained in the literature. However, this discrepancy is also observed in regular language development as it is well admitted that girls generally develop speech and language faster than boys. Yet, this speed difference is significant, up to 30 months (Eriksson et al. 2012).

Regarding the differences related to school level, it is important to note that most children with SSD were in kindergarten and grade 1 (SIL). Many of the first-grade children in this study had failed to progress to the second grade (CP). These results can be interpreted as evidence that SSD is a handicap to children's academic performance. Several studies have linked SSD to children's education and it is now well recognized that they can give rise to learning disabilities such as difficulty learning written language graphemes (e.g. Rvachew 2007). One explanation is that SSD is often related to a phonological awareness deficit which plays a significant role in written language learning. This causal relation is mainly determined by the severity of the disorders profile regarding types of errors (e.g. omission) and error pattern, whether they are typical or atypical among normal developing children Rvachew et al. (2007). Omission errors are considered more severe than substitution as are atypical errors compared to typical ones.

Concerning the speech profile of the disorders in our sample, the main errors were omission and substitution without a significant difference between groups. Omission errors mainly occurred as final consonant omission and consonant group simplification, while the substitution of [ʃ, ʒ] to [s, z] was the most frequent with about 68% of the children, followed by backing, gliding and fronting errors with a 40–60% prevalence rate. According to Rvachew et al. (2007) and Fox & Dodd (2001), all these forms of errors are also typical to normal developing children. Consonants [s, ʃ, z, l, ʁ] and CVC syllables were the most impaired structures. These results are consistent with the literature both regarding type of errors (e.g. Austin & Shriberg 1997; Ruscello et al. 1991) and impaired consonants (e.g. Maurin-Cherou (1993) for French-speaking children; Shriberg & Kwiatkowski (1994) for English-speaking children). Besides, our analysis emphasized the importance of the syllabic structure including the lexical position and environment of consonants. Very few studies (e.g. Rvachew et al. 2007) have examined this aspect while assessment and intervention always include them in order to better evaluate speech difficulties (e.g. Maurin-Cherou 1993).

Regarding the impairment of [ʁ] in this study, all the children had difficulties with its use. This consonant is among the most frequent in French (Genouvrier & Peytard 1970) while it is almost absent in Ghɔmálá' (Mba & Domche 1995). Some of the error forms reported here were the same as those observed in the sociolinguistic context of the children as described by Biloa (2004). However, the difficulties with this sound were not only due to language interference or input given that the errors were not always linked to the sociolinguistic context. In fact, several studies have reported difficulties with this consonant in different linguistic environments. In English (or native English) children, the apical [r] is usually substituted for the glide [w] in initial position (Bowen 2014). As for monolingual Francophones, this is a sound frequently affected by SSD Maurin-Cherou (1993).

3.7 Conclusion

The objective of this study was to analyze child SSD in Cameroon in order to encourage the rehabilitation of language disorders in the public health system. Using a sample of 1127 bilingual children between the ages of four and eight years, the study determined the prevalence and speech profile of these disorders. In a nutshell, 6% of the children presented with SSD without a significant difference between age groups and sociolinguistic context (rural and urban). However, boys were more affected than girls with a ratio of 3.2. On the phonic level, consonants [ʁ, l, s, z, ʃ] were the most impaired (with 30% to 100% of the children screened) and the most frequent errors were omission and substitution. On the syllabic level, complex structures in general and the CVC structure, in particular, were the most impaired with a frequency of more than 90% followed by consonant groups with more than half of the children. The need for intervention no longer needs justification since these disorders have an impact both on individual and school performance. There are some limits to this study regarding the comorbidity of the speech disorders studied. None of the screened children had any difficulty understanding oral language. However, since we did not assess their language abilities (e.g., grammatical knowledge), it is possible that some of them may have a language delay.

Appendix

A sample of Ghɔmálá' words used (IPA)

/phə/ 'bag'
/paʔ/ 'house'
/bjɛ/ 'groundnuts'
/mɔk/ 'fire'
/nàm/ 'sun'
/wâsi/ 'watch'
/sɛdjə/ 'broom'

/bàp/ 'meat'
/dàp/ 'thread'
/nɔk/ 'snake'
/sɔk/ 'soap'
/tʃòʔ/ 'hat'
/ŋkedé/ 'banana'
/tsə/ 'cola nut'

/saʔthə/ 'comb'
/ŋwàʔɲə/ 'book'
/ʤɔm/ 'axe'
/bvʉ/ 'dog'
/púsi/ 'cat'
/ʤə/ 'clothe'
/wɔktə/ 'umbrella'

List of the 64 words (in French) used for picture naming and word repetition tests

ananas	casque	grains	pipe
arachide	chaise	hache	plantain
arbre	chapeau	huile	porte
ardoise	chat	journal	radio
assiette	chaussure	livre	robe
avion	chemise	maison	sac
bague	couscous	marmite	savon
ballon	crayon	montre	serpent
banane	doigt	nourriture	soleil
blanc	drap	œuf	table
bonbon	fenêtre	oignon	tasse
bouteille	feu	oiseau	téléphone
brosse	fleur	orange	télévision
cahier	fourchette	pantalon	train
autocar	gâteau	parapluie	voiture
carte	gomme	peigne	yaourt

Acknowledgements

Special thanks to Dr. John Ogwana for verifying the transcribed data and for all his contributions in this work, to Pr. Geneviève Bengono who performed the medical exam, and to Claire Nkoué, the speech-language therapist who gave us access to the speech and language assessment material used during the survey. Our special thanks also go to the teachers and headmasters of the eight schools for their enthusiasm and willingness to make the survey possible.

References

Austin, Diane & Lawrence D. Shriberg. 1997. *Lifespan reference data for ten measures of articulation competence using the speech disorders classification system (SDCS)*.

Beitchman, J. H., R. Nair, M. Clegg & P. G Patel. 1986. Prevalence of speech and language disorders in five-year-old kindergarten children in the Ottawa-carleton region. *Journal of Speech and Hearing Disorders* 51. 98–110.

Biloa, Edmond. 2004. *La Langue française au cameroun: Analyse linguistique et didactique. 2e edition*. Bern et al.: Peter Lang.

Bishop, Dorothy Vera Margareth & Andrew Edmundson. 1987. Language-impaired 4-year-olds: Distinguishing transient from persistent impairment. *Journal of Speech and Hearing Disorders* 52(2). 156–173.

Bowen, Caroline. 2014. *Children's speech sound disorders.* Oxford, UK: John Wiley & Sons.

Breton, Roland & Bikia Fohtung. 1991. *Atlas administratif des langues nationales du cameroun.* Paris: Agence de coopération culturelle et technique.

Dieu, M. & P. Renaud. 1983. *Atlas linguistique d'afrique centrale (ALAC) : Situation linguistique en afrique centrale. Inventaire préliminaire: Le cameroun.* Paris, Yaoundé: ACCT, CERDOTOLA, DGRST.

Dodd, Barbara. 2013. *Differential diagnosis and treatment of children with speech disorder.* 2nd edn. Oxford, UK: John Wiley & Sons.

Domche, Engelbert & Deborah Hatfield. 1991. *Enquête sociolinguistique sur le ghɔmálá'-jo comme dialecte de référence standard.* Yaoundé: SIL.

Enderby, P. & R. Philipp. 1986. Speech and language handicap: Toward knowing the size of the problem. *British Journal of Disorders of Communication* 21. 151–165.

Eriksson, M., P. B Marschik, T. Tulviste, M. Almgren, M. P. Pereira, S. Wehberg, L. Marjanoviˇc-Umek, F. Gayraud, M. Kovacevic & C Gallego. 2012. Differences between girls and boys in emerging language skills: Evidence from 10 language communities. *British Journal of Developmental Psychology* 30. 326–343.

Fombonne, Eric & S Vermeersh. 1997. Les enfants de la cohorte GAZEl: Ii - Motifs des contacts avec le système médico-éducatif, par âge et sexe". *Revue Epidémiologique de Santé Publique* 45. 107–115.

Fox, Annette V. & Barbara Dodd. 2001. Phonologically disordered German-speaking children. *American Journal of Speech-Language Pathology* 10(3). 291–307.

Genouvrier, Émile & Jean Peytard. 1970. *Linguistique et enseignement du français.* Paris: Larousse.

Hull, Forrest M., P. W. Jr. Mielke, R. J. Timmons & J. A Willeford. 1971. The national speech and hearing survey: Preliminary results. *Asha* 13. 501–509.

Kirkpatrick, E. & J Ward. 1984. Prevalence of articulation errors in new South Wales primary school pupils. *Australian Journal of Human Communication Disorders* 12(1). 55–62.

MacLeod, Andrea, Ann Sutton, Natacha Trudeau & Elin Thordardottir. 2011. The acquisition of consonants in Québécois French: a cross-sectional study of pre-school aged children. *International Journal of Speech-Language Pathology* 13(2). 93–109.

Maurin-Cherou, N. 1993. *Rééducation des troubles articulatoires isolés.* Paris: Ortho Edition.

Mba, Gabriel & Engelbert Domche. 1995. *L'alphabet du ghɔmálá'.* 2nd Edition, Yaoundé: ISH.

McKinnon, David H., Sharynne McLeod & Sheena Reilly. 2007. The prevalence of stuttering, voice and speech-sound disorders in primary school students in Australia. *Language, Speech and Hearing Services in School* 38. 5–15.

Morley, Muriel E. 1972. *The development and disorders of speech in childhood.* Edingburgh & London: Churchill Livingstone.

Nissim, Gabriel. 1981. *Le Bamiléké - Ghɔmálá' (parler de bandjoun, Cameroun). Phonologie-morphologie nominale, comparaison avec des parlers voisins. Coll.* Langue et Civilisation orale, n°45, Paris: SELAF.

Paradis, Johanne, Fred Genesee & Martha B. Crago. 2011. *Dual language development and disorders: A handbook on bilingualism and second language learning (2e éd.)* Baltimore: Paul Brooke Publishing Co.

Peckham, C. S. 1973. Speech defects in a national sample of children aged seven years. *British Journal of Disorders of Communication* 8(1). 2–8.

Ruscello, Dennis M., Kenneth O. St. Louis & Nancy Mason. 1991. School-aged children with phonologic disorders: Coexistence with other speech/language disorders. *Journal of Speech, Language, and Hearing Research* 34(2). 236–242.

Rvachew, Susan, Alexandra Marquis, Françoise Brosseau-Lapré, Marianne Paul, Phaedra Royle & Laura M Gonnerman. 2013. Speech articulation performance of francophone children in the early school years: Norming of the test de dépistage francophone de phonologie. *Clinical Linguistics & Phonetics, 27:* 12. 950–968.

Rvachew, Susan. 2007. Phonological processing and reading in children with speech sound disorders. *American Journal of Speech-Language Pathology* 16. 260–270.

Rvachew, Susan, Pi-Yu Chiang & Natalia Evans. 2007. Characteristics of speech errors produced by children with and without delayed phonological awareness skills. *Language, Speech and Hearing Services in School* 38. 60–71.

Shriberg, Lawrence D. & Joan Kwiatkowski. 1994. Developmental phonological disorders i: A clinical profile. *Journal of Speech and Hearing Research* 37. 1100–1126.

Shriberg, Lawrence D., Bruce Tomblin & Jane L. Mcsweeny. 1999. Prevalence of speech delay in 6-year-old children and comorbidity with language impairment. *Journal of Speech and Hearing Research,* 42. 1461–1481.

Silva, Phil A. 1980. The prevalence, stability and significance of developmental language delay in preschool children. *Developmental Medicine and Child Neurology* 22. 768–777.

Silva, Phil A., Chris Justin, Rob McGee & Sheila M. Williams. 1984. Some developmental and behavioural characteristics of seven-year-old children with delayed speech development. *Developmental Medicine and Child Neurology* 19. 147–154.

Stevenson, Jim & Naomi Richman. 1976. The prevalence of language delay in a population of three-year-old children and its association with general retardation. *Developmental Medicine and Child Neurology* 18. 431–441.

Stothard, Susan E., Margaret J. Snowling, D. V. M. Bishop, Barry B. Chipchase & Carole A. Kaplan. 1998. Language-impaired preschoolers: A followup into adolescence. *Journal of Speech, Language, and Hearing Research* 41. 407–418.

Takam, Aurélie. Unpublished. Développement phonologique du français en milieu multilingue africain.

Topouzkhanian, Sylvia & Moustapha Mijiyawa. 2013. A French-speaking speech-language pathology program in West Africa: Transfer of training between minority and majority world countries. *International Journal of Speech-Language Pathology* 15(1). 58–64.

Van der Linde, Jeannie, Linique Hanekom De Wet Swanepoel, Tasha Lemmer, Karla Schoeman, Frances Page Glascoe & Bart Vinck. 2016. Early detection of communication delays with the PEDS tools in at-risk South African infants. *African Journal of Disability* 5(1). DOI:10.4102/ajod.v5i1.223

Chapter 4

Efik nominal tonal alternations as phrasal morphology

Eleanor Glewwe
University of California, Los Angeles

Certain Efik nominal constructions exhibit fixed tonal melodies that overwrite nouns' underlying tones. Previous analyses of these alternations (Welmers 1973; Kim 1974; Cook 1985) are purely phonological. Working in a constraint-based framework, I propose that the tonal alternations are actually phrasal morphology (McPherson 2014). The tonal melodies are overlays encoded in lexicalized constructional schemas that relate idiosyncratic phrasal phonology with specific syntactic constructions. The constructional schemas are enforced by constraints. The Efik case extends the observed range of phrasal morphology by demonstrating that constructional schema constraints and phonological constraints can interact to determine a construction's surface tones.

1 Efik nominal tonal alternations

Efik (Niger-Congo: Benue-Congo: Cross River) is a language spoken in Cross River State in southeastern Nigeria (Cook 1985). It has two tones, high (H) and low (L), which may combine in a single syllable to produce falling (HL) and rising (LH) tones (Welmers 1968). Additionally, there is a downstepped high tone ($^{\downarrow}$H) whose pitch is lower than H but higher than L. I analyze $^{\downarrow}$H as an H after a floating L.

In certain nominal constructions, including noun-noun compounds, adjective-noun constructions, and genitive constructions, nouns exhibit tonal alternations. For instance, in the noun-noun compound 'dog house,' the underlyingly H-H noun *ébwá* 'dog' is realized as H-L after the underlyingly H-L noun *úfɔ̀k* 'house':

Eleanor Glewwe. 2019. Efik nominal tonal alternations as phrasal morphology. In Samson Lotven, Silvina Bongiovanni, Phillip Weirich, Robert Botne & Samuel Gyasi Obeng (eds.), *African linguistics across the disciplines: Selected papers from the 48th Annual Conference on African Linguistics*, 71–88. Berlin: Language Science Press. DOI:10.5281/zenodo.3520571

(1) /úfɔ̀k ébwá/ → [úfɔ̀k ébwà]
     house dog
     'dog house'

The complete patterns of nominal tonal alternations in compounds are given in Table 1. These patterns were reported by Welmers (1968) and Cook (1985) and confirmed with new data elicited from six native speakers of Efik.

Table 1: Surface tones on the second noun in noun-noun compounds

Underlying tonal shape of first noun		Underlying tonal shape of second noun						
		Group 1				Group 2		
		H-H	H-HL	H-L	L-L	L-H	L-HL[a]	H-↓H
Alternation 1	H-H							
	H-L							
	L-L			H-L				H-↓H
	L-H							
	H-↓H							
Alternation 2	H-HL			L-L				L-H
	L-HL							

[a]L-HL nouns actually preserve their final fall, surfacing as H-↓HL and L-HL under Alternations 1 and 2, respectively.

As Table 1 shows, disyllabic nouns occur in seven tonal shapes: H-H, H-L, L-H, L-L, H-HL, L-HL, and H-↓H (Welmers 1968: 86). Nouns longer than two syllables still exhibit one of these seven tonal melodies. In a noun-noun compound, only the tones of the second (non-head) noun alternate; the tones of the first noun surface unchanged. The seven nominal tonal shapes can be divided into two groups according to the pattern of alternations they exhibit. Group 1 comprises H-H, H-HL, H-L, and L-L nouns while Group 2 comprises L-H, L-HL, and H-↓H nouns (the terms *Group 1* and *Group 2* come from Welmers 1968). Additionally, there are two alternation patterns in compounds, triggered by two different sets of nouns. Alternation 1 is triggered by first nouns with tonal shapes ending in H or L while Alternation 2 is triggered by first nouns with tonal shapes end in HL (*Alternation 1* and *Alternation 2* are also Welmers' terms). Each tonal shape group exhibits a different output under each of the two tonal alternations, yielding a

total of four patterns. After a noun ending in H or L, Group 1 nouns surface as
H-L, and after a noun ending in HL, they surface as L-L. Group 2 nouns surface
as H-↓H after a noun ending in H or L and as L-H after a noun ending in HL.
Thus in (1), the noun *ébwá* 'dog' surfaces as H-L in the compound 'dog house'
because it is a Group 1 noun (with underlying tones H-H) and it occurs after the
noun *úfɔk* 'house,' which ends in L.

While complex, these tonal alternation patterns can be summarized in a few
generalizations. There are essentially two tonal melodies, HL, which corresponds
to Alternation 1, and L, which corresponds to Alternation 2. The melody HL occurs after nouns ending in a level tone (H or L) while the melody L occurs after
nouns ending in a falling tone (HL). The surface melodies H-↓H and L-H exhibit
the melodies HL and L, respectively, but instead of continuing to the end of the
word, the melodies stop before an H that is the final tone of the word. H-↓H
and L-H arise in Group 2 nouns, which differ from Group 1 nouns in that their
tonal shapes contain an H after an L (in H-↓H nouns, the L that the second H
follows is unassociated, manifesting as downstep). Thus in Group 2 nouns the
tonal melodies HL and L extend only as far as the H that followed the original
underlying L and no further, leaving that H to be realized on the second syllable
of the noun.

In (2), I provide a few more compounds that illustrate the tonal alternation
patterns in Table 1:

(2) a. /ùbóm íják/ → [ùbóm íjàk] Alt. 1 Group 1 H-L
        boat   fish
        'fish boat'

    b. /ɔ́fɔ̀ŋ ùsàn/ → [ɔ̀fɔ̀ŋ úsàn] Alt. 1 Group 1 H-L
        cloth dish
        'dish cloth'

    c. /ùsàn ejím/ → [ùsàn é↓jím] Alt. 1 Group 2 H-↓H
        dish   onion
        'onion dish'

    d. /úfɔk ìw̃áŋ/ → [úfɔk í↓w̃áŋ] Alt. 1 Group 2 H-↓H
        house farm
        'farm house'

    e. /íkwâ ébwá/ → [íkwâ èbwà] Alt. 2 Group 1 L-L
        knife dog
        'dog knife'

    f. /àw̃â úkwàk/ → [àw̃â ùkwàk] Alt. 2 Group 1 L-L
       cat iron

       'iron cat'

    g. /íkwâ i↓nwέn/ → [íkwâ ìnwέn] Alt. 2 Group 2 L-H
       knife bird

       'bird knife'

    h. /àw̃â i↓nwεn/ → [àw̃â ìnwεn] Alt. 2 Group 2 L-H
       cat bird

       'bird cat'

Previous analyses of the Efik nominal tonal alternations (Welmers 1973; Kim 1974; Cook 1985) are purely phonological. Only Cook 1985 is fully elaborated. For noun-noun compounds, Cook posits a construction marker /H L/, that is, a high tone followed by a low tone with no segmental material, that occurs between the two nouns of the compound (e.g. /ú-fɔk ´ ` é-bwá/ 'dog house'). He derives the surface tones of the second noun with three phonological rules. Two are tonal assimilation rules triggered by floating tones. Assimilation to Floating L changes each H of a continuous string of Hs to L after a floating L (e.g. /` ó ó ó / → [` ò ò ò ]) while Assimilation to Floating H changes a single L to H after a floating H and applies iteratively (e.g. /´ ` ò ò ò / → [´ ´ ò ò ò] → [´ ´ ó ò ò]) (Cook 1985: 193). These rules seem somewhat arbitrary. Why does a floating L affect a whole string of following Hs (Assimilation to Floating L) while a floating H affects only a single following L but can apply iteratively (Assimilation to Floating H)? Why do floating tones but not associated tones trigger these assimilations?

These two assimilation rules have at least some application outside nominal constructions in Cook's phonology of Efik, but the third rule that derives the tonal alternations in compounds is purely ad hoc. This rule, called L Copying, copies an initial L of a noun when that initial L is preceded by a word boundary and a floating tone. (Specifically, the L copies onto an open transition, a unit specific to Cook's phonological analysis of Efik. An open transition is a segmental phoneme that is not audible but can bear a tone and occurs immediately after the initial vowel of most nouns.) L Copying's sole role in the grammar is to ensure that tonal alternations in compounds and other nominal constructions come out right. In particular, it is needed to derive downstep where it is observed to occur.

While Cook's analysis can account for all four tonal alternation patterns in Table 1, the rules it relies on are unsatisfying. Moreover, it does not capture the generalizations stated above, namely that there are essentially two surface melodies, HL and L, and that consistent tonal properties of the first and second nouns in compounds give rise to the full set of four patterns.

Instead of treating the nominal tonal alternations as purely phonological, I propose a phrasal morphology account for them. This analysis is presented in the following section. I then consider an alternative, constraint-based phonological account and argue that the phrasal morphology account is preferable.

2 A phrasal morphology account

The phrasal morphology account I advocate treats the surface tones in Efik compounds as tonal melodies that are imposed in particular constructions. This approach is reminiscent of Harry & Hyman (2014) approach to Kalabari nouns, which exhibit tonal alternations in many of the same constructions as in Efik. While they do not provide a fully implemented analysis, Harry & Hyman argue for a constructional, rather than a purely phonological, approach in which Kalabari nouns in certain constructions, including compounds and genitive constructions, lose their underlying tones and are assigned a particular tonal melody.

My analysis of Efik is couched in a different constructional framework, that of McPherson 2014. In McPherson's framework, lexicalized constructional schemas relate idiosyncratic phrasal phonology with particular syntactic constructions. For example, in specific syntactic constructions, certain word classes may impose tonal overlays on other words. In the case of Efik noun-noun compounds, it will be the first (head) noun that imposes a tonal overlay on the second (non-head) noun. Recall the generalizations from §1: the second nouns in compounds exhibit two melodies, HL and L, with HL occurring after a first noun ending in a level tone and L occurring after a first noun ending in a falling tone. In keeping with McPherson's framework, there is a constructional schema for Efik noun-noun compounds that specifies a tonal overlay with two allomorphs, {HL} and {L}, and the environment in which each allomorph occurs. The constructional schema is associated with a constraint that enforces the application of the appropriate tonal overlay, and the interaction of this constructional schema constraint with other phonological constraints gives rise to the full range of surface tones seen on the second nouns of compounds.

The constructional schema for Efik compounds is given in Figure 1. Constructional schemas show the correspondence of idiosyncratic phonology, including tonal overlays, with specific syntactic structures. The schema in Figure 1 states that in a noun-noun compound, if the first noun ends in a falling tone HL, the tonal overlay {L} is imposed on the second noun, and if the first noun ends in a syllable with a single tone (H or L) associated to it, the tonal overlay {HL} is imposed on the second noun.

PHON   ↔   NP

ω_i ω_j ω_i ω_j N

...σ [ ]   ...σ [ ] N_i N_j

H   L   {L}   T   {HL}

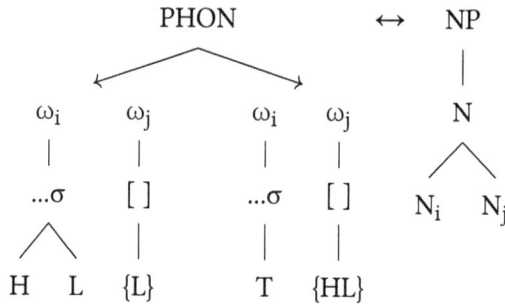

Figure 1: Constructional schema for Efik noun-noun compounds

This schema is enforced with the single constructional schema constraint N $N^{(H)L}$, which is satisfied when the correct allomorph of the tonal overlay is imposed on the second noun of a compound. N $N^{(H)L}$ counts one violation for each associated tone in the output that does not match the overlay (we will see later why its evaluation is not binary). Following McPherson (2014), the complementary faithfulness constraint I use is FAITH(T). One violation of FAITH(T) is incurred when a word's tones in the output do not match its tones in the input.

The tableau in Figure 2 shows the derivation of the surface tone pattern H-L (Group 1 Alternation 1) with the compound *úfɔk ébwà* 'dog house.' A superscript on a word indicates that a tonal overlay has been imposed, whether partially or fully.

/úfɔk ébwá/ | | | | H L H_1 H_2	N $N^{(H)L}$	FAITH(T)
☞ a. úfɔk ébwà^{HL} | | | | H L H_1 L		*
b. úfɔk ébwá | | | | H L H_1 H_2	*!	

Figure 2: Tableau for *úfɔk ébwà*

The first noun in the compound, /úfɔk/, ends in L, so according to the constructional schema in Figure 1 it seeks to impose the overlay {HL} on the second noun, /ébwá/. The constructional schema constraint N $N^{(H)L}$ is violated if the tonal overlay is not exhaustively imposed. Candidate (b), the faithful candidate, only partially satisfies the overlay, realizing it on the first syllable of *ebwa* but not imposing it over the final H of this word. The H on the final syllable of *ebwa* does not match the tonal overlay, so one violation of N N$^{(H)L}$ is incurred. Candidate (a) imposes the overlay exhaustively and so does not violate the constructional schema constraint. It changes the tones of *ebwa*, violating FAITH(T), but since N N$^{(H)L}$ >> FAITH(T), it is the winner. Note that I assume lexical tones can realize tonal overlays. Thus in the winner the first tone of the {HL} overlay is in fact the original first H of *ébwá*; this lexical tone is maintained since it can realize the overlay. The same is true in candidate (b).

The tableau in Figure 3 shows the derivation of the surface tones L-L (Group 1 Alternation 2) with the compound *íkwâ èbwà* 'dog knife'.

/íkwâ ébwá/ ⎧ ∧ ⎫ H H L H₁ H₂	N N$^{(H)L}$	FAITH(T)
☞ a. íkwâ èbwà^L ⎧ ∧ ⎫ H H L L L		*
b. íkwâ ébwá ⎧ ∧ ⎫ H H L H₁ H₂	*!*	
c. íkwâ èbwá^L ⎧ ∧ ⎫ H H L L H₂	*!	*

Figure 3: Tableau for *íkwâ èbwà*

The first noun of the compound, /íkwâ/, ends in HL, so according to the constructional schema it seeks to impose the overlay {L} on /ébwá/. The faithful candidate, (b), does not impose the overlay at all, thereby incurring two violations of N N$^{(H)L}$, and candidate (c) imposes the overlay only partially, incurring one violation of N N$^{(H)L}$. Consequently, they both lose to candidate (a), which exhaustively imposes the overlay.

Having accounted for the surface tones of Group 1 nouns in compounds, I now consider Group 2 nouns. The surface melodies that must be derived are H-↓H and L-H. As discussed in §1, Group 2 nouns (those with the tonal shapes L-H, L-HL, or H-↓H) differ from Group 1 nouns in that they contain an H after an L (the L is floating in H-↓H nouns). After nouns ending in a falling tone, Group 2 nouns have the surface tones L-H (Group 2 Alternation 2). These nouns do exhibit the melody of the {L} allomorph of the tonal overlay, but the noun's original underlying H after the underlying L is preserved. That is, the imposition of the overlay is halted by the H after the L and does not extend beyond it. I therefore propose that an H following an L in the same word is preserved by the following special positional faithfulness constraint:

(3)   PRESERVEHPOSTL: An associated H that follows an L (associated or not) within the same word in the input must be associated in the output.

This constraint, combined with the constructional schema constraint, derives the surface pattern L-H. The idea is that PRESERVEHPOSTL blocks the tonal overlay from proceeding past the H after the L. The tableau in Figure 4 illustrates this with the compound *íkwâ ìnwɛn* 'bird knife'.

/íkwâ i'nwέn/ $\mid \wedge \mid \quad \mid$ H H L H₁L₂H₃	PRESERVEHPOSTL	N N$^{(H)L}$	FAITH(T)
☞ a. íkwâ ìnwέn^L $\mid \wedge \mid \quad \mid$ H H L L L₂H₃		*	*
b. íkwâ i'nwέn $\mid \wedge \mid \quad \mid$ H H L H₁L₂H₃		**!	
c. íkwâ ìnwὲn^L $\mid \wedge \mid \quad \mid$ H H L LL₂L	*!		*

Figure 4: Tableau for *íkwâ ìnwɛn*

Since the first noun of the compound, /íkwâ/, ends in HL, the constructional schema dictates that it impose the overlay {L} on /i↓nwen/. PRESERVEHPOSTL outranks N N$^{(H)L}$ and prevents exhaustive realization of the overlay, eliminating candidate (c). Because N N$^{(H)L}$ counts the number of tones that do not match the overlay, though, non-exhaustive realization, as in candidate (a), is still better than no realization, as in (b), so the winner is [íkwâ ìnwen^L].

The final surface melody to be derived is H-↓H (Group 2 Alternation 1). Group 2 nouns show the H-↓H pattern after nouns ending in H or L, so according to the constructional schema it is the {HL} overlay that is being imposed. The surface tones H-↓H do in fact show the {HL} overlay; the downstep is caused by the presence of an unassociated L. The question is why the L is unassociated. The final H in the H-↓H pattern can be explained by PRESERVEHPOSTL, which prevents the overlay from reaching the end of the word. If the {HL} overlay were fully realized on a Group 2 noun while the H after the L was preserved as well (i.e. if the {HL} overlay were realized on the first syllable of the noun and the H were preserved on the second syllable), the result would be an HLH sequence within a word. This sequence does not surface, so I claim that the constraint *HLH is active:

(4) *HLH: Within a word, don't have the tonal sequence HLH, where all three tones are associated.[1]

*HLH has been proposed for a variety of languages (Cahill 2007; McPherson 2016) and seems to reflect a desire to avoid multiple sharp changes in pitch in close proximity (cf. Hyman's (2007) Principle of Ups and Downs). There is independent evidence that *HLH is active within the word in Efik. As mentioned in §1, there are seven surface tonal shapes for Efik disyllabic nouns. All two-tone combinations of H and L are attested, as are the shapes H-HL, L-HL, and H-↓H, but the shapes H-LH and HL-H are not attested. Additionally, *HLH constrains the surface tones of reduplicated verb forms (Glewwe 2017).

Because realizing the {HL} overlay and preserving a final H would violate *HLH, the L delinks, yielding the surface tones H-↓H. The tableau in Figure 5 shows the derivation of this pattern with the compound *ùsàn é↓jím* 'onion dish'.

/ùsàn èjím/ | | | \ L L L₁H₂	PRESERVEHPOSTL	*HLH	N N⁽ᴴ⁾ᴸ	FAITH(T)
☞ a. ùsàn é↓jím^{HL} | | | \ L L HL₁H₂			*	*
b. ùsàn èjím | | | \ L L L₁ H₂			**!	
c. ùsàn êjím^{HL} | | ∧ \ L L HL₁ H₂	*!		*	*
d. ùsàn éjìm^{HL} | | | | L L H L	*!			*

Figure 5: Tableau for *ùsàn é↓jím*

As it ends in L, /ùsàn/ seeks to impose the overlay {HL} on /èjím/. Candidate (d) fully realizes the overlay, but it violates PRESERVEHPOSTL, so it is eliminated. Candidate (c) preserves the H following the L in /èjìm/ and partially realizes the

---

[1]The domain of *HLH must ultimately be more specific because surface HLH sequences are permitted within a word in, for instance, inflected verb forms like *á-sàŋá* 's/he is walking.'

overlay by imposing the melody HL on the first syllable of *ejim*, but the result violates *HLH. Candidates (a) and (b) respect PRESERVEHPOSTL and *HLH. The winning candidate, (a), delinks the L to avoid violating *HLH but still realizes the {HL} overlay better than the faithful candidate (b). The optimal form is thus the attested [ùsàn é↓jím].

The phrasal morphology account I have presented is able to handle the complete set of tonal alternations seen in Efik compounds. A potential alternative to this account is a purely phonological constraint-based analysis. In the next section, I consider what such an analysis might look like.

3 A constraint-based phonological account

In working out a phonological account of the tonal alternations in Efik compounds, I adopt Cook's (1985) construction marker /H L/, which occurs between the two nouns of a compound. The tones of the construction marker are compelled to surface by REALIZEMORPHEME (Gnanadesikan 1997; Kurisu 2001; van Oostendorp 2005). The interaction of REALIZEMORPHEME with other phonological constraints gives rise to the four different surface patterns.

The tableau in Figure 6 exemplifies the derivation of the surface tones H-L (Group 1 Alternation 1) with the compound *úfɔ̀k ébwà* 'dog house'. Candidates (c) and (d) do not realize both tones of the construction marker, so they are eliminated by REALIZEMORPHEME. *HLH, introduced above in the phrasal morphology account, rules out associating both tones of the construction marker to the first syllable of *ebwa*, as in (b), so (a) is optimal. Note that REALIZEMORPHEME must be defined as being satisfied only if both tones of the construction marker are associated; otherwise, (c) would be as harmonic as (a). This is a departure from well-known formalizations of REALIZEMORPHEME that only require that *some* element of the morpheme's input be realized on the surface to satisfy the constraint (Gnanadesikan 1997; van Oostendorp 2005). One might argue that in candidate (c) the L of the construction marker *is* realized insofar as it has a surface phonological effect, namely, downstep. This would be in the spirit of approaches (e.g. Gnanadesikan 1997) in which any detectable phonological effect of the morpheme counts as realization. However, for candidate (a) to be chosen over candidate (c), REALIZEMORPHEME must require both tones of the construction marker to be *associated*, not merely audible in some way. I return to this subject below.

Next I turn to the surface tones H-↓H (Group 2 Alternation 1). This is one of the patterns exhibited by Group 2 nouns, those with the tonal shapes L-H, L-HL, or H-↓H. The surface pattern H-↓H does show the HL melody of the construction

/úfɔ̀k ébwá/ HLHLH H	RealizeMorpheme	*HLH
☞ a. úfɔ̀k ébwà HLHLH H		
b. úfɔ̀k êbwá HLHLH H		*!
c. úfɔ̀k é'bwá HLHLH H	*!	
d. úfɔ̀k ébwá HLHLH H	*!	

Figure 6: Tableau for *úfɔ̀k ébwà*

marker, but the L is suppressed, appearing only as downstep, while the underlying H after the underlying L is preserved. To derive the behavior of Group 2 nouns, I make use of the constraint PreserveHPostL from the phrasal morphology account.

The surface pattern H-↓H is exemplified by the compound *ùsàn é↓jɨ́m* 'onion dish.' Notice that if the H on the second syllable of /èjɨ́m/ is preserved on the surface, as in [é↓jɨ́m], it means that the L of the construction marker /H L/ has not been associated. That is, only one tone of the construction marker is associated, meaning that this candidate violates RealizeMorpheme as defined above. In that case, one would expect the faithful candidate [ùsàn èjɨ́m], in which *none* of the tones of the construction marker are associated, to win, since this candidate also violates RealizeMorpheme but is more faithful. Overcoming this problem requires a workaround. To ensure that the correct candidate wins, I allow RealizeMorpheme to count units of the morpheme being compelled to realize, so that its evaluation is no longer binary. In this case, the units of the morpheme are tones.

Now the surface tones H-↓H can be derived, as shown in the tableau in Figure 7 for *ùsàn é↓jɨ́m* 'onion dish'. Candidate (d) associates one tone of the construction marker to each syllable of *ejɨm*, but this violates PreserveHPostL. Candidate (c) preserves the underlying H after the L by realizing the construction marker on the first syllable of *ejɨm*, but this violates *HLH. The faithful candidate (b) incurs two violations of RealizeMorpheme while (a) only incurs one by partially realizing the construction marker, so (a) wins.

If the downstep in candidate (a) could qualify as realization of the floating L of the construction marker and therefore exempt candidate (a) from violating RealizeMorpheme, candidate (b) would no longer need to incur two violations of the constraint to lose to candidate (a). The evaluation of RealizeMorpheme could then remain binary. We saw in the derivation of *úfɔ̀k ébwà* (Figure 6) that

/ùsàn èjím/ L L H L LH	Preserve VeHPostL	*HLH	RealizeMorpheme
☞ a. ùsàn é'jím L L H L L H			*
b. ùsàn èjím L L H L LH			**!
c. ùsàn êjím L L H L LH		*!	
d. ùsàn éjìm L L H L LH	*!		

Figure 7: Tableau for *ùsàn é↓jím*

downstep cannot count as realization of the L of the construction marker, though, so this attempt to keep RealizeMorpheme binary will not work.

I turn now to the surface tones L-L (Group 1 Alternation 2). This pattern arises in the compound *íkwâ èbwà* 'dog knife.' Group 1 nouns like *èbwá* 'dog' surface as L-L instead of H-L when the preceding noun ends in a falling tone HL. For some reason, the H of the construction marker does not associate to the first syllable of the second noun when the first noun ends in HL. It seems, then, that the HL#H (falling # high) sequence is avoided, but this structure does not violate *HLH because it is not within a word. Some other markedness constraint must be devised to penalize this structure. I therefore put forth the following constraint:

(5) *HLH<3: Don't have the tonal sequence HLH on fewer than three syllables.[2]

The constraint specifies that the HLH sequence must occur on fewer than three syllables to incur a violation because in a compound like *úfɔ̀k ébwà* 'dog house,' there is an HLH sequence spanning three syllables, and the form is perfectly licit (see McPherson 2016 for another *HLH constraint with a configuration restriction).

---

[2]This constraint must also be restricted to some domain, since HLH sequences on fewer than 3 syllables can arise elsewhere, e.g. on a subject prefix and following verb in *ń-tjě-γé-tjè* 1SG-sit-NEG~FOC 'I'm not *sitting*.'

Realizing the H of the construction marker on the first syllable of the second noun when the first noun ends in the contour tone HL would violate *HLH<3, so the H of the construction marker changes to L. The tableau in Figure 8 shows how the surface tones L-L are derived for the compound *íkwâ èbwà* 'dog knife'. The faithful candidate (e) is eliminated because it violates *HLH<3; it also fails to realize the construction marker. Candidates (c) and (d) both realize the construction marker, but both still violate *HLH<3 (candidate (c) does so twice). Candidate (c) also violates *HLH due to the HLH sequence on *ebwa*. (Note that candidates (d) and (e) do not violate *HLH because *HLH, unlike *HLH<3, only applies to HLH sequences within a word.) Candidate (b) avoids violating *HLH<3 by associating the second tone of the construction marker to both syllables of *ebwa*, but in not associating the first tone of the construction marker it violates REALIZE-MORPHEME. Candidate (a) changes the first tone of the construction marker from H to L, violating IDENT(T), but this faithfulness constraint is lower-ranked, so (a) wins. (Candidates (a) and (b) are homophonous, so analyses other than the one I have opted for here are possible.)

/íkwâ ébwá/ H H L H₁ L₂ H H	*HLH<3	*HLH	REALIZEMORPHEME	ID(T)
☞ a. ikwâ èbwà H H L L₁ L₂ H H				*
b. ikwâ èbwà H H L H₁ L₂ H H			*!	
c. íkwâ èbwá H H L H₁ L₂ H H	*!*	*		
d. íkwâ ébwà H H L H₁ L₂ H H	*!			
e. íkwâ ébwá H H L H₁ L₂ H H	*!		**	

Figure 8: Tableau for *íkwâ èbwà*

The last pattern seen in compounds is when the second noun has the surface tones L-H (Group 2 Alternation 2). A compound that exhibits this pattern is *íkwâ ìnwén* 'bird knife.' In this phonological analysis, the surface tones L-H can be derived through a combination of the effects of PRESERVEHPOSTL and *HLH<3. PRESERVEHPOSTL ensures that the underlying H that occurs after a (floating) L in /íᴸnwén/ is preserved in the surface form [ìnwén], and *HLH<3 prevents *inwɛn* from having an H on its first syllable because after *íkwâ* this would result in an HLH sequence on fewer than three syllables.

4 Comparing the phrasal morphology and phonological accounts

The phrasal morphology account I proposed in §2 and the constraint-based phonological analysis outlined in §3 are both able to derive the tonal alternations seen in Efik compounds, but they differ in their principal mechanism for generating the surface tonal melodies. The phrasal morphology account stipulates two allomorphs of a tonal overlay that is imposed on the second noun of compounds: {L} after nouns ending in HL and {HL} after other nouns. The phonological account posits a construction marker /H L/ between the two nouns of a compound. The phonological account is appealing in not requiring the added apparatus of constructional schemas and the stipulation of two tonal overlays. On the other hand, the phrasal morphology account is appealing in capturing the output-orientedness of the patterns; the data give the impression that nouns should simply have a certain tonal shape in compounds. McPherson (2014) speculates that many cases of phrasal morphology are hidden in the literature because they have been analyzed phonologically.

Both the phonological account and the phrasal morphology account are constraint-based, and the constraint sets they use are quite similar. In particular, both analyses use PRESERVEHPOSTL to capture the difference between Group 1 and Group 2 nouns' surface tones in compounds. There are drawbacks to the constraints used in the phonological account, though. First, the phonological analysis requires the evaluation of REALIZEMORPHEME to be non-binary when it has most commonly been binary (Gnanadesikan 1997; Kurisu 2001; van Oostendorp 2005; Wolf 2007). That is not to say non-binary evaluation is unprecedented. Samek-Lodovici's (1992) original formulation of the morpheme realization constraint, AFFIX REALIZATION, required each specification of an affix to be realized and counted one violation for each unrealized specification. Additionally, Wolf (2007) proposes a constraint MAXFLT that accomplishes the work of REALIZE-MORPHEME but also requires that *all* floating autosegments in the input have output correspondents. Trommer (2012), however, argues that a morphological reanalysis of the data Wolf uses to justify MAXFLT makes the more powerful MAXFLT unnecessary. Therefore the more restrictive, binary REALIZEMORPHEME should be retained.

A full discussion of the proper formalization of morpheme realization constraints is beyond the scope of this paper. For now, I point out that if REALIZEMORPHEME requires all elements of a morpheme to be realized and counts a violation for each unrealized element, as it does in the phonological account, this opens the door to further complications. For instance, when the construction marker is realized by its tones being associated to the second noun of the compound, should the delinked tones of the second noun (e.g. the two delinked Hs of *ebwa* in candidate (a) in Figure 8) also incur violations of REALIZEMORPHEME? If not, why not, when those tones are units of the morpheme consisting of the second noun of the compound?

It should be acknowledged that the phrasal morphology account also requires non-binary constraint evaluation, in this case of the constructional schema constraint N N$^{(H)L}$. This is a departure from McPherson (2014). That said, the non-binary evaluation of N N$^{(H)L}$ is well defined: one violation is incurred per surface tone in the output that does not match the tonal overlay. The non-binary evaluation of REALIZEMORPHEME, in contrast, raises further questions about how it should apply.

Another drawback of the phonological account is that it requires the constraint *HLH<3 in addition to the constraint *HLH. *HLH<3 seems to duplicate *HLH but must specify a domain of two syllables or less while also being allowed to apply across word boundaries. As discussed above, *HLH seems well-motivated for Efik, but there is no independent motivation for *HLH<3. Moreover, it would have to be restricted to compounds because HL#H sequences are permitted in other constructions involving two adjacent nouns, as in the genitive construction in (6) and the double object construction in (7):

(6)   Genitive construction
      àw̃â éjìn
      cat   child
      'the child's cat'

(7)   Double object construction
      ḿ-↓má   ń-nɔ̀   àw̃â íják
      1SG-PAST.AUX 1SG-give cat   fish
      'I gave the cat a fish.'

As pointed out by a reviewer, having to restrict *HLH<3 to compounds would cease to be a problem if we considered a compound to be a single phonological word. In that case, we could simply say that *HLH<3 applies within words. The two nouns composing a compound would then be subject to *HLH<3 while the two nouns composing a genitive construction or a double object construction would not be. This solution will not work, however, because *HLH<3 must also apply to adjective-noun constructions, which are not the focus of this paper but

which also exhibit nominal tonal alternations. The example in (8) illustrates how
*HLH<3 is active in adjective-noun constructions:

(8) /èk͡prî ébwá/ → [èk͡prî èbwà]
     little dog
     'little dog'

The adjective *èk͡prî* 'little' ends in a falling tone, and like nouns ending in
falling tone it triggers Alternation 2 on a following noun. Thus the underlyingly
H-H noun *ébwá* surfaces with the tones L-L. If *ebwa* had retained its initial H after
the final HL of *èk͡prî*, the phrase would violate *HLH<3. While compounds may
constitute a single phonological word, it is unlikely that an adjective followed by
a noun would. Consequently, the elegant solution of restricting *HLH<3 to the
domain of the phonological word is unavailable. Instead, we would have to somehow define *HLH<3 as applying to compounds and adjective-noun constructions
but not to genitive constructions and double object constructions.

Regarding *HLH<3's duplication of *HLH, one might argue that *HLH<3 suf-
fices to derive the tonal alternations in compounds and that *HLH can be gotten
rid of. The losing candidates that violate *HLH in the tableaux in §3 all violate
*HLH<3 as well because the HLH sequence, even when it is within one member
of the compound, never occurs on more than two syllables. However, it is not
the case that a within-word HLH sequence is only illicit on fewer than three syllables in Efik. In reduplicated verb forms, HLH sequences in which each tone is
associated to a different syllable are repaired (Glewwe 2017). For instance, a verb
form that would otherwise be expected to surface with an HLH sequence on the
final three syllables in fact surfaces with an HLL sequence, as exemplified in (9)
(the underlying form of the verb root 'bend down' is /nùyɔ́/):

(9) ì-kí-↓nó~nùyɔ̀   *ì-kí-↓nó~nùyɔ́
     1PL-NEG.PAST.AUX-LEX~bend.down
     'we *bent down*'

Evidence from contrastive verbal reduplication shows that the more general
*HLH is still needed in the grammar of Efik, regardless of whether it is used
in the analysis of the tones of Efik compounds. Thus the grammar would still
have to contain two *HLH constraints, the broader *HLH and the more restricted
*HLH<3.

To sum up, the phonological account relies on an unusual and potentially problematic definition of REALIZEMORPHEME. It also requires an additional constraint

that the phrasal morphology account does not, namely, *HLH<3. This constraint seems ad hoc and is not well motivated for Efik. Broadly speaking, the phonological account resorts to dubious constraints to explain the full range of tonal alternations with just the construction marker /H L/ while the phrasal morphology account allows two allomorphs of the tonal overlay to capture what seem to be the two different surface melodies (HL and L) that arise in compounds. I therefore favor the phrasal morphology account over the phonological account.

That said, many of the types of evidence McPherson (2014) uses to argue for the phrasal morphology account in Dogon languages, such as long-distance imposition of tonal overlays or competition between two words seeking to impose their overlays on an intervening word, are not available in Efik. Further investigation of Efik nominal tonal alternations may yield additional support for one account over the other. In this paper, I have focused on Efik noun-noun compounds, but nouns in genitive constructions and adjective-noun phrases also exhibit the same surface melodies seen on the second noun in compounds, though they differ in which surface melodies arise in which environments. Exploring how both the phrasal morphology account and the phonological account can be extended to the tonal alternations in these other Efik nominal constructions could shed light on their relative merits. Finally, it would also be worthwhile to examine surface tonal patterns in longer phrases containing multiple targets for the tonal alternations.

Acknowledgments

Many thanks to Charles Udoma, Okon Bassey Akpan, Asuquo Edet Ekanem, Udim Ema, Theresa Okon Essien, and Utibe Asuquo Edet for sharing their language with me. Thanks to Travis Major and Harold Torrence for collecting data in Nigeria for me. Thanks to Kie Zuraw, Laura McPherson, Beth Sturman, and audiences at the UCLA Phonology Seminar and ACAL 48 for helpful discussion. Thanks to two anonymous reviewers for their comments and suggestions.

References

Cahill, Michael. 2007. More universals of tone. *SIL Electronic Working Papers.* http://www.sil.org/resources/publications/entry/7816.
Cook, Thomas L. 1985. *An integrated phonology of Efik: Volume I.* Leiden: University of Leiden dissertation.

Glewwe, Eleanor. 2017. An OT analysis of Efik contrastive verbal reduplication. In Karen Jesney, Charlie O'Hara, Caitlin Smith & Rachel Walker (eds.), *Supplemental proceedings of the annual meetings on phonology*, vol. 4. Linguistic Society of America.

Gnanadesikan, Amalia Elisabeth. 1997. *Phonology with ternary scales*. University of Massachusetts, Amherst dissertation.

Harry, Otelemate G. & Larry M. Hyman. 2014. Phrasal construction tonology: The case of Kalabari. *Studies in Language* 38(4). 649–689.

Hyman, Larry M. 2007. Universals of tone rules: 30 years later. In Tomas Riad & Carlos Gussenhoven (eds.), *Tone and tunes, volume 1: Typological studies in word and sentence prosody*, 1–34. Berlin: Mouton de Gruyter.

Kim, Chin-W. 1974. A note on tonal conjunction in Efik. *Studies in the Linguistic Sciences* 4(2). 112–122.

Kurisu, Kazutaka. 2001. *The phonology of morpheme realization*. University of California, Santa Cruz dissertation.

McPherson, Laura. 2014. *Replacive grammatical tone in the Dogon languages*. University of California, Los Angeles dissertation.

McPherson, Laura. 2016. Culminativity and ganging in the tonology of Awa suffixes. *Language: Phonological Analysis* 92(1). e38–e66.

Samek-Lodovici, Vieri. 1992. A unified analysis of crosslinguistic morphological gemination. In *Proceedings of CONSOLE*, vol. 1, 265–283.

Trommer, Jochen. 2012. Constraints on multiple-feature mutation. *Lingua* 122(11). 1182–1192.

van Oostendorp, Marc. 2005. Expressing inflection tonally. *Catalan Journal of Linguistics* 4(1). 107–127.

Welmers, Wm. E. 1968. *Efik*. Ibadan: Institute of African Studies, University of Ibadan.

Welmers, Wm. E. 1973. *African language structures*. Berkeley: University of California Press.

Wolf, Matthew. 2007. For an autosegmental theory of mutation. In Leah Bateman, Michael O'Keefe, Ehren Reilly & Adam Werle (eds.), *Papers in Optimality Theory III* (University of Massachusetts Occasional Working Papers in Linguistics 32), 315–404. Amherst: GLSA.

Chapter 5

Number and animacy in the Teke noun class system

Larry M. Hyman
University of California, Berkeley

Florian Lionnet
Princeton University

Christophère Ngolele
Université Catholique d'Afrique Centrale, Yaoundé

In this paper, we trace the development of Proto-Bantu noun classes into Teke (Bantu B71, Ewo dialect), showing that formal reflexes of classes 1, 2, 5–9, and 14 are detectable. We further show that animacy, abstractness, and number allow us to determine the fate of classes 3, 4, 10, 11 and identify the following singular/plural genders: 1/2 (animate <PB 1/2, some 9/10), 1/8 (inanimate, <PB 3/4), 14/8 (abstract, <PB 14/8), 5/6 (<PB 5/6), 5/9 (<PB 11/10, with 10>9 merger), 7/8 (<PB 7/8), and 9/6 (<PB 9/6). Such reassignments provide a window into probing parallel noun class changes in other Northwest Bantu and Niger-Congo in general.

1 Introduction

In this paper we have two goals. First, we trace the development of the Proto-Bantu (PB) noun classes into a variety of Teke, a group of closely related, understudied B70 languages spoken in Gabon, the Republic of the Congo, and the Democratic Republic of the Congo. Second, we discuss how the Teke facts provide a window into probing parallel noun class changes in other Northwest Bantu, Bantu, and Niger-Congo (NC) in general. In this sense we provide an additional contribution and comparison with past work on the restructuring and loss

Larry M. Hyman, Florian Lionnet & Christophère Ngolele. 2019. Number and animacy in the Teke noun class system. In Samson Lotven, Silvina Bongiovanni, Phillip Weirich, Robert Botne & Samuel Gyasi Obeng (eds.), *African linguistics across the disciplines: Selected papers from the 48th Annual Conference on African Linguistics*, 89–102. Berlin: Language Science Press. DOI:10.5281/zenodo.3520573

of NC noun classes. This includes, among others, the considerable work on mergers and loss in Bantoid (cf. the papers in Hyman 1980 and Hyman & Voorhoeve 1980) and Cross-River (Williamson 1985; Faraclas 1986; Connell 1987; Hyman & Udoh 2006). Of particular interest will be the restructuring which takes place on the basis of animacy, something discussed at great length in Northeastern Bantu (Wald 1975; Contini-Morava 2008) and elsewhere in Bantu (Maho 1999: 122–126). We will show that both phonetic and semantic factors have played a role in the changes which have taken place between PB and Teke. All of the above – and more – is covered in very careful detail in Good (2012).

Crucial to the approach taken here is that synchronic noun classes and genders (singular/plural pairings) are established by concord (agreement markers), not by affixal marking on the noun itself. On the other hand, as pointed out by several of the above studies, attention must be paid to both marking on the noun as well as on agreeing elements. Our attention is on the Ewo dialect of Teke B71 (Republic of the Congo), as spoken by the third author, reporting on a several month study together in Berkeley in Spring 2016. We begin by considering the situation in PB in §2, then turn to Teke in §3. The changes which have taken place between the two are enumerated in §4, followed by a presentation of our conclusions in §5.

2 Proto-Bantu noun classes

The natural starting point for this kind of study is the Proto-Bantu noun class system, both noun prefixes and (pronominal) concordial elements, which Meeussen (1967: 97) identifies as shown in Table 1.[1]

On the basis of the reconstructions, we can make the following observations: (i) Noun prefixes all have L(ow) tone. (ii) Pronominal concord is H(igh) except for (shaded) classes 1 and 9 which are L. (iii) As indicated, some class pairings show some semantic consistency, e.g. 12, 13 and 19 are diminutive classes. In addition, class 6 *mà-* is also used for mass/liquids, and 16, 17, and 18 are locative classes. In short, at least 19 distinct noun classes can be reconstructed in PB.

---

[1] Abbreviations used in the tables are listed at the end of this paper. Vowels are transcribed using IPA symbols, rather than Meeussen's (1967) symbols: /i, ɪ, u, ʊ/ rather than /i̧, i, y, u/. Note that we choose to reconstruct the concordial prefix of class 1 as *ʊ̀- rather than to adopt Meeussen's (1967)'s *jʊ̀-, in which the j- might be a confusion with class 9.

Table 1: Proto-Bantu noun classes and genders

Class	NPfx	Co	Class	NPfx	Co		Sg./Pl. genders
1	*mʊ̀-	*ʊ̀-	11	*lʊ̀-	*lʊ́-	1/2	(humans)
2	*bà-	*bá-	12	*kà-	*ká-	3/4	
3	*mʊ̀-	*gʊ́-	13	*tʊ̀-	*tʊ́-	5/6	
4	*mì-	*gí-	14	*bʊ̀-	*bʊ́-	7/8	
5	*ì-	*lí-	15	*kʊ̀-	*kʊ́-	9/10	(incl. animals)
6	*mà-	*gá-	16	*pà-	*pá-	11/10	
7	*kì-	*gí-	17	*kʊ̀-	*kʊ́-	12/13	(diminutives)
8	*bì-	*bí-	18	*mʊ̀-	*mʊ́-	14/6	(abstract)
9	*Ǹ-	*jì-	19	*pì-	*pí-	15/6	
10	*Ǹ-	*jí-				19/13?	(diminutives)

Table 2: Noun class reflexes in Teke (Ewo dialect)

PB	NPfx	As	Prox	Dist	'two'	SPr	SAgr/_C	SAgr/_V
1	ò-, Ǹ-, ∅-	wà	wù	wâ	—	ndé	∅	∅
2	à-	bá	bà	bâ	bvwóólè	bó	á	bá
5	lè-, ∅	lé	lì	lyâ	—	ló	lé	lé
6	à-	má	mà	mâ	mbvwóólè	mó	á	má
7	kè-	ké	kì	kyâ	—	kó	ké	ké
8	è-	bé	bì	byâ	dzíéélè	jó	é	bé
9	N(-), ∅	yè	yì	yâ	yíéélè	yó	é	yé
14	ò-	bó	bà	bâ	—	ndé	∅	∅

Table 3: Teke genders (sg./pl. pairings)

Gender	PB cl.	Sg. pfx	Pl. pfx	Prox (sg./pl.)	#	Semantics
wà/bá	1/2	ò-, Ǹ-, ∅-	à-	wù/bà	79	animate, human
wà/bé	(1/8)	ò-	è-	wù/bì	52	inanimate
bó/bé	(14/8)	ò-	è-	bà/bì	18	abstract
lé/má	5/6	lè-	à-	lì/mà	92	
lé/bá	(5/2)	lè-	à-	lì/bà	1	'bird'
lé/yè	(5/9)	lè-	N-	lì/yì	12	
ké/bé	7/8	kè-	è-	kì/bì	54	
yè/má	(9/6)	N(-), ∅-	à-	yì/mà	45	

3 Teke (Ewo dialect)

The situation is quite different in Teke.[2] The forms found in the Ewo dialect are presented in Table 2. The PB class numbers in the first column are given for reference. Note that it is not clear whether the initial nasal consonant of class 9 nouns should still be analyzed as a prefix in Teke, or whether it has fused with the root (i.e., class 9 nouns do not have a prefix anymore). This will accordingly be shown in all transcriptions of class 9 nouns with a hyphen in parentheses between the potential nasal prefix and the root.

From these tables the following observations and additional facts can be noted:[3]

(i) Class 3 merged with class 1. We know that the form is historical class 1 because of the L tone associative (only classes 1 and 9 had L tone concord in PB).

(ii) Class 4 merged with class 8, thus producing a 1/8 gender (corresponding to PB 3/4).

(iii) The Teke reflexes of PB class 9 is used both as a singular (with a class 6 plural), but also as the plural of class 5 (from class Proto-Bantu class 11, see below), thus producing the two genders 9/6 and 5/9. Again, we know that the plural form is a reflex of class 9 because of its L tone associative (a reflex of Proto-Bantu class 10 would have a H tone).

(iv) Class 11 merged with class 5. Its plural is now in class 9, hence a 5/9 gender (see above).

(v) PB diminutive classes 12, 13 and 19 and locative classes 16, 17 and 18 are not present in Teke.

(vi) Of the eight singular/plural genders in Teke, those not occurring in PB are in parentheses (Maho 1999: 255–261). As seen, most genders are innovations (five out of eight), as schematized in Figure 1 (the numerals refer to

---

[2] Although Teke languages often have seven (or more) phonetic vowels, e.g. Kukuya (Paulian 1975), we did not find a phonemic contrast in the mid vowels, which we transcribe with *e* and *o*, pronounced as such in noun class markers and other grammatical morphemes, otherwise as [ɛ] and [ɔ].

[3] Note, additionally, that the plural of class 14 nouns is now in class 8 instead of the original class 6 of proto-Bantu, depsite the fact that class 6 still exists in Teke. We do not have an explanation for this change. One may surmise that the similarity of the singular ò- of 1/8 (from Proto-Bantu 3/4), inanimate, may have caused an analogy.

the PB noun classes that the modern Teke classes correspond to historically; the numerals in parentheses refer to the PB classes that merged with
other classes). Examples of each gender follow in Table 4.

Figure 1: Teke genders

As can be seen in the shaded column of Table 2, at most eight distinct classes
are recognizable, which we identify by their associative marker. The singular/
plural pairings ("genders") are presented in Table 3, where the number (#) indicated for each gender is based on a lexicon of 356 singular/plural nouns.

With this established, we now turn to consider how Teke derived from PB.

Table 4: Examples of each Teke gender

Teke	PB	Singular	Plural	
wà/bá	1/2	mwàánà	à-bàánà	'child'
		ò-kúúlù	à-kúúlù	'uncle'
		ǹ-dzìá	à-ǹdzìá	'stranger'
		ǹ-dzòò	à-ǹdzòò	'elephant'
wà/bé	(1/8)	ò-bá	è-bá	'palm tree'
		ò-mbónó	è-mbónó	'leg'
		ò-nywà	è-nywà	'mouth'
		ò-kìlà	è-kìlà	'tail'
bó/bé	(14/8)	ò-yúú	è-yúú	'poverty'
		ò-dzá	è-dzá	'food'
		ò-bvwòó	è-bvòó	'fear'
		ò-nsámbá	è-nsámbá	'judgment'
lé/má[4]	5/6	lè-lémì	à-lémì	'tongue'
		kélé	à-kélé	'stone'
		dzìíní	mìíní	'tooth'
		dzíírì	mbíírì	'eye'
lé/bá	(5/2)	lè-nyòní	à-nyòní	'bird'

Teke	PB	Singular	Plural	
lé/yè	(5/9)	lè-nkíí	n(-)kíí	'neck'
		lè-sálá	n(-)tsálá	'feather'
		lè-ntsèrè	n(-)tsèrè	'straw'
		lè-ndèlì	n(-)dèlì	'beard'
ké/bé	7/8	kè-kàì	è-kàì	'hand'
		kè-kàlá	è-kàlá	'mat'
		kè-bàá	è-bàá	'wall'
		kè-yìrí	è-yìrí	'bone'
yè/má	(9/6)	n(-)dzó	à-ndzó	'house'
		bí	à-bí	'egg'
		n(-)dzálí	à-ndzálí	'river'
		m(-)bàà	à-mbàà	'fire'

4 From Proto-Bantu to Teke

As summarized in §2, the noun classes inherited from PB have undergone a number of mergers. PB classes 3, 4 and 11 all merged their noun and agreements with classes 1, 8 and 5, respectively. Class 14, on the other hand has merged its *bʊ̀-prefix with class 1 (and 3) ò-, but maintains a separate agreement. Similarly, PB class 2 *bà- and class 6 *mà- have merged their noun prefix as *a-*, but maintain distinct agreements. It is likely therefore that the noun prefixes merged first, and later their agreements. We survey these changes in this section. However, we first begin by considering the three genders that were inherited directly from PB. Table 5 presents examples of PB and later regional reconstructions, as well as their current reflexes in Teke.[5]

As seen in Table 5, the major change has been the loss of the initial consonant of PB class 2 *ba-, class 6 *ma- and class 8 *bɪ-. The Teke 5/6 examples show that class 5 nouns can be marked by *lè-* or ∅. Nouns in 5/6 are roughly equally divided; those in 5/9 always take *lè-*, since they all derive from PB class 11 *lʊ̀-.

---

[4]Gender *lé/má* (5/6) contains a few nouns whose class can be identified through initial consonant alternation rather than the regular Teke prefixes *lè-* and *à-*, e.g. *dzìnì/mììnì* 'tooth', *dzíírì/mbíírì* 'eye'. Such words are rare, and constitute exceptional forms in the language (we have not been able to identify any phonological conditioning). Note that the plural of 'tooth' *mbíírì* starts with a (historically unexpected) [mb] cluster rather than the expected [m].

[5]Proto-Bantu reconstructions are taken from Bastin et al. (2002) (noun roots), and Meeussen (1967) (noun class prefixes, cf. Table 1).

Table 5: Genders inherited from Proto-Bantu (Pfx-Noun + Assoc.)

PB (sg./pl.)		Teke (sg./pl.)		
*1/2		1/2 wà/bá		
*mʊ̀-kádɪ́ ʊ̀-	*bà-kádɪ́ bá-	ò-kálí wà	à-kálí bá	'woman'
*mʊ̀-gìà ʊ̀-	*bà-gìà bá-	ò-yìà wà	à-yìà bá	'slave'
*5/6		5/6 lé/má		
*ɪ̀-jícò lɪ́-	*mà-jícò gá-	dzíírì lé	mbíírì má	'eye'
*ɪ̀-jʊ́ì lɪ́-	*mà-jʊ́ì gá-	dzúì lé	à-dzúì-má	'voice'
*ɪ̀-kájá lɪ́-	*mà-kájá gá-	lè-káyà lé	à-káyà má	'tobacco'
*7/8		7/8 ké/bé		
*kɪ̀-dìbà gɪ́-	*bì-dìbà bí-	kè-dìà ké	è-dìà bé	'pool'
*kɪ̀-gàdá gɪ́-	*bì-gàdá bí-	kè-kàlá ké	è-kàlá bé	'mat'

While the above genders have been stable, four class mergers directly explain two of the new genders: The first, gender 1/8 *wà/bé*, is the formal merger of *3 > 1 and *4 > 8. Thus, as seen in Table 6, PB 3/4 now corresponds to Teke 1/8 *wà/bé*:

Table 6: Gender *wà/bé* (*3/4 > 1/8)

PB (sg./pl.)		Teke (sg./pl.)		
*3/4		1/8 wà/bé		
*mʊ̀-nʊ̀à gʊ̀-	*mì-nʊ̀à gɪ́-	ò-nywà wà	è-nywà bé	'mouth'
*mʊ̀-gʊ̀ndà gʊ̀-	*mì-gʊ̀ndà gɪ́-	ò-kùùnà wà	è-kùùnà bé	'field'
*mʊ̀-kɪ́dà gʊ̀-	*mì-kɪ́dà gɪ́-	ò-kílà wà	è-kílà bé	'tail'
*mʊ̀-tímà gʊ̀-	*mì-tímà gɪ́-	ò-tímà wà	è-tímà bé	'heart'

Similarly, gender 5/9 *lé/yè* derives from the merger of *11 > 5 and *10 > 9 (Table 7).[6]

---

[6]The same *10 > 9 merger seems to have occurred in Latege, another B71 dialect (Ruth Raharimanantsoa and Pauline Linton, p.c.), but not in Kukuya (Paulian 1975), Ngungwel, or Eboo (Ruth Raharimanantsoa p.c.). This merger thus seems to be a characteristic of B71 dialects only.

Table 7: Gender *lé/yè* (*11/10 > 5/9)

PB (sg./pl.)		Teke (sg./pl.)		
*11/10		5/9 lé/yè		
*lʊ̀-dèdù lʊ̌-	*Ǹ-dèdù yí	lè-ndèlì lé	n(-)dèlì yè (*yé)	'beard'[a]
*lʊ̀-cádá lʊ̌-	*Ǹ-cádá yí	lè-sálá lé	n(-)tsálá yè (*yé)	'feather'

[a]Note that the initial [n] in the singular form *lè-n̠dèlí* might be an indication that the singular was also initially in class 9, and then reassigned to class 5.

As discussed above, these mergers appear to be the result of regular sound changes affecting noun prefixes, e.g. the systematic loss of prefix-initial [b] or [m] (prefix-initial [l] and [k] are not affected), followed by the realignment of agreement patterns, as illustrated in Table 8 for the *4 > 8 merger:[7]

Table 8: Hypothesized steps of *4 > 8 merger

4 *mì-kídà gí-	>	4 ì-kídà gí-	> (...) >	8 è-kídà bé
8 *bì-dìbà bí-	>	8 ì-dìbà bí-	> (...) >	8 è-dìà bé

The origin of 5/9, and 9/6 can be traced back to class/gender reassignment following the consequences of the *10 > 9 merger, i.e. the loss of a number distinction for N- initial nouns. This again shows the importance of a prior prefix merger in motivating changes in noun class assignments. Former *9/10 nouns could have become a number-insensitive 9/9 gender, but did not. Instead, the *10 > 9 merger led to a class/gender reassignment based on the semantic property of animacy. Animate *9/10 nouns were reassigned to 1/2 *wà/bá*, merging with the human nouns in that class, as shown in Table 9.[8]

As also seen in Table 9, one noun, *lè-nyòní* 'bird', shifted into gender 5/2 *lé/bá*. Note that this is the only noun illustrating both this shift, and the inquorate

---

[7]The fact that only prefix-initial labial consonants are targeted does not necessarily contradict the Neogrammarian principle of sound change regularity: stem-initial prominence, which plays an important role in Teke and more generally Northwestern Bantu languages (cf. Paulian (1975), Hyman (1987), Idiatov & Van de Velde (2016), a.o.) is not unlikely to have protected stem-initial consonants (and possibly other non-prefix consonants?) from this change. A detailed account of such sound changes in Teke is, however, outside the scope of this paper.

[8]Most of the former class 9 nouns that were reassigned to class 1 or class 5 start with a nasal consonant, which is a trace of the former nasal prefix of class 9, now part of the root. We have indicated the historical origin of this nasal consonant as a prefix with a hyphen in parentheses.

gender 5/2 *lé/bá*. On the other hand, inanimate *9/10 nouns either became 9/6 *yè/má* (plural reassignment only) or 5/6 *lè/má* (complete gender reassignment), as shown in Table 10.

Table 9: Animate *9/10 > 1/2 *wà/bá* (+ 1 case of 5/2 *lé/bá*)

PB (sg./pl.)		Teke (sg./pl.)		
*9/10		1/2 wà/bá		
*Ǹ-ɲàmà yì-	*Ǹ-ɲàmà yí-	nyàmà wà	à-nyàmà bá	'animal'
*Ǹ-jògʊ̀ yì-	*Ǹ-jògʊ̀ yí-	n(-)dzòò wà	à-ndzòò bá	'elephant'
*Ǹ-bʊ́à yì-	*Ǹ-bʊ́à yí-	m(-)bvà wà	à-mbvà bá	'dog'
*Ǹ-gòmbè yì-	*Ǹ-gòmbè yí-	n(-)gómbè wà	à-ngómbè bá	'cow'
*Ǹ-gàndʊ́ yì-	*Ǹ-gàndʊ́ yí-	n(-)gàndí wà	à-ngàndí bá	'crocodile'
*Ǹ-gòì yì-	*Ǹ-gòì yí-	n(-)gò wà	à-ngò bá	'leopard'
*Ǹ-gʊ̀mbá yì-	*Ǹ-gʊ̀mbá yí-	n(-)gùùmà wà	à-ngùùmà bá	'porcupine'
*Ǹ-kímà yì-	*Ǹ-kímà yí-	n(-)kímà wà	à-nkímà bá	'monkey'
*Ǹ-gùbʊ́ yì-	*Ǹ-gùbʊ́ yí-	n(-)gùbú	à-ngùbú bá	'hippo'
*Ǹ-pʊ́kʊ̀ yì-	*Ǹ-pʊ́kʊ̀ yí-	m(-)púù wà	à-mpúù bá	'rat'
*Ǹ-pídì yì-	*Ǹ-pídì yí-	m(-)pílì wà	à-mpílì bá	'snake sp.'
*Ǹ-cúì yì-	*Ǹ-cúì yí-	n(-)tsú wà	à-ntsú bá	'fish'
		5/2 lé/bá		
*Ǹ-jʊ̀nì yì-	*Ǹ-jʊ̀nì yí-	lè-nyòní lé	à-nyòní bá	'bird'

Table 10: Inanimate *9/10 > 9/6 *yè/má* or 5/6 *lè/má*

PB (sg./pl.)		Teke (sg./pl.)		
*9/10		9/6 yè/má		
*Ǹ-jàdà yì-	*Ǹ-jàdà yí-	n(-)dzàlà yè	à-ndzàlà má	'hunger'
*Ǹ-jʊ̀ngʊ̀ yì-	*Ǹ-jʊ̀ngʊ̀ yí-	n(-)dʒùngù yè	à-ndʒùngù má	'pot'
*Ǹ-jìdà yì-	*Ǹ-jìdà yí-	n(-)dzìlà yè	à-ndzìlà má	'path'
		5/6 lé/má		
*Ǹ-gì yì-	Ǹ-gì yí-	lè-ngìngì lé	à-ngìngì má	'fly'
*Ǹ-dʊ́ngʊ́ yì-	Ǹ-dʊ́ngʊ́ yí-	lè-ndúú lé	à-ndúú má	'pepper'
*Ǹ-tʊ́dʊ̀ yì-	Ǹ-tʊ́dʊ̀ yí-	lè-ntúlù lé	à-ntúlù má	'chest'

In addition, a few *9/10 inanimate nouns became either 1/8 *wà/bé* or 5/9 *lé/yè*, as can be seen in Table 11.

Table 11: Inanimate *9/10 > 1/8 *wà/bé* or 5/9 *lé/yè*

PB (sg./pl.)		Teke (sg./pl.)		
*9/10		wà/bé		
*Ǹ-gòdí yì-	Ǹ-gòdí yí-	ò-ngòrí wà	è-ngòrí bé	'liana'
		lé/yè		
*Ǹ-jʊ̀gʊ́ yì-	Ǹ-jʊ̀gʊ́ yí-	lè-ndzú lé	n(-)dzú yè	'groundnut'
*Ǹ-kíngó yì-	Ǹ-kíngó yí-	lè-nkíí lé	ŋ(-)kíí yè	'neck'

Finally, a few former *9/10 nouns alternate between 5/6 *lé/má* and 5/9 (< *10) *lé/yè*, e.g. *lè-mpàmbù lé / à-mpàmbù má ~ m(-)pàmbù yè* 'worm'. Note that all former *9/10 nouns reassigned to 1/2 *wà/bá*, 5/6 *lè/má*, 9/6 *yè/má*, 1/8 *wà/bé*, or 5/9 *lè/yè* have kept the historical N- prefix. The cause of all of the above *9/10 class/gender reassignments is presumably the need to maintain a singular/plural distinction, with animacy exploited as the guiding criterion for reassignment.

Animacy plays a potential role in other places in the Teke noun class system. Recall that singular nouns marked by the prefix *ò-* today may represent the merger of PB *1 and *3 (with the same agreements) or class *14 (with its distinct agreements). From the semantics one can almost perfectly predict whether an *ò-*prefixed noun will be in gender 1/2, 1/8 or 14/8. As before, animate nouns will all be in 1/2. Inanimates will either be in 14/8 *bó/bé* if they represent an abstract quality (as in PB *14), otherwise in 1/8 *wà/bé*. Representative examples are provided in Table 12.

Table 12: Animacy-based gender assignment of *ò-* nouns

Animate → 1/2 *wà/bá*					
ò-lúmì	'husband'	→	ò-lúmì wá	/	à-lúmì bá
ò-tèé	'Teke person'	→	ò-tèé wá	/	à-tèé bá
Abstract → 14/8 *bó/bé*					
ò-bvwòó	'fear'	→	ò-bvwòó bó	/	è-mbvwòó bé
ò-yúú	'poverty'	→	ò-yúú bó	/	è-yúú bé
Concrete inanimate → 1/8 *wà/bé*					
ò-bá	'palmtree'	→	ò-bá wà	/	è-bá bé
ò-sià	'rope'	→	ò-sià wà	/	è-sià bé

Table 13 shows the number of animate nouns that occur in each gender.

Table 13: Genders and animacy [bracketed number = nouns with human referent]

		Animate [incl. human]	Inanimate	Total
1/2	wà/bá	73 [34]	6	79
5/2	lé/bá	1	0	1
1/8	wà/bé	5 [1]	47	52
14/8	bó/bé	0	18 (abstract)	18
5/6	lé/má	9 (insects, 'frog', 'tortoise')	83	92
5/9	lé/yè	2	10	12
7/8	ké/bé	11 [5, kin]	43	54
9/6	yè/má	0	45	45
		Total: 353		

As seen in Table 13, the total number of animates is 101 out of 353 total nouns. Of these 101, 73 occur in 1/2 *wà/bá*. In fact, virtually all humans are in 1/2. Of the rest only 28 animate nouns occur outside 1/2. Interestingly, no animate noun has a class 9 *yè* singular (gender 9/6 *yè/má*). All PB *9/10 animate nouns were reassigned, mostly to 1/2 *wà/bá*.

To conclude this section, we note with considerable interest the variation in former *11 (and some *9) nouns that have been reassigned to class 5 *lé*. These have kept the former class 10 plural N- form, even though it has the L tone agreement *yè* of *9. However, as we have noted, an N- noun is ambiguous in terms of number, and may be interpreted either as singular or as plural. It can be the plural class 9 of a class 5 *lé* singular (from *11) or the singular of 9/6 *yè/má* and 1/2 *wà/bá*. In addition, nearly half of class 5/6 nouns alternate between a prefixed *lè-* and a ∅ or N- singular form, approximately half in our lexicon occur without *lè-*. (Recall that all 5/9 nouns require *lè-* on their singular.) This is illustrated in Table 14.

Table 14: *lè-* vs. ∅ sg. prefix in 5/6 *lé/má* nouns

Optional ∅			
(lè-)mpéì lé	/	à-mpéì má	'chin'
(lè-)sàánì lé	/	à-sàánì má	'plate'
Obligatory ∅			
(*lè-)kfúrú lé	/	à-kfúrú má	'hole'
(*lè-)bìlà lé	/	à-bìlà má	'leprosy'

As a result this has produced several cases where the same N- noun can be interpreted as either singular or plural, paired with an appropriate noun class of opposite number, as shown in Table 15.

Table 15: N- nouns as singular or plural

Plural class 9 *yè* (singular = class 5 *lé*)			
lè-mbàlà lé	/	m(-)bàlà yè	'civet cat'
lè-ŋkíí lé	/	ŋ(-)kíí yè	'neck'
Singular class 5 *lé* (plural = class 2 *bá* if animate)			
m(-)bàlà lé	/	à-mbàlà bá	'civet cat'
Singular class 5 *lé* (plural = class 2 *má* if inanimate)			
ŋ(-)kíí lé	/	à-ŋkíí má	'leprosy'

5 Conclusion

As seen above, an identical prefix shape can not only lead to merger of noun classes (e.g. class *1 and *3, *4 and *8, *5 and *11), but can cause a noun to function in two different genders, one as a singular, the other as a plural. This too can be expected to lead to further realignments as the noun classes prepare for their next move.

In the preceding sections, we have seen that the Teke noun class system has undergone important restructuring with loss of eleven of the nineteen PB classes, four class mergers, and many gender reassignments. As we have shown, only three out of eight genders are inherited from PB. Three variables have played an important role in this evolution: (i) prefix shapes; (ii) animacy; (iii) number. Number and animacy have played a major role in this restructuring, in particular in the class and gender reassignment of PB *9/10 nouns. These become 1/2 *waà/bá* if animate, 5/6 *lé/má* or 9/6 *yè/má* if inanimate (occasionally also 1/8 *wà/bé* and 5/9 *lé/yè*). Animacy also plays an important role in synchrony. As we have shown, singular *ò-* is interpreted as 1/2 *wà/bá* if animate, 14/8 *bó/bé* if abstract, and 1/8 *wà/bé* if concrete inanimate. In addition, a noun with the prefix sequence *à-N-* is unambiguously class 2 *bá* if animate, class 6 *má* if inanimate. The relevance (and potential conflict) of animacy in the synchronic and diachronic marking of noun classes is attested elsewhere in Bantu (Wald 1975; Maho 1999; Contini-Morava 2008; among others), even to the extent of entirely replacing the inherited noun class system, as in Nzadi (Crane et al. 2011). What is particularly interesting in the Teke case is the conspiracy between prefix shape and animacy. Noun classes are reassigned on the basis of animacy. As prefixes merge, noun class agreements merge, even those accompanying singular and plural 9/10. This shows that Teke speakers are paying attention not only to the semantics, but are impressively influenced by the forms. Such interplay in the reassignments which we have enumerated should be considered in probing parallel noun class changes in other Northwest Bantu and Niger-Congo in general.

Abbreviations

As	Associative	Prox	proximal demonstrative
Co	concord		'this/these'
Dist	distal demonstrative 'that/those'	SA	Subject agreement
NPfx	noun prefix	SPr	Subject pronoun

References

Bastin, Yvonne, Andre Coupez, Evariste Mumba & Thilo Schadeberg (eds.). 2002. *Bantu lexical reconstructions 3 / Reconstructions lexicales bantoues 3.* Tervuren: Musée Royal de l'Afrique Centrale. http://linguistics.africamuseum.be/BLR3.html, accessed 2017-3-31.

Connell, Bruce. 1987. Noun classification in Lower Cross. *Journal of West African Languages* 17. 110–125.

Contini-Morava, Ellen. 2008. Human relationship terms, discourse prominence, and asymmetrical animacy in Swahili. *Journal of African Languages and Linguistics* 29. 127–171.

Crane, Thera M., Larry M. Hyman & Simon Nsielanga Tukumu. 2011. *A grammar of Nzadi [B865]: A language of Democratic Republic of Congo* (University of California Publications in Linguistics). Berkeley: University of California Press. http://escholarship.org/uc/item/846308w2.

Faraclas, Nicholas. 1986. Cross River as a model for the evolution of Benue-Congo nominal class/concord systems. *Studies in African Linguistics* 17. 40–54.

Good, Jeff. 2012. How to become a "Kwa" noun. *Morphology* 22. 293–335.

Hyman, Larry (ed.). 1980. *Noun classes in the Grassfileds Bantu borderland* (Southern California Occasional Papers in Linguistics 8). University of Southern California: Los Angeles.

Hyman, Larry M. 1987. Prosodic domains in Kukuya. *Natural Language and Linguistic Theory* 5. 311–333.

Hyman, Larry M. & Imelda Udoh. 2006. Relic noun class structure in Leggbo. In Larry M. Hyman & Paul Newman (eds.), *West African linguistics: Papers in honor of Russell G. Schuh* (Supplement 11 to Studies in African linguistics), 75–99.

Hyman, Larry M. & Jan Voorhoeve (eds.). 1980. *L'Expansion bantoue, volume 1: Les classes nominales dans le bantou des Grassfields.* (Actes du colloque international du CNRS, Viviers (France), 4-16 avril 1977.). Paris: SELAF.

Idiatov, Dmitry & Mark Van de Velde. 2016. *Stem-initial accent and C-emphasis prosody in North-Western Bantu.* Presentation given at the 6th international conference on Bantu Languages, 6 June 2016, Helsinki, Finland.

Maho, Jouni F. 1999. *A comparative study of Bantu noun classes.* Gothenburg, Sweden: University of Gothenburg dissertation.

Meeussen, A. E. 1967. *Bantu grammatical reconstructions.* Tervuren: Musée Royal de l'Afrique Centrale.

Paulian, Christiane. 1975. *Le kukuya: Langue teke du Congo.* Paris: SELAF.

Wald, Benji. 1975. Animate concord in Northeast Coastal Bantu: Its linguistic and social implications as a case of grammatical convergence. *Studies in African Linguistics* 6. 261–314.

Williamson, Kay. 1985. How to become a Kwa language. In A. Makkai & Melby A. K. (eds.), *Linguistics and philosophy: Essays in honor of Rulon S. Wells*, 427–443. Amsterdam: Benjamins.

Chapter 6

Tone, orthographies, and phonological depth in African languages

Michael Cahill

SIL international

Marking of tone in African orthographies has historically been a challenge, not only for linguistic and analytical reasons, but also because most designers of these orthographies have been educated in non-tonal languages. After a review of lexical vs. grammatical tone, this paper examines various strategies that have been used for marking both lexical and grammatical tone in several East and West African languages, as well as cases in which tone is not marked. The question of the desired phonological depth of an orthography is discussed, especially when applied to tonal processes. Many phonologists do not apply theory more recent than Chomsky and Halle & Chomsky (1968) to orthographies. However, the more recent bifurcation of rules into lexical and postlexical provides a psycholinguistically supported phonological level at which tone marking can be based: the output of the lexical level. Experimental evidence supports this LEXICAL level as more readable than either a PHONEMIC or a DEEP level. A tonal typology of languages also guides what types of languages more predictably would need lexical tone marking. Recommendations for orthographical implementation are given in the conclusion.

1 Introduction

Marking of tone in African orthographies was considered problematic even before the 1928 Rejaf Language Conference, where permission was rather grudgingly given to mark tones in Sudanese languages when absolutely necessary: "For tonal representations, the consensus was that only high tones should be marked, with an acute accent, and only if necessary for a particular language" (Miner 2003).

One reason for this rather tepid approval was that most developers of orthographies either were Europeans or were educated in European languages, which

Michael Cahill. 2019. Tone, orthographies, and phonological depth in African languages. In Samson Lotven, Silvina Bongiovanni, Phillip Weirich, Robert Botne & Samuel Gyasi Obeng (eds.), *African linguistics across the disciplines: Selected papers from the 48th Annual Conference on African Linguistics*, 103–123. Berlin: Language Science Press. DOI:10.5281 zenodo.3520575

of course are not tonal. The result was that many writing systems for African languages avoided tone marking, and tone was often not studied in any depth. Matters improved only somewhat two years after Rejaf with a cross-continental proclamation:

> In books for Africans, tones, generally speaking, need only be marked when they have a grammatical function, or when they serve to distinguish words alike in every other respect; and even then they may be sometimes omitted when the context makes it quite clear which word is intended. As a rule, it will suffice to mark the high or the low tone only. (International Institute of African Languages and Cultures 1930: 14, referring to Rejaf and 12 other documents)

This guidance sounds strikingly modern, both in what it says and does not say. Note that this statement specifies books "for Africans," not for foreigners, so it primarily has local literacies in mind. It laudably distinguishes grammatical from lexical tone, and for the latter, advocates what is called "selective tone marking" today – marking tone only on minimal pairs, and even then, only when they are words likely to be confused in context. Tone marking is still considered a challenge today. It is not uncommon for orthography developers to not mark tone at all, either for principled reasons, or because they cannot deal with it, or because they do not consider it important (see Cahill 2000 for a critique of omitting all tone markings).

This paper begins (§2) with a review of the distinction between lexical and grammatical tone. §3 examines methods that have been used to represent both lexical and grammatical tone (or not) in various African orthographies. In §4, I examine two major topics for assisting decisions in tone marking: the appropriate phonological level for orthographies, and a two-fold typological division of African languages. I close in §5 with some recommendations for representing tone in African orthographies, and a brief re-examination of the selective tone marking issue.

2 Lexical vs. grammatical tone: Review

Lexical tone is a difference in pitch that distinguishes one *lexeme* from another. Samples of this are given in (1).[1]

---

[1] I follow a common notation for tone transcriptions that indicates tone levels with various diacritics: á = high, à = low, ā = mid, â = falling, ǎ = rising, and ꜝá = downstepped high. An un-

(1) Lexical tone differences in nouns

    a. Kɔnni (Cahill 2007: 306)

kpááŋ	*kpá'áŋ*	*kpàáŋ*
'oil'	'guinea fowl'	'back of head'

    b. Mono [mnh] (D. R. Congo) (Olson 2005: 198)

áwá	*āwā*	*àwà*
'diarrhea'	'road'	'fear'

Grammatical tone, on the other hand, distinguishes one *grammatical category* from another. There are many grammatical categories which can be thus distinguished. Some of the more common ones are given in (2–6) and Table 1. Not every person distinction is differentiated by tone in these or other languages; it is typically only two pronouns of the set that are so distinguished.

(2) Person distinguished by grammatical tone

    a. Jur Modo [bex] (Sudan) (Persson 2004: 80)

nì	*ní*
'her'	'their'

    b. Lyele [lee] (Burkina Faso) (Kutsch Lojenga 2014: 57)

ń	*ǹ*
2SG	3SG

In some languages (e.g., Tarok in Table 1), tone distinguishes singulars from plurals in only a subset of nouns, while in others (e.g., Koro Waci, Ndrulo), tone change is the normal method of making plurals from singular nouns. It appears that in the majority of languages which exhibit tone change to mark plural nouns, the plural nouns are in some way higher toned than the singular. However, this is not universal, as will be seen in Karaboro in section §3.3.

    Though verbal aspect may be the most common grammatical category distinguished by tone, as in (3), other categories are not rare. (4) shows an example of tone distinguishing a locative from the bare noun, (5) exemplifies the syntactic subject/object feature distinguished solely by tone, and (6) exhibits a miscellany of language-specific grammatical relations distinguished by tone.

---

marked tone is generally mid in a 3-level system. Unless indicated by other labeling, phonetic transcriptions are enclosed in square brackets [a], while orthographic representations are in angle brackets ⟨a⟩. ISO codes for languages are noted in the usual square brackets, e.g., [kma] for Kɔnni in (1).

Michael Cahill

Table 1: Singular/plural nouns distinguished by grammatical tone

Singular	Plural	Gloss
a. Ndrulo [led] (Uganda) (Kutsch Lojenga 2014: 60)		
vìnì	vínì	'his sister/s'
djānì	djánì	'his father/s'
b. Koro Waci [bqv] (Nigeria) (Rachelle Wenger, p.c.)		
ìsŏr	ísŏr	'he-goat/s'
ìtómì	ítómì	'work/s'
ibŭr	íbûr	'slime/s'
c. Tarok [yer] (Nigeria) (Longtau 2008: 90–91)		
ifàng	īfáng	'fingers/s'
ìnà	īnà	'cow/s'
ǹtúng	ńtúng	'hyena/s'

(3) Verbal aspect distinguished by grammatical tone
Mbembe [mfn] (Nigeria) (Barnwell 1969)

ɔ̀kɔ̂n 'you sang'   ɔ́kɔ́n 'you should sing'   móchí 'he will eat'
ɔ́kɔ̀n 'you have sung'   ɔ́k!ɔ́n 'if you sing'   mòchí 'he will not eat'

(4) Locative distinguished by grammatical tone
Fur [fvr] (Sudan) (Kutsch Lojenga 2014: 61)

bàrù 'country'   bàrú 'in the country'
dɔ́ŋá 'hand'   dɔ́ŋà 'in the hand'
ʊ̀tʊ́ 'fire'   ʊ̆tʊ̀ 'in the fire'

(5) Subject/object relations distinguished by grammatical tone
Sabaot [spy] (Uganda) (Kutsch Lojenga 2014: 66)

kɪbakaac kwàán 'his father left him'
kɪbakaac kwáán 'he left his father'

(6) Other relations
Lugungu [rub] (Uganda) (Moe & Mbabazi 1999: 10)

mulogo muhandú 'an old witch'
múlógó muhandú 'the witch is old'
múlógô muhandú 'the witch, (she) is old'

3 How tone is marked

Local orthography developers and outside linguists have developed astonishingly varied and sometimes creative ways of marking tone in languages. In contrast, some languages do not mark tone at all, even if they are distinctly tonal, and I start with these.

3.1 No tone marking

Here I look at a few languages with no orthographic tone marking at all. Interestingly, sometimes tone marking appears to be crucial to reading, and in other cases less so.

The consensus among linguists I have spoken to is that the common way of writing Hausa in (7) (there are other systems) is quite difficult to read. This is especially due to the fact that the *grammatical* tone, as in the example, is not marked, and there are many situations where this ambiguity is impossible to resolve by the context.

(7)   Various verbal aspects
      Hausa [hau] (Nigeria) (Harley 2012)

[jáá tàfí]	[jáà tàfí]	[jà tàfí]
⟨ya tafi⟩	⟨ya tafi⟩	⟨ya tafi⟩
'he went'	'he may go'	'he should go'

Kumam [kdi] (Uganda) has both lexical and grammatical tone: *abe* can mean either 'an egg' or 'a lie,' while *ebedo* can mean either 'he lives' or 'he lived.' However, tone is not marked at all in Kumam, and 60% of people surveyed agreed that it is more difficult to read the Kumam Bible than Bibles in other languages (Edonyu 2015).

Kɔnni [kma] (Ghana) orthography does not mark tone. However, in contrast to the above languages, this seems not to make a significant difference in readability (my personal observation). In this language minimal pairs are few, so there is a fairly small functional load for lexical tone. Furthermore, there is very little grammatical tone in the language. People are able to read aloud fluently.

3.2 Marking lexical tone

Lexical tone, if it is marked, is marked by diacritics more frequently than not. Rangi [lag] of Tanzania, for example, marks lexical High tone, but only on nouns (e.g., *ikúfa* 'bone', Stegen 2005). Similarly, Akoose marks High tone (e.g., *edíb* [èdíb] 'river') and contours (e.g., *kɔ́d* [kɔd] 'age'), but leaves Low unmarked (Hedinger 2011: 13).

In a few cases, tone has been marked by punctuation marks before each word, especially in Côte d'Ivoire (e.g., Bolli 1978). Examples of the punctuation marks used are displayed in Table 2.

Table 2: Lexical tone notation for Côte d'Ivoire languages (Kutsch Lojenga 2014: 58)

extra high	high	mid	low	extra low	mid-low falling	low-high rising	high-low falling
"CV	'CV	CV	-CV	=CV	CV-	-CV'	'CV-

This system can handle up to five tone levels, necessary in some languages of Côte d'Ivoire. This is exemplified as follows in Attié, which has four contrastive levels of tone (but does not have extra low).

(8) Attié (Matthew 6:30a)
'Pɛte "yi "fa, 'fa "kan'a 'lö "a -bë ko fon- 'tshɛn'a tɔ, 'eyipian -Zö -wɔ' sɛn 'e hɛn dzhi ko ...

3.3 Marking grammatical tone

Different languages have used a wide variety of strategies for indicating grammatical tone. One strategy is using diacritics, and often these mark a phonetic tone which instantiates a particular grammatical category, as in (9), with the Daffo variety of Lis Ma Ron.

(9) Diacritic showing both phonetics and meaning
Lis Ma Ron [cla] (Nigeria) (Harley 2012)

á à
'you (male)' 'he'

Akoose exhibits a somewhat unusual pattern in that the singular and plural nouns for class 9/10 are identical, but the distinction is made by tone on the agreement prefix of the following *verb*:

(10)   Akoose (Hedinger 2011: 13)

    a. [ngù: èdélé]

      nguu edélé

      'the pig is heavy'

    b. [ngù: édélé]

      nguu édélé

      'the pigs are heavy'

Some languages indicate grammatical tone by letters which are otherwise un-used. For example, Gangam [gng] (Togo) marks grammatical tone, not phoneti-cally, but with other symbols to indicate the *meaning*. The imperfective is marked with the letter ⟨h⟩ and the perfective with an apostrophe ⟨'⟩ (See Higdon et al. 2000, also Roberts et al. 2013 for more examples. Phonetic transcription is from Jean Reimer p.c.).

(11)   Gangam (Higdon et al. 2000)

    a. *N bɛnge' [béŋge] Miganganm ya kaanm.*

      'I learned to read Gangam.'

    b. *N laan bɛngeh [bēŋgé] Miganganm ya kaanm nɛ.*

      'I am learning to read Gangam.'

Similarly, Etung (12) uses ⟨h⟩ to differentiate pronouns which differ only by tone.

(12)   Pronouns in Etung [etu] (Nigeria, Harley 2012)

    a. [á]   b. [à]

      ⟨ah⟩   ⟨a⟩

      'they'   'he'

Other languages double some letters to differentiate pronouns which differ only by tone (13).

(13)   Pronouns in Jur Modo [bex] (Sudan, Persson 2004)

    a. [nì]   b. [ní]

      ⟨nï⟩   ⟨nnï⟩

      'her'   'their'

A number of languages indicate various grammatical tone functions by means of punctuation or other non-alphabetic marks. Karaboro, as displayed in (14), uses a word-final hyphen to indicate plurals (in those cases which are not indicated by a segmental marker), which all happen to end in a low tone.

(14) Plurals in Karaboro [xrb] (Burkina Faso, SIL 2009, as cited in Roberts et al. 2013)

a. [kāī, kāì]	b. [gjɔɔ, gjɔɔ]	c. [sàὰpjé, sàápjè]
⟨kai, kai-⟩	⟨jɔɔ, jɔɔ-⟩	⟨saapye, saapye-⟩
'affair, affairs'	'net, nets'	'rabbit, rabbits'

The old Ejagham orthography, now changed to a different system, used punctuation extensively to indicate various verbal aspectual forms (3).

Table 3: Old Ejagham orthography [etu] (Nigeria & Cameroon) (Bird 1999a, corrected by John Watters, p.c.)

Orthographic Rule	Phonetic	Orthography	Gloss
colon = PERFECT	[émè]	⟨e:me⟩	'we have swallowed'
space = PERFECTIVE	[èmê]	⟨e me⟩	'we swallowed'
apostrophe = HORTATIVE	[éme]	⟨e'me⟩	'let us swallow'
hyphen = CONDITIONAL	[émĕ]	⟨e-me⟩	'when we swallow'
no symbol = NOUN	[èmè]	⟨eme⟩	'neck'

The Bokyi orthography (Table 4) uses a system that appears rather unusual to most readers in its employment of a variety of non-alphabetic symbols, but it is currently in use.

The Bungu language is one of the more complex illustrations of grammatical tone marking. It uses both diacritics and punctuation marks to indicate the interaction of person and aspect in the verbal system. Many words are segmentally identical, and vowel length is not contrastive, putting a greater load on tone. At this point, no lexical tone is marked (though the orthography is still being adjusted), and Table 5 does not give the entire picture of grammatical tone. Other complexities exist as well, such as tone marking of objects.

3.4 Marking both lexical and grammatical tone with diacritics

Zinza [zin] (Echizinza) marks both lexical and grammatical tone, with accent marks for high, rising, and falling (see 15).

Table 4: Bokyi [bky] (Nigeria) orthography (Harley, p.c.)

Phonetic	Orthography	Gloss
[ǹtsè]	⟨nce⟩	'going'
[ǹtsâ]	⟨n-ca⟩	'I go'
[ńtsè]	⟨n/ce⟩	'I went'
[n̄ńtsè]	⟨nn/ce⟩	'I have gone'
[ńtʃì ǹ-tsâ]	⟨n/chi n-ca⟩	'I will go'
[n̄ńtséē]	⟨n*-ce*⟩	'I don't go'
[ǹdátsèē]	⟨n*da/ce*⟩	'I didn't go'
[m̄ḿbátʃì ǹtsáā]	⟨n*ba/chi n-ca*⟩	'I will not go'

Table 5: Bungu [wun] (Tanzania, Katterhenrich & Gray 2016) (Low tone is unmarked). Key: Colon: COMPLETIVE; Carat: PROGRESSIVE; Umlaut: 2SG.SUBJ.PAST; Accent: 3SG.SUBJ.PAST; Double vowel: 3PL.SUBJ.PAST.

Orthography		Gloss
⟨wäkala⟩	[wàkála]	'you bought (recent)'
⟨wákala⟩	[wákála]	'he bought (recent)'
⟨waakala⟩	[wa:kála]	'they bought (recent)'
⟨wakala⟩	[wakála]	'they will buy'
⟨^wakala⟩	[waˇkala]	'they are buying'
⟨:wäkala⟩	[wákala]	'you have already bought'
⟨:wákala⟩	[wakála]	'he has already bought'
⟨:waakala⟩	[wǎ:kala]	'they have already bought'
⟨:nakala⟩	[nákala]	'I have already bought'
⟨^nakala⟩	[nǎkala]	'I am buying'

(15) Marking both lexical and grammatical tone with accent in Zinza
(Matthews 2010)

    a. lexical tone

enzóka	*omuyănda*
'snake'	'child, youth'

    b. grammatical tone

aleeba	*aléeba*
'he looked'	'he (habitually) looks'

4 Phonological theory and orthography

The above discussion has assumed that tones are completely stable, i.e., that underlying tones and surface tones are the same. The question of when or if to mark the results of *tone rules* offers more challenges. For example, in a Bantu language, if a prefixal High tone spreads for three syllables, does one mark the initial prefix syllable alone, or the result of the spreading rule? Or, in west Africa, if underlying tones in a word are /HLH/, but surface as [H'HH], what is the appropriate marking? The major question that involves both of these situation is: what *depth* of phonological representation should be the basis for marking tone? This section addresses those questions.

Tone studies have advanced in the decades since the 1928 Rejaf conference, especially with Autosegmental Phonology (Goldsmith 1976) and Lexical Phonology (Pulleyblank 1986). However, as Snider (2014) notes, many people do not apply phonological theory more recent than Halle & Chomsky (1968) to orthographies. Rather, the main distinctions that most orthographers have in mind are "deep" vs. "shallow" orthographies. However, as we will see, there are other options.

A shallow orthography is close to or identical with the surface pronunciation, after most or all of the rules have applied. This has certain consequences and raises the following issues.

- The same word will appear with different tone marks *depending on its context*. A "constant word image" (useful for quick word recognition) is not maintained.

- It tends to be cumbersome and hard to read. Bird (1999b) showed that an exhaustive shallow tone marking was actually less readable than no marking in Dschang.

- How are multiple downsteps represented, when the tone can have several decreasing phonetic levels?

A deep orthography represents the sounds before the rules have applied. Very broadly, this is what linguists think of as the "underlying form." This also has certain consequences. A deep orthography has certain characteristics.

- It retains a constant word image, aiding quicker visual recognition of a word;

- It can sometimes be adapted better across dialects, since dialectal differences can be attributed to varying rule application;

- It can be significantly different than any person's actual pronunciation, including pronunciation in isolation.

If a particular language has few tone processes, there will be little or no difference between a shallow and deep orthography. The above does not exhaust the possibilities; Bird (1999a) and Roberts et al. (2013) give a number of other variations on marking tone.

4.1 Lexical phonology as a useful framework

I have mentioned "rules," but what kind of rules do I mean? There is a rich history of types of rules and their interactions, and one would expect that a narrowing of types of rules would likely be helpful in determining tone orthographies. And so it is.

Lexical Phonology (e.g., Pulleyblank 1986) is now disfavored as a comprehensive phonological theory, but the notion of *lexical* vs. *postlexical* processes is still invoked in contemporary theories such as Stratal Optimality Theory (Kiparsky 2000; Goldsmith et al. 2014). I argue that Lexical Phonology offers a level of psycholinguistic realism that is helpful in determining which level to refer to in deriving orthographic representations.

In Lexical Phonology, the output of the lexical level is the *psychologically real* level. This level is similar to but not precisely the same as the "phonemic level" of earlier theories. Following Snider (2014), I propose that this is the most appropriate phonological level for orthography in general. Specifically for this paper, it is proposed that this level is the most fruitful level in applying the results of tone rules to an orthography.

Snider (2014) is a major advocate of the above. One does not need to adopt the entire theory of Lexical Phonology to profit from its main benefits. The main

Michael Cahill

question in dealing with a phonological rule that may make a difference in orthographic representation is whether a rule is lexical or postlexical. Several diagnostic questions can be fruitfully applied to determine this, which I have adapted with minor modification from Snider (2014). These questions are:

- Are there lexical exceptions to the process?

- Does a given process lack phonetic motivation?

- Does the process have to apply across a *morpheme* boundary? (not a word boundary)

If one or more answers to the above are "yes," then the rule is a lexical rule; write the output of that rule. Other diagnostic questions:

- Is the new sound the rule produces a *non*-contrastive sound in the language?

- When a given process has applied, do native speakers think that the sound that results is the same as the sound that underwent the process?

- Does the process apply across *word* boundaries?

If one or more answers to the above are "yes", then the rule is postlexical; write the sound at the level *before* the rule applies. Also, if there is no apparent reason to categorize a rule as lexical, Snider advises assuming it is postlexical.

> The above questions are a starting point for tentative decisions that should be held somewhat loosely; all orthographic decisions need to be actually tested.[2]

The experimental evidence from Kabiye (Roberts et al. 2016) on two tone processes which were marked differentially in test orthographies supports this. The authors tested what they termed the *Lexical Orthography Hypothesis*, that is, that the lexical level (i.e., the output of the lexical phonology) offers the most promising level of phonological depth upon which to base a phonographic tone orthography that marks tone exhaustively.[3]

---

[2] Gudschinsky (1958: 342–343) gives an interesting example of a Mazatec man (Mexico) who was quite aware of the results of tone processes *within* words (lexical rules), but insisted that the tones of two particular *phrases* were different, though they were phonetically tonally identical (result of *postlexical* rules).

[3] "Exhaustive tone marking" is marking the tone on every syllable. There is reason to believe that this is not the most effective way to mark tone, but it was adopted for the purposes of having a more controlled experiment.

They tested 97 tenth-graders with orthographies that represented two tonal processes in three different ways. The rules were:

Lexical rule of L-spread: in the Kabiye verb, the L tone of a prefix spreads rightwards onto a H verb root until it is blocked by a singly linked H tone. This is shown to be lexical because it applies only across a specific morpheme boundary and is limited to within a word. Results of this rule are illustrated in Table 6.

Postlexical rule of HLH plateauing: a singly linked L between two H tones delinks, and the second H spreads left and has a downstepped register. This is shown to be postlexical by the fact that it applies across word boundaries as well as within words. Results of this rule are illustrated in Table 7.

The researchers tested 3 orthographies:

Phonemic: the pronunciation minus application of any allophonic processes

Lexical: (output of lexical phonology) the phonemic level minus application of any postlexical processes

Deep: (input of lexical phonology) the lexical level minus application of any lexical processes, a morphographic representation.

Examples of the orthographic output of these different systems are shown in Tables 6 and 7.

Note that because of the specific processes chosen, the results of the Low-Spread rule distinguish a Deep orthography from the others. Is the Deep or the Lexical/Phonemic representation better? The results of the HLH Plateauing rule distinguish the Phonemic orthography from the others; is the Phonemic or the Deep/Lexical representation better? Table 8 shows the expected results if the Lexical Orthography Hypothesis is correct. Note that the experiment focused on the oft-neglected domain of *writing* as well as reading.

The reader is referred to the paper for full results, but on the whole, the Lexical Orthography Hypothesis was supported. Lexical and Phonemic orthographies worked better in dealing with one tone process, and Lexical and Deep orthographies worked better in dealing with the other tone process. So the Lexical orthography fared well in both processes, while the others did worse in one orthography or the other. Specifically, those writing the Lexical orthography:

Table 6: Low-spread and Kabiye orthographies

Speech	Deep orthography	Lexical and phonemic orthographies	Gloss
[wélésí-∅] listen-IMP	⟨wélési⟩	⟨wélésí⟩	'listen!'
[e-welesí-na] 3SG-NC1-listen-COM	⟨ewélésína⟩	⟨ewelesína⟩	'he listened'
[te-welesí-na] NEG-listen-COM	⟨tewélésína⟩	⟨tewelesína⟩	'didn't listen'

Table 7: HLH plateauing and Kabiye orthographies

Speech	Deep and lexical orthographies	Phonemic orthography	Gloss
[sɛ́-tʊ] thanks-NC9	⟨sétʊ⟩	⟨sétʊ⟩	'thanks'
[féyɩ́] there_is_no	⟨féyɩ⟩	⟨féyɩ⟩	'there is not'
[sɛ́tʊ́ féyɩ́] thanks-NC9 there_is_no	⟨sétʊ féyɩ⟩	⟨sɛ́'tʊ́ féyɩ́⟩	'don't mention it!'

Table 8: Expected results from three experimental orthographies

Orthography	Lexical L tone spreading	Post-lexical HLH plateauing
Phonemic	Written as pronounced (easier)	Written as pronounced (harder)
Lexical		Written without post-lexical processes (easier)
Deep (harder)	Written morphographically	

- scored fewer errors writing an appropriate accent on a vowel than those writing the Deep orthography;

- scored fewer errors writing post-lexical non-automatic downstep than those writing the Phonemic orthography;

- experienced less degradation of performance on a later test than those writing the Deep and Phonemic orthographies;

- were more absorbed with the task of writing accents correctly than those writing the Deep and Phonemic orthographies (though this often caused them to write long vowels incorrectly).

One caveat for the experiment is that there is not universal acceptance by researchers what the underlying (deep) tones of Kabiye actually are. Also, as mentioned before, this experiment focuses on lexical tone, exhaustively marked. Other less exhaustive methods of tone marking were not explored.

4.2 Language typology as a useful guide

Besides the largely theoretical insights of the Lexical Orthography Hypothesis, another promising tool for deciding how to mark tone is a more typological one. Kutsch Lojenga (2014) proposes two main types of tone languages. In her terminology, these are "stable tone languages" and "movable tone languages."

Stable tone languages are those in which tone rules do not change an underlying tone. They tend to have a cluster of properties:

- These languages tend to have shorter words, and more tone levels.

- Tone generally has a heavy functional load, both lexically and grammatically.

- Grammatical tone can be looked at as tone replacement.

- Writing tone on every syllable is possible and straightforward.

- Teaching phonetic tone awareness is (relatively) easier, and a constant word image can be maintained.

Ndrulo and Attié, cited earlier, are examples of stable tone languages.

Movable tone languages are those in which the tones change according to the context, due to a variety of tone sandhi rules. These also tend to have a cluster of properties which differ from the stable tone languages:

- These languages tend to have longer words and fewer tone levels.

- They generally have a lighter load for lexical tone, but often a heavy functional load for grammatical tone.

- Thus it may be less important to mark lexical tone, but it is important that *grammatical* tone distinctions be differentiated.

- Teaching tone awareness could focus on grammatical notions rather than phonetics

Sabaot, Lugungu, and many Bantu languages are examples of movable tone languages.

Of course, these language types are prototypical. Many languages do not fall neatly into these categories. However, this can serve as a general first approximation and guide to the type of orthographic tone marking that may prove fruitful.

5 Conclusions and recommendations

I conclude this paper with several recommendations – some definite and others more tentative – and an open question on "selective tone marking."

5.1 Recommendations

Some practices in orthography development have been confirmed enough by experienced people that I can definitely recommend these.

1. First, work with the community! The emphasis in this paper has been on usability of the orthography, based on linguistic factors. However, if for any reason, the language community does not *want* to use a particular orthography, linguistic perfection becomes irrelevant. Various sociopolitical factors that can be relevant in different situations are discussed in Cahill (2014).

2. All decisions on marking tone need to be tested. Unforeseen factors, including incomplete analysis, may result in one's orthography not being as useable as anticipated. Whether the testing be formal or informal, one needs to check it with people who use the language (see Karan 2014 for details).

3. If it is decided to mark lexical tone in the orthography, mark the output of the lexical level, as discussed in §4.1

4. When marking grammatical tone of whatever sort, prioritize marking the *meaning*, not the phonetics (in Roberts et al.'s 2013 term, "semiographically"). Readers and writers have meaning "in their heads" more than they do the abstract sound. Also, a particular grammatical meaning such as "recent past" may have several phonetic implementations. Figuring these out is a challenging task, but one which, as far as orthography goes, is unnecessary.

5. Consider how to *teach* the orthography. Even if speakers know their language is tonal, they often do not have a high awareness of the specifics of tone, let alone how to represent this. Each tone mark should be taught in a separate lesson, just as any consonant or vowel. Also, lexical and grammatical tone should be taught separately.

> ... a tone orthography needs to be accompanied by a well thought-through methodology for awareness raising of tonal contrasts and for teaching people to read with the symbols chosen to mark tone in a language. (Kutsch Lojenga 2014: 52)

6. Make the orthography compatible with electronic devices – phones, tablets, internet, and computers in general. A Unicode-compatible orthography[4] will be very helpful in the long run. Non-alphabetic symbols (e.g., * = +) are appealing for marking grammatical tone, but a warning here is appropriate. The advantages of these marks is that they are already present on the keyboard, they can be written in line with the other characters rather than going back to add a diacritic, and they can mark an easily recognized *meaning* rather than the harder to process phonetics. However, the Unicode *characteristics* of these symbols mean that many programs will not treat them as part of the word, but will split them off from the usual consonants and vowels. Publishing can potentially be hindered if this issue is neglected.

7. Finally, consider the writer as well as the reader. Active literacy in a language involves simplicity of writing as well as reading.

The following are additional factors to consider as possibilities in orthography design, though I do not suggest them as firmly as the above recommendations. These seem reasonable, but have not been proven through practical experience to the extent that the definite recommendations above were.

---

[4]Unicode is the international standard for encoding text in electronic data. Major software assumes user input uses Unicode characters and not a custom font. "Unicode-compatible" in our context means first, that only Unicode characters are used, and second, that they are used in accordance with their defined set of properties. One of those properties is whether it is treated as a "word-forming" character. The usual equals sign (=, Unicode U+003D) is not word-forming, but a shortened equals sign (꞊, Unicode U+A78A) has been defined as word-forming.

Michael Cahill

When extra symbols are needed, consider writing them *in line* with other letters, rather than accents above the letter (e.g., *^baba*, not *bába*). These are easier to write, since the pencil or pen does not have to be lifted to a separate tier (think of writing an English word like *constitution*, which requires dotting ⟨i⟩s and crossing ⟨t⟩s.) More testing and experience is needed, but this may also be possibly easier to read.

> Once the initial strangeness of such symbols in the orthography [Bokyi, see Table 4] has been overcome, and their function is understood, teams learn to use them quite quickly and can get quite excited about them. But teaching phonetic tone-marking using accents is always a struggle here, and very, very few ever master it. (Harley, p.c.)

If both grammatical and lexical tone are to be marked, mark them with different systems. Testing in Togo (Kabiyé language), Roberts marked lexical tone with accents, and grammatical tone with other characters. Roberts comments that readers seemed to "feel" the grammar more than the sound system.

5.2 A closing question

One convention that has been fairly widely practiced, but also has been opposed for theoretical reasons, is "selective tone marking." Selective tone marking applies tone marking only to one word of a minimal tone pair, leaving the other unmarked. Thus if a language has two words [bóbò] and [bóbó], with different meanings, they could be written as ⟨bóbo⟩ and ⟨bobo⟩. Selective tone marking thus contrasts with marking tone more extensively or exhaustively.

Wiesemann (1989: 16) and Longacre (1953: 132–133) assert that selective tone marking should be avoided. Wiesemann gives the following reason for rejecting selective tone marking:

> It should be mentioned here that a system which marks tone where it is minimally different in individual words is not a good system. In such a system, for each individual word one must learn whether it carries a tone mark or not. To mark low tones only on words where there is a minimal tone pair makes the teaching of tone a matter of memory, rather than a matter of rules linked to pronunciation.

Longacre (1953: 133) adds the point that selective tone marking "presupposes that one has already made a list of all the words in the language to see which ones are minimal pairs. Such a claim is pretentious since most newly written languages do not have good dictionaries."

Thus two reasons for avoiding selective tone marking are 1) the memory load of having to know all the individual words which must be marked and 2) the improbability of the orthography designer knowing all such word pairs (or triplets, or more) that need to be marked.

However, dictionaries that include a large percentage of lexemes in a language are easier to produce now than in past years (http://www.rapidwords.net/). Also, the preference for rules rather than memorization a) is possibly a relic of Western education, with its bias against rote memorization, and b) ignores the fact that much of our successful (!) English orthography also depends on memorization rather than rules, as the examples in Table 9 show.

Table 9: Variable English pronunciation of same spellings

Spelling of ⟨ough⟩ words	Phonetics	Spelling of ⟨ear⟩ words	Phonetics
cough	[ɑf]	*hear*	[iɹ]
though	[o]	*heard*	[ɚ]
through	[u]	*heart*	[ɑɹ]

English orthography is far from being an ideal model, but if such a widely-used orthography can depend so much on memorization, then the argument based on memory loses its force. So a better case can probably be made for selective tone marking than previous scholars have argued.

Acknowledgments

This paper was first presented at the Academic Forum of the Graduate Institute of Applied Linguistics, Dallas, before its presentation at the 48th Annual Conference on African Languages at Indiana University. I am grateful for comments and interesting discussion from both audiences. I also acknowledge valuable comments from two reviewers in preparation for the ACAL proceedings.

References

Barnwell, Katherine G. L. 1969. *A grammatical description of Mbembe (Adun dialect): A Cross River language.* London, UK: University of London dissertation.

Bird, Steven. 1999a. Strategies for representing tone in African writing systems. *Written Language & Literacy* 2(1). 1–44.

Bird, Steven. 1999b. When marking tone reduces fluency: An orthography experiment in Cameroon. *Language and Speech* 42(1). 83–115.

Bolli, Margrit. 1978. Writing tone with punctuation marks. *Notes on Literacy* 23. 16–18.

Cahill, Michael. 2000. Avoiding tone marks: A remnant of English education? *Notes on Literacy* 26(1). 1–11.

Cahill, Michael. 2007. *Aspects of the morphology and phonology of Konni.* Austin, Texas: SIL International.

Cahill, Michael. 2014. Non-linguistic factors in orthographies. In Michael Cahill & Keren Rice (eds.), *Developing orthographies for unwritten languages,* 9–25. Austin, Texas: SIL International.

Edonyu, Richard. 2015. *The impact of sociolinguistic factors on the use of vernacular scriptures in Kumam.* Nairobi, Kenya: Africa International University MA thesis.

Goldsmith, John A. 1976. *Autosegmental phonology.* Cambridge, Massachusetts: Massachusetts Institute of Technology dissertation.

Goldsmith, John A., Jason Riggle & Alan C.L. Yu. 2014. *The handbook of phonological theory.* 2nd edn. John Wiley & Sons.

Gudschinsky, Sarah C. 1958. Native reactions to tones and words in Mazatec. *Word* 14(2–3). 338–345.

Halle, Morris & Noam Chomsky. 1968. *The sound pattern of English.* New York: Harper & Row.

Harley, Matthew. 2012. *Guidelines for marking tone in Nigerian languages.* Presentation at 3rd West Kainji languages workshop.

Hedinger, Robert. 2011. *Akoose orthography guide.*

Higdon, Lee, Lamboni Gnanlé André, Lossoule Kolani, Namoni Nambaré, N'Touame Pakdembé, Tchanate Kodjo & Namoine Emanuel. 2000. *Apprendre a lire et a écrire le Gangam: Guide pour les scolarisés.* Togo: SIL.

International Institute of African Languages and Cultures. 1930. *Practical orthography of African languages.* Oxford: Oxford University Press. www.bisharat. net/Documents/poal30.htm, accessed 2017-5-30.

Karan, Elke. 2014. The ABD of orthography testing: Practical guidelines. *Work Papers of the Summer Institute of Linguistics. University of North Dakota Session* 54. http://arts-sciences.und.edu/summer-institute-of-linguistics/work-papers/_files/docs/2014-karan.pdf, accessed 2017-5-30. Accessed May 30, 2017.

Katterhenrich, Stephen & Hazel Gray. 2016. *Bungu orthography statement, revised.* SIL Uganda-Tanzania.

Kiparsky, Paul. 2000. Opacity and cyclicity. *The linguistic review* 17(2-4). 351–366.

Kutsch Lojenga, Constance. 2014. Orthography and tone: A tone system typology with implications for orthography development. In Michael Cahill & Keren Rice (eds.), *Developing orthographies for unwritten languages* (SIL International Publications in Language Use and Education 6), 49–72. Dallas, TX: SIL International.

Longacre, Robert E. 1953. A tone orthography for Trique. *The Bible Translator* 4(1). 8–13.

Longtau, Selbut R. 2008. *The Tarok language: Its basic principles and grammar.* Dart-Jos: Developments Alternatives, Research & Training (DART).

Matthews, Tom. 2010. *Echizinza orthography guide.* Dorien Kamphuis (ed.). SIL Uganda-Tanzania.

Miner, Edward. 2003. *The development of Nuer linguistics.* http://www.dlib.indiana.edu/collections/nuer/edward/linguistics.html, accessed 2017-5-30.

Moe, Ron & James Mbabazi. 1999. *Lugungu orthography guide: Preliminary version.* Document de travail, Nairobi, SIL.

Olson, Kenneth. 2005. *The phonology of Mono* (SIL and UTA Publications in Linguistics 140). Dallas, TX & Arlington, TX: SIL International & the University of Texas at Arlington.

Persson, Janet. 2004. Bongo-Bagirmi languages in Sudan. *Occasional papers in the study of Sudanese languages* 9. 77–84.

Pulleyblank, Douglas. 1986. *Tone in lexical phonology.* Vol. 4 (Studies in Natural Language and Linguistic Theory). Dordecht: Springer.

Roberts, David, S Borgwaldt & T Joyce. 2013. A tone orthography typology. *Typology of writing systems* 51. 82–108.

Roberts, David, Stephen L Walter & Keith Snider. 2016. Neither deep nor shallow: A classroom experiment testing the orthographic depth of tone marking in Kabiye (Togo). *Language and Speech* 59(1). 113–138. DOI:10.1177/0023830915580387

Snider, Keith. 2014. Orthography and phonological depth. In Michael Cahill & Keren Rice (eds.), *Developing orthographies for unwritten languages*, 27–48. Dallas, TX: SIL International.

Stegen, Oliver. 2005. *Tone in eastern Bantu orthographies.* Dallas, TX. https://www.academia.edu/2155341/Tone_in_Eastern_Bantu_Orthographies. Presented at SIL Bantu orthography meeting.

Wiesemann, Ursula. 1989. Orthography matters. *Notes on Literacy* 57. 14–21.

Chapter 7

Prosodic restructuring in Somali nominal constructions

Laura J. Downing

Morgan Nilsson
University of Gothenburg, Sweden

This paper investigates variability in the realization of High tones in some nominal constructions of Somali. Previous work on Somali tone suggests that most determiners and all nominal modifiers should realize a High tone when they combine with the noun they modify. However, our study finds that there is considerable variability in the realization of High tones on nominal determiners and modifiers, with the High tone often not realized. This phenomenon of variability in tone realization is quite reminiscent of Swedish, which shares with Somali the property that tone realization is culminative within some prosodic domain. Recent work on Swedish has argued that variable non-realization of High tone is best analyzed as prosodic restructuring: reducing the number of culminative tonal domains in a construction necessarily leads to a reduction in the number of surface High tones. We argue that prosodic domain restructuring also provides the most plausible analysis of High tone reduction in Somali nominals.

1 Introduction

It is uncontroversial that the Somali tonal system has canonical stress-like properties, as defined in Downing (2010) and Hyman (2006; 2011; 2012; 2014). Work by Hyman (1981; 2006; 2012); Le Gac (2003); Green & Morrison (2016), and Saeed (2004) agrees that High tone is *culminative*: no more than one High tone can occur per (minimal Phonological) Word (PWord). The position of High tones is, roughly, *demarcative*: they occur on either the penult or final mora of a PWord. Only some proper names have a High tone in another position (Saeed 1999: 22).

Laura J. Downing & Morgan Nilsson. 2019. Prosodic restructuring in Somali nominal constructions. In Samson Lotven, Silvina Bongiovanni, Phillip Weirich, Robert Botne & Samuel Gyasi Obeng (eds.), *African linguistics across the disciplines: Selected papers from the 48th Annual Conference on African Linguistics*, 125–142. Berlin: Language Science Press.
DOI:10.5281/zenodo.3520577

How to account for these generalizations, which hold for PWords in isolation, is more controversial. Some possibilities are: underlying accent (Banti 1988; Green & Morrison 2016; Le Gac 2003), (underlying) High tone (Andrzejewski 1964; 1979; 1981; Armstrong 1934; Hyman 2006; 2014; Le Gac 2016), or no underlying tone or accent, rather surface tone is the result of morphological tone/accent assignment principles (Hyman 1981; Mous 2009). Addressing this problem in detail is outside the scope of this particular paper. However, we do assume that Somali is a tonal language, not an (underlyingly) accentual one.

The goals of our investigation are twofold: to document the realization of High tones in some nominal constructions, and to account for the position and number of High tones that occur within these constructions in terms of matches and mismatches between morphosyntactic structure and prosodic structure.[1] The central empirical finding of the paper is presented in §2, which shows that a number of Somali nominal constructions in our corpus do not have the tone pattern expected from the previous literature because the expected High tone on the determiner or modifier is "missing". In §3, we argue that familiar tone or intonation processes like the Obligatory Contour Principle (OCP) or Final Lowering do not plausibly account for the missing High tones. In §4, we propose that prosodic restructuring provides a better account: a reduction in the number of prosodic domains a construction is parsed into leads to a reduction in the number of High tones that can be realized in the construction when High tone is a culminative property of the domain. We draw a parallel between the prosodic restructuring found in Somali and the prosodic adjunction processes that have been proposed by Myrberg & Riad (2015) and Riad (2016) for Swedish, a language with a surprising number of prosodic properties in common with Somali.

2 Data to be accounted for

This paper presents preliminary results of a study of the prosody of some nominal constructions of Somali, based on recently collected elicitation data. We begin by summarizing the sources of High tones expected in nominal constructions for the data we investigated. Then we present the tone patterns attested in our data and give more information about our corpus.

---

[1]We adopt the approach to defining mismatches between morphosyntactic and prosodic structure developed in work like: Downing (1999; 2016); Inkelas (1993; 2014); Itô & Mester (2012; 2013); Nespor & Vogel (1986); Riad (2012); Selkirk (1986; 2011); Vigário (2010), and Vogel (2010). See Green & Morrison (2016) for a recent alternative analysis of Somali prosody within this general framework.

2.1 Expected High tones in (non-subject) nominal constructions from the literature

Hyman (1981); Saeed (1993; 1999) and Green & Morrison (2016) show that all Somali nouns in isolation have a High tone on either the penult or the final mora.
That is, High tone is obligatory in certain morphosyntactic constructions. The
position is determined by morphological factors (e.g., declension class; "gender";
singular vs. plural), not phonological factors. We give a few examples in (1); note
that compounds have a single High tone, on either the penult or the final mora:

(1) Somali nominals

  a. tonal minimal pairs

ínan	'boy'	vs.	*inán*	'girl'
béer	'liver'	vs.	*beér*	'garden'
éy	'dog'	vs.	*eý*	'dogs'

  b. tone on penult vs. ultima in phonologically analogous words

  dukáan 'shop'
  caleén 'leaf'
  sonkór 'sugar'
  kibís   'bread'
  súbag   'butter'
  mindí   'knife'
  gúri   'house'

  c. compounds
  dayaxgacméed 'satellite' (cf. *dáyax* 'moon'; *gacmeéd* 'of hands')
  lacagháye 'cashier' (cf. *lacág* 'money'; *hay-* 'have, hold'; *-e* agentive)
  caanagéel 'camel milk' (cf. *caanó* 'milk'; *géel* 'camels')
  madaxweýne 'president' (cf. *mádax* 'head'; *weýn* 'big')

Nouns can be followed by a number of determiners. As shown in the list in
(2), while the definite determiner is toneless, the other determiners introduce a
High tone:[2]

---

[2] The **k**/g/h/∅ vs. **t**/d/sh alternations in the Somali determiner system illustrated in our data
is conditioned by gender agreement: masculine nouns take the k/g/h/∅ series of determiners,
while feminine nouns take the t/d/sh series. The allomorphy found in both series of determiners
is phonologically conditioned. See, e.g., Saeed (1993; 1999), for detailed discussion of this sandhi
phenomenon.

(2) Somali determiner types (Saeed 1999: 111–117)

    a. Definite *-ka/-ta*

    b. Remote definite *-kií/-tií*

    c. Interrogative *-keé/-teé* 'which'

    d. Possessives *-káyga/-táyda* 'my', *-káaga/-táada* 'your (sg.)', *-kíisa/-tíisa* 'his', *-kéeda/-téeda* 'her', *-kayága/-tayáda* 'our (excl.)', *-kéenna/-téenna* 'our (incl.)', *-kíinna/-tíinna* 'your (pl.)', *-kóoda/-tóoda* 'their'

    e. Demonstrative *-kán/-tán* 'this', *-kaás/-taás* 'that'

According to work like Green & Morrison (2016); Hyman (1981), and Saeed (1993; 1999), when the High-toned determiners occur in combination with a noun, they retain their High tone, as illustrated in (3). While Hyman (1981: 191) mentions a process of accent (High tone) reduction on possessive determiners following a noun, only an example or two is provided. None of the determiners change the tone of the base noun, except *-keé/-teé* 'which?' (3h, 3i).

(3) Somali nouns with determiners (Saeed 1993: 160–168)

    a. *nín* 'man' | *nín-ka* 'the man'

    b. *naág* 'woman' | *naág-ta* 'the woman'

    c. *nín* 'man' | *nín-kán* 'this man'

    d. *naág* 'woman' | *naág-tán* 'this woman'

    e. *sáddex* 'three' | *sáddex-daás* 'those three'

    f. *shúqul* 'work' | *shúqul-káyga* 'my work'

    g. *lacág* 'money' | *lacág-táada* 'your money'

    h. *nín* 'man' | *nin-keé* 'which man?'

    i. *naág* 'woman' | *naag-teé* 'which woman?'

Green & Morrison (2016); Hyman (1981), and Saeed (1993) observe that the modifier in a Noun+modifier phrase ⭢Noun+Noun or Noun+Adjective – is also expected to be realized with a High tone when the phrases are pronounced in isolation.[3] This is illustrated in (4), where we see that a High tone is assigned to the final vowel of the (indefinite) postnominal modifier, while the modified

---

[3] Noun+Noun (N+N) modifier phrases are called "genitive constructions" by Hyman (1981) and Saeed (1993). Green & Morrison (2016) refer to N+N modifier phrases as "associative constructions" and, following Saeed (1993), use the term "attributive adjective" for the Noun+adjective construction. See Saeed (1993) for detailed discussion of Noun+modifier constructions in Somali.

noun keeps its base High tone pattern.[4] Note that numbers are considered nouns (Saeed 1993: 123) and can head Noun+modifier phrases, as shown in (4b, 4c).

(4) Somali Noun+modifier phrases (Hyman 1981; Green & Morrison 2016; our elicitation notes)

    a. *géed wiíl* 'a tree of a boy' (cf. *wíil* 'boy')

    b. *áfar buúg* 'four books' (cf. *búug* 'book')

    c. *labó sabuurad-oód* 'two blackboards' (cf. *sabuurád* 'blackboard')

    d. *gacán-ta midíg* 'the right hand' (cf. *mídig* 'right side')

    e. *mindí-da Maxaméd* 'the knife of Maxamed' (cf. *Maxámed*)

    f. *gaarí cusúb* 'a new car'

    g. *shúqul adág* 'hard work'

In sum, many nominal constructions are expected to have two High tones: one on the noun and one on the following determiner or modifier (noun or adjective).

In keeping with the one High tone per Prosodic Word (PWord) principle, Green & Morrison (2016) propose that Noun+determiner (H-toned) and Noun+modifier constructions have the same prosodic representation: namely, they are both parsed as independent PWords from the noun they modify. The representations in (5) adapt Green & Morrison's (2016) analysis by abstracting away from the PWord-min vs. PWord-max distinction they argue for; surface High-toned morphemes are **bolded**:

(5) Prosodic structures for Somali nominals; parentheses indicate PWords (adapting Green & Morrison 2016)

    a. N+definite (N)$_{\text{PWord}}$ def

    b. N+H-toned determiner (N)$_{\text{PWord}}$ (**Det**)$_{\text{PWord}}$

    c. compound ((N) (N))$_{\text{PWord}}$

    d. N+modifier (N)$_{\text{PWord}}$ (**Modif**)$_{\text{PWord}}$

Notice the parallelism in the structure of N+determiner (5b) and N+modifier (5d). These representations form the starting point for our investigation.

---

[4]Only a few adjectives, e.g., *dhéer* 'long', *wéyn* 'big' (Saeed 1999: 105–106), and some female proper names seem to constitute exceptions to the generalization that modifiers in Noun+modifier phrases have a High tone on the final mora.

2.2 Our data

The new data discussed in this paper were collected in 2016 through elicitation at the University of Gothenburg, working mainly with one speaker from Kismayo and two speakers from Mogadishu. The overall corpus comprises 10,002 individual utterances (tokens) representing 2,970 different types. The NPs were provided both in isolation and in short sentences, in morphosyntactic contexts where the variable High tone is expected to consistently occur.

What we find in these data is that the nominal constructions in (5b) and (5d) do not consistently have the High tone patterns expected from previous work on Somali prosody. Instead, the High tone on the determiner or nominal modifier is often "missing". For example, the possessive determiner is seldom realized with its expected High tone. Out of a total of 1,068 instances of N+possessive constructions in our corpus,[5] 929 (87%) do not realize a High tone on the possessive suffix. This is illustrated in (6).

(6) a. *biyá-hayga* 'my water' (~ *biyá-háyga*)
   b. *dhég-tiisa* 'his ear' (~ *dhég-tíisa*)
   c. *mindí-diisa* 'his knife' (~ *mindí-díisa*)
   d. *webí-gooda* 'their river' (~ *webí-góoda*)
   e. *biyó-hooda* 'their water' (~ *biyó-hóoda*)
   f. *bisád-deeda* 'her cat' (~ *bisád-déeda*)

The pitch pattern of a typical possessive with the High tone missing, like (6f), is shown in Figure 1.

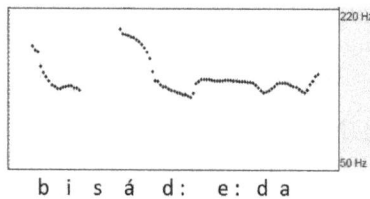

Figure 1: *bisáddeeda* 'her cat'

Our data thus tends to confirm Hyman's (1981) observation that the possessive undergoes accent (High tone) reduction, except that High tone reduction is variable in our corpus: it does not occur 100% of the time.

---

[5]This set of 1,068 excludes constructions containing the shorter (indefinite) possessive suffixes, in which tonal differences reflect the distinction between a non-focused subject and other syntactic functions.

Interestingly, our data shows that the likelihood of realization of the determiner's High tone is construction specific. For example, the demonstrative suffixes also often lack a High tone: out of a total of 635 instances of Noun+demonstrative constructions in our corpus, 369 (58%) do not realize a High tone on the demonstrative suffix. This variation is illustrated in (7):

(7) a. *wíil-kan* 'this boy' *(~wíil-kán)*

  b. *gaarí-gaas* 'that car' *(~gaarí-gaás)*

  c. *Talaadá-daas* 'that Tuesday' *(~ Talaadá-daás)*

This is a significantly lower proportion of missing High tones, however, than found with the possessive suffixes.

In contrast, the remote definite suffix more generally realizes its High tone. Out of 997 instances of Noun+remote definite constructions in our corpus,[6] only 358 (36%) do not realize a High tone on the remote definite suffix. This variation is illustrated in (8):

(8) a. *mindí-dii* 'that (remote) knife' *(~ mindí-dií)*

  b. *nín-kii* 'that (remote) man' *(~ nín-kií)*

  c. *qoraallá-dii* 'those (remote) texts' *(~ qoraallá-dií)*

Finally, Noun+modifier constructions should have a High tone assigned to the final syllable of the second word.[7] Yet, in our data, this High tone is again often missing. Out of 571 instances of Noun+indefinite Noun constructions in our corpus,[8] 391 (68.5%) do not realize a High tone on the second noun. This variation is illustrated in (9a, 9b); recall that numbers are nouns in Somali. Out of 599 instances of Noun+Adjective constructions, in contrast, only 297 (50%) do not realize a High tone on the modifier. This variation is illustrated in (9c, 9d):[9]

---

[6]This set of 997 excludes constructions where the remote definite suffix occurs in a non-focused subject NP.

[7]Nouns can be followed by more than one modifier, and it is the final modifier which should realize a final High tone. We consider here only nouns followed by a single modifier, for ease of comparison with the Noun+determiner data.

[8]This number excludes feminine nouns – mostly personal names and place names – with a fixed (exceptional) accent on a non-final mora, which show much less variability in their tonal behavior.

[9]This set of 599 excludes constructions where the adjective either has the subject suffix *-i* or has an exceptional, fixed penult accent (in our data: *wéyn* 'big', *dhéer* 'long', *macáan* 'sweet'), which show almost no variability in their tonal behavior.

(9) a. *hál litir* 'one liter' (~ *hál litír*)

　　 b. *gúri-ga Muuse* 'Musa's house' (~ *gúri-ga Muusé*)

　　 c. *biyó badan* 'much water' (~ *biyó badán*)

　　 d. *subáx-dií hore* '(in) the early morning' (~ *subáx-dií horé*)

To sum up this section, High tones on determiners and nominal modifiers are often not realized. All the speakers exhibit the same range of variation, so it cannot be attributed to dialectal or individual differences. In the next section, we take up two untenable phonological accounts – the OCP and Final Lowering – for why these High tones are missing before arguing for an alternative analysis in §4.

3 Why the OCP and Final Lowering cannot account for the missing High tones

3.1 The OCP

Looking at Figure 1, above, one might propose that the High tone on the possessive suffix – and other determiners – is deleted as an OCP effect (Leben 1973): in a sequence of adjacent High tones, one is deleted. However, this explanation faces the problem that the OCP is not a general principle of the Somali tone system. When two consecutive High tones occur, they are normally realized on almost the same pitch level. This is illustrated in the pitch track for (9d), *subáxdií hore* '(in) the early morning' given in Figure 2.

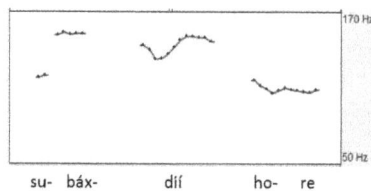

Figure 2: *subáxdií hore* '(in) the early morning'

Therefore, tonal reduction on possessives and other determiners is not plausibly motivated by the OCP. Furthermore, the OCP is not relevant in the case of the missing High tones on the final vowels of modifiers in Noun+modifier constructions, such as *hore* 'early' in this example.

3.2 Final Lowering

The Somali tone literature (Andrzejewski 1981; Armstrong 1934; Hyman 1981; Le Gac 2003; Saeed 1993; 1999) notes that High tones are lowered phrase-finally/pre-pausally/post-focally. Since the "missing" High tones in our data – in both Noun+determiner and Noun+modifier constructions – often occur in phrase-final position, one might propose that Final Lowering is responsible for giving the impression that the High tones have been deleted. However, Final Lowering does not provide a general explanation for the missing High tones in our data. First, the expected High tone on the possessive suffix (e.g., *dhég-tíisa* 'his ear') is not associated with the final syllable or mora, so Final Lowering is not relevant here. Second, final High tones are not deleted in our data in other morphosyntactic contexts, such as lexical words in isolation (10) and in sentence final position (11), where the final High tone is expected to be realized. Non-lowered final High-toned vowels are bolded:

(10)   Words in isolation

     a. *tukayaá**l*** 'crows'

     b. *ubaxy**ó*** 'flowers'

     c. *lafdhabarr**ó*** 'spines'

(11)   Sentence final position

     a. *Wáxaan arkay rat**í**.* 'I saw a camel.'

     b. *Waxaan lá kulmay Sahr**ó**.* 'I met with Sahra.'

     c. *Hooyadáa waa macallim**á**d.* 'Your mother is a teacher.'

     d. *Libáax ayáa dila**ý** dawac**ó**.* 'A lion killed a fox.'

That is, final High tones are not systematically deleted. Only High tones on (some) postnominal determiners and modifiers are.

Third, High tones can be deleted from the word-final syllable of a determiner or a modifier even when the word is not phrase-final or pre-pausal:

(12)   Vowels with "missing" non-final High tones are bolded

     a. *labá dúmar ah oo qurúx bad**an** oo kalíya*
        'just two beautiful women' (cf. *labá* 'two'; *dúmar* 'women'; *qurúx* 'beauty'; *badán* 'much'; *kalíya* 'only')

     b. *sánnad-k**ii** hore ~ sánnad-k**ií** hore*
        'last year' (cf. *sánnad* 'year'; *horé* 'previous')

     c. *bisád-d**aa**s yar ~ bisád-da**ás** yar*
        'that little cat' (cf. *bisád* 'cat'; *yár* 'small')

To sum up this section, neither the OCP nor Final Lowering can account for the missing High tones in N+determiner and N+modifier constructions, because neither of these processes applies generally in Somali. Instead, High tone deletion/non-realization appears to be construction specific. Further, High tones are often deleted when the context for neither the OCP or Final Lowering is met.

4 Tone "deletion" as prosodic restructuring

4.1 Parallels with Swedish prosody

Coming from a Swedish background, one is struck by the similarities between the prosodic systems of Somali and Swedish, another language with a stress-like tone system. As argued for in recent work by Riad (2012; 2016) and Myrberg & Riad (2015), Swedish has prosodic culminativity of stress at the PWord$_{(min)}$ level and culminativity of tone at the PWord$_{(max)}$ level; compounds are a single tone realization/assignment domain; and some affixes are stressed, while others are not. Data illustrating these properties for Swedish are given in (13–15); all of the data are cited from Myrberg & Riad (2015). In (13), we see that Swedish does not have secondary stress, unlike English or German:

(13) PWord culminativity for stress

    a. American English and Swedish stress

        i. (ˈmoneˌtary)$_\omega$ (moneˈtär)$_\omega$min=max

        ii. (toˌtaliˈtarian)$_\omega$ (totaliˈtär)$_\omega$min=max

        iii. (ˈabˌstract)$_\omega$ (abˈstrakt)$_\omega$min=max

    b. German and Swedish stress

        i. (ˌmiliˌtariˈsieren)$_\omega$ (militariˈsera)$_\omega$min=max

        ii. (ˌonoˌmatopoˈetisch)$_\omega$ (onomatopoˈetisk)$_\omega$min=max

        iii. (ˌuniˌversiˈtät)$_\omega$ (universiˈtet)$_\omega$min=max

The data in (14) shows that compounds have two stresses but a single tonal accent (accent 2, indicated with a diacritic superscripted before the compound) realized over the entire compound and replacing the isolation tone pattern of the words making up the compound:

(14) Compounds

    a. sommar-lov ^{2}((ˈsommar$_2$)$_\omega$min(ˌlov$_1$)$_\omega$min)$_\omega$max
        'summer break'

b. jul-lovs-morgon $^2((\text{'jul}_1)_\omega\min(\text{,lov}_1\text{-s})_\omega\min(\text{,morgon}_2)_\omega\min)_\omega\max$
'Christmas break morning'

c. jul-klapp $^2((\text{'jul}_1)_\omega\min(\text{,klapp}_1)_\omega\min)_\omega\max$
'Chistmas present'

The data in (15) illustrates that some affixes bear a stress and takes part in the realization of a tonal accent 2 in the construction, while others – (15c) – bear neither stress nor tone:

(15)   Affixes

a. tvätt-bar $^2((\text{'tvätt})_\omega\min(\text{,bar})_\omega\min)_\omega\max$ 'washable' **tonic suffix**

b. o-nödig $^2((\text{'o})_\omega\min(\text{,nöd-ig})_\omega\min)_\omega\max$ 'unnecessary' **tonic prefix**

c. för-ändra (för-$^1(\text{'ändra})_\omega\min)_\omega\max$ 'to change'

All of these properties also characterize Somali's prosodic system, as we have seen in the preceding sections. Table 1 summarizes the similarities in the prosodic systems of the two languages.

Table 1: Comparison of the prosody of Swedish and Somali

	Somali	Swedish
PWord culminativity	✔[a]	✔[b]
compounds are 1 tone realization domain	✔	✔
stressable/tone bearing affixes	✔	✔

[a]tone
[b]stress (PWord$_{\min}$); tonal accent (PWord$_{\max}$)

4.2 Prosodic restructuring in Swedish

Another property the Swedish and Somali prosodic systems have in common is that a tone (accent) is obligatory. In Swedish, tonal accent is obligatory for all PWord$_{(\max)}$, and in Somali, for all nominals and modifiers when pronounced in isolation. Yet, in both languages, an expected High tone (or accent) is sometimes "missing". We illustrated the "missing" High tones of Somali in §3. For Swedish, as work like Garlén (1988); Myrberg & Riad (2015) and Riad (2016) reports, words in some short phrases, which sometimes are even structurally similar to those in our Somali data, variably lose their tonal accent. This phenomenon is illustrated in (16). As we can see in this data, the input tone-accent is sometimes simplified. Accent 2 can be reduced to accent 1 – as in (16a). The examples in (16b–16c) illustrate that often only the accent of the rightmost PWord in the phrase is consistently realized. (In this data set, subscripted numbers indicate the input tonal accents. Superscripted numbers indicate the tonal accents realized under prosodic adjunction):

(16) Prosodic restructuring in Swedish (Myrberg & Riad 2015)

    a. Prosodic adjunction in morphology and syntax
       morphology: $(\text{för-}^1(\text{ändra}_2)_\omega)_\omega$max 'to change'
       syntax: $(\text{för }^1(\text{liten}_2)_\omega)_\omega$max 'too small'
       $(\text{för }^1(\text{många}_2)_\omega)_\omega$max 'too many'
       $(\text{för }^1(\text{länge}_2)_\omega)_\omega$max 'too long'

    b. Lexicalized phrases with prosodic adjunction
       $((\text{'röd-a}_2)_\omega \,^2(\text{'matt-an}_2)_\omega)_\omega$max 'red carpet' (lexicalised phrase)
       $((\text{'Röd-a}_2)_\omega \,^1(\text{'Kors-et}_1)_\omega)_\omega$max 'Red Cross' (name, lexicalised)
       $((\text{'hopp-a}_2)_\omega \,^1(\text{'upp}_1)_\omega)_\omega$max 'jump up' (particle verb)
       $((\text{'hel-a}_2)_\omega (\text{'lång-a}_2)_\omega \,^1(\text{'dag-en}_1)_\omega)_\omega$max 'all day, lit. whole long day'

    c. Local deaccentuation as the result of prosodic adjunction
       $((\text{'liten}_2)_\omega \,^2(\text{'smuts-ig}_2)_\omega)_\omega$max $^2(\text{'gryt-a}_2)_\omega$min=max 'little dirty pot'
       $((\text{'lag-a}_2)_\omega (\text{be-}^1(\text{'gagn-ade}_2)_\omega)_\omega\text{'})_\omega$max $(\text{kopia}^1\text{'torer}_1)_\omega$min=max
       'repair used copying machines'

To account for this variation in output accent realization, Myrberg & Riad (2015) and Riad (2016) propose that both words and affixes can be incorporated into a single PWord$_{(\text{max})}$ via prosodic restructuring (adjunction). (Their restructuring analysis is illustrated in the prosodic representations in (16).) Prosodic restructuring accounts for the tonal reduction found, given the culminative one tonal accent per PWord$_{(\text{max})}$ principle which Riad (2016) shows holds for Swedish. Reducing the number of PWord$_{(\text{max})}$ in a phrase necessarily reduces the number of tonal accents that can be realized.

4.3 Prosodic restructuring in Somali

What we propose is that Somali High tone reduction is the result of prosodic restructuring, analogous to what has been proposed for Swedish by Myrberg & Riad (2015) and Riad (2016) and illustrated in the preceding section. We also adopt from their analysis a distinction between PWord$_{(\text{min})}$ and PWord$_{(\text{max})}$.[10]

---

[10]Following Myrberg & Riad (2015) and Riad (2016), we adopt a distinction between PWord-min and PWord-max as defined in work like Itô & Mester (2012; 2013).

We follow work like Green & Morrison (2016); Hyman (1981; 2006; 2012); Le Gac (2003) and Saeed (2004) in assuming that a culminative one High tone per PWord principle holds for Somali. For High-toned determiners like the possessive to be realized with a High tone, we propose that they must therefore be parsed in a separate PWord$_{(min)}$ from the noun they modify. However, High-toned determiners are arguably parsed in the same PWord$_{(max)}$ domain as a preceding noun, because they undergo segmental sandhi processes which do not apply across PWord$_{(max)}$ boundaries. The representations in (17) illustrate our analysis:[11]

(17) a. ((dhég)$_{\text{PWord-min}}$ (tíisa)$_{\text{PWord-min}}$)$_{\text{PWord-max}}$ 'his ear'

   b. ((mindí)$_{\text{PWord-min}}$ (díisa)$_{\text{PWord-min}}$)$_{\text{PWord-max}}$ 'his knife'

Note that the alternation between *-diisa* and *-tiisa* in (17) is an example of a sandhi process that only applies across a PWord-min boundary within PWord-max in our analysis. (See Saeed 1999: 28–31 for detailed discussion of these segmental sandhi processes.)

In the variable pronunciation where the possessive, for example, has lost its High tone, we propose that the construction has the same recursive PWord structure as the toneless definite determiner suffix – cf. (5a). That is, the construction has undergone prosodic restructuring like that found in Swedish (16), so that the possessive suffix is not an independent PWord$_{(min)}$, but rather is adjoined to the preceding noun within PWord$_{(max)}$, as shown in (18) – cf. (17a) and (18b):

(18) a. ((dhég)$_{\text{PWord-min}}$ ta)$_{\text{PWord-max}}$ 'the ear'

   b. ((dhég)$_{\text{PWord-min}}$ tiisa)$_{\text{PWord-max}}$ 'his ear'

Since High tone is culminative and obligatory within the PWord$_{(min)}$ domain, reducing the number of PWord$_{(min)}$ within a PWord$_{(max)}$ domain necessarily leads to a reduction in the number of High tones realized within PWord$_{(max)}$.

We propose that Noun+modifier phrases that have "lost" the High tone on the modifier have a similar analysis. They also undergo prosodic restructuring, but they are parsed into a different prosodic domain from the restructured determiners. Following Vigário (2010) and Vogel (2010), we assume a Complex Word Group (CWG) constituent, which is the domain of, for example, tone assignment to compounds. Recall from (1c), above, that compounds in Somali form a single tonal realization domain; more examples are given in (19):

---

[11]See Green & Morrison (2016) for an alternative account of similar Somali data. Space does not permit a careful critical comparison of our analysis with theirs. The interested reader is directed to their work for details.

(19) a. *madax-weýn-e* (m.) 'president' (cf. *mádax* (m.) 'head'; *wéyn* 'big'; *-e* agentive suff.)

  b. *cod-kác* (m.) 'tonal accent' (cf. *cód* (m.) 'voice'; *kac-* 'rise')

  c. *biya-dhác* (m.) 'waterfall' (cf. *biyó* (pl.) 'water'; *dhac-* 'fall')

  d. *bad-wéyn* (f.) 'ocean' (cf. *bád* (f.) 'sea'; *wéyn* 'big')

  e. *magaala-mádax* (f.) 'capital' (cf. *magaálo* (f.) 'town'; *mádax* (m.) 'head')

  f. *laf-dhábar* (f.) 'spine' (cf. *láf* (f.) 'bone'; *dhábar* (m.) 'back')

We propose that restructured Noun+modifier phrases are also parsed into a CWG, as illustrated in (20) – cf. (5d), above:

(20) ((hál)$_{PWord-max}$ litir)$_{CWG}$ 'one liter'

It is interesting to note that tonal reduction results in a High tone on the leftmost word of the Noun+modifier construction, whereas compounding typically results in a single High tone on the rightmost word. We conclude that these two constructions must have a different prosodic representation. As illustrated in (21), prosodic restructuring of a Noun+modifier leads to a left-headed construction, whereas compounds are right headed:[12]

(21) prosodic restructuring: ((hál)$_{PWord-max}$ litir)$_{CWG}$ 'one liter'
  vs.
  compound: (cod (kác)$_{PWord-max}$)$_{CWG}$ 'tonal accent'

Both CWG constructions are posited to contain a PWord-max in order to account for the fact that segmental sandhi processes do not occur across the words in the CWG domain:

(22) No segmental sandhi in the CWG domain
  prosodic restructuring:
  ((labá)$_{PWord-max}$ tuug)$_{CWG}$ (*labá duug) 'two thieves'
  vs. compound:
  (keli (tális)$_{PWord-max}$)$_{CWG}$ (* keli dális) 'dictatorship'
  (cf. kéli (m.) 'being alone'; tális 'government')

---

[12] A reviewer notes that another difference between restructured N+modifier phrases and compounds is that the tonal accent (and prosodic structure) assigned to compounds never varies. We propose that the lack of variation in compounds is due to the fact that they are lexicalized forms, morphosyntactically non-compositional. High tone variation in our data is found in compositional forms.

To account for tone assignment in these constructions, we propose that, in nominal CWGs, the High tone assigned to a CWG is realized on the internal PWord$_{(max)}$. This is again analogous to Swedish, which only allows one tonal accent to be assigned both to a compound or compound-like construction, as well as to a construction that has undergone prosodic restructuring. The accent assignment principles for compounds and restructured words and phrases are not identical in Swedish. Note that this also generally holds true for Somali.

One last point in favor of our analysis is that it accounts for why determiners are added only to the rightmost word in a compound, whereas each noun in a Noun+Noun construction can have its own determiner, as shown in (23).

(23)   compound   Noun+Noun
   a.   *guri-márti-ga* 'the guesthouse'   *gúri-ga martí-da* 'the guests' house'
   b.   *caana-géel-a* 'the camel milk'   *caaná-ha géel-a* 'the camels' milk'

Recall that compounds and Noun+Noun constructions are also potentially distinguished by tone, as shown in (23). Noun+Noun constructions can have two High tones, one for each PWord, when they are not restructured, while compounds, which contain only one PWord, only have one High tone:

(24)   compound   Noun+Noun
   a.   (guri(márti)$_{PWord\text{-}max}$)$_{CWG}$ b.   (gúri)$_{PWord\text{-}max}$
        'guesthouse'   (martí)$_{PWord\text{-}max}$ ~
                                                          ((gúri)$_{PWord\text{-}max}$ marti)$_{CWG}$
                                                          'guests' house' (cf. *gúri*
                                                          'house'; *martí* 'guests')

   c.   (caana(géel)$_{PWord\text{-}max}$)$_{CWG}$ d.   (caanó)$_{PWord\text{-}max}$
        'camel milk'   (geél)$_{PWord\text{-}max}$ ~
                                                          ((caanó)$_{PWord\text{-}max}$ geel)$_{CWG}$
                                                          'camels' milk' (cf. *caanó*
                                                          'milk'; *géel* 'camels')

We propose that a determiner takes a PWord as its base. Since compounds contain only one PWord, as shown in (24a, c), they can take only one determiner. However, each noun in a Noun+Noun construction can be parsed as a PWord, as shown in (24b, d), and so each can take a determiner. Strikingly, Noun1-determiner+Noun2-determiner constructions cannot be restructured; the High tone of the second noun is always realized. The determiner, which requires a PWord base, appears to block tonal reduction in Noun2. In our analysis, this falls out from proposing that both the determiner and the High tone require a PWord base. When Noun2 is not parsed as a PWord, under restructuring (see 25d), it can bear neither a determiner nor a High tone.

Our analysis is summarized schematically below (cf. 5, above); 'X' in compounds indicates that compounds can be made up of a combination of lexical words (X):

(25)   Summary of our analysis

    a. N+definite: $((N)_{PWord\text{-}min}\ def)_{PWord\text{-}max}$

    b. N+H-toned determiner: $((N)_{PWord\text{-}min}\ (Det)_{PWord\text{-}min})_{PWord\text{-}max}$
       OR restructured $((N)_{PWord\text{-}min}\ Det)_{PWord\text{-}max}$

    c. compound: $(X\ (X)_{PWord\text{-}max})_{CWG}$

    d. N+modifier: $(N)_{PWord\text{-}max}\ (Modif)_{PWord\text{-}max}$
       OR restructured $((N)_{PWord\text{-}max}\ Modif)_{CWG}$

5 Conclusion and topics for future research

Many nominal constructions in Somali do not realize the expected High tones on the determiner or modifier; that is, they undergo tonal reduction. We argue that tonal reduction in Somali is the consequence of prosodic restructuring, rather than as the result of tone deletion or tonal lowering processes. Since High tone is culminative within the $PWord_{(min)}$ domain, prosodic restructuring which reduces the number of $PWord_{(min)}$ automatically reduces the number of High tones which can be realized in the domain. It is striking that prosodic restructuring in Somali so closely parallels prosodic restructuring in Swedish. This leads us to propose that restructuring is typical of these kinds of tonal systems: i.e., with tonal culminativity within a prosodic domain. An important question for future research is whether Somali High tones are underlying or assigned to $PWord_{(min)}$ (depending on morphosyntactic information, à la Hyman 1981). While our analysis shows that High tone realization is conditioned by prosodic domain structure, the source of the High tones in the representation requires further investigation.

Acknowledgements

We thank our Somali language consultants for their patience in teaching us about their language. We are grateful to to Nina Hagen Kaldhol, two anonymous reviewers and a proofreader for thoughtful comments. We thank the ACAL audience for helpful feedback. We would like to acknowledge a grant from the Swedish Science Foundation (Vetenskapsrådet) which supports our research on Somali prosody.

References

Andrzejewski, Bogumil W. 1964. *The declensions of Somali nouns.* London: SOAS.

Andrzejewski, Bogumil W. 1979. *The case system in Somali.* London: SOAS.

Andrzejewski, Bogumil W. 1981. *Tone in Somali.* Ms. SOAS.

Armstrong, Lilias E. 1934. *The phonetic structure of Somali.* Ridgewood, NJ: Gregg Press Inc. Republished 1964.

Banti, Giorgio. 1988. Two Cushitic systems: Somali and Oromo nouns. In Harry van der Hulst & Norval Smith (eds.), *Autosegmental studies on pitch accent*, 11–50. Dordrecht: Foris Publications.

Downing, Laura J. 1999. Prosodic stem ≠ prosodic word in Bantu. In Tracy Alan Hall & Ursula Kleinhenz (eds.), *Studies on the phonological word*, vol. 174, 73–98. Amsterdam: John Benjamins.

Downing, Laura J. 2010. Accent in African languages. In *A survey of word accentual patterns in the languages of the world*, 381–427. Mouton de Gruyter.

Downing, Laura J. 2016. The prosodic hierarchy in Chichewa: How many levels? *Prosodic Studies* 1. 1–44.

Garlén, Claes. 1988. *Svenskans fonologi.* Lund: Studentlitteratur.

Green, Christopher R. & Michelle E. Morrison. 2016. Somali wordhood and its relationship to prosodic structure. *Morphology* 26. 3–32.

Hyman, Larry M. 1981. *Noni grammatical structure with special reference to verb morphology.* Los Angeles, CA: University of Southern California.

Hyman, Larry M. 2006. Word-prosodic typology. *Phonology* 23(2). 225–257.

Hyman, Larry M. 2011. Tone: Is it different? In John Goldsmith, Jason Riggle & Alan C. L. Yu (eds.), *The handbook of phonological theory*, 2nd edn., vol. 75, 197–239. Cambridge, MA: John Wiley & Sons.

Hyman, Larry M. 2012. In defense of prosodic typology: A response to Beckman and Venditti. *Linguistic Typology* 16(3). 341–385.

Hyman, Larry M. 2014. Do all languages have word accent? In Harry van der Hulst (ed.), *Word stress: Theoretical and typological issues*, 56–82. Cambridge, UK: Cambridge University Press.

Inkelas, Sharon. 1993. Deriving cyclicity. In *Studies in lexical phonology* (Phonetics and Phonology 4), 75–110. Boston: Academic Press.

Inkelas, Sharon. 2014. *The interplay of morphology and phonology.* Vol. 8. Oxford: Oxford University Press.

Itô, Junko & Armin Mester. 2012. Recursive prosodic phrasing in Japanese. In *Prosody matters: Essays in honor of Elisabeth Selkirk*, 280–303. Sheffield: Equinox Publishers.

Itô, Junko & Armin Mester. 2013. Prosodic subcategories in Japanese. *Lingua* 124. 20–40.

Le Gac, David. 2003. Tonal alternations in Somali. In Jacqueline Lecarme (ed.), *Research in Afroasiatic grammar II: Selected papers from the fifth conference on Afroasiatic Languages, Paris, 2000* (4), 287–304. Amsterdam; Philadelphia: John Benjamins.

Le Gac, David. 2016. *Somali as a tone language.* Presented at the workshop on Approches sociolinguistique et linguistique des langues de Mayotte et Djibouti, Université de Rouen.

Leben, William Ronald. 1973. *Suprasegmental phonology.* Massachusetts Institute of Technology dissertation.

Mous, Maarten. 2009. *The typology of tone in Cushitic.* Presented at WOCAL 6.

Myrberg, Sara & Tomas Riad. 2015. The prosodic hierarchy of Swedish. *Nordic Journal of Linguistics* 38(2). 115–147.

Nespor, Marina & Irene Vogel. 1986. *Prosodic phonology* (Studies in Generative Grammar 28). Dordrecht: Foris Publications.

Riad, Tomas. 2012. Culminativity, stress and tone accent in Central Swedish. *Lingua* 122(13). 1352–1379.

Riad, Tomas. 2016. Underpinnings of prosodic grouping in Swedish. In *Word order variation at the interfaces*, 13–15. Beer-Sheva: Ben-Gurion University of the Negev.

Saeed, John. 1993. *Somali reference grammar.* 2nd revised edition. Kensington, MD: Dunwoody Press.

Saeed, John. 1999. *Somali.* Vol. 10. Amsterdam: John Benjamins Publishing.

Saeed, John. 2004. The focus structure of Somali. In *Role and reference grammar (RRG) Book of proceedings.*

Selkirk, Elisabeth. 1986. On derived domains in sentence phonology. *Phonology* 3. 371–405.

Selkirk, Elisabeth. 2011. The syntax-phonology interface. In John A. Goldsmith, Jason Riggle & Alan C. L. Yu (eds.), *The handbook of phonological theory*, 2nd edn., 435–483. Wiley Blackwell.

Vigário, Marina. 2010. Prosodic structure between the prosodic word and the phonological phrase: Recursive nodes or an independent domain? *The Linguistic Review* 27. 485–530.

Vogel, Irene. 2010. The phonology of compounds. In Sergio Scalise & Irene Vogel (eds.), *Cross-disciplinary issues in compounding* (Current Issues in Linguistic Theory 311), 145–163. Amsterdam, Netherlands: John Benjamins.

Chapter 8

DP-internal structure and agreement in Nafara

Bertille Baron
Georgetown University

Senufo Nafara DPs show the particularly rare unmarked word order [N AP Def Dem Numeral]. In this cartographic account, the proposed derivation uses spec-to-spec movement operations to generate this word order (Cinque 2005). This analysis relies on two main claims: there is a domain ΣP under Num (Aboh 2004) in which two distinct categories of adjectives (high and low following Cinque 1994) merge to modify the noun. It is this same ΣP domain that undergoes spec-to-spec movement, motivated for agreement purposes. Oppositely, all elements structurally above ΣP remain in situ.

1 Introduction

Nafara is a Senufo language[1] spoken in Korhogo, Côte d'Ivoire. Determiner phrases in the language show the canonical word order [N Adj D Dem Num], like in (1) below.

(1) lo   tã   -gəl   gal   kɔrʃi
     mango sweet -DEF.3.PL DEM.3.PL seven
     N   Adj   -D   Dem   Num

     'these seven sweet mangoes'[2]

---

[1]Although there is some controversy over its classification (Manessy 1975; Naden 1989), Senufo is traditionally defined as a branch of the Niger-Congo, Gur subgroup (Westermann & Bryan 1970; Bendor-Samuel 1971).

[2]The data introduced and analyzed throughout this paper was elicited from a native speaker of Senufo Nafara.

Bertille Baron. 2019. DP-internal structure and agreement in Nafara. In Samson Lotven, Silvina Bongiovanni, Phillip Weirich, Robert Botne & Samuel Gyasi Obeng (eds.), *African linguistics across the disciplines: Selected papers from the 48th Annual Conference on African Linguistics*, 143–158. Berlin: Language Science Press. DOI:10.5281/zenodo.3520579

As we see here, attributive adjectives usually directly follow the noun. While they do not seem to show agreement, adjectives are apparently the host for the number and gender specific determiner.[3] The demonstrative directly follows the determiner, and inflects for number and gender also. Numerals are DP-final in the language, and do not show concord.[4]

The DP word order in (1) is highly unexpected, as argued by Cinque (2005). First, cross-linguistically, Numerals in DP-final position are noticeably rare. Then, syntactically speaking, the derivation of this word order is usually considered marked (Cinque 2005).

This paper accounts for both the syntactic structure and derivation of Nafara DPs, assuming the universal functional hierarchy [Dem > Num > Adj > N] adopted by Greenberg (1963), Cinque (2005) and others. In §2.1, I first discuss the location of each DP-internal element. I also draw distinctions between two separate categories of adjectives (that I refer to as high and low, corresponding to Cinque's (2010) indirect and direct modification respectively). In §2.2, I motivate the movement of adjectives and noun only, responsible for the surface word order. Finally, in §2.3, I show that such movement is motivated for agreement purposes.

2 DP structure and word order

2.1 Assumptions and data

2.1.1 The functional structure of DPs

In a cartographic approach to DP structure, Greenberg (1963) and Cinque (2005) argue that the only possible initial order capable of universally generating the DP word orders attested in natural language is [Dem > Num > Adj > N]. Assuming the underlying structure in Figure 1, Cinque accounts for all possible word orders as the result of some type of movement of NP. Namely, he argues for combinations of successive Spec-to-Spec movements with or without pied-piping of NP up the DP spine.

Note here that, in Cinque's account, Num, Dem, and A are heads of their own functional projections (henceforth FPs) above NP. Those FPs merge in the Specifier of phrases (here WP, XP, and YP) that are all sisters to an Agree node, head of

---

[3]The noun classification adopted in this paper is adapted from those provided by both Manessy (1996: 22) and Carlson (1990: 76) for other Senufo varieties. Nafara shows a 5-gender system, where genders 1, 2, and 3 consist of countable nouns, and genders 4 and 5 are for non-count nouns. Considering the scope of this paper, I will limit my discussion to countable nouns.

[4]This is true of all numerals except 'one' which shows gender agreement, as shown in §2.1.4.

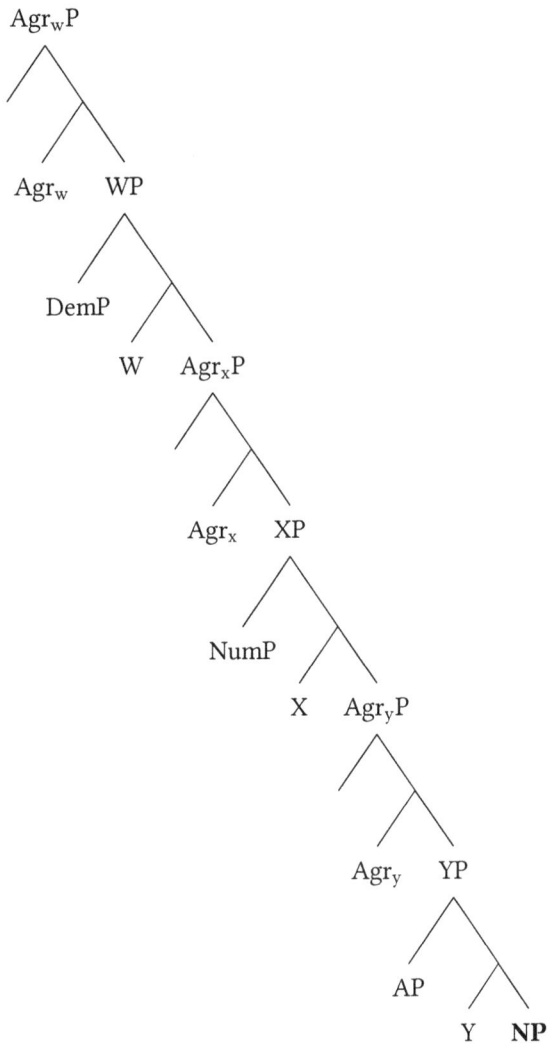

Figure 1: the cartographic representation of DPs (adapted from Cinque 2005: 2).

an AgrP where NP potentially lands when undergoing movement. From a Mini-malist perspective (Chomsky 1995), such a structure violates the economy prin-ciple by assuming that additional and potentially unnecessary elements merge into the syntactic structure. Therefore, and in an effort to preserve Cinque's hi-erarchy, I assume the syntactic structure in (2) below, where functional elements all merge directly above NP and below D as heads of their own projections, and where AgrPs are eliminated.[5] Adjectives are not included in (2). Their location and behavior will be discussed more thoroughly in §2.1.5.

(2)   [DP ... D [DemP ... Dem [NumP ... Num [NP ... N]]]]

The remainder of §2.1 will focus on the distribution and properties character-istic of each functional and lexical category represented in Nafara DPs.

2.1.2 Determiners

Nafara determiners agree in gender and number with the noun they determine. They obligatorily attach to the right edge of the noun in simple DPs, as in (3). However, in the presence of AP, they attach to the AP final element, as in (4). It is important to note here the variable placement of the adverb in the AP.

(3)   a.   lo   -gəl
            mango -**DEF.3.PL**
            'the mangoes'
      b. * gəl   lo
            DEF.3.PL mango
            'the mangoes'

(4)   lo   [(dɛl) tã   / tã   (tɛl)] -gəl
      mango [(very) sweet / sweet (very)] -**DEF.3.PL**
      'the very sweet mangoes'

Cinque (2005) does not account for determiners and how or where they surface in the DP. Because they are separate morphemes in Nafara, and because it is the only DP-internal element encoding definiteness, I take the definite marker to be the realization of the D head, merging as the sister to the highest DP-internal functional projection, as in (2) above. That D head is spelled out *in situ*, cliticizing to the final extended noun phrase element located in its specifier, as shown in §2.2.

---

[5]The present analysis for the surface DP word order in Nafara does not justify the need for AgrPs to be generated in the syntax.

2.1.3 Demonstratives

Demonstratives also inflect for number and gender. They necessarily follow the determiner, as shown in (5).

(5) a. pɔm tã   -bɛl   **bal**
         apple sweet -DEF.1.PL **DEM.1.PL**

         'these sweet apples'

     b. * pɔm **bal**   tã   -bɛl
         apple **DEM.1.PL** sweet -DEF.1.PL

         'these sweet apples'

Following Cinque's (2005) account, I assume that they merge rather high in DP, as the head of a functional projection DemP.

2.1.4 Numerals

As shown below, numerals occur in DP-final position. Because the literature on numerals has not led to any consensus on their syntax, both cross-linguistically and within languages, and due to the fact that I have no further evidence to motivate a more elaborate account for the distribution and properties of numerals in Nafara, I follow Cinque (2005) in assuming that they merge as the head of a functional projection NumP.[6]

(6) 'one'
     a. pɔm -u   **nuã**
         apple -DEF.1.SG **one.1**

         'the one apple'

     b. ʧi   -g   **nuŋɔ**
         tree -DEF.2.SG **one.2**

         'the one tree'

     c. lo   -n   **nunã**
         mango -DEF.3.SG **one.3**

         'the one mango'

---

[6]Cross-linguistically, numerals have either been analyzed as lexical or functional categories, showing great cross-linguistic differences (Danon 2012; Ionin & Matushansky 2006, among others).

(7) 'seven'

    a. pɔm -u   kɔrʃi

       apple -DEF.1.PL **seven**

       'the seven apples'

    b. ʧi -i   kɔrʃi

       tree -DEF.2.PL **seven**

       'the seven trees'

    c. lo   -gel   kɔrʃi

       mango -DEF.3.PL **seven**

       'the seven mangoes'

Note here that while 'seven' in (7) – as well as any other number in the language – does not inflect for gender, the number 'one' in (6) along with all numbers compounded with 'one' do. For this reason, I argue that 'one' merges in Num with an unvalued gender feature [uGEN]. Following both Greenberg (1963) and Cinque (2005), I assume NumP to be below DemP in the functional projection hierarchy. The DP word order in Nafara is [N A D Dem Num] as in (1), repeated in (8) below.

(8) lo   tã   -gəl   gal   kɔrʃi

    mango sweet -DEF.3.PL DEM.3.PL seven

    N   Adj -D   Dem   Num

    'these seven sweet mangoes'

2.1.5 Adjectives

So far, I have argued that attributive adjectives directly follow the noun they modify, as in (9a) below. The ungrammaticality of (9b) and (9c) shows that attributive adjectives that occur in postnominal position (that is to say most adjectives in the language) cannot occur in prenominal position.

(9)   a.   lo   tã   -gəl

          mango **sweet** -DEF.3.PL

          'the sweet mangoes'

     b. * tã   lo   -gəl

          sweet mango -DEF.3.PL

          'the sweet mangoes'

c. * tã   -gəl   lo
    sweet -DEF.3.PL mango

'the sweet mangoes'

There are however certain adjectives that can only occur prenominally. It is the case for adjectives of nationality, as shown in (10a).

(10)   a.   **kodivware** ʃju -u
             Ivorian   man -DEF.3.SG

             'the Ivorian man'

        b. * ʃju -u   **kodivware**
             man -DEF.1.SG **Ivorian**

             'the Ivorian man'

        c. * ʃju   **kodivware** -u
             man **Ivorian**   -DEF.1.SG

             'the Ivorian man'

        d. * **kodivware** -u   ʃju
             Ivorian   -DEF.1.SG man

             'the Ivorian man'

In (10b) and (10c), we see that the same adjective cannot occur after the noun, either preceding or following the determiner. This does not result in a semantic alteration of the DP, but in complete ungrammaticality. (10d) shows that such adjectives cannot be the host for the determiner clitic.

Cinque (1994) argues that adjective phrases merge in the Specifier position of functional projections occurring in a fixed order above NP based on a strict hierarchy, as in (11).

(11)   [$_{FP}$ AP F [AP F [AP F [$_{NP}$ N]]]]

The data above is somewhat surprising, as it contradicts the semantic hierarchy for adjectives proposed by Cinque (1994) according to which adjectives of nationality merge lower than adjectives of quality (Cinque 1994: 96). One major difference here is that Nafara postnominal adjectives are ordered freely, as in (12) below. Therefore, as is, the data does not allow us to posit any specific ranking of adjectives of nationality relatively to other types of adjectives.

(12) a. pɔm tã   ʧɛ ɲe -bɛl   c. pɔm ʧɛ ɲe tã   -bɛl
         apple sweet good red -DEF.1.PL   apple good red sweet -DEF.1.PL
         'the sweet good red apples'   'the sweet good red apples'

      b. pɔm ʧɛ   tã   ɲe -bɛl   d. pɔm ɲe tã   ʧɛ -bɛl
         apple good sweet red -DEF.1.PL   apple red sweet good -DEF.1.PL
         'the sweet good red apples'   'the sweet good red apples'

Due to the fact that both pre- and postnominal adjectives exist in Nafara, and because postnominal adjectives can be ordered freely, I follow Cinque (2010) in differentiating between two types of adjectives merging in two distinct positions in the syntax. While postnominal (low) adjectives merge as adjuncts inside NP (which explains their free ordering), prenominal (high) adjectives merge higher in the structure. Following Cinque, the latter are in fact reduced relative clauses (henceforth RC) merging in the Specifier of a projection above NP.

Applying this analysis to Nafara, I propose the syntactic representation in (13) below, where the few semantically selected reduced RC adjectives in the language merge in the specifier of the extended nominal domain that I call ΣP following Aboh (2004).[7]

(13) [$_{DP}$ ... D [$_{DemP}$ ... Dem [$_{NumP}$ ... Num [$_{\Sigma P}$ [A_{high}P] Σ [$_{NP}$ ... [$_{NP}$ N] [A_{low}P]]]]]]

Considering the word order [A_{high} N A_{low} D Dem Num] in (14), I argue that high and low adjectives all remain in situ within ΣP during the entire derivation.[8]

(14) kodivware lo   ʧɛ   tã   -gəl   gal   kɔrʃi
      Ivorian   mango good sweet -DEF.3.PL DEM.3.PL seven
      A_{high} N A_{low} A_{low} -D   Dem   Num
      'these seven good sweet Ivorian mangoes'

In the following section, I show that only ΣP moves up the DP spine, generating the surface word order. I will illustrate this derivation, and motivate it in §3.

---

[7]In his account for Gungbe – and ultimately for Gbe languages, Aboh (2004) argues in favor of an extended noun phrase that he calls ΣP. In Gbe (also Niger-Congo), ΣP constitutes the inflectional nominal domain, and ΣP alone undergoes movement up the DP spine for agreement purposes, landing in Spec,DP. While ΣP in Nafara does not apparently constitute a particular inflectional domain, I posit its existence in the language as the extended noun phrase once the higher adjectives have merged.

[8]Further data regarding complements to N is called for. The question is left aside and will be the object of future research.

2.2 Underlying structure and derivation

In his DP typology, Cinque (2005) argues that all attested word orders are the result of NP undergoing some type or combination of movements. According to him, total roll-up movement (also referred to as Spec-to-Spec movement with pied-piping) is the least marked type of movement available. Regarding the word order [N A Dem Num] (which is the one we observe here in Nafara DPs), Cinque argues that it is rather rare, but derived as in (15).

(15) **(N A Dem Num[eral])** has a derivation in which NP raises past A, followed by pied-piping of the *whose picture* type past Num[eral], followed by raising of [N A] without pied-piping (**marked**) past Dem. (Cinque 2005: 323(6l))

Cinque argues that what makes this word order rather uncommon is that it is somewhat marked. NP undergoes a combination of roll-up and Spec-to-Spec movement, as shown in Figure 2, adapted from Cinque (2005).

In §2.1.5, I have established that low adjectives are adjuncts inside NP, and high adjectives merge in Spec,ΣP, an extended nominal projection. Therefore, NP no longer needs to raise past AP and then raise along with AP past Num. Instead, the entire ΣP, including the high and low attributive adjectives, moves up. Figure 3 is a tree representation of the phrase in (16) where this movement is illustrated.

(16) kodivware lo dɛl tã -gəl gal kɔrʃi
      Ivorian mango very sweet -DEF.3.PL DEM.3.PL seven
      'these seven very sweet Ivorian mangoes'

The syntactic structure in Figure 3 clearly shows that, to obtain the desired word order [A_{high} N A_{low} D Dem Num], ΣP must move up without pied-piping and eventually reach Spec,DP (to precede D, Dem, and Num in that order). Therefore, and contra Cinque in (15) and Figure 2, I argue that ΣP undergoes a uniform Spec-to-Spec movement without pied-piping all the way up. However, this movement must be correctly motivated.

In §2.3, I demonstrate that movement is triggered by syntactic agreement with N. Due to some agreement effects that I will explain, ΣP is the phrase that gets selected, and raises to Spec,DP by way of Spec-to-Spec movement.

Agr$_w$P

Agr$_w$ WP

DemP

W   Agr$_x$P

No pied-piping: marked   Agr$_x$ XP

NumP

X   Agr$_y$P

Agr$_y$ YP

AP

Y   **NP**

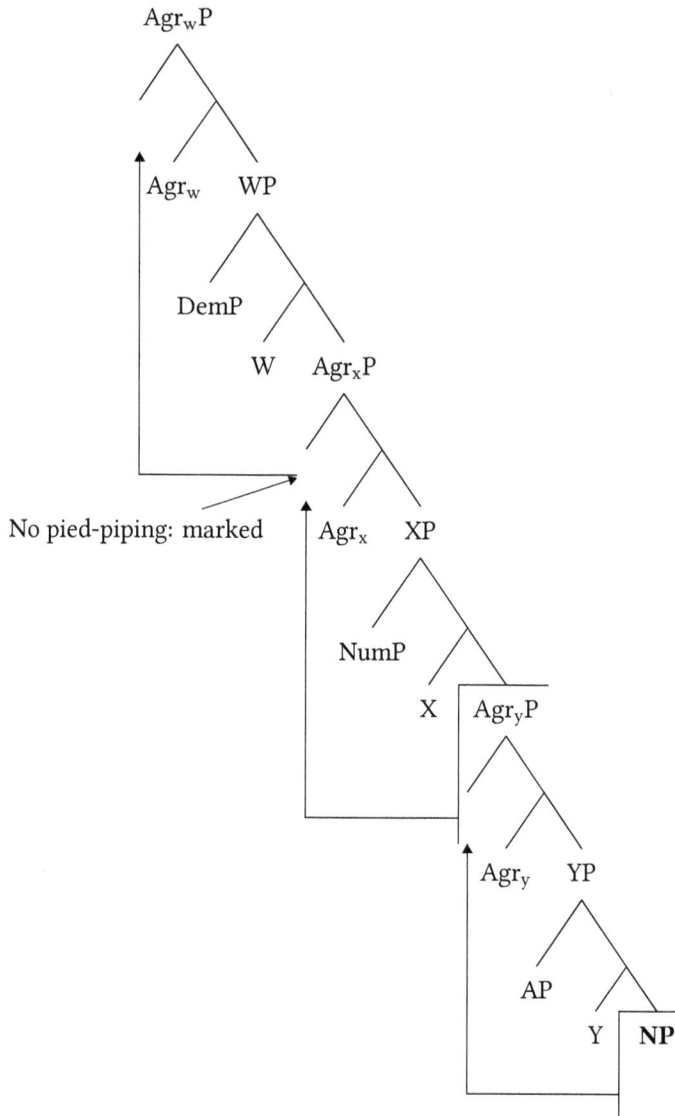

Figure 2: Syntactic derivation for the word order N A Dem Num (adapted from Cinque 2005)

DP
[DEF]
[GEN]
[NUM]

D'
[DEF]

D   DemP
gə̄l

Dem'

Dem   NumP
gal

Num'

Num   ΣP
kɔrʃi

AP   Σ'

kodivware   Σ   NP

N'

N'   AP

N   dɛl tã
lo

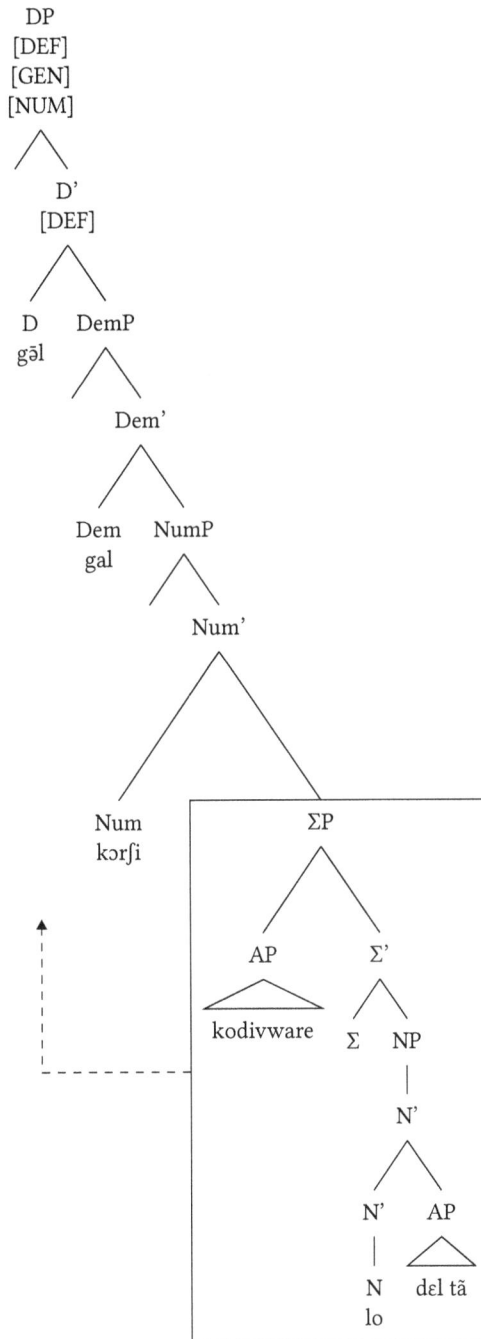

Figure 3: Feature Percolation in Nafara DPs.

2.3 Agree and DP word order

2.3.1 Agree

As previously mentioned, number and gender are active features of Nafara nominal concord. The phrase in (1), repeated here in (17), shows that both the determiner and the demonstrative agree in number and gender.

(17) lo   tã   -gəl   gal   kɔrʃi
      mango sweet -DEF.3.PL DEM.3.PL seven

      'these seven sweet mangoes'

Debatably, nominal concord has been argued to be the result of an operation called Agree (Chomsky 2000; 2001) also considered responsible for subject-verb agreement (Baker 2008; Carstens 2001; Collins 2004, among others). One version of the operation is provided in (18).

(18)   Agree (Norris 2014: 26)
       A probe X establishes an Agree relation with a goal YP, where:
       a. X c-commands YP,
       b. X lacks values for uninterpretable features that can be supplied by the values of matching features on Y,
       c. Y lacks values for uninterpretable features that can be supplied by X,
       d. No potential goal intervenes between X and Y,
       e. X and Y are in the same phase.
       Agree supplies the values of each category's uninterpretable features from matching features of the other category, with the two features coalescing into a single shared feature.

Let us now see how this operation can account for DP-internal agreement and word order in Nafara.

2.3.2 Agree, EPP, and ΣP movement

I argue here that D merges with a set of features that contains at least one valued feature: definiteness [DEF], and two unvalued features: number [NUM] and gender [GEN]. Additionally, D merges with an EPP feature. Similarly, Dem merges with unvalued [NUM] and [GEN] features, and the numeral arguably merges as the head of NumP with a gender feature that is unvalued (that is at least the case for 'one', overtly inflecting for gender as shown in (6)).

By way of Agree, all these functional elements look down their c-command domain for the missing values. As N comes from the lexicon with both [NUM] and [GEN], it is the best possible goal for all of them to probe down to.

While N is the best potential goal, it is ΣP that moves up. In fact, the same Agree relation through which DP-internal functional elements probe down to N selects ΣP to move up to Spec,DP. In his account for Estonian concord, Norris (2014) argues that the DP-internal agreement pattern observed in the language is made possible by a syntactic principle called Feature Percolation, presented here in (19).

(19)   Feature Percolation (Norris 2014: 135 (242))
   a. All projections of a head X^0 have the feature-value pairs that X^0 has.
   b. Let [F:val] be a valued feature on XP.
      Let Z^0 be a head lacking the feature [F].
      Let X^0 and Z^0 be members of the same extended projection (i.e., both [+N]).
      When Z^0 merges with XP, projecting ZP, ZP also has the valued feature [F:val].

According to (19), as heads merge into the structure with valued features, those same features percolate to the phrase those heads project. In Figure 4, I show how this principle applies in the Nafara DP. By way of Feature Percolation, and due to the fact that ΣP is nominal, I argue that the features [GEN] and [NUM] percolate all the way up to ΣP.

Since agreement with N occurs all the way up the DP spine, I argue that ΣP undergoes Spec-to-Spec movement up to Spec,DP where the EPP feature on D is satisfied.

3 Conclusions

In this paper, I have accounted for the structure and word order occurring in Nafara DPs. Following Cinque (2005), I argue for D > Dem > Num > A > N to be the DP-internal hierarchy. Additionally, and following Cinque (2010), I argue that there are two distinct types of attributive adjectives, that I refer to as high and low, and that do not seem to be interchangeable in the language. Finally, I argue that the surface word order is derived by moving ΣP to Spec,DP, for agreement purposes and due to the presence of an EPP feature on D. Because it is structurally higher than ΣP, Num does not undergo movement. For this reason, it surfaces in DP-final position. The Spec-to-Spec movement of ΣP is illustrated in (20) below.

DP
[DEF]
[GEN]
[NUM]

D'
[DEF]

D
[DEF]
[uGEN]
[uNUM]
EPP

DemP

Dem'

Dem
[uGEN]
[uNUM]

NumP

Num'

Num
[uGEN]

ΣP
[GEN]
[NUM]

AP

...A_{high}...

Σ'
[GEN]
[NUM]

Σ

NP
[GEN]
[NUM]

N'
[GEN]
[NUM]

N'
[GEN]
[NUM]

N
[GEN]
[NUM]

AP

...A_{low}...

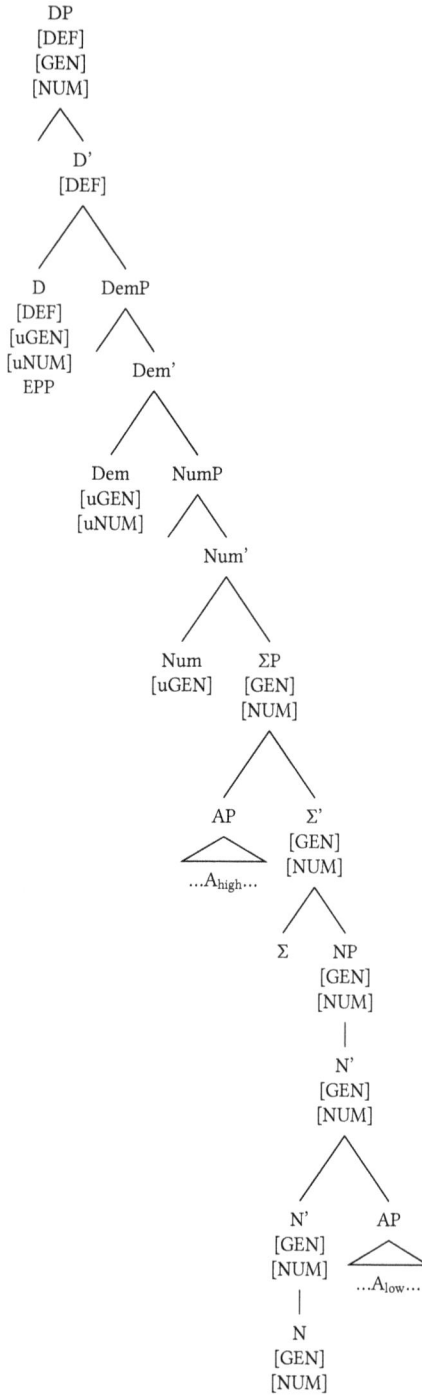

Figure 4: Feature Percolation in Nafara DPs

(20)   [$_{DP}$ D$_{[EPP]}$ [$_{DemP}$ **Dem** [$_{NumP}$ **Num** $\boxed{[_{\Sigma P} \, [_{AP} \, \textbf{A}_{high}] \, \Sigma \, [_{NP} \, \text{N} \, [_{AP} \, \textbf{A}_{low}]]]}$]]]

Abbreviations

A(dj)	adjective	D	determiner	Num	numeral
1	gender1	DEF	definite	PL	plural
2	gender2	Dem	demonstrative	SG	singular
3	gender3	INDEF	indefinite		

References

Aboh, Enoch Oladé. 2004. *The Morphosyntax of complement-head sequences.* Oxford: Oxford University Press.

Baker, Mark. 2008. *The syntax of agreement and concord.* Cambridge: Cambridge University Press.

Bendor-Samuel, John T. 1971. Niger-Congo, Gur. *Current Trends in Linguistics* 7. 141–178.

Carlson, Robert. 1990. *A grammar of Supyire. Volume 1: Kampwo dialect.* University of Oregon dissertation.

Carstens, Vicki. 2001. Multiple agreement and case deletion. *Syntax* 4(3). 147–163.

Chomsky, Noam. 1995. *The Minimalist program.* Cambridge: MIT Press.

Chomsky, Noam. 2000. Minimalist inquiries: The framework. In Roger Martin, David Michaels & Juan Uriagereka (eds.), *Step by step: Essays on minimalist syntax in honor of Howard Lasnik,* 89–155. Cambridge: MIT Press.

Chomsky, Noam. 2001. Derivation by phase. In Michael Kenstowicz (ed.), *Ken Hale: A life in language,* 1–52. Cambridge: MIT Press.

Cinque, Guglielmo. 1994. On the evidence for partial N movement in the Romance DP. In Anne Zribi-Hertz, Guglielmo Cinque, Jan Koster, Jean-Yves Pollock, Luigi Rizzi & Raffaella Zanuttini (eds.), *Paths toward Universal Grammar,* 85–110. Washington, DC: Georgetown University Press.

Cinque, Guglielmo. 2005. Deriving Greenberg's universal 20 and its exceptions. *Linguistic Inquiry* 36. 315–332.

Cinque, Guglielmo. 2010. *The syntax of adjectives.* Cambridge: MIT Press.

Collins, Chris. 2004. The agreement parameter. In Anne Breitbarth & Henk van Riemsdijk (eds.), *The agreement parameter,* vol. 75, 115–136. Berlin, Germany: Walter de Gruyter.

Danon, Gabi. 2012. Two structures for numeral-noun constructions. *Lingua* 122. 1282–1307.

Greenberg, Joseph. 1963. Some universals of grammar with particular reference to the order of meaningful elements. In Joseph Greenberg (ed.), *Universals of language.* 73–113. Cambridge, MA: MIT Press.

Ionin, Tania & Ora Matushansky. 2006. The composition of complex cardinals. *Journal of Semantics* 23. 315–360.

Manessy, Gabriel. 1975. *Les langues oti-volta: Classification généalogique d'un groupe de langues voltaïques.* Vol. 15. Leuven: Peeters Publishers.

Manessy, Gabriel. 1996. La détermination nominale en senoufo. *Linguistique africaine* 16. 53–68.

Naden, Anthony. 1989. Gur. In John Bendor-Samuel & Rhonda L. Hartell (eds.), *The Niger-Congo languages: A classification and description of Africa's largest language family,* 140–168. Lanham, MD: University Press of America.

Norris, Mark. 2014. *A theory of nominal concord.* UC Santa Cruz dissertation.

Westermann, Diedrich & M. A. Bryan. 1970. *The languages of West Africa.* Oxford: Oxford University Press (for the International African Institute).

Chapter 9

Complement clause C-agreement beyond subject phi-agreement in Ikalanga

Rose Letsholo

University of Botswana

Ken Safir

Rutgers University

In this essay, we provide a rich description and analysis of C-agreement and complement clause complementizer (CCC) distributions in Ikalanga which reveals a highly articulated set of relationships between matrix clause properties and the morphology of an agreeing complementizer. In particular, we show that the agreeing CCC is sensitive not only to matrix subject phi-features, but to matrix voice and tense as well. Although the agreeing Cs are limited to a small set of predicates that are not fully predictable from meaning, the agreement facts are the same wherever an agreeing C is possible.

1 Introduction

Complementizer agreement with matrix verb subjects in languages like Lubukusu (Diercks 2013) raises many issues concerning the syntax of agreement and the status of agreeing complementizers, but rich descriptions beyond Lubukusu are rare. In addition to Lubukusu, C-agreement with the matrix subject has been attested for Kinande and Ibibio (Baker 2008), Mande languages (Idiatov 2010), Luvale, Luchazi, Chokwe and Lunda (Kawasha 2007), Limbum (Nformi 2017) and Kipsigis (Diercks & Rao 2019). Only the recent account of Kipsigis, however, comes close to the thorough description Diercks provides for Lubukusu. In this

Rose Letsholo & Ken Safir. 2019. Complement clause C-agreement beyond subject phi-agreement in Ikalanga. In Samson Lotven, Silvina Bongiovanni, Phillip Weirich, Robert Botne & Samuel Gyasi Obeng (eds.), *African linguistics across the disciplines: Selected papers from the 48th Annual Conference on African Linguistics*, 159–186. Berlin: Language Science Press. DOI:10.5281/zenodo.3520581

paper we provide a rich description and analysis of C-agreement and complement clause complementizer (CCC) distributions in Ikalanga, which uncovers a much more articulated set of relationships between matrix clause properties and the morphology of an agreeing complementizer. In particular, we show that the agreeing CCC is sensitive not only to matrix subject phi-features, but matrix voice and tense as well. Although we suggest an analysis, our main goal in this essay is to set boundary conditions on what any truly explanatory treatment must account for.

2 The Ikalanga pattern

Ikalanga CCCs for non-infinitival clauses include invariant *kuti* and *kuyi*, and two CCCs that agree with matrix subjects, AGR-*ti* and AGR-*yi*. The morpheme -*ti* is identical to the verb 'say' -*ti* and neither AGR-*ti*, nor any other CCC, is possible with main verb -*ti*. However, AGR-*ti*, when it occurs with other verbs, not only agrees with matrix subjects, but also partially agrees with matrix tense. We will argue further that both *kuti* and *kuyi* are also based on the -*ti* 'say' root which has the suppletive form -*yi* when it is passive. *Kuyi*, in at least some of its distribution, agrees for passive voice with the matrix verb. The *ku*- of *kuti* and *kuyi* is a default form where the c17 prefix *ku*- affixes to -*ti* (and suppletive -*yi*) in the absence of agreement. We argue that all the -*ti*-based complementizers are essentially the same form and that they are not verbs – grammaticalization is incomplete in an interesting way. This pattern has consequences for what the assumed locality relations are between matrix T(ense) and elements inside vP. Although sensitivity to voice and subject phi-features is feasible within the vP-phase in minimalist reasoning, interaction of a CCC with matrix T raises interesting questions that require further assumptions which we will explore.

The following examples show that what we are calling the AGR-*ti* complementizer agrees with the matrix subject for person and noun class. Examples (1a–1b) show agreement for noun classes c1 and c2 and examples (1c–1d) show agreement for noun class and person. The vowel /e/ in *eti* (1a) and *beti* in (1b) is underlyingly /a/ before regressive assimilation. The rest of the examples in (1) illustrate agreement for c3 through c10. The presence of -*ka*- as in -*kati* will be addressed later.[1]

---

[1]Our glosses diverge slightly from Leipzig Glossing Conventions in that we follow Afranaph Project glossing (Afranaph Project Ongoing) and in particular subject agreement is treated as *subject marker* (SM) to avoid prejudging the agreement or pronominal status of subjects in Bantu languages and more generally (also OM for *object marker*). Noun class numbers are pre-

(1) a. ú-nó-dw-à   Néó è-tí   á-téng-é   lórì
          SM.c1-PRS-tell-fv Neo SM.c1-that SM.c1-buy-SBJV c9.car
          'He/she is telling Neo that she should buy a car/to buy a car.'

     b. íbò   b-á-dw-á   Nchídzì bè-tí   á-tèng-è   lórì
          PRN.c2 SM.c2-PST1-tell-fv Nchidzi SM.c2-that SM.c1-buy-SBJV c9.car
          'They (pl) told Nchidzi that he should buy a car/to buy a car.'

     c. nd-ó-dw-à   Néó ndì-tí   á-tèng-è   lórì
          SM.c1.1[st]-PRS-tell-fv Neo SM.c1.1[st]-that SM.c1-buy-SBJV c9.car
          'I am telling Neo to buy a car.'

     d. ìswì   t-à-dw-á   Nchídzì tì-tí   á-tèng-è
          PRN.c2.1[st] SM.c2.1[st]-PST1-tell-fv Nchidzi SM.c2.1[st]-that SM.c1-buy-SBJV
          lórì
          c9.car
          'We told Nchidzi that he should buy a car/to buy a car.'

     e. mpání   w-áká-dw-à   nsú   ú-kàtì   ú-ízèl-é
          mophane.c3 SM.c3-PST2-tell-fv acacia-c3 SM.c3-that SM.c3-sleep-SBJV
          'The mophane tree told the acacia tree to sleep.'

     f. mipání   y-áká-dw-à   nsú   í-kàtì   ú-ízèl-é
          mophane.c4 SM.c4-PST2-tell-fv acacia-c3 SM.c4-that SM.c3-sleep-SBJV
          'The mophane trees told the acacia tree to sleep.' (lit. The mophane
          trees told the acacia tree that it (the acacia tree) should sleep.)

Additional examples illustrating agreement for c5–c10 are to be found in Afranaph Project (Ongoing), see example IDs #15250–15255.

2.1 The Lubukusu pattern

Our expectations of what C-agreement with matrix subject phenomena look like have been largely set by Diercks' (2013) analysis of Lubukusu, and so we outline some key features of the Lubukusu pattern as a background comparison for our

---

ceded by "c" to facilitate Afranaph searches, as are other departures from Leipzig conventions. Person is marked with 1st and 2nd and noun class glosses determine plurality, as in SM.c1.1[st] which is first person singular where c2 would be plural. Third person is treated as default. Please see the list of abbreviations on page 184 for other glosses. Associative plural, *bo-* in Ikalanga, is informally glossed as "&". INF (infinitive) is used instead of c17 in Ikalanga, which it may be identical to. For Kinande, IV is *initial vowel*.

account of Ikalanga. Lubukusu has three sorts of complementizers that are typically used for indicative complement clauses: invariant *bali, mbo,* and AGR-*li,* the last of which agrees with the matrix subject.

A. The root -*li* of AGR-*li* is related either to a copula or a c5 agreement marker. Indicative clausal subjects show c5 agreement with matrix subject agreement markers (SMS).

B. A fairly wide class of verbs (at least 19), including verbs of speaking, desire, perception and epistemic verbs, take indicative or subjunctive complement clauses that can have AGR-*li.*

C. Lubukusu AGR-*li* agrees with the matrix subject of the verb selecting the complement clause, whether the matrix subject is an active agent or experiencer, or if it is the passivized object.

D. Direct objects of double complement verbs do not block C-agreement with the matrix subject and the agreement is not keyed to perspectives. Diercks (2013) shows C-agreement with the matrix subject, not the information source in prepositional object position, as in (2) (glossing from source).

(2) Khw-a-ulila khukhwama khu Sammy **khu-li**/*ali ba-limi
    1PLS-PST-hear from   LOC 1Sammy 1PL-that   2-farmers
    ba-a-funa   ka-ma-indi.
    2S-PST-harvest 6-6-maize

    'We heard from Sammy that the farmers harvested the maize.'

2.2 The role of the 'say' root in Ikalanga -*ti* based complementizers

One difference from Lubukusu is that the lexical root of the Ikalanga agreeing CCC is morphologically identical to the root of a verb meaning 'say'. When -*ti* is used as a matrix verb, no -*ti* complementizer is possible, be it *kuti, kuyi* or AGR-*ti.*

(3) a. nd-à-tí   Néó w-á-téng-à   lórì
       SM.c1.1st-PST1-say Neo SM.c1-PST1-buy-fv c9.car.

       'I said that Neo has bought a car.'

    b. ù-kà-tì   Nchídzì w-á-énd-à
       SM.c1.2nd-PRS-say Nchidzi SM.c1-PST1-go-fv

       'You say/are saying Nchidzi is gone/has left.'

c. à-kà-tì   Nchídzì w-á-énd-à
   SM.c1-PRS-say Nchidzi SM.c1-PST-go-fv
   'He says/is saying Nchidzi is gone/has left.'

d. Néó ú-nòò-tì   b-àná bá-zh-è.
   Neo SM.c1-FUT-say c2-child SM.c2-come-SBJV
   'Neo will say (that) the children should come.'

Since many languages have grammaticalized 'say' complementizers (see, e.g., Heine & Kuteva 2002), a natural hypothesis might be that AGR-*ti* not only looks like a verb, it is one, and that is why it is missing when the main verb means 'say'. There are a number of reasons that we do not analyze AGR-*ti* as a synchronic verb.

One is that the morphology borne by AGR-*ti* is impoverished by comparison with main verb -*ti*. For example, recent past (PST1) of main verb -*ti* (3a), the present (3b), and the future (3d), are never used on the 'AGR-*ti*' that introduces a complement clause (whenever the main verb is not -*ti*). The suppletive -*kà*- which is PRS for only the verb -*ti* in (3b) can occur on AGR-*ti*, but only in concordance with remote past.[2]

Additional evidence that AGR-*ti* is not acting as a verb comes from contexts where the verb -*ti* is embedded after AGR-*ti*. [based on Afranaph Project Ongoing: ID559]

(4) Edgar w-ákà-dw-à   Bill à-kà-tì   á-tí   Mary
     Edgar SM.c1-PST2-tell-fv Bill SM.c1-PST2-that SM.c1-say Mary
     ú-noò-n-dá
     SM.c1-PRS-OM.c1-love
     'Edgar told Bill to say that Mary loved him.'

If *àkàtì* were sufficient to embed the verb 'say', then we would not expect *átí* to follow it. In fact, there is another verb meaning 'say' or 'speak' in Ikalanga that requires AGR-*ti* as its complementizer. If AGR-*ti* were a main verb it would be redundant in (5).

(5) Néó w-ákà-leb-a   (à)-kà-ti   Nchidzi w-ákà-téng-á   lórì
     Neo SM.c1-PST2-say-fv SM.c1-PST2-that Nchidzi SM.c1-PST2-buy-fv car
     'Neo said it that Nchidzi had bought a car.'

---

[2]Remote past (PST2) might be morphologically composed of recent past (PST1) -*a*- and remote past (PST2) -*ka*- but we will represent it as undecomposed -*aka*-. This morphological analysis is not crucial in our discussion of C distributions.

Moreover, all matrix verbs that take subjunctive or indicative complements require that the CCC be either AGR-*ti, kuti,* or *kuyi,* an observation most naturally stated as (6) rather than a semantically inappropriate claim that every finite complement clause is introduced by the verb meaning 'say'.[3]

(6) In Ikalanga, C is obligatory for any non-infinitival complement clause, unless the main verb is -*ti*.

We conclude that -*ti*-based C in Ikalanga is not a verb, however closely it is historically related to the verb -*ti,* and -*ti*-based complementizers are fully distinguishable from the verb -*ti*. We return to the relationship between -*ti*-based C and the verb -*ti* in §3.4, however.

2.3 Sensitivity of AGR-*ti* to Tense

Ikalanga departs from what we know of the other C-agreement languages in that AGR-*ti* is sensitive to the tense of the matrix verb. However, as just remarked, AGR-*ti* morphology is often impoverished; Tense agreement on AGR-*ti* only matches the matrix verb for remote past -*aká-*. For any other matrix tense there is no tense affix on AGR-*ti*. Where -*ti* cannot bear PST2, the non-agreeing *kuti* is used.

(7) a. Maria w-ákà-dw-a   Nchídzì (á)-kà-tì   á-bík-è
       Maria SM.c1-PST2-tell-fv Nchidzi SM.c1-PST2-that SM.c1-cook-SBJV
       'Maria told Nchidzi that he should cook.'

   b. bo-Maria b-ákà-dw-à   Nchídzì bá-kà-tì
      &-Maria SM.c2-PST2-tell-fv Nchidzi SM.c2-PST2-that
      á-bík-è
      SM.c1-cook-SBJV
      'Maria and others told Nchidzi that he should cook.'

---

[3]There are some verbs that take a slightly different -*ti*-based 'as that' complementizer (similar to the one found in Kinande) which we do not discuss.

   (i) bo-Nchidzi ba-no-zwi-tham-a   se-u-nga-ti   ba-no-lil-a
       &-Nchidzi SM.c2-PRS-RFM-make-fv as-SM.c1-as-that SM.c2-PRS-cry-fv
       'Nchidzi and others are pretending to be crying.'
       Or: 'Nchidzi and others are pretending like they are crying.'

(8) a. Néó w-á-zwí-bùzw-à   (á)-kà-tì   à   Nchídzì
         Neo SM.c1-PST1-RFM-ask-fv SM.c1-PST2-that Q-part Nchidzi
         w-ákà-téng-á   lórì
         SM.c1-PST2-buy-fv car
         'Neo wondered whether Nchidzi had bought a car.'

    b. *Néó ú-nò-zwí-bùzw-à   (á)-kà-tì   à   Nchídzì
         Neo SM-c1-PRS-RFM-ask-fv SM.c1-PST2-that Q-part Nchidzi
         w-á-kà-téng-á lórì
         SM.c1-PST2-buy car
         'Neo wonders whether Nchidzi had bought a car.'

    c. Néó ú-nòò-zwí-bùzw-à   kuti à   Nchídzì w-ákà-téng-á
         Neo SM.c1-FUT-RFM-ask-fv that Q-part Nchidzi SM.c1-PST2-buy-fv
         lórì tshwá
         car new
         'Neo will wonder whether Nchidzi bought a new car.'

Thus in addition to the phi-features of the matrix subject, the shape of AGR-*ti* is also sensitive to tense.

2.4 Sensitivity to Voice

When a verb taking a clausal complement is passivized, the form of the CCC is typically *kuyi*, which does not permit any subject or tense agreement (9b is after ID654 in Afranaph), but some speakers (probably older ones) also accept agreeing AGR-*yi* (which we have verified allows agreement for all persons and noun classes, not illustrated here).

(9) a. (ìmì) nd-àká-dw-à   Nchídzì ndí-kà-tì   á-téng-é
         I   SM.c1.1[st]-PST2-tell-fv Nchidzi SM.c1.1[st]-PST2-that SM.c1-buy-SBJV
         lórì.
         car
         'I told Nchidzi that he should buy a car.'

    b. (ìmì) nd-àká-dw-íw-à   kù-yí   Mary
         I   SM.c1.1[st]-PST2-tell-PASS-fv SM.c1.1[st]-that Mary
         à-á-tó-ndí-d-á
         NEG-SM.c1-PST1-OM.c1.1[st]-like-fv
         'I was told that Mary did not like me.'

c. ìmì nd-àká-dw-íw-à   ndì-yí   Mary
I   SM.c1.1[st]-PST2-tell-PASS-fv SM.c1.1[st]-that Mary
à-á-tó-ndí-d-á
NEG-SM.c1-PST1-OM.c1.1[st]-like-fv
'I was told that Mary did not like me.'

Even verbs like *-budz-* that allow both *kuti* and AGR-*ti* in the active favor the
-yi form when the immediately superordinate verb is passivized, though *kuti* is
always possible, as in (10a). Verbs that do not allow AGR-*ti* like *-dum-* also can
take *kuyi* (but not AGR-*yi*) when they are passivized – compare (10c, 10d).

(10)   a. Néó ú-nò-èmùl-à   kù-búdz-íw-á   kùyí/kùtí á-tèng-é   lórì
         Neo SM.c1-PRS-wish-fv INF-tell-PASS-fv that   SM.c1-buy-SBJV car
         'Neo wishes to be told to buy a car.'

     b. Néó ú-nò-èmùl-à   kù-búdz-íw-á   è-yí   á-tèng-é   lórì
         Neo SM.c1-PRS-wish-fv INF-tell-PASS-fv SM.c1-that SM.c1-buy-SBJV car
         'Neo wishes to be told to buy a car.'

     c. Néó ú-nò-dùm-à   kùyí/kùtì Nchídzì w-ákà-bál-á
         Neo SM.c1-PRS-believe-fv that   Nchidzi SM.c1-PST2-read-fv
         búkà
         book.c9
         'Neo believes that Nchidzi read a book.'

     d. ku-ó-dùm-ìw-à   kùyí/kùtì Nchídzì w-ákà-bál-á
         SM.c17-PRS-believe-PASS-fv that   Nchidzi SM.c1-PST2-read-fv
         búkà
         book.c9
         'It is believed that Nchidzi read a book.'[4]

A number of points emerge in this data. First, both *kuti* and *kuyi* Cs are possible for passivized verbs and for some speakers AGR-*yi* is also possible. However,
AGR-*yi* is not normally possible when the matrix verb is not passivized. Also, notice that the forms like (10b) suggest that agreement for voice and agreement with
the 'subject' are both distinct from tense agreement. (10b) shows c1 agreement
on AGR-*yi* even though the infinitive has no subject agreement – it is marked
only with the invariant c17 marker for infinitives. Thus the C must be agreeing

---

[4]The SM.c17 appears to be *ku-* where /u/ becomes a glide before /a/ and deletes before /o/. Nothing turns on this.

with the PRO subject of the 'to be told' infinitive, determined to be c1 because it is controlled by *Neo*. This fact generalizes to AGR-*ti*, which also can agree for noun class with a controlled infinitival subject.

(11) Néó wá-kà-bé-è-shák-à   kù-dw-á   bàìsáná è-tí
      Neo SM.c1-PST2-AUX-SM.c1-want-fv INF-tell-fv c2.boys SM.c1-that
      bá-tèng-é   lórì
      SM.c2-buy-SBJV car
      'Neo wanted to tell the boys that they should buy a car.'

Subject clauses always take *kuti*. When an active verb like -*sup*-, 'prove', that takes only *kuti* in its complement clause is passivized, it can take either *kuti* or *kuyi* in its postverbal clausal complement. However, when the passivized clause is in sentential subject position (as marked by subject agreement on the verb), the C must be *kuti*, as in (12c), and it cannot be *kuyi*.

(12) a. nsèkísì   w-ákà-súp-à   kùtì Nchídzì w-ákà-kwíb-á
          prosecutor.1 SM.c1-PST2-prove-fv that Nchidzi SM.c1-PST2-steal-fv
          márí
          c6.money
          'The prosecutor proved that Nchidzi stole the money.'
      b. ku-ákà-súp-íw-à   kùtì/kùyí Nchídzì w-ákà-kwíb-á
          c17-PST2-prove-PASS-fv that   Nchidzi SM.c1-PST2-steal-fv
          márí
          c6.money
          'It was proved that Nchidzi stole money.'
      c. kùtì Nchídzì w-ákà-kwíb-á   márí   kw-ákà-súp-íw-à   né
          That Nchidzi SM.c1-PST2-steal-fv c6.money c17-PST2-prove-PASS-fv by
          nsèkísì
          prosecutor
          'That Nchidzi stole the money was proved by the prosecutor.'

This shows that the distribution of *kuyi* and AGR-*ti* is sensitive to voice. It suggests that *kuti* is necessary in subject position because passive does not c-command it. Notice further, that -*sup*- is a verb that does not take AGR-*ti*. Thus, even verbs that only co-occur with *kuti* in their active form also license *kuyi*. This shows that the *kuti/kuyi* alternation is independent of the *kuti*/AGR-*ti* alternation. The agreement and distributions of -*ti* and -*yi* are summarized in Tables 1 and 2, respectively.

Table 1: Summary of the C-agreement morphemes

Agreement features	*-ti*	*-yi*
Subject Agr	✓	✓
Tense Agr	✓	✓

Table 2: Complementizer distribution of *-ti* in comparison with *-yi*

Distribution		*-ti*	*-yi*
Voice:	Active	✓	✗
	Passive	✓	✓
Mood:	Subjunctive	✓	✓
	Interrogative	✓	✗
Introducing clausal complement		✓	✗

2.4.1 Suppletion of *-ti*

What makes it clear that there is an agreement relation between passive voice and *kuyi* or AGR-*yi*, however is the *-yi* shape itself. When main verb *-ti* is passivized, the root is suppletive, taking the form *-yi*, as illustrated in (13b), and unlike the AGR-*yi* C, it can be inflected for tense.

(13) a. ku-ákà-yì   Nchídzì à-á-pò
          SM.c17-PST2-say.PASS Nchidzi Neg-SM.c1-there

          'It was said that Nchidzi was not there.'

     b. kó-ò-yì   Nchídzì á-tèng-è   lórì tshwá
          SM.c17-FUT-say.PASS Nchidzi SM.c1-buy-SBJV car new

          'It will be said that Nchdizi should buy a new car.'

Thus it seems that AGR-*yi* could be a form of suppletion parallel to the *-ti/-yi* alternation of the main verb *-ti*. It is plausible to see this as a form of morphological concord or agreement, especially since phi-agreement on AGR-*yi* is also possible when it is a complementizer (as in 14). Moreover, AGR-*yi*, just like AGR-*ti*, also permits tense agreement for PST2.

(14) Néó w-ákà-dw-iw–á   á-ká-yì   á-tèng-é   lórì
      Neo SM.c1-PST2-tell-PASS-fv SM.c1-PST2-that SM.c1-buy-SBJV car
      'Neo was told to buy a car/Neo was told that she should buy a car.'

It appears that verbs that most favor AGR-*ti* are those that permit AGR-*yi*, but we have not checked every case.

2.4.2 *Kuyi* without passive concord

Kuyi can be used for emotive complement clauses in the absence of passive morphology, but in these cases, it appears to simply be an infinitival passive complement of the matrix verb. Thus no complementizer preceding infinitival *kuyi* is expected. *Kuyi* is functioning as a main verb, and as such, it is the one verb that does not introduce a C before its complement clause. Consistent with the infinitival passive analysis, AGR-*yi* is not possible for any of (15a–15d) as illustrated by (15e).

(15) a. Néó ú-nòò-chénám-à   kù-yí   á-tèng-é   lórì
          Neo SM.c1-FUT-surprised-fv INF-say.PASS SM.c1-buy-SBJV car
          'Neo will be surprised to be told that she should buy a car.'

      b. Néó ú-nòò-gwádzík-à kù-yí   á-tèng-é   lórì
          Neo SM.c1-FUT-hurt-fv INF-say.PASS SM.c1-buy-SBJV car
          'Neo will be hurt to be told that she should buy a car.'

      c. Néó ú-nòò-sháth-á   kù-yí   á-tèng-é   lórì
          Neo SM.c1-FUT-happy-fv INF-say.PASS SM.c1-buy-SBJV car
          'Neo will be happy to be told that she should buy a car.'

      d. Néó ú-nòò-d-á   kù-yí   á-tèng-é   lórì
          Neo SM.c1-FUT-happy-fv INF-say.PASS SM.c1-buy-SBJV car
          'Neo will be happy to be told that she should buy a car.'

      e. *Néó ú-nòò-chénám-à   è-yí   á-tèng-é   lórì
          Neo SM.c1-FUT-surprise-fv SM.c1-say.PASS SM.c1-buy-SBJV car
          'Neo will be surprised to be told that she should buy a car.'

Other cases that may be instances where *kuyi* acts like a passivized infinitival complement may include instances where it functions as an evidential.

(16) Néó w-ákà-wh-á   kùtì/kùyí Nchídzì w-ákà-téng-á   lórì tshwá
      Neo SM.c1-PST2-hear-fv that   Nchidzi SM.c1-PST2-buy-fv car new
      'Neo heard that Nchidzi had bought a new car.'

In these contexts, it appears that the truth of the proposition introduced by *kuyi* may have some sort of evidential import. Verbs like *wh-* 'hear' can also take *kuti*, as in (16), but when *kuyi* is used, the source of the information is evaluated differently. While (16) with *kuti* does not indicate how the information came to the matrix subject hearer (someone could have made this claim directly to the matrix subject), with *kuyi* it indicates that that the matrix subject heard that it was said that Nchidzi had bought a car. This indicates further distance between the matrix subject and the evidence.[5]

At present, it is not clear that the infinitival passive complement analysis is appropriate for (17a–17b), that is, whether the agreement is about what is said or about what is believed. These examples require further study.

(17) a. Néó w-ákà-dúm-à   kùyí Nchídzì w-ákà-téng-á   lórì tshwá
      Neo SM.c1-PST2-agree-fv that Nchidzi SM.c1-PST2-buy-fv car new
      'Neo agreed that Nchidzi had bought a new car.'

     b. ìngwì m-ó-lándùl-à   kùyí Nchídzì w-ákà-téng-á   lórì tshwá
      You.pl SM.c2-PRS-refute-fv that Nchidzi SM.c1-PST2-buy-fv car new
      'You (PL) refute that Nchidzi has bought a new car.'

Apart from instances where *kuyi* is a passivized infinitive (and cases like 17a–17b), however, the concord approach to the appearance of *kuyi* in place of AGR-*ti* still seems like the best generalization, especially given the sentential subject facts. The generalization in (18) seems to capture the central pattern.

(18) The -*ti*-based complementizers are allomorphs.

In addition to the fact that all of these -*ti*/-*yi*-based forms are almost in complementary distribution (if the optionality of (10a), (10d) and (12b) arise from competing analyses), they also all occur in the same high clausal position, above the question particle that can introduce a matrix yes-no question as well as an indirect yes-no question. The verb -*buzw*- can take either AGR-*ti* (as in 8a) or invariant *kuti*. The presence of the Q-particle, also used in matrix questions, is obligatory.

---

[5]Moreover, it is possible for a source phrase to be licensed for (16), though it is not clear whether it is *kuyi* or 'hear' itself that makes the source phrase possible, since *kuti* is also possible here.

    (i)   Néó w-ákà-wh-á   kùyí Nchídzì w-ákà–téng-á   lórì ndí John
        Neo SM.c1-PST2-hear-fv that Nchidzi SM.c1-PST2-buy-fv car by John
        'Neo heard from John that Nchidzi had bought a car.'

(19) a. Néó w-ákà-zwí-bùzw-à   (à)-kà-tì   à   Nchídzì
       Neo SM.c1-PST2-RFM-ask-fv SM.c1-PST2-that Q-part Nchidzi
       w-ákà-téng-á   lórì tshwa
       SM.c1-PST2-buy-fv car new

       'Neo wondered whether Nchidzi had bought a new car.'

    b. Néó w-ákà-zwí-bùzw-à   kùtì à   Nchídzì w-ákà-téng-á
       Neo SM.c1-PST2-RFM-ask-fv that Q-part Nchidzi SM.c1-PST2-buy-fv
       lórì tshwá
       car new

       'Neo wondered whether Nchidzi had bought a new car.'

    c. *Néó w-ákà-zwí-bùzw-à   kùtì Nchídzì w-ákà-téng-á   lórì tshwá
       Neo SM.c1-PST2-RFM-ask-fv that Nchidzi c1-PST2-buy-fv car new

       'Neo wondered whether Nchidzi had bought a car.'

    d. Néó w-ákà-búzw-ìw-á   kùyí à   Nchídzì w-ákà-téng-á
       Neo SM.c1-PST2-ask-PASS-fv that Q-part Nchidzi SM.c1-PST2-buy-fv
       lórì
       car

       'Neo was asked whether Nchidzi had bought a car.'

2.5 More on the morphology of AGR-*ti*

There are some deformations in the shape of AGR-*ti* that do not simply result from morphologically composing the SM, the (remote past) tense, and -*ti*. Although we alert the reader to them here, they do not change the basic generalization, namely, that the possible forms of AGR-*ti* (and AGR-*yi*) are entirely predictable from the SM and tense of the matrix verb.

We have shown that remote past -*(a)ká*- shows up on AGR-*ti* when it also appears on the matrix verb. However, if the matrix verb is negated then the shape of matrix remote past tense is affected, surfacing as *zo*- instead of -*ká*. In this case, *ká*- can still appear on AGR-*ti*, as in (20a).

(20) a. Néó à-á-zò-dw-à   Nchídzì á-kà-tì
       Neo NEG-SM.c1-NEG.PST-tell-fv Nchidzi SM.c1-PST2-that
       á-tèng-è   lórì
       SM.c1-buy-SBJV car

       'Neo did not tell Nchidzi that he should buy a car.'

b. Néó à-á-zò-dw-à   Nchídzì è-tí   á-tèng-è   lórì

Neo NEG-SM.c1-NEG.PST-tell-fv Nchidzi SM.c1-that SM.c1-buy-SBJV car

'Neo did not tell Nchidzi that he should buy a car.'

c. (ìwè) à-ú-zò-dw-à   Nchídzì ú-tí

You NEG-SM.c1.2nd-NEG.PST-tell-fv Nchidzi SM.c1.2nd-that

á-tèng-è   lórì

SM.c1-buy-SBJV car

'You did not tell Nchidzi that he should buy a car.'

In (20b) where *ka-* optionally does not appear, SM *a-* will regressively assimilate raising to front *e-* (we do not know why the /*a*/ of *ka-* does not undergo regressive assimilation before the /*i*/ of *kati*). The high *u-* of SM.c1.2nd would not be affected, as in (20c).

The paradigm for the SM followed by the complementizer *-ti* is presented in Table 3 (the tone of *-ti* is influenced by its context).[6]

Table 3: SM paradigm

SM.c1.3rd	SM.c1.1st	SM.c1.2nd	SM.c2.3rd	SM.c2.1st	SM.c2.2nd
ú/wá/á	ndì	ù	bá	tì	mù

It is not clear whether or not SM.c1, which is 3rd if unmarked, is *wá-* when it precedes PST configuration or if it is just /*ú*/ fused with the PST1 *-a-* that follows it (as suggested in Letsholo 2002), raising the tone on /*a*/. For subjunctive, interrogative and negated sentences, c1 C-agreement appears to have the form *a-*.

The paradigm for SM-*ti* combinations when there is no PST2 matching with the AGR-*ti* is as in Table 4. When the matrix has SM.c2, the /*a*/ of *ba-* regressively assimilates to /*e*/ before the /*i*/ of *-ti*, as does SM.c1 when it is *a-*.

If *ká* occurs on AGR-*ti* matching matrix PST2, the outputs in Table 5 are possible (note that the SM we are treating as *a-* is the only one that is optional before *-ka*).

Where *ka* cannot appear, the corresponding forms in Table 2 are possible. We assume that *hàtì* is a suppletive option.

We stress, however, that the morphological details of the forms of AGR-*ti* do not obscure the main point that interests us in this essay, namely, that the possi-

---

[6]See also Chebanne (2010: 73). For more complete accounts of subject agreement and their relations to tense, see Mathangwane (1999) and Letsholo (2002).

Table 4: SM-*ti* paradigm without PST2

SM.c1-*ti*	SM.c1.1st-*ti*	SM.c1.2nd-*ti*	SM.c2-*ti*	SM.c2.1st-*ti*	SM.c2.2nd-*ti*
ú/è-tí	ndì-tí	ù-tí	bè-tí	tì-tí	mù-tí

Table 5: SM-PST2-*ti* paradigm

SM.c1.3rd -PST2-*ti*	SM.c1.1st -PST2-*ti*	SM.c1.2nd -PST2-*ti*	SM.c2.3rd -PST2-*ti*	SM.c2.1st -PST2-*ti*	SM.c2.2nd -PST2-*ti*
(á)-kà-tì	hàtì/ndì-kà-tì	ù-kà-tì	bá-kà-tì	tí-kà-tì	mú-kà-tì

ble forms of AGR-*ti* are entirely determined by its relation to matrix tense, phi-features and voice.[7]

---

[7]There are one or two deviations from the facts as described that we do not understand, such as the following example, where *ka* appears in AGR-*ti* when we do not expect it to.

> (i) (ìwè) ù-nó-léb-á   ù-kà-tì   Nchídzì w-ákà-téng-á   lórì
>   you SM.c1.2nd-PRS-say-fv SM.c1.2nd-PRS-that Nchidzi SM.c1-PST2-buy-fv car
>   'You are saying that Nchidzi bought a car.'

It is possible that this is an instance where the suppletive *kàtì* form for main verb PRS-*ti* is echoed on AGR-*ti*, in which case we also see tense concord for PRS, at least in these cases. We have no more to say about such examples, though they deserve more research. It has been suggested to us that -*ka*- could be understood as a consecutive marker of some kind, both in its position on the verb stem and its position on the CCC. It is also the case in Ikalanga that *ka* can be a consecutive marker as in other Bantu languages, as illustrated in the examples below (tones omitted):

> (ii) Neo w-aka-tem-a   miti,   ka   kubunganya maswazwi, ka   a-pisa
>   Neo SM.c1-PST2-cut-fv c4.tree CONS gather   c6.branches CONS OM.c6-burn
>   'Neo cut the trees, gathered together the branches and burned them.'

> (iii) Ingwi   m-aka-tem-a   miti,   mu-ka   kubunganya maswazwi,
>   PRNC2.2nd SM.c2.2nd-PST2-cut-fv c4.tree SM.c2-CONS gather   c6.branches
>   mu-ka-a-pis-a
>   SM.c2.2nd-CONS-OM.c6-burn-fv
>   'The men cut the trees, gathered together the branches and burned them.'

We are not sure if the events in (i) can be said to be consecutive in nature in the way that examples (ii) and (iii) are. We do not see a way to relate these observations to *ka* on C.

2.6 The paucity of AGR-*ti*-taking verbs vs. invariant *kuti*

It would seem that selection for AGR-*ti* is a largely lexical affair limited to only a few verbs, including the roots -*buzw*- 'ask', and -*leb*- 'speak, say', -*budz*- 'tell' (21c) and -*dw*- 'tell' (an instruction), which have all been exemplified, in addition to -*dum*- 'concede/agree/believe', -*landul*- 'disagree', and -*alakan*- 'think' (not illustrated here). By comparison, recall that Diercks cites at least 19 Lubukusu verbs which permit AGR-*li*.

(21)   a.   Néó w-ákà-dúm-à   (à)-kà-tì   Nchídzì
              Neo SM.c1-PST2-agree/concede-fv SM.c1-PST2-that Nchidzi
              w-ákà-téng-á   lórì
              SM.c1-PST2-buy-fv car

              'Neo conceded that Nchidzi had bought a car.'

       b.   Néó w-ákà-lándúl-à   (à)-kà-tì   Nchídzì
              Neo SM.c1-PST2-disagree-fv SM.c1-PST2-that Nchidzi
              à-á-zò-téng-á   lórì
              NEG-SM.c1-PRS-buy-fv car

              'Neo disagreed (saying?) that Nchidzi has not bought a new car.'

       c.   nd-àká-kú-búdz-à   ndì-tí   ú-tèng-è   lórì
              SM.c1.1[st]-PST2-OM.c1.2[nd]-tell-fv SM.c1.1[st]-that SM.c1.2[nd]-buy-SBJV car

              'I told you to buy a car.'

Consultants differ as to whether or not -*dw*- can also take *kuti* complements, but they agree that -*leb*-, -*budz*-, and -*buzw*- can (see 19a–19b for *buzw*-).

(22)   a.   Néó w-ákà-léb-á   kùtì Nchídzì w-ákà-téng-á   lórì tshwá
              Neo SM.c1-PST2-tell-fv that Nchidzi SM.c1-PST2-buy-fv car new

              'Neo said that Nchidzi bought a car.'

       b.   (ìmì) nd-àká-kú-búdz-à   kùti/hà-tì
              I   SM.c1.1[st]-PST2-OM.c1.2[nd]-tell-fv that/SM.c1.1[st]-that
              ú-tèng-è   lórì
              SM.c1.2[nd]-buy-SBJV car

              'I told you to buy a car.'

However, as we saw in the case of (12a–12b), whatever determines the distribution of *kuyi* concord applies more generally than whatever determines which verbs allow AGR-*ti*.

So far, we have no indication that there is a successful generalization about verbs that take *kuti*, other than that *kuti* may be a default for verbs that take indicative or subjunctive complements when AGR-*ti* is not available. In some cases it is still available even when AGR-*ti* is a possible choice. Evidence that *kuti* is, at least in some contexts, a default form, is that it is always used for sentential subjects, where the clause determines SM.c17, even for a verb like -*dum*- that we know to be an AGR-*ti*-taking verb (in contrast to -*sup*- in 12b).

(23) kùtì bàthù   bà-njínjí   à-bá-tó-thòph-à
      that c2.people c2.Agr-many NEG-SM.c2-NEG.PRS-vote-fv
      kw-áká-dúmí-gw-àn-à
      SM.c17-PST2-agree-PASS-RCM-fv
      'That many people don't vote was agreed on.'

As noted earlier, this suggests that in clausal subject position, *kuti* is in a position where there is no c-commanding tense, voice, or subject to agree with.

2.7 The status of the allomorphy hypothesis

We suggested in (18) that all -*ti*-based Cs are allomorphs of each other, and at this point, there is reason to believe that the distribution of AGR-*ti*, AGR-*yi*, and *kuti* is predictable from the voice, tense and subject phi-features of the matrix verb, once we determine which predicates permit AGR-*ti*. We have treated *kuyi* as potentially in concord with passivized verbs in some contexts, but in others where it appears to be evidential, we treat it as the infinitival passive form of AGR-*ti*.

3 Theoretical questions about locality

If syntactic relations like agreement are always phase-internal, a central tenet in minimalist theorizing, then we must determine whether all the agreement relations we posit are phase-local. In typical phase-based accounts, C and v or Voice are the phase heads. There is discussion in the literature (Kratzer 1996; Harley 2013; Legate 2012; Safir & Bassene 2017) concerning whether the phase edge is the functional head v, which determines that a root is verbal or a higher Voice head (which takes vP as a complement). Following Kratzer and others, we assume that Voice selects vP and can introduce the external argument (EA). Alternatively, it might be assumed that the EA is introduced in Spec vP and can raise to Spec

VoiceP (in parentheses in 24), thus inhabiting the phase edge.[8] Thus the maximal span of locality extends from the edge of the VoiceP downward to the edge of the CP (C, Spec CP, and adjunctions to CP, if these are different from Spec CP) The Voice phase does not include the higher (bolded) T or anything above it, nor anything below AGR-*ti* (C) such as the lower (bolded) TP.

(24)   [T [$_{VoiceP}$ (EA) [$_{Voice}$ Voice [$_{vP}$ EA v ...[$_{CP}$ ...AGR-*ti* [$_{TP}$ ...]]]]]]

In §3.1 we examine the phase-internal relations between the EA and Voice with respect to AGR-*ti* and in §3.2–3.3 we suggest an analysis based on Voice agreement that could instantiate the allomorphy analysis proposed in (18).

Notice now that matrix T and AGR-*ti* do not share a phase in (24). Thus we would not ordinarily expect any agreement relation to hold between those two heads, unless AGR-*ti* or a phrase below Voice that contains AGR-*ti* somehow escapes to the edge of VoiceP. We consider "escape" strategies in sections §§3.3–3.5.

3.1 Agreement internal to the VoiceP

On the view that a passivized object passes through Spec VoiceP (and perhaps through Spec vP, where v selected by passive Voice does not assign an EA), we may expect that agreeing C in some languages would be sensitive to whatever inhabits the argument position that is most local to the Voice head. In Lubukusu (25) (from Diercks 2013: 368, glosses ours), the verb agrees with the passivized subject.

(25)   a.   (Ese) n-a-bol-el-a   Nelsoni   **n-di**   ba-keni
              I   SM.c1.1st-PST1-say-APPL-fv c1.Nelson SM.c1.1st-that c2-guests
              ba-a-ch-a
              SM.c2-PST1-go-fv

              'I told Nelson that the guests left.'

        b.   Sammy   ka-bol-el-w-a   **a-li**   ba-keni b-ol-a
              c1.Sammy SM.c1-say-APPL-PASS-fv c1-that 2-guests SM.c2-arrive-fv

              'Sammy was told that the guests arrived.'

---

[8]It is possible that VoiceP is always the phase edge, but only occasionally introduces the EA. We will assume that only some light verbs are banned from introducing their EA in Spec V, such as CAUS, while most other verbs assign their EA in Spec vP. Arguments against assigning EA to Spec vP in Pylkkänen (2008) are primarily based on evidence about CAUS. Any argument exiting VoiceP will have to pass through its edge, however. See also Safir & Bassene (2017) for discussion of the left periphery of the verbal domain.

That such a relationship between Spec VoiceP is possible in both active and passive is what would be expected, but this is not what we find in Kinande, nor is it what we always find in Ikalanga. In Kinande, another C-agreement language, agreeing C (agreeing with matrix subject only) in the active reverts to default non-agreeing form in the passive, which suggests that it is primarily sensitive to passive voice, not agreement with a DP. Thanks to Prof. Philip Ngessimo Mutaka for these Kinande examples.

(26) a. Yoháni mwásirisyákumbusy' abakolhw' ati bálwé b'erisom' echapítre 2

      Yohani mo-a-sirisya-buki-a   a-ba-kolho   a-ti   ba-lue

      John   mo-SM.c1-FUT-remind-fv IV-c2-student SM.c1-COMP SM.c2-AUX

      ba   e-ri-som-a   e-chapitre 2

      c2.LK IV-INF-read-fv IV-chapter 2

      'John reminded the students that they should read chapter 2.'

    b. abakolhó móbásirisyabukibw' ambu bálwé b'erisom echapítre 2

      a-ba-kolho   mo-ba-sirisya-buk-i-bu-a   ambu

      IV-c2-student mo-SM.c2-FUT-remember-CAUS-PASS-fv COMP

      ba-lue   ba   e-ri-som-a   e-chapitre 2

      SM.c2-AUX c2.LK IV-INF-read-fv IV-chapter 2

      'The students were reminded that they should read chapter 2.'

However, the shift to *ambu* has a semantic consequence, namely, it removes the speaker's responsibility for the following proposition, and which echoes a similar distinction related to non-agreeing voice in Ikalanga perception complements. Nonetheless, the shift from the agreeing C to the non-agreeing C suggests that it is passive Voice in Kinande that fails to facilitate C-agreement with the matrix subject.

3.2 What we know so far

The strongest theory of the distribution of *kuti*, *kuyi*, AGR-*ti* and AGR-*yi* is that they are allomorphs (apart from the infinitival passive *kuyi*), as this imposes certain analytic requirements that stipulated distributions do not. By definition, the form of the C should be predicted by its syntactic and/or morphological context, so it is a rule that determines the allomorph. After all, the AGR-*yi*/AGR-*ti* alternation is not a predicate specific relation even if the availability of AGR-*ti* is predicate specific and must be stipulated somehow. These, then, are the alternations predicted.

(27) The allomorphy theory as driven by Voice

    a. AGR-ti alternates with AGR-*yi* when the superordinate verb is active or passive, respectively.

    b. Kuti is almost always available as a default where the superordinate verb is active or passive.

    c. Kuyi is possible when the superordinate verb is passive

We have distinguished two kinds of verbs that take finite CP complements in terms of the C alternation that they permit. There is a small class of verbs that select AGR-*ti* and those verbs participate in the AGR-*ti*/AGR-*yi* alternation. Just about all verbs can take kuti complements. Passivized, these verbs allow for a *kuyi* C when the CP is postverbal. Some verbs take *kuyi* complements that are understood as impersonal infinitival passives, but *kuyi* is acting as a verb in these cases.

We have also established certain relations that have to be captured in any analysis of the Iklalanga phenomena.

(28)   a. C-Agreement for voice is independent of agreement for tense (see 10b).

    b. C-Agreement for phi-features with active or passive voice is independent of tense (see 10b and 11).

    c. C-Agreement for phi-features is independent of matrix agreement on T (as in 10b and 11).

    d. C-Agreement for tense is only possible if there is agreement for phi-features.

In what follows, we argue that (28a–28c) are captured by tying C-agreement relations to Voice, and we postpone discussion of (28d), which is licensed by a different locality relation, until §3.5.

3.3 Modeling Voice agreement with C

Up to this point, we have been making the case that the relation between Voice and -*ti* complementizers is one of agreement in a descriptive sense, that is, the -*ti*/*yi* alternation covaries with passive marking on the verb. Although Diercks (2010: 353–370) discusses and rejects modeling Lubukusu C-agreement as agreement with Voice, we believe modeling C-agreement as a Voice-C relation is the best account of Ikalanga and perhaps correct for Lubukusu as well. As Diercks points out, a Voice-C relation suggests why direct objects or other intervening nominals do not shift agreement to non-subjects, since Voice only agrees with the nominal closest to it, namely, the EA or a passivized nominal that passes through Spec-VoiceP (or Spec-vP). Diercks rejects the Voice-C model, however, because he assumes that the causative affix (CAUS) takes VoiceP complements, and if so, the affected subject, rather than the subject of CAUS, should control agreement. Under different assumptions about the position of the EA, Voice-C relation may actually produce the right result. If most predicates assign EAs to Spec vP, but only certain light verbs like CAUS (a species of v) assign their EA in Spec VoiceP (see fn. 8), then CAUS can take a vP complement that has an EA, but would not embed a Voice projection below it. The structure is illustrated in (29).

(29) $[_{\text{VoiceP}}$ EA $[$ Voice $[_{\text{vP}}$ $[_{\text{v}}$ CAUS $[_{\text{vP}}$ EA $[_{\text{v}}$ V... $[_{\text{CP}}$ $[$ C... $]]$ $]]$ $]]$ $]]$

If this approach is viable, then only the causer argument can antecede Voice, so only the causer argument can control C-agreement. This is the right prediction for Lubukusu, but in Ikalanga (30) the introduction of a causative affix blocks C-agreement altogether, perhaps as a form of defective intervention that neither the movement theory nor our agreement theory fully predicts.

(30) ba-isana b-aka-buzw-is-a   Neo mme-abe   kuti kene
      c2-boys SM.c2-PST2-ask-CAUS-fv Neo mother-hers that whether
      b-aka-teng-a   ma-bisi.
      SM.c2a-PST2-buy-fv c6-melons
      'The boys made Neo ask her mother whether they had bought
      watermelons.'

Thus treating the Voice-C relation as the core of C-agreement has advantages,[9] especially in Ikalanga, where we have morphological evidence that the voice of C covaries with the voice of the immediately superordinate verb.

At this point, more technical issues arise as to how "agreement" is to be modeled within a theoretical approach. In minimalist theories, such as Chomsky (2001), agreeing heads with unvalued features are "probes" which search for "goals" (typically nominals) in order to value their (probing) features. This probing operation is called "Agree". Theorists divide over whether all Agree is

---

[9]Diercks (2010: 367–369) rejects the Voice-C relation as a model for C-agreement in Lubukusu in favor of a control analysis, in part because of examples where C-agreement holds for clausal complements to direct object nouns. These cases, also found in Ikalanga, are indeed puzzling, but they are so for all accounts, including the proposal of Diercks et al. (2017), discussed in §3.5.

downward-looking, upward looking, or both.[10] They also disagree about whether or not Agree is the operation that ensures that anaphors agree with their antecedents. Following Rooryck & van den Wyngaerd (2011), Diercks et al. (2017) assume that anaphoric features of AGR-*ti* raise to adjoin to the vP (or VoiceP) phase head where they can probe down to get the features of the EA. Then these agreement features are morphologically realized only in the C position, not the higher vP adjoined position. The inheritance of morphologically realized features downward to a copy does not follow from Agree or copy theory, however. The only overt evidence they offer for C-movement to vP is the behavior of 'say' verbs in languages like Ikalanga that don't allow C to follow them. Although we adopt a version of their analysis for the Lubukusu 'say' verb below, the motivation we provide does not justify generalized C-to-vP (or VoiceP) adjunction.

We agree with Diercks et al. that Voice and C are in an antecedent-anaphor relation, but we do not treat the antecedent-anaphor relation as an Agree relation. Rather it is a morphological relation that results from anaphoric elements that find their antecedent features within the same phase, as proposed in Safir (2014). The relation between Voice and the EA may also be seen as anaphoric. Thus Voice gets phi-features from the EA or whatever passes through its Spec VoiceP, and then an anaphoric voice feature on C is anteceded by Voice along with its agreement features that were anaphorically valued by Spec VoiceP. On this model, phi-agreement on AGR-*ti* and AGR-*yi* only proceeds by virtue of agreement with Voice. When Voice is active, the agreeing C is AGR-*ti* and when Voice is passive, we get AGR-*yi*. Since we could not find a semantic generalization that characterizes the small class of verbs that license agreeing C, selection for agreeing C must be treated as a lexical matter. There are various ways to stipulate this, but how that is done need not require anything special, so we do not address it here.

Our account predicts that agreement on Voice is independent of agreement introduced by finite T. As (11) illustrates, this is the correct prediction, since AGR-*ti* agrees with the subject of an infinitive (presumably PRO) in the absence of finite agreement introduced by T.

---

[10]As Diercks et al. (2017) point out, the "delayed valuation" of Carstens (2016), which allows a probe to search "up" if there is no agreement goal locally c-commanded by the probe, appears to predict that nominals intervening between C and the superordinate subject should result in agreement with non-subjects. Carstens argues that the intervention does not occur due to independent factors, but those factors deserve further scrutiny. Both Diercks et al. and the proposal made here do not require additional mechanisms to make the right prediction with respect to this intervention.

There are few verbs, if any, that take finite complements and are completely incompatible with *kuti*. We propose that the *kuti/kuyi* alternation arises when the anaphoric feature on *-ti* has no phi-feature, so the anaphoric feature on *-ti* is only sensitive to passive/active. The absence of an anaphoric feature on *-ti* also yields *kuti*, as in cases where there is a finite sentential subject. The C of the CP subject is not anteceded by Voice and so cannot successfully agree.

Voice sensitivity ascribed to AGR-C may provide insight into what is going on in Kinande and Lubukusu. In Lubukusu, C-agreement with the subject is also possible with matrix active verb subjects as well as passivized subjects. As in Diercks's (2010) hypothetical account of Voice agreement, we assume that phi-agreement is parasitic on Voice in Lubukusu, but unlike Ikalanga, voice has no morphological exponent on C. Kinande, like Lubukusu, has no C-morphology for voice. In Kinande, however, when the matrix verb is passivized, C-agreement is blocked. This would follow if passive Voice in Kinande is not anaphoric for phi-features, thus has none to transmit.[11]

3.4 Raising of *-ti* to v

Diercks et al. (2017) suggest that the reason 'say' verbs in some languages resist taking any complementizer is that the 'say' C in those languages raises into the matrix clause. In their account, it is raising to an adjoined position on vP or VoiceP and it is independent of whether or not there is a lexical matrix verb. By contrast, we propose to limit the raising of 'say' C by permitting it only when it fills an empty v position in the matrix clause. Both our account and Diercks et al., however, assume that the *-ti* root begins as a complementizer, not as a verb, as 'say' complementizers are more commonly speculated to be. In Ikalanga, this would be manifested by the *-ti* root taking on verbal status and being licensed to bear verbal morphology, which it cannot do when it remains the head of C.

(31) a. [TP T [VoiceP EA [Voice [vP [v v [CP *-ti* [TP ...]]]]]]]
      b. [TP T [VoiceP EA [Voice-v-*ti* [vP [v v-*ti*... [CP *-ti* [TP ...]]]]]]]

Raising of C to v is illustrated in (31b) (copies bolded), presumably with subsequent raising of v to Voice, part of the phase edge, where agreement with T

---

[11]A further challenge is raised by C-agreement in Limbum. Nformi (2017) reports that direct objects block c-agreement in Limbum, which otherwise looks just like Lubukusu in the relevant respects. Accounts designed for the Lubukusu and Ikalanga patterns so far do not account for Limbum. Nformi proposes that the direct object blocks Agree between upward-probing C and the EA (see also Carstens 2016, on Lubukusu).

is possible. This limited account of 'say' C-raising is thus morphologically motivated, but there is an independent reason to suppose that the v corresponding to 'say' might often be morphologically null.

Grimshaw (2015) proposes that the semantics of 'say' verbs follows a strikingly regular semantic decomposition based on what she calls the 'say' schema. She notes that English *say* is a kind of vanilla report of a particular form of speech act that has at least two arguments, a source and a "linguistic material" argument that amounts to content of what was said (setting aside the addressee or goal argument). One can talk nonsense or speak words, but neither of these two speech acts involves a linguistic material argument, as the direct objects have no propositional content. She then notes that three classes of verbs are based on the 'say' schema, namely, 'say by means' (*mutter, shriek, mumble*), 'say with attitude' (*bitch, gripe*) and 'discourse role' verbs (*ask, announce, comment, remark, tell*). She points out that the three classes do not overlap, in that there are no monomorphemic verbs that mean 'announce by shrieking', 'ask in a bitching way' or 'mutter by bitching', etc. She proposes that all three sets of verbs modify the same single mutable feature of the 'say' schema to create other verbs. The 'say' schema itself is just a template of argument places waiting for suitable morphology. Our suggestion is that in languages like Ikalanga, the predicate is filled by a complementizer from the argument that distinguishes the 'say' schema by virtue of the presence of a linguistic material argument.[12]

If this proposal is on the right track, then the suggestion by Diercks et al. that C raises to become main verb 'say' is essentially correct, but it does not support their proposal that movement of C to matrix vP or VoiceP is in any way general.

3.5 Locality between matrix T and AGR-*ti*

The more challenging locality relation for phase theory is the relationship between T and the complement clause C, insofar as they are separated by a phase boundary. At least two different approaches come to mind that might address this puzzle.

One way is to motivate (covert) movement of AGR-C into the periphery of the VoiceP phase in order to be high enough to agree with T. In the past, anaphors that can only agree with subjects and never with objects have been posited to move to the matrix T where only the Spec-TP locally c-commands them (on "hoisting" analyses, see Safir 2013). The motivation for moving nominal anaphors

---

[12] This proposal grew out of a discussion with Jane Grimshaw, personal communication.

in this way was always thin, driven by the needs of the locality of binding, rather than any morphological property of tense apparent on the element that moves.[13]

This proposal, essentially that of Diercks et al. (2017), is anaphor movement, except what moves has no nominal character. The vestige of T-agreement on C is a posited residue of covert head-movement of AGR-*ti* to the edge of VoiceP, as in (32) (bolding=copies).

(32)   [$_{TP}$ T [$_{VoiceP}$ **AGR-*ti*** [$_{VoiceP}$ EA [$_{Voice}$ ...[$_{CP}$ **AGR-*ti*** [$_{TP}$ ...]]]]]]]]

The AGR-*ti* adjoined to VoiceP is an unpronounced higher copy resulting from movement. Adjoined to the VoiceP, abstract AGR-*ti* is then in the VoiceP phase edge and local to T. A serious problem for such an account is that Spell-out should apply to the lower copy of AGR-*ti* (the one that is overt) as soon as the VoiceP phase is complete. T is outside the VoiceP phase, however, so the lowest C copy of the complement clause could only get its tense agreement by a counter-cyclic operation of inheritance down into the closed VoiceP phase. This counter-cyclic Spell-out breaches the Phase Impenetrability Condition (Chomsky 2001).

An alternative account would be to assume that the complement clause can extrapose to a position at the edge of VoiceP where the edge of the complement clause CP phase would be visible to T in the matrix clause CP phase. Notice that it is possible for a complement clause to be separated from adjacency to the verb by an adverb.

(33)   Néó w-ákà-léb-á   chósèlélè (à)-kà-tì   Nchídzì
       Neo SM.c1-PST2-say-fv indeed   SM.c1-PST2-that Nchidzi
       w-ákà-téng-á   lórì
       SM.c1-PST2-buy-fv car
       'Neo said it definitely that Nchidzi had bought a new car.'

If the complement clause can extrapose by adjunction to VoiceP, where C is on the edge of CP, and CP is on the edge of VoiceP, then C is in the same phase as T.

(34)   [T [$_{VoiceP}$ [$_{VoiceP}$ ...(EA) [$_{Voice}$ v [$_{VP}$ ...[$_{CP}$ AGR-C [TP]]]]]] [$_{CP}$ <u>AGR-C</u>
       [TP]]]

---

[13]Diercks et al. attempt to motivate movement of anaphoric features to adjoined vP (or VoiceP) position on the basis of creating "referential" vPs, which, to avoid crashing, must have no meaningful, but unvalued features in them. It is unclear how they can account for cases like *The men considered themselves to have praised themselves*, where the EA of *praise* has no valued features to contribute, so movement of anaphoric features of the direct object to vP is not motivated or helpful. Such derivations should crash in their account.

The (underlined) overt copy of AGR-C in the extraposed CP at the edge of the complement clause domain is no longer separated from T by a phase boundary in (34). The underlined AGR-C can thus agree with Voice in the higher phase if Voice (and v) is incorporated into T, as is usually assumed in Bantu (but clausal subjects would still be outside the c-command domain of T, so would not agree in voice, as shown in (23)). Thus T-agreement (from anaphoric tense features parasitic on agreeing C) would be direct, not indirect via copy inheritance down, as in (32).

Rackowski & Richards (2005) have proposed extraposition of exactly the sort we propose to make the CP phase edge susceptible to wh-extraction, and in particular, with accompanying agreement relations established with the extraposed clause. We set aside investigation of this parallel (pointed out to us by Michael Diercks, personal communication) for future investigation.

4 Conclusion

Although our approach holds out the promise of applying more generally to other C-agreement systems, empirical studies of matrix C-agreement are still sparse and our proposals will have to be tested against the additional patterns that may be discovered (including Diercks & Rao 2019, not addressed here). Nonetheless, the relations between voice and tense and subordinate C-agreement uncovered in Ikalanga will have to be accounted for in any future approach.

Abbreviations

&	associative plural		OM	object marker
AUX	auxiliary		PASS	passive
C	noun class		PRN	pronoun
CAUS	causative		PRS	present
fv	final vowel		PST1	recent past
FUT	future		PST2	remote past
INF	infinitive		RCM	reciprocal verbal affix
IV	initial vowel		RFM	reflexive verbal affix
LOC	locative		SBJV	subjunctive
NEG	negation		SM	subject marker

Acknowledgements

The authors acknowledge the support of NSF BCS #1324404 which was crucial for this research. We would also like to thank Michael Diercks whose commentary considerably influenced our revisions and Samson Lotven for his good advice and forbearance.

References

Afranaph Project. Ongoing. *Afranaph Database: Ikalanga data.* Ken Safir (ed.). http://www.africananaphora.rutgers.edu.

Baker, Mark. 2008. *The syntax of agreement and concord.* Cambridge: Cambridge University Press.

Carstens, Vicki. 2016. Delayed valuation: A reanalysis of goal features, "upward" complementizer agreement, and the mechanics of case. *Syntax* 19(1). 1–42.

Chebanne, Andy. 2010. Kalanga phonology, morpho-phonology and the occurrence of some "peculiar" phonological realizations. *Zimbabwe International Journal of Languages and Cultures* 1(1). 35–60.

Chomsky, Noam. 2001. Derivation by phase. In Michael Kenstowicz (ed.), *Ken Hale: A life in language*, 1–52. Cambridge: MIT Press.

Diercks, Michael. 2010. *Agreement with subjects in Lubukusu.* Georgetown University dissertation.

Diercks, Michael. 2013. Indirect agree in Lubukusu complementizer agreement. *Natural Language & Linguistic Theory* 31(2). 357–407.

Diercks, Michael & Meghana Rao. 2019. Upward-oriented complementizer agreement with subjects and objects in Kipsigis. In Emily Clem, Peter Jenks & Hannah Sande (eds.), *Theory and description in African Linguistics: Selected papers from the 47th Annual Conference on African Linguistics*, 369–393. Berlin: Language Science Press. DOI:10.5281/zenodo.3367166

Diercks, Michael, Marjo van Koppen & Michael Putnam. 2017. *Agree probes down: Anaphoric feature valuation and phase reference.* Pomona College, Utrecht University, Penn State University. Ms.

Grimshaw, Jane. 2015. The light verbs say and SAY. In Ida Toivonen, Piroska Csúri & Emile van der Zee (eds.), *Structures in the mind: Essays on language, music, and cognition.* Cambridge: MIT Press.

Harley, Heidi. 2013. External arguments and the mirror principle: On the distinctness of voice and v. *Lingua* 125. 34–57.

Heine, Bernd & Tania Kuteva. 2002. *World lexicon of grammaticalization.* Cambridge: Cambridge University Press.

Idiatov, Dmitry. 2010. Person–number agreement on clause linking markers in Mande. *Studies in Language.* 34(4). 832–868.

Kawasha, Boniface. 2007. Subject-agreeing complementizers and their functions in Chokwe, Luchazi, Lunda, and Luvale. In *Selected proceedings of the 37th Annual Conference on African linguistics*, 180–190. Somerville, MA: Cascadilla Proceedings Project.

Kratzer, Angelika. 1996. Severing the external argument from the verb. In J. Rooryck & L. Zaring (eds.), *Phrase structure and the lexicon*, 109–137. Dordrecht: Kluwer.

Legate, Julie Anne. 2012. Subjects in Acehnese and the nature of the passive. *Language* 88(3). 495–525.

Letsholo, Rose. 2002. Subjects, their (dis)location and agreement in Ikalanga. *Linguistic Analysis* 32. 505–543.

Mathangwane, Joyce. 1999. *Ikalanga phonetics and phonology: A synchronic and diachronic study* (Stanford Monographs in African Languages). Standford: CSLI Publications.

Nformi, Jude. 2017. Complementizer agreement and intervention effects. Ms. University of Leipzig.

Pylkkänen, Liina. 2008. *Introducing arguments.* Cambridge: MIT Press.

Rackowski, Andrea & Norvin Richards. 2005. Phase edge and extraction: A Tagalog case study. *Linguistic Inquiry* 36(4). 565–599.

Rooryck, Johan & Guido van den Wyngaerd. 2011. *Dissolving binding theory.* Oxford: Oxford University Press.

Safir, Ken. 2013. Syntax, binding and patterns of anaphora. In Marcel den Dikken (ed.), *Cambridge handbook of generatve syntax*, 515–576. Cambridge: Cambridge University Press.

Safir, Ken. 2014. One true anaphor. *Linguistic Inquiry* 45(1). 91–124.

Safir, Ken & Mamadou Bassene. 2017. Morphosyntax and movement: Verb stems in Jóola Eegimaa. *Natural Language & Linguistic Theory* 35(3). 839–897.

Chapter 10

Optional past tense in Wolof

M. Ryan Bochnak
University of Konstanz

Martina Martinović
University of Florida

In this paper, we discuss the interpretation of the past temporal marker *oon* in Wolof (Niger-Congo; Senegal), in light of recent claims in the literature regarding its status as a so-called "discontinuous past." We show that the cessation inference associated with *oon* is a conversational implicature. Thus, *oon* can receive an analysis as a plain semantic past tense.

1 Introduction

There has been some debate in the recent literature regarding the semantic nature of so-called "discontinuous past" markers. On the one hand, Plungian & van der Auwera (2006), to whom the term "discontinuous past" is due, characterize its meaning as "past and not present" or "past with no present relevance."

On the other hand, Cable (2017) argues that the apparently discontinuous semantics of the Tlingit (Na Dene, Alaska and British Columbia) decessive form (Leer 1991) is actually a defeasible implicature, i.e., not part of the conventional semantics of the tense form. Cable assigns a plain past tense semantics, and the implicature of "not present" or "no present relevance" is derived via competition with temporally unmarked clauses, which can receive either a past or present interpretation. Cable further observes that discontinuous pasts are found exclusively in languages where overt past marking is optional,[1] and thus calls into

---

[1] By "optional" past, we are referring to the fact that past temporal reference can also grammatically be achieved with temporally unmarked clauses. Speakers may nevertheless make use of optional past markers for specific rhetorical purposes, as highlighted by Plungian & van der Auwera (2006).

M. Ryan Bochnak & Martina Martinović. 2019. Optional past tense in Wolof. In Samson Lotven, Silvina Bongiovanni, Phillip Weirich, Robert Botne & Samuel Gyasi Obeng (eds.), *African linguistics across the disciplines: Selected papers from the 48th Annual Conference on African Linguistics*, 187–202. Berlin: Language Science Press. DOI:10.5281/zenodo.3520583

question whether the category of discontinuous past exists at all in natural language.

In this paper, we contribute to this discussion by examining the past temporal marker *oon*[2] in Wolof (Niger-Congo; Senegal; see Church 1981; Robert 1991). This tense marker was identified by Plungian & van der Auwera (2006) as a discontinuous past, and the Wolof data formed an important part of their argument for the existence of discontinuous pasts in the world's languages. The main evidence for this claim comes from a cessation inference associated with the use of *oon* in contrast with temporally unmarked past-referring sentences.[3] For instance, comparing (1) and (2), the addition of *oon* in (2) gives rise to a cessation inference that the result state of the event (here, the subject being gone) no longer holds at present.[4]

(1) Dem-na-∅ Ndar.
    go-C-SCL.3SG Saint-Louis
    'He left for Saint-Louis (and is still there).'
    'Il est parti à Saint-Louis (c'est toujours vrai, il n'est pas là).'
    (Robert 1991: 279)

(2) Dem-**oon**-na-∅ Ndar.
    go-PST-C-SCL.3SG Saint-Louis
    'He had left for Saint-Louis (and has since come back).'
    'Il était parti à Saint-Louis (et en T_0, il est revenu).'   (Robert 1991: 279)

The use of *oon* with stative predicates gives rise to the inference that the state no longer holds in the present, as illustrated by the translations in (3–4).

(3) Tiit-na-a.
    afraid-C-SCL.1SG
    'I am afraid.'
    (Torrence 2012: 25)

---

[2]The past marker surfaces as *oon* if the preceding element ends in a consonant, and as *woon* if it ends in a vowel, as a result of a phonological hiatus repair.

[3]Like Cable, we follow Altshuler & Schwarzschild (2012) in using the terminology of "cessation" to describe this inference.

[4]In examples taken from other sources, we modify the morpheme glosses according to the analysis of Martinović (2015). For examples from Robert 1991, we keep the original French translation and add our own colloquial English translation. The translations do not represent our analysis of the Wolof forms.

(4) Tiit-óon-na-a.
    afraid-PST-C-SCL.1SG

    'I was afraid (but I am not now).'   (Torrence 2012: 26)

The analysis of *oon* as a discontinuous past contrasts with that of the past tense in languages like English, which makes no claim about the state of affairs at present. For instance, in (5), we have a discourse about a past time, and the past tense is used in each clause. These uses of the past tense in English simply refer to the topical past time, and make no claims about the state of affairs at the speech time. For instance, the sentence in (5c) only makes a claim about the past topic time (the time of looking in the room), and not about the present; intuitively, the book is still in Russian at the speech time (if it still exists).

(5) Context: A judge poses question (a) to a witness, who replies with (b–c):
    a. What did you notice when you looked in the room?
    b. The light was on. There was a book on the table.
    c. It was in Russian.   (Klein 1994)

In this paper, we argue that *oon* is in fact not a discontinuous past, but rather a past marker with a conventional meaning parallel to the past tense in English. Using diagnostics similar to those that Cable (2017) used in his study of Tlingit, we show that the cessation inference of *oon* is not part of its conventional meaning, but rather is a conversational implicature, arising due to competition with temporally unmarked clauses (see also Bochnak 2016 on optional past in Washo (Hokan/isolate, California and Nevada)). In this respect, Wolof *oon* is similar to other optional past markers in other languages, as has been argued in the recent literature. In this respect, we concur with Church (1981), who also showed that *oon* does not always have a "discontinuous" interpretation (though with different terminology and analytical tools).

The paper proceeds as follows. In §2, we discuss the temporal interpretation of tenseless clauses in Wolof, while in §3 we turn to the interpretation of *oon* and show that it behaves like an ordinary past tense marker. §4 contains our analysis, including a proposal for deriving the cessation implicature associated with *oon*. In §5 we survey some syntactic evidence that suggests that *oon* does not behave syntactically like a tense head. §6 concludes.

Unless noted otherwise, all the data in the paper were obtained by the second author in Saint-Louis, Senegal, during March 2016 and April–May 2017. All speakers were native speakers of Wolof, and Wolof was their first language. The data represent judgments of nine speakers, age 30 to 68. We use direct elicitation in order to replicate as closely as possible the data used in previous works on so-called discontinuous pasts in other languages (Bochnak 2016; Cable 2017).

2 Temporal interpretation of tenseless clauses

Wolof finite indicative clauses have an obligatory complementizer layer (Martinović 2015). There are several types of complementizers with different syntactic and information-structural properties; these differences do not concern us here as they do not affect the temporal interpretation. We therefore gloss all complementizers as C.

Tense marking and negation in Wolof are only possible in the presence of a complementizer (Njie 1982). Wolof also has *minimal clauses* (Sauvageot 1965; Church 1981; Dialo 1981; Robert 1991; Zribi-Hertz & Diagne 2003), which can be used in a narrative context and appear to be smaller than TPs.[5] The temporal interpretation of such clauses is determined with respect to a previously introduced temporal anchor. In this paper we are therefore only concerned with clauses that contain the CP and TP layers.

In clauses with no overt tense/aspect marking, stative predicates receive a present interpretation by default, as in (6–7).

(6) Baax-na-∅.
    good-C-SCL.3SG
    'It is good.'/ #'It was good.'

(7) Da-ma   mer.
    do.C-SCL.1SG angry
    'I am angry.'/ #'I was angry.'

Meanwhile, eventive predicates receive a default past interpretation, as in (8–9). As shown in (10), activities pattern with other eventive predicates, rather than states.

(8) Xale yi   lekk-na-ñu   ceeb.
    child the.PL eat-C-SCL.3PL rice
    'The children ate rice.'/ #'The children are eating rice.'

---

[5] Zribi-Hertz & Diagne (2003) consider them to be *v*Ps, but they can contain imperfective aspect, which suggests they are at least as big as an AspP.

(9) Musaa dem-na-∅.
     Moussa leave-C-SCL.3SG
     'Moussa left.'/ #'Moussa is leaving.'

(10) Musaa fécc-na-∅.
     Moussa dance-C-SCL.3SG
     'Moussa danced.'/ #'Moussa is dancing.'

However, these defaults are not tied to the aspectual class of the predicate per se. Derived statives (e.g., eventive predicates co-occurring with 'imperfective' *di*) can also have present temporal reference, as in (11–12).[6]

(11) Usmaan-a di (>Usmaanay) gis Musaa.
     Oussman-C IMPF   see Moussa
     'It's Oussman who sees Moussa.'

(12) Daf-a-∅   di (>dafay) añ,   mën-ul ñëw.
     do-C-SCL.3SG IMPF   eat.lunch, can-NEG come
     'He is eating lunch, he cannot come.'
     'Il est en train de manger, il ne peut pas venir.'   (Robert 1991: 263)

To account for these facts, we follow the principles of Smith & Erbaugh (2005); Smith et al. (2007) for default temporal interpretation of tenseless clauses. These principles were developed to account for temporal interpretation of the tenseless language Mandarin (Smith & Erbaugh 2005), and have been applied to other tenseless languages, such as Navajo (Smith et al. 2007) and Hausa (Mucha 2013). The three main principles – the Deictic Principle, the Simplicity Principle of Interpretation, and the Bounded Event Constraint – are given in (13–15):

(13) Deictic Principle
     Situations (events) are located with respect to UT
     (i.e., utterance time is the default reference point)

(14) Simplicity Principle of Interpretation
     Choose the interpretation that requires the least information added or inferred.

---

[6]In the examples, *-y* is an allophonic realization of *di*; see Dunigan 1994, Torrence (2005; 2012), Martinović (2015).

Hierarchy of Simplicity:

a. RT = UT: Present time reference is the simplest kind of temporal reference since (i) an utterance event always provides a time interval to which an RT variable can be anchored, namely UT; (ii) present interpretation requires no displacement of either the time or world of evaluation

b. RT < UT: Past time reference is more complex since it requires the displacement of RT from the concrete utterance event

c. RT > UT: Future time reference involves both RT shifting but also modal displacement, and thus increases the level of abstraction

(ensures that present is preferred over past, which is in turn preferred over future)

(15) Bounded Event Constraint
Bounded events are not located in the present. Speakers follow a tacit convention that communication is instantaneous. The present perspective is incompatible with the report of a bounded event, because the bounds would go beyond that moment.
(bounded events cannot be located in the present)

The Deictic Principle states that the utterance time is the default reference point for temporal interpretation. Together with (14a), this predicts a present interpretation as a default. However, by (15), bounded events – which cover (perfective) eventive predicates – cannot be located in the present. These are then shifted to a past interpretation, given (14b). This setup also predicts that future reference with tenseless clauses is dispreferred. In many tenseless languages, additional morphology must be used to achieve future time reference (Matthewson 2006; Tonhauser 2011; Bochnak 2016). This is indeed also the case for Wolof, where the imperfective marker *di* is used for future reference, as in (16).[7]

(16) Di-na-a   toog ceeb-u-jën.
      IMPF-C-SCL.1SG cook rice-GEN-fish

      'I will cook ceebujën.'

---

[7]See Bochnak & Martinović 2018 for discussion and an analysis of imperfective *di* and its future uses.

3 The interpretation of *oon*

Turning to the semantics of *oon*, we argue that it is a regular past tense marker. The main pieces of evidence for this claim are that clauses with *oon* are obligatorily interpreted as past, and the cessation inference (i.e., "discontinuous" interpretation) does not always occur with *oon*. We also show that *oon* is not an English-style perfect, and that *oon* is found in counterfactual conditionals.

First, we find that *oon* is only compatible with past time reference. In addition to the examples we have already seen, we add (17–18) below.

(17) Baax-**oon**-na-∅.
good-PST-C-SCL.3SG

'It was good.'/ #'It's good.'

(18) Xale yi lekk-**oon**-na-ñu ceeb.
child the.PL eat-PST-C-SCL.3PL rice

'The children ate rice.'/ #'The children are eating rice.'

Second, the cessation inference associated with *oon* is not always present for all speakers.[8] Recall the data in (1–2), repeated here, which show that the use of *oon* can trigger a cessation inference.

(19) Dem-na-∅ Ndar.
go-C-SCL.3SG Saint-Louis

'He left for Saint-Louis (and is still there).'
'Il est parti à Saint-Louis (c'est toujours vrai, il n'est pas là).'
(Robert 1991: 279)

(20) Dem-**oon**-na-∅ Ndar.
go-PST-C-SCL.3SG Saint-Louis

'He had left for Saint-Louis (and has since come back).'
'Il était parti à Saint-Louis (et en T_0, il est revenu).' (Robert 1991: 279)

---

[8]There is both interspeaker and intraspeaker variation in this. Some speakers insist on the cessation inference in some contexts but not in others, and for some speakers it is never present. We have not found any speakers for whom the cessation inference is obligatory in all contexts that we tested.

However, when a past topic time is overtly specified, e.g., by a time adverbial as in (21), there is no cessation implicature.[9]

(21) Musaa jënd(-**oon**)-na-∅   oto bu bees at   bi jáll, waye
      Moussa buy(-PST)-C-SCL.3SG car c new year c past but

      mu-angi (> mungi) ko   di (> koy) dawal ba   léegi.
      SCL.3SG-C   OCL.3SG IMPF   drive until now

      'Moussa bought a new car last year, but he is still driving it.'

With predicates such as *xaru* 'kill oneself', many speakers report that the use of *oon* implies that Moussa is now alive again, or that the suicide attempt was unsuccessful (i.e. a cessation inference is detected). However, this effect is reported to go away for some speakers in particular contexts; e.g. if (22) is said as part of the story of Moussa's life, or if we are retelling the events of, for example, last week.

(22) Musaa xaru(-**woon**)-na-∅   ayubés bi weesu.
      Moussa kill.oneself(-PST)-C-SCL.3SG week   c past

      'Moussa killed himself last week.'

The example (5) from Klein (1994) is also felicitous in Wolof for most of our speakers, as shown in (23). Even though the book presumably still exists and is still in Wolof, *oon* can be used in the answer in (23c).

(23) Context: A judge poses question (a) to a witness, who replies with (b–c):
      a. Lan nga   gis bi   nga   xool-e   neeg bi?
         what C.SCL.2SG see when SCL.2SG look.at-ANT room the.SG

         'What did you see when you looked at the room?'

      b. Làmp bi   tàkk-oon-na-∅.   Am-oon-na-∅   benn téeré
         lamp the.SG be.alight-PST-C-SCL.3SG. have-PST-C-SCL.3SG one   book

         bu ubbeeku si kaw taabal bi.
         c be.open on top table the.SG

         'The light was on. There was an open book on the table.'

      c. Téeré wolof la-∅   (woon).
         book Wolof C-SCL.3SG (PST).

         'It was/is in Wolof.'

---

[9]We place *oon* in brackets to indicate that the sentences with and without *oon* are accepted by speakers in the context provided.

Since the cessation inference is not always present, we conclude that it is not part of the lexical semantics of *oon*. Therefore, we do not consider it a "discontinuous past" in the sense of Plungian & van der Auwera (2006), since is not part of its conventional meaning that a state of affairs fails to hold at speech time.

Third, we observe that *oon* does not behave like an English-style perfect.[10] The English perfect does not co-occur with temporal frame adverbials (Klein 1992), see (24). However, we have already seen in (21) that *oon* can co-occur with temporal adverbials.

(24) #I have bought a car yesterday/last year/on December 1, 2010.

The English perfect also displays so-called lifetime effects (McCawley 1971). The sentence in (25) is apparently infelicitous because Christopher Columbus is no longer living. However, as shown in (26), Wolof *oon* does not have this property.

(25) #Christopher Columbus has discovered America.

(26) Colombo féeñal(-**oon**)-na-∅ Amerik.
      Columbus find-(PST)-C-SCL.3SG America
      'Columbus found America.'

Another property of the English perfect (and of so-called terminative aspects more generally, see Bohnemeyer 2002), is that they assert that the result state of the perfect-marked event still holds. This means continuations like in (27) are infelicitous. These types of examples are nevertheless felicitous in Wolof with *oon*, as shown in (28).

(27) I have lost my glasses, #and now I (have) found them.

(28) Sama   lunettes réer(-**oon**)-na-∅-ma, ,   waye
      POSS.1SG glasses lose(-PST)-C-SCL.3SG-OCL.1SG but
      gis(-**oon**)-na-a-ko.
      see(-PST)-C-SCL.1SG-OCL.3SG
      'I lost my glasses, but I found them.'

---

[10]We acknowledge that perfects in many languages do not have these properties.

Fourth, we find *oon* in counterfactual conditionals. Past tense marking is common cross-linguistically in counterfactual conditionals (Iatridou 2000; Halpert & Karawani 2012), including in English. The sentence in (29) has a present topic time (by the presence of *right now*), but has past morphology in the antecedent. We also see this in Wolof, where *oon* appears in counterfactual conditionals, as in (30).[11]

(29)   If I was in Paris right now, I would be eating a croissant.

(30)   Su-ma   ragal-**oon**   rabi, di-na-a   tiit   léegi.
       if-SCL.1SG be.afraid.of-PST spirit, IMPF-C-SCL.1SG be.afraid now

       'If I was afraid of spirits, I would be afraid now.'

Although the role of the past tense in counterfactuals is a matter still very much under debate, it is certainly striking that Wolof uses this marker in counterfactuals, just like in many other typologically unrelated languages.

In sum, apart from its optionality, *oon* behaves like a regular past tense, where the apparent discontinuous semantics are not part of its conventional meaning. We therefore propose to analyze it semantically as a regular past tense, just like other optional pasts in Washo (Bochnak 2016) and Tlingit (Cable 2017).

4 Analysis

We define tense as a morpheme whose conventional meaning relates a reference or topic time with the speech time, or possibly another evaluation time (Reichenbach 1947; Klein 1994). We assume a pronominal or referential theory of tense, whereby the reference time of a clause is represented as a temporal pronoun located in the T head (e.g., Abusch 1997; Heim 1994; Partee 1973, among many others). Like other pronouns, it bears an index, and receives its value from an assignment function *g*. Every finite clause contains a reference time pronoun, regardless of whether there is an overt tense morpheme or not. We treat *oon* as a tense feature which modifies the temporal pronoun, placing a presupposition on its possible values (i.e., restricting it to times in the past of the speech time).

---

[11]We do not intend this point as an argument against a discontinuous past analysis, but rather as evidence that *oon* behaves quite similarly to non-discontinuous pasts in more familiar languages.

We propose that a sentence such as (31) has the clause structure given in Figure 1.[12] Semantically, AspP denotes a predicate of times as in (32a), where we assume arguments of the verb are interpreted in their base position. The temporal argument slot is filled in by the reference time pronoun. When *oon*, defined in (32c), surfaces, it adds the presupposition that the reference time is located in the past of the speech time t_c. (In the absence of a morphological tense, we assume the value of the reference time pronoun in T is restricted by the principles outlined in §2.) The result is a proposition meaning, given in (32d).[13]

(31)   Colombo daf-a-∅   féñaal-oon Amerik.
       Columbus do-c-scl.3sg discover-pst America
       'Columbus DISCOVERED America'

(32)   a. $[\![\text{ AspP }]\!]^{g,c} = \lambda t \lambda w.\textbf{discover}(a)(c)$ at t in w

       b. $[\![\text{ T}_1]\!]^{g,c} = g(1)$

       c. $[\![\text{ oon }]\!]^{g,c} = \lambda t.t$; defined only if $t < t_c$

       d. $[\![\text{ TP }]\!]^{g,c} = \lambda w.\textbf{discover}(a)(c)$ at $g(1)$ in w ; defined only if $g(1) < t_c$

Under this analysis, cessation is not part of the lexical semantics of *oon*, contra Plungian & van der Auwera (2006). Instead, *oon* only adds a plain past presupposition, just like the past tense in English. The question, then, is how to account for the robust intuition, both by native speakers and previous authors, that the use of *oon* in many contexts generates a cessation inference.

We suggest that the cessation inference is a conversational implicature derived by the Gricean Maxim of Manner (cf. Altshuler & Schwarzschild 2012; Cable 2017, for whom cessation inferences are analyzed as *scalar* implicatures). Following Levinson (2000), a marked message indicates a marked situation. We assume

---

[12]The example (31) is of a predicate focus sentence with *do*-support in C. We choose this clause type for illustration as the verb here stays low, unlike in some other cases when it raises to C taking *oon* with it. The clause structure in Figure 1 is somewhat simplified from what Martinović (2015) assumes; any differences are not relevant for our analysis here. For example, the non-pronominal subject in these clauses is in the left periphery (Spec,CP), and it is doubled by a subject clitic which is here represented in Spec,TP (the clitics all move to adjoin above TP at a late stage in the syntax). The details of the doubling are not relevant here; we assume that the non-pronominal argument is generated in the subject position in Spec,*v*P (omitted for simplicity). Additionally, the verb also raises through the Asp head and carries it on to T, but we also omit this here.

[13]Robert (1991) analyzes *oon* as a relative past, in which case the reference time can be related to an evaluation time other than the speech time, i.e., t_c in (32c) can be distinct from the speech time.

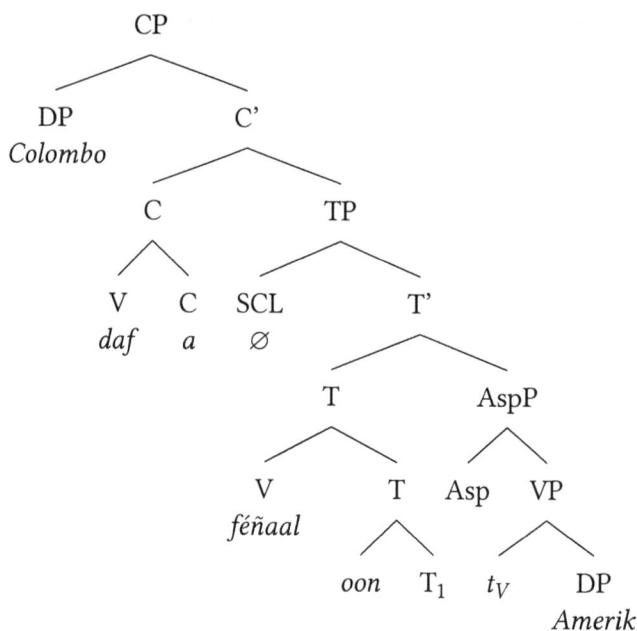

Figure 1: Wolof clause structure

that a past-referring clause containing *oon* is "marked" in comparison to a past-referring tenseless clause. A Gricean chain of reasoning proceeds as follows.[14] A sentence with *oon* is morphologically more marked than a sentence without *oon*. Given that past marking is not required by the grammar of Wolof, the speaker (in most situations) could have used an unmarked form for past temporal reference. Since the speaker used a marked form, the hearer infers that the speaker must believe that the situation is marked. That is, more than just a plain past meaning is intended by the speaker. The hearer infers that the state of affairs described does not hold at present, otherwise the simpler form could have been used. Therefore, cessation is an inference derived from the fact that *oon* is optional, and temporally unmarked clauses can also have past interpretations.

If the implicature calculation is based on Manner, whereby a marked message leads to pragmatic enrichment, the question arises as to why a *cessation* implicature in particular is calculated. Why could some other inference not be calculated? Apparently, other inferences are in fact possible and attested. For instance,

---

[14] A reviewer points out the possibility that Gricean conversational maxims may not be followed in all cultures. At this point, we have no reason to believe they do not apply in Wolof, but leave further investigation into this question for later work.

Church (1981) claims that the use of *oon* often gives rise to a *remoteness* inference as well. Our speakers also seem to prefer *oon* when talking about a time in a more distant past. Some speakers even report they *must* use *oon* in those cases (e.g. when speaking about an event that occurred last year). This inference would also be a conversational implicature, and not part of the lexical semantics of *oon*, given examples like (33), where *oon* is possible with *demb* 'yesterday' (assuming one day ago does not count as 'distant').

(33) Musaa jënd(-**oon**)-na-∅ oto bu bees démb
      Moussa buy-PST-C-SCL.3SG car c new yesterday.

      'Moussa bought a new car yesterday.'

5 Is *oon* a tense head?

There is some indication that *oon* is syntactically not a head. First, in clauses in which the verb raises to C, *oon* is affixed onto it in affirmative cases, as in (34) but skipped over in the presence of negation, shown in (35). Martinović (2015; 2016) proposes an analysis of the affixation of *oon* in which she argues that *oon* affixes onto the verb postsyntactically (at PF) in a certain syntactic configuration, but not in others. Crucially, for her analysis to go through, *oon* cannot be a head, as it would then always be picked up by head movement. She therefore suggests that *oon* is a phrasal morpheme in Spec,TP.

(34) Xale yi   lekk-**oon**-na-ñu jën.
      child the.PL eat-PST-C-SCL.3PL fish

      'The children ate fish.'

(35) Xale yi   lekk-u(l)-∅-ñu   **woon** jën.
      child the.PL eat-NEG-C-SCL.3PL PST   fish

      'The children didn't eat fish.'

The second piece of evidence that casts doubt on the treatment of *oon* as a T head is that it can occur apparently affixed onto non-verbal elements, as reported by Torrence (2012).

(36) Kan-ati-**woon** la-ñu   dóor?
      who-again-PST C-SCL.3PL hit

      'Who did they hit again?'   (Torrence 2012: 24)

Given the examples above, it is possible that *oon* is not a tense morpheme, but a particular type of a temporal adverbial (cf. Tonhauser 2006 on an optional past adverbial in Paraguayan Guaraní). We leave this only as a speculation at this point, as the matter requires further research. Given that our definition of tense in §4 only makes reference to semantic notions, the question of whether *oon* behaves syntactically like a T head is orthogonal to the core aspects of our semantic analysis, where *oon* is treated as a tense (i.e., relating a reference time to speech time).

6 Conclusion

We have argued that *oon* in Wolof marks past temporal reference, and can be given an analysis of a semantic past tense. The cessation inference detected by Church (1981) and Robert (1991), and analyzed as discontinuous past by Plungian & van der Auwera (2006), is not present in all uses of *oon*, and we argue this is a conversational implicature. Given that the same conclusion was reached for the optional tense languages Washo (Bochnak 2016) and Tlingit (Cable 2017), the status of discontinuous past as a grammatical category is therefore called into question.

Acknowledgements

We wish to thank our Wolof consultants Abdou Aziz Djakhate, Magatte Bocar Ndiaye, Louis Camara, Mbaye Diop, Jean Léo Diouf, Ibrahim Gise, Alioune Kebe, Ismail Kebe, Tapha Ndiaye for their time and dedication. We also thank the audience at ACAL 48 for their helpful comments. All errors are our own.

Abbreviations

ANT	anterior		PL	plural
C	complementizer		POSS	possessive
GEN	genitive		REL	relative
IMPF	imperfective		SCL	subject clitic
NEG	negation		SG	singular
OCL	object clitic			

References

Abusch, Dorit. 1997. Sequence of tense and temporal de re. *Linguistics and Philosophy* 20(1). 1–50. DOI:10.1023/A:1005331423820

Altshuler, Daniel & Roger Schwarzschild. 2012. Moment of change, cessation im-
plicatures and simultaneous readings. In Emmanuel Chemla, Vincent Homer
& Grégoire Winterstein (eds.), *Proceedings of Sinn und Bedeutung 17*, 45–62.
Available online at http://semanticsarchive.net/sub2012.

Bochnak, M. Ryan. 2016. Past time reference in a language with optional tense.
Linguistics and Philosophy 39. 247–294.

Bochnak, M. Ryan & Martina Martinović. 2018. The case of Wolof imprerfective
di. In Uli Sauerland & Stephanie Solt (eds.), *Proceedings of Sinn und Bedeutung
22*, vol. 1, 223–240.

Bohnemeyer, Juergen. 2002. *The grammar of time reference in Yukatek Maya*. Mu-
nich: Lincom.

Cable, Seth. 2017. The implicatures of optional past tense in Tlingit and the implications for discontinuous past. *Natural Language and Linguistic Theory* 35(3).
635–681.

Church, Eric. 1981. *Le système verbal du wolof*. Université de Dakar, Documents
Linguistiques.

Dialo, Amadou. 1981. *Structures verbales du wolof contemporain*. Dakar, Senegal:
Centre de Linguistique Appliquée de Dakar.

Dunigan, Melynda. 1994. *The clausal structure of Wolof: A study of focus and cliti-
cization*. Chapel Hill, NC: University of North Carolina dissertation.

Halpert, Claire & Hadil Karawani. 2012. Aspect in counterfactuals from A(rabic)
to Z(ulu). In *Proceedings of WCCFL 29*. Tucson, AZ: Cascadilla Proceedings
Project.

Heim, Irene. 1994. Comments on Abusch's theory of tense. In Hans Kamp (ed.),
Ellipsis, tense, and questions, 143–170. Amsterdam: University of Amsterdam.

Iatridou, Sabine. 2000. The grammatical ingredients of counterfactuality. *Linguistic Inquiry* 31. 231–270.

Klein, Wolfgang. 1992. The present perfect puzzle. *Language* 68. 525–552.

Klein, Wolfgang. 1994. *Time in language*. New York: Routledge.

Leer, Jeff. 1991. *The schetic categories of the Tlingit verb*. Chicago: University of
Chicago dissertation.

Levinson, Stephen C. 2000. *Presumptive meanings: The theory of generalized conversational implicature*. Cambridge, MA: MIT Press.

Martinović, Martina. 2015. *Feature geometry and head-splitting: Evidence from the
morpho-syntax of the Wolof clausal periphery*. Chicago: University of Chicago
dissertation.

Martinović, Martina. 2016. Interleaving syntax and postsyntax: Spell-out before
syntactic movement. Ms. University of Leipzig.

Matthewson, Lisa. 2006. Temporal semantics in a superficially tenseless language. *Linguistics and Philosophy* 29. 673–713.   DOI:10.1007/s10988-006-9010-6

McCawley, James. 1971. Tense and time reference in English. In Charles Fillmore & D. Terence Langendoen (eds.), *Studies in linguistic semantics*, 96–113. New York: Holt, Reinhart, & Winston.

Mucha, Anne. 2013. Temporal interpretation in Hausa. *Linguistics and Philosophy* 36. 371–415.   DOI:10.1007/s10988-013-9140-6

Njie, Codu Mbassy. 1982. *Description syntaxique du wolof de Gambie*. Dakar, Senegal: Les Nouvelles Editions Africaines.

Partee, Barbara. 1973. Some structural analogies between tenses and pronouns in English. *Journal of Philosophy* 70(18). 601–609.   DOI:10.2307/2025024

Plungian, Vladimir & Johan van der Auwera. 2006. Towards a typology of discontinuous past marking. *Sprachtypologie und Universalienforschung* 59(4). 317–349.   DOI:10.1524/stuf.2006.59.4.317

Reichenbach, Hans. 1947. The tenses of verbs. In *Elements of symbolic logic*, 287–298. New York: The Macmillan Company.

Robert, Stéphane. 1991. *Approche énonciative du système verbale: Le cas du wolof*. Paris: Editions du CNRS.

Sauvageot, Serge. 1965. *Description synchronique d'un dialecte wolof: Le parler du dyolof*. Dakar, Senegal: IFAN.

Smith, Carlota S. & Mary Erbaugh. 2005. Temporal interpretation in Mandarin Chinese. *Linguistics* 43(4). 713–756.   DOI:10.1515/ling.2005.43.4.713

Smith, Carlota, Ellavina Perkins & Theodore Fernald. 2007. Time in Navajo: Direct and indirect interpretations. *International Journal of American Linguistics* 73(1). 40–71.   DOI:10.1086/518334

Tonhauser, Judith. 2006. *The temporal semantics of noun phrases: Evidence from Guaraní*. Stanford University dissertation.

Tonhauser, Judith. 2011. Temporal reference in Paraguayan Guaraní, a tenseless language. *Linguistics and Philosophy* 34(3). 257–303.   DOI:10.1007/s10988-011-9097-2

Torrence, Harold. 2005. *On the distribution of complementizers in Wolof*. Los Angeles, CA: University of California dissertation.

Torrence, Harold. 2012. *The clause structure of Wolof: Insights into the left periphery*. Amsterdam: John Benjamins.

Zribi-Hertz, Anne & Lamine Diagne. 2003. Deficience flexionnelle et temps totopic en wolof. In *Typologies des langues d'Afrique et universaux de la grammaire, vol. 2: Benue-kwa, soninke, wolof*, 205–231. Paris: Presses Universitaires de Vincennes/Éditions de l'Harmattan.

Chapter 11

The Syntax of experiencers in Sereer-Siin

Khady Tamba

Université Cheikh Anta Diop

The special grammatical status of experiencers has been at the center of various studies within linguistics for several decades (Belletti & Rizzi 1988; Ameka 1990; Pesetsky 1995). This attention is due to the fact that there are specific syntactic features that are only associated with experiencers (Landau 2010). This study investigates object experiencers in Sereer-Siin – a dialect of Sereer, a West Atlantic language of the Niger Congo family spoken in Senegal. I show that object experiencers in Sereer can be classified in two groups according to their syntactic behavior. In this study I provide evidence that Sereer experiencers can be used to extend Belletti and Rizzi's traditional classification of experiencers. Using data from Italian, Belletti and Rizzi have classified object experiencers in two groups. The first one they refer to as class II, has a nominative theme and an accusative experiencer whereas the second one, class III, has a nominative theme and a dative experiencer. In Sereer, like in Italian, different properties of object experiencers account for asymmetries noted with respect to constructions like passive, antipassive and nominalization.

1 Introduction

1.1 Language Background

Sereer-Siin (Sereer) is a West Atlantic language of the Niger Congo family spoken in Senegal. It is genetically related to Wolof and Pulaar (Simons & Fennig 2017). There are various dialects of Sereer. This variety, considered the standard, is spoken in the areas traditionally known as Siin and Saalum. The basic word order of Sereer is SVO. Sereer is an agglutinative language; this is exemplified in (1).

Khady Tamba. 2019. The Syntax of experiencers in Sereer-Siin. In Samson Lotven, Silvina Bongiovanni, Phillip Weirich, Robert Botne & Samuel Gyasi Obeng (eds.), *African linguistics across the disciplines: Selected papers from the 48th Annual Conference on African Linguistics*, 203–217. Berlin: Language Science Press. DOI:10.5281/zenodo.3520585

(1) a. o njaač onqe ɓog -u -ir -k -at -ir -an
        CL child CL_DEF wash -REF -INST -IPFV -IT -NEG -3OBJ
        'The child will not wash him/herself with this again'

     b. xa caač axe ɓog -u -ir -k -at -ir -an
        CL_PL child CL_DEF-PL wash -REF -INST -IPFV -IT -NEG -OBJ
        'The children will not wash him/herself with this again'

There are various studies dealing with the noun class system in Sereer (Fal 1980; Faye 1979; Faye 2013; Renaudier 2012); however there is no agreement about the number of noun classes found in Sereer. For instance, Faye (2013) argues that Sereer has nine noun classes, whereas for Fal (1980) and McLaughlin (1992), Sereer has thirteen noun classes. Table 1 from McLaughlin (1992: 284) gives a list of the different noun classes found in Sereer.

Table 1: Sereer noun classes

Class	Prefix	Clitic determiner	Class content
1	o-	oxe	human singular
2	ø-	we	human plural
3a	a-	ale	singular
3b	a-	ale	augmentative singular
4	a-	ake	plural
5	ø -	le	singular
6	ø-	ne	singular
7	ø -	fee	singular
8	fo-	ole	plural
9	ø-	ke	plural
10	o-	ole	singular
11	xa-	axe	plural

Indefiniteness is shown with the presence of a noun class marker (*prefix* in Table 1) before the noun whereas definiteness is shown through the presence of a prenominal and a postnominal class marker (*clitic determiner* in Table 1).

Consonant mutation is another important characteristic of Sereer. It is used to show subject-verb agreement with regard to number; it is also used for inflectional and derivational processes (see McLaughlin for a detailed analysis on consonant mutation in Sereer). Finally, in Sereer, object pronouns are suffixes incorporated to the noun (Baier 2018).

1.2 Experiencers in Sereer

There are different types of experiencers. An example of subject experiencer is shown in (2a) with the verb *bug* 'love'. Object experiencers are shown in (2b–d) with the verbs *diidlat* 'be scared', *bet* 'surprise' and *sooɓ* 'miss' respectively.

(2)   a. Subject Experiencer
            Faatu a   bug -a   Maamkoor
            Faatu 3SG love -PERF Maamkoor
            'Faatu loves Mamkoor'

        b. Object Experiencer
            Awa a   diid   -lat -a o fes   ole
            Awa 3SG be.scared -CAUS PERF CL young.man CL_{DEF}
            'Awa frightened the young man'

        c. Object Experiencer
            Faatu a   bet   -a   o njaac onqe
            Faatu 3SG surprise -PERF CL child CL_{DEF}
            'Faatu surprised the child'

        d. Object Experiencer
            o fes   ole   a sooɓ a   o tew   oxe
            CL young.man CL_{DEF} 3SG miss PERF CL woman CL_{DEF}
            'The woman misses the young man'

In (2b) the psych verb appears with a causative suffix whereas in (2c) and (2d) the verb does not bear any extra morphology. The rest of this paper is on object experiencers (2b–d).

2 Previous Studies

In their seminal work on experiencers, Belletti & Rizzi (1988) use Italian to posit three classes of experiencers. They are illustrated in (3) from Belletti & Rizzi (1988: 291–292).

(3)   Italian (Indo-European; Belletti & Rizzi 1988)

        a. Gianni teme questo
            'Gianni fears this'

        b. Questo preoccupa Gianni
            'This worries Gianni'

    c. A Gianni piace questo
       'Gianni pleases this'

    d. Questo piace a Gianni
       'This pleases to Gianni'

Belletti & Rizzi (B & R) make the claim that (3a) and (3b) are syntactically similar as they can both be related to transitive structures. Thus verbs like *temere* in (3a) belong to a class of experiencer verbs which have an experiencer as a subject and a theme as an object. In contrast, in (3b) with *preoccupare* type verbs, the experiencer is in object position whereas the theme is in subject position. Finally, in (3c) with experiencer verbs of the *piacere* class, the verb appears with a dative experiencer as a subject and a nominative theme, however these arguments of the verb can appear in a different order as shown in (3d).

In his study on the syntax of experiencers, Pesetsky (1995) puts aside the expression "theme" in B & R and argues for the following:

- Subject argument with object experiencers are always *Causer.*

- Object experiencers always have one of these roles: Target of Emotion or Subject Matter of Emotion.

Landau (2010: 3) builds on B & R and uses the three classes of experiencers to classify English experiencers.

- Class I: Nominative experiencer, accusative theme.
  John loves Mary.

- Class II: Nominative theme, accusative experiencer.
  The show amused Bill.

- Class III: Nominative theme, dative experiencer.
  The idea appealed to Julie.

Landau argues that experiencers are mental locations (locatives) and that universally "object experiencers behave like oblique arguments, whether their governing preposition is overt or not" Landau (2010: 127). He further makes the claim that in some languages object experiencers are overtly quirky and for that reason can occur in subject position.

Throughout this paper I use B & R's classification of Italian experiencers and adapt it to classify Sereer experiencers.

2.1 Classifying Sereer experiencers using B & R

In this section, I show that Sereer experiencer verbs come in three classes (adapted from B & R). Verbs in the first class come with a nominative experiencer and an accusative theme whereas the verbs in the second class appear with a nominative causer, accusative experiencer. Finally, the last class of experiencer verbs have a nominative theme and a dative experiencer. These different classes of experiencers are illustrated next.

2.1.1 Class I: Nominative experiencer, accusative theme

In this class, verbs like *bug* 'love' and *and* 'know' are found, they have the structure of a regular transitive verb.

(4)   a. Faatu a   bug -a   Maamkoor
           Faatu 3SG love -PERF Maamkoor
           'Faatu loves Mamkoor'

        b. o tew oxe a   and   a   Maamkoor
           CL lady CL_DEF 3SG know PERF Maamkoor
           'The lady knows Mamkoor'

In (4a) and (4b) the entity undergoing a psychological experience is in subject position. The next two classes describe object experiencers.

2.1.2 Class II: Nominative causer, accusative experiencer

These experiencer verbs come in two types. The first type must appear with a causative suffix whereas the second type does not occur with a causative suffix. Note that this is different from B & R's Class II. Even though they do not use "causer", my assumption is that a causer role is added to the subject of experiencer verbs of Class II. In (5a) and (5b) the verbs *diidlat* 'frighten' and *jaaxdat* 'worry' are used transitively and are morphological complex.

(5)   a. Awa a   diid   -lat -a   o fes   ole
           Awa 3SG be.scared -CAUS PERF CL young.man CL_DEF
           'Awa frightened the young man'

        b. Faatu a   jaax   -ɗat -a   o tew oxe
           Faatu 3SG be.worried -CAUS PERF CL lady CL_DEF
           'Faatu made the woman worried'

In (5a) and (5b), the experiencers are in object position. The other type of object experiencer in this class is shown in (6).

(6) a. Faatu a   bet   a   o njaac onqe
         Faatu 3SG surprise PERF CL child CL$_{DEF}$

         'Faatu suprised the child'

     b. Faatu a   weg   a   o tew oxe
         Faatu 3SG be.unlucky PERF CL lady CL$_{DEF}$

         'Faatu brought bad luck to the woman'

In (6a) and (6b) there is no overt causative suffix on the verb. My assumption is that there is a silent causative suffix. As will be show in §3 these verbs behave the same in some syntactic environments. Object experiencers, according to Pesetsky (1995), add an additional causer argument. In addition, the argument related to the "cause" must be realized as the subject (Grimshaw 1990).

Verbs of this class (Class II) behave like regular transitive verbs projecting a light verb headed by an overt or a silent causative.

2.1.3 Class III: Nominative theme, dative experiencer

Arguments of verbs of this class, shown in (7), appear in the same order as the ones of verbs of Class II described (6).

(7) a. o fes   ole   a   soo6 a   o tew   oxe
         CL young.man CL$_{DEF}$ 3SG miss PERF CL woman CL$_{DEF}$

         'the woman misses the young man'

     b. Awa a   fel   a   o njaac onqe
         Awa 3SG appeal PERF CL boy   CL$_{DET}$

         'Awa appeals to the boy'

In (7a) and (7b) the verbs do not have a causative component associated with them. These verbs have been argued to be stative/unaccusative. My assumption is that the object experiencers of these verbs are introduced by a silent preposition making them oblique. As will be shown, these objects behave like typical datives. The different classes of experiencers in Sereer are summarized in Table 2.

The remainder of this paper focuses on Class II and Class III experiencers by discussing syntactic differences between the two types of object experiencers that account for the classification in Table 2. More specifically, I show that they behave differently with respect to passivization, nominalization and antipassivization.

Table 2: Sereer experiencers

Class I	Nominative experiencer	Accusative theme
Class II	Nominative causer	Accusative experiencer
Class III	Nominative theme	Dative experiencer

3 Distinguishing between the two object experiencers in Sereer

3.1 Passivization test

In Sereer, passive is shown through the promoting of the verb internal argument to subject position whereas the external argument is demoted through suppression. Passive construction is marked through the use of the suffix -*el*[1] on the infinitive verb (Faye 1979; Renaudier 2012; Faye 2013), however, this suffix has various allomorphs conditioned by aspect, tense and/or negation.

(8) a. Awa a   ñaam a   maalo fe
        Awa 3SG eat   PERF rice   CL$_{DEF}$

        'Awa ate the rice'

     b. maalo fe   a   ñaam-e? (*Awa)
        rice   CL$_{DEF}$ 3SG eat-PASS Awa

        'the rice was eaten'

As seen in (8), with a regular transitive verb, the demoted external argument *Awa* cannot appear in passive constructions. Passivizing experiencer verbs yields different results according to the nature of the object.

Sereer Class II object experiencers can successfully undergo passivization. This is illustrated in (9) and (10) with the verbs *diidlat* 'frighten' and *bet* 'surprise'.

(9) a. Awa a   diid   -lat   a   o fes   ole
        Awa 3SG be.scared -CAUS PERF CL young.man CL$_{DEF}$

        'Awa frightened the young man'

     b. o fes   ole   a   diid   -lat   -e?
        CL young.man CL$_{DEF}$ 3SG be.scared -CAUS -PASS

        'The young man was frightened'

---

[1]This suffix is referred to in Faye & Mous (2006) as anticausative.

In (9b) derived from (9a) the object experiencer is promoted to subject position and the verb, which is morphologically complex, must appear with a passive morpheme. A similar situation can be observed in (10a–b) with the verb *bet* 'surprise' which is morphological simple. Note however that I mentioned earlier that this verb is semantically similar to *diidlat* 'frighten' as they both have the "cause" component.

(10)   a. Faatu a   bet   -a   o njaac onqe
          Faatu 3SG surprise PERF CL child CL_{DEF}
          'Faatu surprised the child'

       b. o njaac onqe a   bet   -e?
          CL child CL   3SG surprise -PASS
          'the child was surprised'

In (10) the verb behaves as expected since it allows passivization. The object experiencer can move to subject position along with a demotion of the original subject through suppression.

Next I show that Class III object experiencers cannot undergo passivization. This is illustrated in (11) with the verb *soob* 'miss'.

(11)   a. o fes   ole   a soob a   o tew   oxe
          CL young.man CL_{DEF} 3SG miss PERF CL woman CL_{DEF}
          'the woman misses the young man'

       b. * o tew   oxe   a soob -e?
            CL woman CL_{DEF} 3SG miss -PASS
          'The woman was missed' (intended)

(11b) shows that passive morphology is incompatible with verbs of this class, that is the object experiencers cannot be promoted to subject position. This is evidence that they are different from the ones in Class II. (12) follows a similar pattern with the verb *fel* 'appeal to'.

(12)   a. Awa a   fel   -a   o njaac onqe
          Awa 3SG appeal PERF CL child CL_{DEF}
          'Awa appeals to the boy'

       b. * o   njaac onqe -a fel   -e?
            CL chile CL_{DEF} 3SG appeal.to -PASS
          'The child was appealed to' (intended)

After this passivization test, I use another test which consists of nominalizing the clause containing an object experiencer.

3.2 Nominalization test

Grimshaw (1990) argues that nominalization and passivization are related in that in both cases the external argument is optional and as such, can be suppressed. Indeed in English, for instance, the external argument in such constructions is optional as (13) shows.

(13) a. The door was opened (by John)

  b. The opening of the door (by John)

These sentences show that in English the external argument can be suppressed in nominalization and passivization. In Sereer, a similar situation can be observed, however the suppression of the external argument in these constructions is mandatory as mentioned earlier with passsives. If these two constructions (i.e. passivization and nominalization) are related, one should expect to see results similar to the ones observed with the passivization test.

In Sereer, Class II experiencer verbs can successfully undergo nominalization as (14) shows.

(14) a. Awa a   diid   -lat -a   o fes   ole
      Awa 3SG be.scared -CAUS PERF CL young.man CL_{DEF}

      'Awa frightened the young man'

  b. Nominalization
      o diid   -lat ole   no o fes   ole
      CL be.scared -CAUS CL_{DEF} P CL young.man CL_{DEF}

      'The frightening of the young man'

In (14b) the nominal derived from (14a) appears with noun class markers. In addition, the internal argument of the verb, the object experiencer, is introduced by the preposition *no*. A similar pattern can be observed in (15) with the verb *bet* 'surprise'.

(15) a. Faatu a bet   -a   o njaac onqe
      Faatu 3SG surprise PERF CL child CL_{DEF}

      'Faatu surprised the child'

  b. Nominalization
      o bet   ole   no o njaac onqe
      CL surprise CL_{DEF} P CL child CL_{DEF}

      'the surprising of the child'

Just like in the previous example, in (15) the object experiencer appears in a prepositional phrase whereas the nominalized verb occur with nominalizers (i.e. noun class markers).

Class III experiencer verbs fail to undergo nominalization. This is illustrated in (16).

(16) a. Awa a sooɓ -a o tew   oxe
          Awa 3SG miss PERF CL woman CL_DEF

          'Awa misses the woman'

      b. *o sooɓ ole   no no tew   oxe
          CL miss CL_DEF P CL woman CL_DEF

          'The woman being missed' (intended)

In (16b), derived from (16a), nominalizing the verb results in ungrammaticality. This is expected since the verb does not assign accusative case to the object experiencer. A similar situation is can be noted in (17).

(17) a. Awa a fel   -a o tew   oxe
          Awa 3SG appeal.to PERF CL woman CL_DEF

          'Awa appeals to the woman'

      b. *o fel   ole   no no tew   oxe
          CL appeal.to CL_DEF P CL woman CL_DEF

          'The woman being appealed to' (intended)

In (17) the verb *fel* 'appeal to' cannot be nominalized as the ungrammaticality of (17b) shows. Surprisingly, if the passive morphology *-el* appears with a verb of this type (Class III) nominalization is possible as shown in (18).

(18) a. Awa a fel   a o   njaaƈ onqe
          Awa 3SG appeal PERF CL boy CL_DEF

          'Awa appeals to the boy'

      b. o pel   -el ole   no o njaaƈ onqe
          CL appeal -PASS CL_DEF P CL boy CL_DEF

          'The appealing to the young man' (intended)

      c. *o pel   ole   no o njaaƈ onqe
          CL appeal CL_DEF P CL boy CL_DEF

          'The young man being appealed to'

Faye (2013) argues that another use of the passive marker *-el* is to derive nominals from stative verbs. The behavior of Class III experiencer verbs with respect to nominalization shows that these verbs are different from the ones of Class II.

These types of experiencer verbs are superficially transitive but underlyingly unaccusative (Belletti & Rizzi 1988; Pesetsky 1995; Landau 2010).

In the next subsection, I use antipassivation to further distinguish between the two types of object experiencers.

3.3 Antipassivization test

The term "antipassive" is generally used to refer to a characteristic of voice in ergative languages (Crystal 2008). In antipassive constructions, the verb is semantically transitive but does not project a direct object (Polinsky 2017).

Polinsky further argues that crosslinguistically, antipassive can be diagnosed through case marking, noun incorporation, agreement, word order, verbal affixation. She also provides evidence that antipassive can be found in accusative languages (see also Heaton 2017).

In Sereer (Renaudier 2011), and related languages like Wolof (Creissels & Nouguier-Voisin 2008) antipassive is marked through verbal suffixation.

(19)   a.   o ɓox ole   a   ŋat -a   o njaac onqe
            CL dog CL$_{DEF}$ 3SG bite PERF CL boy   CL$_{DEF}$
            'The dog bit the boy'

       b.   o ɓox ole   kaa   ŋat -a   -a   (*o njaac onqe)
            CL dog CL$_{DEF}$ IPFV.3SG bite -ANTIP -PERF
            'The dog bit'

In Sereer, the suffix *-a* is used on the verb to mark the antipassive construction. The antipassive morpheme is very productive (not only related to verbs of transfer and ditransitives as argued in Renaudier).

With respect to experiencer verbs, different results are noticed according to the type of object being dealt with. Verbs belonging to Class II can undergo antipassivization, that is they can appear with the passive marker along with a suppression of the object experiencer. This is shown in (20) and in (21).

(20)   a.   Awa a   diid   -lat   a   o fes   ole
            Awa 3SG be.scared -CAUS PERF CL young.man CL$_{DEF}$
            'Awa frightened the young man'

b. Awa kaa   diid -lat   -a   -a

Awa IPFV.3SG be   scared -CAUS -ANTIP - PERF

'Awa frightened'

(21)   a. Faatu a   bet   -a o njaac̉ onqe

Faatu 3SG surprise PERF CL child CL$_{DEF}$

'Faatu surprised the child'

b. Faatu kaa   bet   -a   -a

Faatu IPFV.3SG surprise -ANTIP PERF

'Faatu surprised'

These examples show that experiencer verbs of Class II behave like regular transitive verbs in that they can undergo antipassivization. In both (20b) and in (21b) the object experiencer argument is suppressed.

Contrary to Class II verbs, verbs of Class III cannot occur with the antipassive marker -*a*.

(22)   a. Awa a   fel   -a o tew   oxe

Awa 3SG appeal PERF CL woman CL$_{DEF}$

'Awa appeals to the woman'

b. * Awa kaa   fel   -a   -a

Awa IPFV.3SG appeal -ANTIP -PERF

'Awa appealed to' (intended)

In (22b) the verb *fel* 'appeal to' appear with the antipassive marker and this yields ungrammaticality. The same situation can be observed in (23b).

(23)   a. *o njaac̉ onqe a   soob́ a   o tew   oxe*

CL boy   CL$_{DEF}$ 3SG miss PERF CL woman CL$_{DEF}$

'The woman misses the boy'

b. * o njaac̉ onqe kaa   soob́ -a

o njaac̉ CL$_{DEF}$ IPFV.3SG miss -antip

In this section I have used various tests (i.e. passivization, nominalization and antipassivization) to substantiate the claim that Sereer object experiencers come into two classes, Class II and Class III.

4 Conclusion

The main aim of this study was to describe object experiencers in Sereer in light of Belletti & Rizzi (1988). I have shown that they come in two types, Class II and Class III. Contrary to Landau (2010), I have shown that Class II object experiencers are not oblique and behave like regular transitive verbs. In contrast, Class III object experiencers are oblique and as such do not display typical object properties. It is my assumption that these objects are introduced by a silent preposition. This is in line with B & R's analysis of experiencers of this type as being assigned an inherent dative case. This study is not only a contribution to the literature of experiencers but is also a contribution to the study of argument structure in Sereer. Table 3, repeated from above, summarizes the different properties of the experiencer verbs found in Sereer.

Table 3: Sereer experiencers

Class I	Nominative experiencer	Accusative theme
Class II	Nominative causer	Accusative experiencer
Class III	Nominative theme	Dative experiencer

Abbreviations

ANTIP	antipassive	NEG	negation
CAUS	causative	PASS	passive marker
CL	noun class marker	P	preposition
CL$_{DEF}$	definite	PERF	perfective
FOC	focus	REF	reflexive
INST	instrument	3OBJ	third person object pronoun
IPFV	imperfective	3SG	third person singular
IT	iterative		

Acknowledgements

Special thanks to my consultant Dr Mamecor Faye for his patience and availability. I would also like to thank the following persons for their support: Pr Enoch Aboh (University of Amsterdam), Dr Mamadou Bassene (UCAD), Dr Kelly Berkson (Indiana University) and Pr Amadou Abdoul Sow (Dean of UCAD School and Arts and Humanities) for the financial support. Finally, I would like to thank two anonymous reviewers for their comments that helped improve the quality of this paper.

References

Ameka, Felix K. 1990. The grammatical packaging of experiencers in Ewe: A study in the semantics of syntax. *Australian Journal of Linguistics* 10(2). 139–181.

Baier, Nico. 2018. Object suffixes as incorporated pronouns in Seereer. In Jason Kandybowicz, Travis Major, Harold Torrence & Philip T. Duncan (eds.), *African linguistics on the prairie: Selected papers from the 45th Annual Conference on African Linguistics*, 253–268. Berlin: Language Science Press. DOI:10.5281/zenodo.1251738

Belletti, Adriana & Luigi Rizzi. 1988. Psych-verbs and θ-theory. *Natural Language & Linguistic Theory* 6(3). 291–352.

Creissels, Denis & Sylvie Nouguier-Voisin. 2008. The verbal suffixes of Wolof coding valency changes and the notion of coparticipation. In Ekkehard König & Volker Gast (eds.), *Reciprocals and reflexives: Theoretical and typological explorations*, vol. 192, 289–306. Berlin, Germany: Walter de Gruyter.

Crystal, David. 2008. *A dictionary of linguistics and phonetics*. 6th edn. Maldan, MA, USA: Blackwell Publishing.

Fal, Arame. 1980. *Les nominaux en sereer-siin: Parler de Jaxaw*. Dakar: Les Nouvelles Editions Africaines.

Faye, Souleymane. 2013. *Grammaire dialectale du seereer*. Bruxelles: La maison du livre universel (ELU).

Faye, Souleymane & Maarten Mous. 2006. Verbal system and diathesis derivations in Seereer. *Africana Linguistica* 12. 89–112. DOI:10.3406/aflin.2006.963

Faye, Waly Coly. 1979. *Etude morphosyntaxique du sereer singandum (région de Jaxaaw-Ñaaxar), thèse de 3ème cycle*. Dakar: Université Cheikh Anta Diop.

Grimshaw, Jane. 1990. *Argument structure*. Cambridge: MIT press.

Heaton, Raina. 2017. *A typology of antipassives, with special reference to Mayan*. Honolulu: University of Hawai at Manoa dissertation.

Landau, Idan. 2010. The explicit syntax of implicit arguments. *Linguistic Inquiry* 41. 357–388.

McLaughlin, Fiona. 1992. Consonant mutation in Sereer-Siin. *Studies in African Linguistics* 23(3). 279–313.

Pesetsky, David. 1995. *Zero syntax experiencers and cascades*. Cambridge: MIT Press.

Polinsky, Maria. 2017. Antipassive. In Jessica Coon, Diane Massam & Lisa de-Mena Travis (eds.), *The Oxford handbook of ergativity*, 1–27. Oxford: Oxford University Press.

Renaudier, Marie. 2011. The antipassive in accusative languages: The case of Sereer (senegal, atlantic). Université Lyon 2 – Dynamique du Language.

Renaudier, Marie. 2012. *Dérivation et valence en sereer variété de Mar Lodj (Sénégal)*. Université Lyon 2 dissertation.

Simons, Gary F. & Charles D. Fennig (eds.). 2017. *Ethnologue: Languages of the world*. 20th edn. SIL International.

Chapter 12

Focus in Limbum

Laura Becker
Leipzig University

Imke Driemel
Leipzig University

Jude Nformi Awasom
Leipzig University

In this paper, we discuss the realization of focus in Limbum (Grassfields Bantu, Cameroon), a language which shows a so-far unattested pattern of focus marking, where two distinct focus constructions are realized by two different particles, *á* and *bá*, which express information focus on the one hand and contrastive focus on the other. Strikingly, the former is realized by a structurally more complex construction (particle + fronting) – the inverse pattern of what is attested cross-linguistically (Fiedler et al. 2010; Skopeteas & Fanselow 2009). A biclausal cleft structure underlying the *á* strategy can be argued to be implausible. Instead, we adopt a Q/F particle analysis (Cable 2010) which proposes the existence of a particle independent of a higher functional head mediating between that head and the focused phrase. Limbum provides overt evidence for both, the head and the particle.

1 Introduction

The present paper discusses two focus strategies in Limbum (Grassfields Bantu, Cameroon) that can be distinguished on the basis of different focus markers and the types of focus they convey. The constructions and their respective focus markers are shown in (1)[1] below.

---

[1]Translations are modeled after the interpretations the focus strategies come with. Small capitals, as in (1a), signals pitch accent, an intonation strategy English makes use of. A cleft structure is chosen as a translation if the sentence conveys an exhaustive meaning, see (1b).

Laura Becker, Imke Driemel & Jude Nformi Awasom. 2019. Focus in Limbum. In Samson Lotven, Silvina Bongiovanni, Phillip Weirich, Robert Botne & Samuel Gyasi Obeng (eds.), *African linguistics across the disciplines: Selected papers from the 48th Annual Conference on African Linguistics*, 219–237. Berlin: Language Science Press. DOI:10.5281/zenodo.3520587

(1) a. á   Nfor (cí)   mè bí   tū
         FOC Nfor COMP 1SG FUT1 send

     'I will send NFOR.'

     b. mè bí   tū   bá Nfor
         1SG FUT1 send FOC Nfor

     'It is Nfor whom I will send.'[2]

The sentence in (1a) shows the focus marker *á*, consistently followed by the fronted constituent that is focused, in turn followed by an optional element, which we label *complementizer* for now. Note that this element occurs exclusively with this type of focus construction, which we will address in more detail in §3.2. The second strategy, shown in (1b), involves the marker *bá*, which consistently occurs left adjacent to the focused constituent.

We will show that the *á* construction, although appearing similar to cleft constructions, does not mark contrastive/exhaustive focus, but rather information focus.[3] For exhaustive focus, only the *bá* strategy is felicitous.[4] This is rather surprising, since the structurally more complex construction with *á* and fronting of the focused constituent is used to convey the "simpler" kind of focus, i.e. focus without any additional semantic or pragmatic restrictions. This goes against the trend of focus marking observable cross-linguistically, where information focus is expressed with a canonical focus structure and contrastive focus with a relatively more marked structure (Zimmermann 2011). §2 briefly discusses semantic evidence for the focus constructions to necessarily express different types of focus. In §3, we turn to the syntactic analysis of the *á* strategy where we argue against an underlying cleft structure and eventually adopt a feature-driven focus movement analysis along the lines of Cable (2010).

2 Focus in Limbum: Interpretation

Before we turn to the two constructions at stake, this section provides a brief overview of focus in general. Following Zimmermann & Féry (2010: 2), focus is

---

[2] All Limbum data in this paper are our own. They are based on the judgement of two native speakers of Limbum from Nkambe.

[3] Note that Limbum also has the option of leaving focus completely unmarked. This strategy mostly patterns with *á*. The *á* strategy, however, imposes an existence assumption (Dryer 1996) on the context which is not required in the absence of a focus marking particle. For reasons of space, we cannot go into detail here, but see Driemel & Nformi (2018a).

[4] While *bá* necessarily expresses exhaustivity, it is not the only strategy Limbum offers to express such a type of focus. Example (17) presents a cleft structure which is also able to trigger an exhaustive interpretation.

"a classical semantic notion expressing that a focused linguistic constituent is selected from a set of alternatives", i.e. focus marks the presence of alternatives (Rooth 1992; Krifka 2008). Focus is generally said to be involved in question-answer congruence, correction, and the marking of contrast, among other contexts.

The literature often distinguishes two main types, namely information focus and contrastive focus. The former signals the presence of contextual alternatives and often introduces new information. Therefore, we will use question-answer pairs to test for information focus. The latter type of focus comprises a number of subtypes, all of which add semantic and/or pragmatic conditions on the alternatives laid out by the presence of focus. In this paper, we will consider:[5]

Information focus: marks the presence of alternatives

(2) Who$_F$ stole the cookie?
[PEter]$_F$ stole the cookie.

Contrast: an explicit alternative is present; often within the same utterance

(3) An [AMErican]$_F$ farmer talked to a [CaNAdian]$_F$ farmer.

Correction: an explicit alternative from a previous utterance is rejected by giving a new explicit alternative

(4) [PEter]$_F$ stole the cookie.
No, [MAry]$_F$ did it.

Exhaustivity: one (set of) alternative(s) is selected; all non-selected alternatives are false (Szabolcsi 1981; Kiss 1998; Vallduví & Vilkuna 1998; Horvath 2010; 2013), e.g.

(5) Hungarian
Anikó a templomba ment be, (máshová nem ment be).
Anikó the church.into went in.PRV elsewhere not went in.PRV
'It was the CHURCH that Anikó entered (and nowhere else).'

---

[5]For reasons of brevity, we cannot discuss all possible types with respect to the focus strategies in Limbum in the present paper. To just name a few other important types, *selection* features an explicit set of alternatives, from which one or more alternatives can be chosen; *exclusivity* has one (set of) alternative(s) selected, where at least one of the non-selected (set of) alternative(s) is false (van der Wal 2011; 2014), or only stronger alternatives on some scale are false (Beaver & Clark 2008; Coppock & Beaver 2012); *unexpectedness* involves the selected alternative to stand out (Zimmermann 2008; 2011; Hartmann 2008; Skopeteas & Fanselow 2009; 2011; Frey 2010; Zimmermann 2011; Destruel & Velleman 2014).

In this section, we will look at three context tests that show how the two focus markers are felicitous in different contexts in Limbum. Then, we will address exhaustivity in more detail and provide evidence for *bá* involving exhaustivity, while *á* does not.

New information can be modeled with the help of an inquisitive context. Imagine the following scenario:

(6) *Context:* A and B are talking on the phone, the connection is really bad. A was telling B that she was going to meet someone, but B could not understand the person's name. B asks A to repeat whom she is going to meet.

> A: á Ngàlá (cí) mè bí kɔ̄nī
> FOC Ngala COMP 1SG FUT1 meet
>
> 'I will meet NGALA.'

> A′: # mè bí kɔnī bá Ngàlá
> 1SG FUT1 meet FOC Ngala
>
> 'It is Ngala whom I will meet.'

In such a context, A can clarify who she is going to meet with the *á* marker, but not use *bá*. The latter, as will be shown in (7) and (8), requires an additional contrastive component.

Corrective contexts require an utterance with an explicit alternative, which is followed by another alternative in a second utterance, automatically canceling the first one. In such contexts, the *bá* strategy is obligatory:

(7) *Context:* A bought a pair of shoes. B does not remember correctly and tells someone that A bought a dress. A corrects B saying that she bought shoes (instead).

> B: í bá yū cɛ̀?
> 3SG PST2 buy dress
>
> 'She bought a dress.'

> A: # á blábáʔ (cí) mè bā yú
> FOC shoes COMP 1SG PST2 buy
>
> 'I bought SHOES.'

> A′: mè bā yū bá blábáʔ
> 1SG PST2 buy FOC shoes
>
> 'It is shoes that I bought.'

In order to correct B's statement, example (7) shows that *bá* now becomes licit, while *á* cannot be used to mark focus any longer in the presence of correction.

A similar effect can be observed with the expression of contrast. Again, only *bá* is felicitous for contrasting two arguments, *á* being not acceptable in this context.

(8)   a.   Tánkó kí   nɔ̄   mndzīp, Ngàlá cí   nɔ̄   bá blēē
            Tanko HAB drink water   Ngala but drink FOC blood

            'Tanko drinks water but it is blood that Ngala drinks.'

     b.   * Tánkó kí   nɔ̄   mndzīp, á   blēē   cí   Ngàlá nɔ̄
            Tanko HAB drink water   FOC blood but Ngala drink

            'Tanko drinks water but Ngala drinks BLOOD.'

To test for exhaustivity, we will apply tests that have been proposed by Kiss (1998): combining exhaustively focused constituents with *also* or universal quantifiers is infelicitous since they both semantically contradict exhaustivity. As examples (9B)[6] and (10B) show for the subject and object, respectively, the *á* strategy is able to occur with *also* scoping over the constituent in focus. The marker *bá*, on the other hand, does not allow for focused constituents including an *also* phrase, see (9B′)[7] and (10B′). This behaviour is consistent with contrast and correction scenarios, given in (8) and (7), i.e. contexts that involve exhaustivity.

(9)   A: Nfò à   mū yū rkār.
           Nfor 3SG PST2 buy car

           'Nfor bought a car.'

     B: á   Ngàlá fɔ́ŋ à   mū yū rkār.
           FOC Ngala also 3SG PST2 buy car

           'NGALA bought a car, too.'

     B′:   # à   mū yū bá Ngàlá rkā fɔ́ŋ.
           EXPL PST2 buy FOC Ngala car also

           'It was also Ngala who bought a car.'

---

[6]While *í* encodes a 3SG pronoun, both *à* and *í* seem to function as 3SG subject markers, i.e. they can optionally co-occur with NP subjects. 3SG pronoun *í* can be seen in (7B), (10B-B′), and (21a). 3SG subject markers are realized either as *à*, see (9A-B), (10A), (14a), (16), (17), and (31), or as *í*, see (13a), (18), and (19).

[7]As can be observed in (9), subject focus comes with an additional restriction for *bá* focused constituents, in that they can only occur postverbally. Glossing *à* as EXPL is only one option and might not be the most convincing one, since typical expressions involving expletives such as weather verbs, locative inversions, or existential constructions do not occur with *à*. An alternative is to analyze *à* as a default marker since it is identical to the 3SG subject marker.

(10) A: Nfò à mū yū rkār.
          Nfor 3SG PST2 buy car

          'Nfor bought a car.'

      B: á ntùmntùm fɔ́ŋ í mū yú.
          FOC motorbike also 3SG PST2 buy

          'He bought a MOTORBIKE, too.'

      B′: #í mū yū bá ntùmntùm fɔ́ŋ.
          3SG PST2 buy FOC motorbike also

          'It was also a motorbike he bought.'

Using a universal quantifier inside of the focused constituent, we get the same effect: the universal quantifier is incompatible with exhaustivity because it inherently makes reference to all alternatives from a set, whereas exhaustivity entails that some alternative is selected from the set, excluding others. Again, examples (11) and (12) illustrate for focused subjects and objects that *á*, as predicted, is compatible with universal quantifiers, while *bá* is not:

(11) a. á ŋwὲ nsìp (cí) à bā zhē bāā   subject focus
          FOC person all   COMP 3SG PST1 eat fufu

          'EVERYBODY ate fufu.'

      b. *à bā zhē bá ŋwὲ nsìp bāā
          EXPL PST1 eat FOC person all   fufu

          'It is everybody who ate fufu.'

(12) a. á ŋwὲ nsìp (cí)   mὲ bí kɔ̄nī   object focus
          FOC person all (COMP) I FUT1 meet

          'I will meet EVERYBODY.'

      b. *mὲ bí kɔnī bá ŋwὲ nsìp
          I FUT1 meet FOC person all

          'It is everybody that I will meet.'

3 The syntax of *á*

Focused constituents that are preceded by the focus marker *á* have to occur clause-initially. They can be followed by what we have so far glossed as the complementizer *cí*.

(13)   a.   á   Nfò (cí)   í   bā   zhē bāā   subject focus
           FOC Nfor COMP 3SG PST1 eat fufu

           'NFOR ate fufu.'

       b.   á   Ngàlá (cí)   mè bí   kōnī   object focus
           FOC Ngala COMP 1SG FUT1 meet

           'I will meet NGALA.'

       c.   á   àyàŋsè   (cí)   sì   bífū yέ Shey   adverbial focus
           FOC tomorrow COMP 1PL.INCL FUT2 see Shey

           'We will see Shey TOMORROW.'

Similar to many West African languages (Koopman 1984; Ameka 1992; Manfredi 1997; Biloa 1997; Aboh 1998; 2006), verb focus in Limbum is realized by doubling of the verb. Note that the higher copy of the verb differs from the lower copy in that it is prefixed with a noun class marker.[8]

(14)   Verb focus:[9]

       a.   á   r-gwè (cí)   ndāp fɔ̄   à   Ø   gwè   intransitive
           FOC 5-fall COMP house DET 3SG PERF fall

           'The house FELL.'

       b.   á   r-yū (cí)   njíŋwè fɔ̄ bí   yú msāŋ   transitive
           FOC 5-buy COMP woman DET FUT1 buy rice

           'The woman will BUY rice.'

3.1 Against a biclausal structure

As was shown in the previous section, the *á* strategy contrasts with the *bá* strategy in that it is compatible with non-exhaustive contexts. This provides our first argument against an underlying biclausal cleft structure, as those are typically found with an exhaustive meaning component (Horn 1981; Percus 1997). In this section, we provide three syntactic arguments against a cleft structure.

Based on sentences like (15) in which *á* seems to act like a copula, Fransen (1995: 301) concludes that the high focus marker strategy constitutes a cleft.

---

[8]Nouns which are formed from verbs via prefixing of the noun class 5 marker *r-* are generally the gerundive form of the verb (Nformi 2017). In such derivations, the tone of the noun class prefix lowers the tone of the verb root if it is a H tone verb (14b). The infinitive form of the verb in the language also looks similar to the gerundive but differs in that it has the infinitive marker *à*.

[9]This focus construction cannot be used to express TAM focus. It can, however, express VERUM focus.

(15) á rtēē
      ? palm.tree
      'It is a palm tree.'

An alternative analysis of (15) takes copulas to be silent while *á* acts as a focus particle. This idea predicts copulas to show up as soon as they have to act as hosts for negation and/or tense affixes. Adding an overt tense marker to *á* is ungrammatical, see (16). As predicted, the only way to save the structure is by using a copula and an expletive, see (17).

(16) (*mū) á   (*mū) bāā (cí)   Nfò à   bā   zhē
      PST2   FOC PST2   fufu COMP Nfor 3SG PST1 eat
      'Nfor ate FUFU.'

(17) à   mū   bā   bāā Nfò à   mū   zhē
      EXPL PST2 COP fufu Nfor 3SG PST2 eat
      'It was a fufu that Nfor ate.'

Our second and third argument concern the cleft clause. *Extraposition* (Akmajian 1970; Gundel 1977; Percus 1997) as well as *predicative approaches* (Svenious 1998; Hedberg 2000; Reeve 2011) uncontroversially take cleft clauses to be embedded relative clauses. In Limbum, there is ample reason to doubt the existence of a relative clause in an *á* construction. While the complementizer *cí* is optionally spelled out following the focused constituent, it cannot, however, act as a relative pronoun.

(18) mū   zhǐ / *cí   í   mū   zhéé mŋgɔ̀mbé
      child REL / COMP 3SG PST2 eat   plantains
      'the child who ate plantains'

Furthermore, relative clauses can optionally co-occur with the right-headed demonstrative marker *nà* (Fransen 1995; Mpoche 1993), shown in (19). Crucially, the demonstrative is prohibited in the *á* strategy, see (20).

(19) mū   zhǐ í   mū   zhéé mŋgɔ̀mbé (nà)
      child REL 3SG PST2 eat   plantains DEM
      'the child who ate plantains'

(20) á   ŋkfúú (cí)   mè   bí   kɔ̄nī (*nà)
      FOC chief COMP 1SG FUT1 meet   DEM
      'I will meet the CHIEF.'

To sum up, a biclausal cleft structure requires a copula and and a relative clause, neither of which seems to be present in the *á* construction.

3.2 Focus movement analysis

In line with what has been argued for question particles in Japanese (Hagstrom 1998), Sinhala (Kishimoto 2005), and Tlingit (Cable 2010) on the one hand and focus fronting in Hungarian (Horvath 2007; 2010; 2013) on the other, we propose that the focus particle *á* merges with a constituent that is focused (or at least contains a constituent that is focused). The particle heads its own projection FP and bears an •F• feature. This feature projects up to FP enabling the contained constituent to be focused. A higher functional head, optionally spelled out as *cí*, probes for the feature, finds it on FP and, as a consequence, attracts FP (and everything contained in it) to its specifier, see Figure 1.[10]

The alternative proposal in which *á* itself spells out the focus head and attracts the focused constituent to its specifier, sketched in (21b), can be refuted based on the linear order of the structures: *á* would be predicted to follow the focused constituent, contrary to fact. An ad-hoc movement step of *á* to a higher (possibly) C or Force head is ruled out based on the behaviour of focused constituents in embedded clauses.

(21) a. í   bā lá nè   á   rkár fɔ́ (cí)   ndū   zhì à m̀ yú
          3SG PST1 say COMP FOC car DET COMP husband her 3SG PST3 buy
          'She said that her husband bought the CAR.'

   b. * ...[$_{VP}$ [$_V$ lá][$_{CP}$ [$_C$ nḛ̀] [$_{FocP}$ rkár fɔ́ [$_{Foc}$ á] [$_{FinP}$ [$_{Fin}$ cí]]]]]
       '------- ✗ -------'

The complementizer *nè* would block movement of *á* to C, nevertheless *á* precedes the focused constituent. Hence, we assume the left periphery of the embedded clause in (21a) to be composed as shown in Figure 1.

Support for the FP analysis comes from the fact that *cí* can only occur in clauses realizing the *á* strategy. Thus, *cí* seems to be tied to the presence of *á* focus. Under the account, presented in (21b), this obligatory co-occurrence would be a coincidence. Limbum, therefore, is strikingly different from Japanese, Sinhala, Tlingit,

---

[10]The exact nature of feature *F* and *FocP* and how they differ from focus on the contained constituents that needs to be interpreted is not entirely worked out in this paper. Based on the claim in footnote 3, it is possible to reanalyze *F* and *FocP* as triggers for movement that have a semantic impact, in the spirit of Horvath (2007; 2013). This analyzes will have consequences for the information focus status of the *á* strategy and its relation to contrastive focus, both of which are explored in Driemel & Nformi (2018a,b).

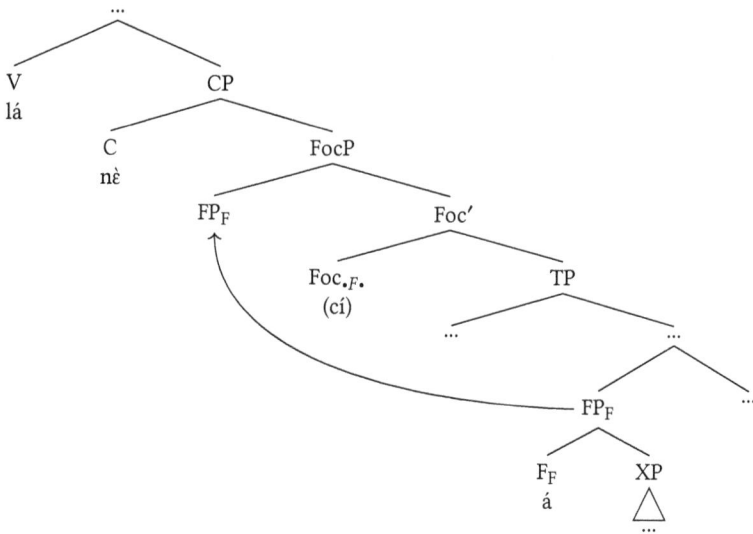

Figure 1: Focus movement of FP

and Hungarian in that it provides overt evidence for both the locally merged particle as well as the higher functional head which causes overt movement. The functional head must be different from C, since an additional complementizer can co-occur with *cí*, as (21a) shows. Moreover, *cí* can never act as a complementizer on its own, it is dependent on the occurrence of *á*.

Limbum patterns with Tlingit, in that the particle takes the focused phrase as a complement rather than adjoining to it. FP as a projection of F bears the F-feature probed for by the Foc head. Since FP properly contains the focused phrase, the entire FP is expected to move to spec,FP, including possibly non-focused material. In other words, focus movement is predicted to pied-pipe. (22) shows the inability of possessors to be extracted by themselves, they obligatorily have to pied-pipe the possessum.

(22) *Context:* A heard B telling someone on the phone that B would pick up someone's brother from the bus station. A couldn't properly understand whose brother B will pick up.

   A: á   ndúr   ndā (cí)   à   bí   lɔ̀rī
       FOC brother who COMP 2SG FUT1 pick.up
       'Whose brother will you pick up?'

B: á ndúr Tánkó (cí) mὲ bí lɔ̀rī
FOC brother Tanko COMP 1SG FUT1 pick.up

'I will pick up TANKO's brother.'

B′: *á Tánkó (cí) mὲ bí lɔ̀rī ndúr
FOC Tanko COMP 1SG FUT1 pick.up brother

'I will pick up TANKO's brother.'

An alternative account like the one shown in (21b) cannot predict pied-piping without assuming further constraints on movement. Whichever phrase is focused, and thus bears an F feature, would be predicted to move to spec,FocP, see (23) for an illustration.

(23) * [... á$_1$ [$_{FocP}$ [$_{DP}$ Tánkó$_F$]$_2$ [$_{Foc}$ t$_1$] [$_{TP}$ ... [$_{DP}$ [$_{D'}$ [$_{NP}$ ndúr] Ø$_D$] t$_2$]...]]

In the current analysis the FP is the closest goal the Foc head sees. It is therefore the entire FP that gets attracted to the specifier of FocP, making it impossible for a focused phrase contained in an FP to move to spec,FocP on its own, see (24).

(24) [$_{FocP}$ [$_{Foc}$ cí] [$_{TP}$ ... [$_{FP}$ á [$_{DP}$ [$_{D'}$ [$_{NP}$ ndúr] Ø$_D$] Tánkó$_F$]]...]]

Extractions of the type shown in (23) can potentially be ruled out by general constraints on movement since they seem to be marked cross-linguistically (Corver 1990; Bošković 2005). We would like to point out, however, that possessor extraction is not banned per se, since it is allowed in topic configurations, shown in (25a), albeit with a resumptive pronoun. A base-generation approach seems implausible since topicalization is less acceptable out of islands, shown e.g. in (25b) for a complex noun phrase.

(25) a. à mbò Tanko, mὲ mū yὲ̄ nfɨ̀ zhɨ̀
as for Tanko 1SG PST2 see brother his

'As for Tanko, I met his brother.'

b. ?à mbò Tanko, mὲ rìŋ ŋwe zhɨ̀ mū kɔ́ní nfɨ̀ zhɨ̀
as for Tanko 1SG know man REL PST2 meet brother his

'As for Tanko, I know a man who met his brother.'

Since the possessor can, in principle, move out of the DP it is contained in, we conclude that it must be the focus particle á merged with the entire DP that prevents the possessor from moving to spec,FocP alone.

Another environment in which we can observe the pied-piping property of focus movement concerns prepositional phrases, shown in (26). Prepositions cannot be stranded if the phrase they merge with is narrowly focused.

(26) *Context:* A heard B telling someone on the phone that B shot an animal with something but it is not clear to A with what.

> A: á nɨ kɛ̄ (cí) wè mū tā nyà à?
> FOC with what COMP 2SG PST2 shoot animal Q
>
> 'With what did you shoot the animal?'
>
> B: á nɨ ŋgār (cí) mè mū tā nyà
> FOC with gun COMP 1SG PST2 shoot animal
>
> 'I shot the animal with a GUN.'
>
> B': *á ŋgār (cí) mè mū tā nyà nɨ
> FOC gun COMP 1SG PST2 shoot animal with
>
> 'I shot the animal with a GUN.'

Similar to the possessor case, the alternative account in which the focus particle *á* spells out the FOC head would predict the complement of P to be attractable to spec,FocP, in case it is the constituent that carries the F feature.

(27) *[... á₁ [FocP [DP ŋgār_F]₂ [Foc t₁] [TP ... [PP [p nɨ] t₂]...]]

In contrast, the FP analysis predicts FP to be the goal that checks the F feature on the FOC head. Hence, the entire PP has to move to spec, FocP.

(28) [FocP [Foc cí] [TP ... [FP á [PP [p nɨ] ŋgār_F]...]]

Again, conditions on preposition stranding can be independently motivated, since this kind of movement seems to be banned in a number of languages (Abels 2003; Heck 2008). The FP analysis, however, offers an explanation for the lack of preposition stranding and possessor extraction simultaneously.

At this point, it is important to answer the question why the focus particle cannot merge directly with the narrowly focused constituent in (24) and (28). Here we follow Cable (2010) by adopting the *QP-Intervention Condition* reformulated for FPs.

(29) *FP-Intervention Condition:* (adapted from Cable 2010: 57)
An FP cannot intervene between a functional head α and a phrase selected by α. (Such an intervening FP blocks the selectional relation between α and the lower phrase.)

By assumption, functional heads *c-select* for their arguments, while lexical heads *s-select* for their arguments (Cable 2010: 62). An FP can intervene between a lexical head and the phrase selected by that head because the F particle does not change the semantic type of the phrase it merges with. An FP cannot, however, intervene between a functional head and the phrase it selects for since the F particle indeed changes the category of the phrase it merges with. Hence, *á* cannot merge with the embedded XP of a prepositional phrase because it would intervene between the functional head P and XP. Neither can *á* directly merge with a possessor because the functional element D c-selects its possessor and *á* would act as an intervener.

Further support for (29) comes from VP-fronting, here analyzed as remnant *v*P-fronting. If *á* were to take *v*P as its complement, the particle would intervene between *v*P and the higher functional head T. As a consequence, VPs cannot (per se)[11] be focused with the *á* strategy.

(30) A: á   kɛ̄   (cí)   njíŋwɛ̀ fɔ́   bí   à
FOC what COMP woman DET FUT1 Q
'What will the woman do?'

B: *á   (r-)yū msāŋ (cí)   njíŋwɛ̀ fɔ́ bí
FOC 5-buy rice COMP woman DET FUT1
'The woman will BUY RICE.'

While the ban on P-stranding and possessor extraction might be reducible to the interplay of the *PIC* (Chomsky 2000) and *Anti-locality* (Abels 2003; Erlewine 2016), this crucially does not apply to the lack of VP fronting because TPs are uncontroversially denied phasehood status. The impossibility to front a VP in (30), thus, requires an independent explanation. In contrast, the FP analysis can capture all three properties of the *á* strategy.

---

[11]There is, however, a way to repair the structure using do-support:

(i) á   r-yū msāŋ (cí)   njíŋwɛ̀ fɔ́ bí   gī
FOC 5-buy rice COMP woman DET FUT1 do
'The woman will BUY RICE.'

At this point, it is unclear to us why do-support is able to save the construction.

Finally, a note on verb focus is in order. As (14a) and (14b) show, verb focus requires doubling on the one hand and a noun class marker prefixing the higher copy on the other hand. The latter suggests that the focus particle *á* c-selects for nominal phrases, so that verbs have to be nominalized in order to be merged with *á*. The behaviour of the focus particle is not unusual for Limbum since coordinators seem to make the same kind of distinction. As (31) shows, the choice of coordinator correlates with the categories of the conjuncts.[12]

(31)   a.   Shey à   mū ró   Njobe b<u>á</u> Shey
          Shey 3SG PST2 search Njobe and Shey

          'Shey searched for Njobe and Shey.'

    b.   Shey à   mū ró   Njobe mà ntāā   <u>bá</u> kò là?
          Shey 3SG PST2 search Njobe at   market and at   home

          'Shey searched for Njobe at the market and at home.'

    c.   Shey à   mū cāŋ <u>á</u>   gwè
          Shey 3SG PST2 run and fall

          'Shey ran and fell.'

Since categorical sensitivity shows up elsewhere in the language, we tentatively conclude that the noun class prefix in verb focus constructions is due to a selectional restriction of *á*. Attaching a noun class prefix to one of the copies could potentially serve as a reason for multiple spell out, i.e. doubling. A detailed analysis, however, is still missing and left for future research.

4 Summary and future work

In this paper, we have shown that the two focus strategies in Limbum, involving two different markers, also clearly differ in their functions: the marker *á* is linked to information focus (i.e. focus with no further semantic/pragmatic conditions), while *bá* occurs in contexts that involve contrast and exhaustivity. The interpretation effects that the *á* strategy triggers are compatible with the syntactic analysis: the lack of tense marking on copulas, the behaviour of the complementizer *cí*, and the ban on right peripheral demonstrative markers provide evidence against an underlying cleft structure. The current proposal, therefore, models *á* focus as focus movement, where the focus particle is directly merged

---

[12]Limbum shows a great deal of homophony (compare also the use of *cí* as a sentence coordinator in (8) vs. the general use of *cí* with respect to focused *á* phrases), which could account for the fact that *á* and *bá* can act as coordinators as well as focus particles. Alternatively, coordinators and focus particles could also be related diachronically. This issue must be left open for now.

with the focused phrase and attracted to the left periphery by a higher functional head, pied-piping the focused constituent. While this type of analysis has been proposed for other languages (Hagstrom 1998; Cable 2010), albeit for questions, Limbum crucially provides morphological evidence for the existence of a particle (*â*) as well as the higher functional head (*cí*).

Even though a cleft analysis is ruled out, the Limbum patterns, shown in this paper, nevertheless present a so-far unattested opposition of focus strategies: information focus, being less marked semantically, is expressed by a complex strategy consisting of a particle and fronting, whereas contrastive/exhaustive focus, although imposing additional semantic restrictions on the focus alternatives, is realized by a particle only. The reasons why Limbum shows the reverse picture in terms of structural markedness and complexity of interpretation need to be explored further in future work.[13]

One last point concerns the syntax of *bá*. In contrast to the *á* strategy, the *bá* construction does not seem to provide overt evidence for the existence of a higher functional head. The behaviour of focused subjects, however, indicates certain positional restrictions a focused phrase has to obey. Future work will explore whether the FP analysis can be extended to the *bá* strategy.

Acknowledgements

We would like to thank the audience at ACAL 48, Indiana University, and two anonymous reviewers for helpful comments.

Abbreviations

1,2,3	1st, 2nd, 3rd person	PL	Plural
1-,2-,5-,	Noun classes	PREP	Preposition
COMP	Complementizer	PRV	Preverb
COP	Copula	PST1	Recent past tense
DET	Determiner	PST2	Distant past tense
DEM	Demonstrative	PST3	Remote past tense
EXPL	Expletive	REL	Relative pronoun
FOC	Focus marker	SG	Singular
FUT1	Near future tense	´	High tone
HAB	Habitual	`	Low tone
INCL	Inclusive	‾	Mid tone
PERF	Perfective		

---

[13]Although see Driemel & Nformi (2018a) for a possible explanation.

References

Abels, Klaus. 2003. *Successive cyclicity, anti-locality and adposition stranding.* University of Connecticut dissertation.

Aboh, Enoch Oladé. 1998. Focus constructions and the focus criterion in Gungbe. *Linguistique Africaine* 20. 5–50.

Aboh, Enoch Oladé. 2006. When verbal predicates go fronting. In Ines Fiedler & Anne Schwarz (eds.), *Papers on information structure in African languages,* vol. 46 (ZAS Papers in Linguistics), 21–48. Berlin: ZAS.

Akmajian, Adrian. 1970. On deriving cleft sentences from pseudo-cleft sentences. *Linguistic Inquiry* 1. 149–168.

Ameka, Felix K. 1992. Focus Constructions in Ewe and Akan. In Chris Collins & Victor Manfredi (eds.), *Proceedings of the Kwa Comparative Syntax Workshop,* vol. 17 (MIT Working Papers in Linguistics), 1–25. Cambridge: MIT Press.

Beaver, David & Brady Clark. 2008. *Sense and sensitivity: How focus determines meaning* (Explorations in Semantics). Oxford: Wiley-Blackwell.

Biloa, Edmond. 1997. *Functional categories and the syntax of focus in Tuki* (Lincom Studies in African Linguistics 2). Newcastle: Lincom Europa.

Bošković, Željko. 2005. On the locality of left branch extraction and the structure of NP. *Studia Linguistica* 59. 1–45.

Cable, Seth. 2010. *The Grammar of Q. Q-Particles, Wh-Movement, and Pied-Piping.* Oxford: OUP.

Chomsky, Noam. 2000. Minimalist inquiries: The framework. In Roger Martin, David Michaels & Juan Uriagereka (eds.), *Step by step: Essays on minimalist syntax in honor of Howard Lasnik,* 89–155. Cambridge: MIT Press.

Coppock, Elizabeth & David Beaver. 2012. Sole sisters. In Neil Ashton, Anca Chereches & David Lutz (eds.), *Proceedings of SALT 21,* 197–217. New Brunswick, New Jersey.

Corver, Norbert. 1990. *The syntax of left branch extractions.* Tilburg University dissertation.

Destruel, Emilie & Leah Velleman. 2014. Refining contrast: Empirical evidence from the English *it*-cleft. In Christopher Piñón (ed.), *Empirical Issues in Syntax and Semantics,* vol. 10, 197–214. http://www.cssp.cnrs.fr/eiss10/.

Driemel, Imke & Jude Nformi. 2018a. Focus strategies in Limbum. In Elizabeth Bogal-Allbritten & Liz Coppock (eds.), *Proceedings of TripleA 4.* Tübingen: Universität Tübingen.

Driemel, Imke & Jude Nformi. 2018b. On pure focus movement in syntax: Observations from Limbum. Handout, Talk at GLOW 41, Hungary.

Dryer, Matthew. 1996. Focus, pragmatic presupposition, and activated presuppositions. *Journal of Pragmatics* 26. 475–523.

Erlewine, Michael. 2016. Anti-locality and optimality in Kaqchikel agent focus. *Natural Language and Linguistic Theory* 34. 429–479.

Fiedler, Ines, Katharina Hartmann, Brigitte Reineke, Anne Schwarz & Malte Zimmermann. 2010. Subject focus in West African languages. In Malte Zimmermann & Caroline Féry (eds.), *Information structure: Theoretical, typological, and experimental perspectives*, 234–257. Oxford: Oxford University Press.

Fransen, Margo. 1995. *A grammar of Limbum: A Grassfields Bantu language.* Vrije Universiteit te Amsterdam dissertation.

Frey, Werner. 2010. Ā-Movement and conventional implicatures: About the grammatical encoding of emphasis in German. *Lingua* 120. 1416–1435.

Gundel, Jeanette K. 1977. Where do cleft sentences come from? *Language* 53. 543–559.

Hagstrom, Paul. 1998. *Decomposing questions.* MIT dissertation.

Hartmann, Katharina. 2008. Focus and emphasis in tone and intonational languages. In Anita Steube (ed.), *The discourse-potential of underspecified structures*, 389–411. Berlin/New York: de Gruyter.

Heck, Fabian. 2008. *On pied-piping – Wh-movement and beyond* (Studies in Generative Grammar 98). Berlin/New York: Mouton de Gruyter.

Hedberg, Nancy. 2000. The referential status of clefts. *Language* 76. 891–920.

Horn, Larry. 1981. Exhaustiveness and the semantics of clefts. In Virginia Burke & James Pustejovsky (eds.), *Proceedings of NELS 11*, 124–142. Amherst: GLSA.

Horvath, Julia. 2007. Separating "Focus Movement" from Focus. In Simin Karimi, Vida Samiian & Wendy K Wilkins (eds.), *Phrasal and clausal architecture: Syntactic derivation and interpretation. In honor of Joseph E. Emonds*, 108–145. Amsterdam: John Benjamins.

Horvath, Julia. 2010. "Discourse-features", syntactic displacement and the status of contrast. *Lingua* 120. 1346–1369.

Horvath, Julia. 2013. On focus, exhaustivity and Wh-interrogatives: The case of Hungarian. In Johan Brandtler, Valéria Molnár & Christer Platzak (eds.), *Approaches to Hungarian: Papers from the 2011 Lund conference*, vol. 13, 97–132. Amsterdam: John Benjamins.

Kishimoto, Hideki. 2005. Wh-in-situ and movement in Sinhala questions. *Natural Language and Linguistic Theory* 23. 1–51.

Kiss, Katalin É. 1998. Identification focus versus information focus. *Language* 74(2). 245–273.

Koopman, Hilda. 1984. *The syntax of verbs: From verb movement rules in the Kru languages to Universal Grammar.* Dordrecht: Fortis.

Krifka, Manfred. 2008. Basic notions of information structure. *Acta Linguistica Hungarica* 55(3-4). 243–276.

Manfredi, Victor. 1997. Aspectual licensing and object shift. In Rose-Marie Déchaine & Victor Manfredi (eds.), *Object positions in Benue-Kwa*, 87–122. The Hague: Holland Academic Graphics.

Mpoche, Kizitus. 1993. *The Limbum noun phrase: A generative approach*. Université de Yaoundé MA thesis.

Nformi, Jude. 2017. Register lowering and tonal overwriting in Limbum deverbal nouns. Handout at Annual Conference on African Linguistics, ACAL 48, Indiana University.

Percus, Orin. 1997. Prying open the cleft. In Kiyomi Kusumoto (ed.), *Proceedings of NELS 27*, 337–351. McGill University.

Reeve, Matthew. 2011. The syntactic structure of English clefts. *Lingua* 121. 142–171.

Rooth, Mats. 1992. A theory of focus interpretation. *Natural Language Semantics* 1. 75–116.

Skopeteas, Stavros & Gisbert Fanselow. 2009. Focus types and argument asymmetries: A cross-linguistic study in language production. In Carsten Breul & Edward Göbbel (eds.), *Contrastive Information Structure*, 169–198. Amsterdam: Benjamins.

Skopeteas, Stavros & Gisbert Fanselow. 2011. Focus and the exclusion of alternatives: On the interaction of syntactic structure with pragmatic inference. *Lingua* 121. 1693–1706.

Svenious, Peter. 1998. Clefts in Scandinavian: An investigation. *ZAS Papers in Linguistics* 10. 163–190.

Szabolcsi, Anna. 1981. Compositionality in focus. *Folia Linguistica Societatis Linguisticae Europaeae* 15. 141–162.

Vallduví, Enric & Maria Vilkuna. 1998. On Rheme and Kontrast. In Peter Culicover & Louise McNally (eds.), *The limits of syntax*, 79–106. New York: Academic Press.

van der Wal, Jenneke. 2011. Focus excluding alternatives: Conjoint/disjoint marking in Makhuwa. *Lingua* 121. 1734–1750.

van der Wal, Jenneke. 2014. Subordinate clauses and exclusive focus in Makhuwa. In Rik van Gijn, Jeremy Hammond, Dejan Matic, Saskia van Putten & Ana Vilacy Galucio (eds.), *Information structure and reference tracking in complex sentences* (Typological Studies in Language 105), 45–70. Amsterdam: John Benjamins.

Zimmermann, Malte. 2008. Contrastive focus and emphasis. *Acta Linguistica Hungarica* 55. 347–360.

Zimmermann, Malte. 2011. The grammatical expression of focus in West Chadic: Variation and uniformity in and across languages. *Linguistics* 49. 1163–1213.

Zimmermann, Malte & Caroline Féry. 2010. Introduction. In Malte Zimmermann & Caroline Féry (eds.), *Information structure: Theoretical, typological, and experimental perspectives*, 1–11. Oxford: Oxford University Press.

Chapter 13

Universal quantification in the nominal domain in Kihehe

Kelly Kasper-Cushman

Indiana University

This study provides a description of the universal quantifiers *mbe-*AGR2-*li* 'all' and *kila* 'every' in Kihehe, a Bantu language spoken in south-central Tanzania. Following a description of general properties of these quantifiers, this study analyzes how the Kihehe data bear on the phenomena of collectivity and distributivity, and situates the Kihehe data with regard to recent crosslinguistic work on the typology of quantifiers (Matthewson 2013).

1 Introduction

This paper presents a description of the universal quantifiers *mbe-*AGR2-*li* 'all' and *kila* 'every' in Kihehe (G.62; Maho 2009), a Bantu language spoken in south-central Tanzania around the town of Iringa. Regarding quantification in Bantu, Zerbian & Krifka (2008: 383) note that "few studies exist which touch upon quantification [in (whatever) Bantu languages]" (but see Landman 2016; 2019 for two recent works). Additionally, this documentation contributes to an understanding of quantifiers crosslinguistically, and to the development of a typology of quantifiers, as called for by Matthewson (2013) (for recent studies on quantification in natural languages, see the works in Gil et al. 2013; Keenan & Paperno 2012; Matthewson 2008 and Paperno & Keenan 2017).

§2 and §3 describe general properties of *mbe-*AGR2-*li* 'all' and *kila* 'every,' respectively. §4 considers how the data in Kihehe bear on the properties of collectivity and distributivity associated with the universal quantifiers (see, e.g., Szabolcsi 2010). Finally, §5 situates the Kihehe data with regard to three crosslinguistic typological generalizations of quantifiers put forth in Matthewson (2013).

Kelly Kasper-Cushman. 2019. Universal quantification in the nominal domain in Kihehe. In Samson Lotven, Silvina Bongiovanni, Phillip Weirich, Robert Botne & Samuel Gyasi Obeng (eds.), *African linguistics across the disciplines: Selected papers from the 48th Annual Conference on African Linguistics*, 239–256. Berlin: Language Science Press. DOI:10.5281/zenodo.3520591

2 *Mbe-AGR2-li* 'all'

This section provides an overview of the universal quantifier *mbe*-AGR2-*li* 'all.'[1] It starts with a discussion of general agreement patterns before providing a description of coordination and the partitive construction.

2.1 General properties

The quantifier *mbe*-AGR2-*li* follows the noun it modifies and agrees with it in noun class, as shown in (1) in which it modifies the plural Class 2 noun *vanu* 'people.' The agreement marker, labeled AGR2, is an infix.

(1) vá-nu   mbé-va-li
     2-person all-2-all

     'all people'/'all of the people'[2]

The morphological form of the agreement marker for this quantifier patterns with that for demonstratives, numbers, and possessives, as shown in (2a). This is unlike the morphological form of the agreement marking on adjectives, which is identical in form to the noun class marker, as in (2b) (this latter pattern includes the quantificational adjectives *-olofu* 'many/much,' *-ongefu* 'many/much,' and *-kefu* 'few'; however, *-ngi* 'other' patterns with demonstratives). When other modifiers are present in the NP, as in (2a), *mbe*-AGR2-*li* appears last.

(2) a. i-mi-biki   gi-tayi mbe-ge-li
         PPF-4-tree 4-four all-4-all

         'all four trees'

     b. i-mi-biki   my-ongefu
         PPF-4-tree 4-many

         'many trees'

A singular noun can be modified by *mbe*-AGR2-*li*. Example (3) shows a noun from Class 3; here, *all* + N is translated as 'the whole N.'

---

[1]The meaning of the individual components *mbe-* and *-li* is not clear; these components always appear together with an infixed agreement marker in this construction.

[2]Tone is marked on examples where transcription is reliable. Data are transcribed using orthographic conventions based on Kiswahili. Vowel length is not typically marked. Syllabic nasals are marked.

(3) ṃ-víli mbé-gu-li
     3-body all-3-all
     'a/the whole body'

Mbe-AGR2-*li* can take locative noun class agreement. With the Class 16 agreement (*pa-*), for example, the quantifier translates as 'all of the time.'

(4) mbé-pa-li
     all-16-all
     'all of the time'

The quantifier can agree with a plural personal subject (see also Jerro 2013).

(5) Tu-bít-e   mbé-tu-li!
     1PL-go-IMP all-1PL-all
     'Let's all go!'

There is no separate lexical item to express *both*; *mbe*-AGR2-*li* is used in this context. If disambiguation is necessary, the number *-vili* 'two' is inserted, as in (6).

(6) A-v-ana   va-vílî mbe-va-li va-támw-a.
     PPF-2-child 2-two all-2-all 2-be_sick-FV
     'Both of the children are sick.'

In citation form, the head noun modified by *mbe*-AGR2-*li* can optionally occur with the pre-prefix. However, when the head noun is an argument, the head noun must appear with the pre-prefix; compare example (7) with example (1); see also the discussion in §5 and Gambarage (2016).

(7) A-v-ána   mbé-va-li va-támw-a.
     PPF-2-child all-2-all 2-be_sick-FV
     'All of the children are sick.'

Note that the pre-prefix is required even if a demonstrative is present as in (8) (see also the discussion in Matthewson 2013: 32–33).

(8) A-va-na   i-v-o   mbe-va-li va-tamw-a.
     PPF-2-child PROX.DEM-2-ADD all-2-all 2-be_sick-FV
     'All of those children are sick.'

Mbe-AGR2-*li* can stand alone as a pronoun, as shown in (9–10). Example (10) shows a copular structure with a predicate noun.

(9)   Mbé-se-li sí-fw-e.
      all-10-all 10-die-PST.FV
      'All (of them) died.'

(10)   Mbé-va-li v-ana.
       all-2-all   2-child
       'All are children.'

Finally, an example of the universal quantifier in a text is given in (11). The example is from Luwuko (2011: 9:25), the Kihehe translation of the Book of Exodus.

(11)   Kihehe (Luwuko 2011: 9:25)
       Na i-ndonya i-nya-ma-ganga y-a-denyanz-ile
       and PPF-9.rain PPF-of-6-stone   9-P3-strike_down-PST
       i-fi-melo   **mbe-fi-li i-fy-a**   **mu=mi-gunda,**
       PPF-8-seedling all-8-all   PPF-8-ASSOC LOC=4-field,
       y-a-nanz-ile   **i-mi-biki mbe-gi-li i-j-a**
       9-P3-destroy-PST PPF-4-tree all-4-all   PPF-4-ASSOC
       mu=mi-gunda.
       LOC=4-field
       'Then the hail struck down **all of the seedlings in the fields**, and destroyed **all of the crops in the fields**.'

2.2 Coordination with *mbe*-AGR2-*li*

In a coordinate structure such as *all of the N₁ and N₂*, *mbe*-AGR2-*li* can modify either N_1 or both N_1 and N_2. *Mbe*-AGR2-*li* can be placed after either the first noun or the second noun in the coordinate structure and have the interpretation 'all N_1 and all N_2,' although the most natural reading will be that of *mbe*-AGR2-*li* modifying the closest N (compare 12a with 12b). To disambiguate, *mbe*-AG2-*li* can be placed after both nouns, as in (12c).

(12)   a.   Structure: *all N₁ and N₂*
           a-va-kwámisi mbé-va-li n(a) a-vá-híìnza
           PPF-2-boy   all-2-all   and PPF-2-girl

           Most natural interpretation: 'all of the boys and some (not all) of the girls'
           Possible interpretation: 'all of the boys and all of the girls'

       b.   Structure: *N₁ and all N₂*
           a-va-kwamisi n(a) a-va-híìnza mbe-va-li
           PPF-2-boy   and PPF-2-girl   all-2-all

           Most natural interpretation: 'some (not all) of the boys and all of the girls'
           Possible interpretation: 'all of the boys and all of the girls'

       c.   Structure: *all N₁ and all N₂*
           a-va-kwamisi mbe-va-li n(a) a-va-híìnza mbe-va-li
           PPF-2-boy   all-2-all   and PPF-2-girl   all-2-all

           'all of the boys and all of the girls'

In the examples in (12), both nouns in the coordinate structure belong to the same noun class. Nouns from different noun classes can be coordinated using the structure *all of the N₁ and N₂*, but the most natural interpretation of that structure is 'all of the N₁ and some of the N₂.' When the intended meaning is 'all of the N₁ and all of the N₂,' it is more felicitous to modify both nouns with *all*.

(13)   a.   a-va-nu   mbe-va-li n(a) i-senga
           PPF-2-person all-2-all   and PPF-10.cow

           Most natural interpretation: 'all of the people and some (not all) of the cows'
           Possible interpretation: 'all of the people and all of the cows'

       b.   a-va-nu   mbe-va-li n(a) i-senga   mbe-se-li
           PPF-2-person all-2-all   and PPF-10.cow all-10-all

           'all of the people and all of the cows'

2.3 Partitive constructions with *mbe-*AGR2*-li*

In English, there is a surface difference between quantified nouns in partitive constructions (e.g., *all of the N*) and non-partitive constructions (*all N*); for example, *I went to a party last night and talked to *all linguists/all of the linguists* (example adapted from an example in Matthewson 2001: 170; see Matthewson

2001, and Matthewson 2013, for a discussion of the debate regarding the partitive construction and the semantic denotation of quantifiers). In Kihehe, there is no overt morphological element corresponding to *of* in English partitive constructions. Additionally, all nouns modified by *mbe-*AGR2-*li* must first combine with the pre-prefix. Thus, we find a lack of surface contrast between contexts in which the quantified noun is contextually restricted versus non-contextually restricted, for both count nouns, as in (14), and mass nouns, as in (15).

(14) a. Generic
      I-senga   **mbe-se-li** s-ay-i-ly-(a)   a-ma-soli.
      PPF-10.cow all-10-all 10-HAB-PRS-eat-FV PPF-6-grass
      'All cows do eat grass.'

    b. Contextually restricted
      Ke=nyele   ku=m̦-nada   n-gus-is(e) **i-senga**   **mbe-se-li.**
      AUX=1SG.go.PST LOC=3-auction 1SG-sell-PST PPF-10.cow all-10-all
      'I went to the auction and sold all of the cows.'

(15) a. Generic
      Nd-i-wend-(a) **i-fy-ayi** **mbe-fe-li.**
      1SG-PRS-like-FV PPF-8-tea all-8-all
      'I like all tea.'

    b. Contextually restricted (Context: I made two pots of tea a while ago.)
      I-fy-ayi **mbe-fe-li** fy-e=nelike   fi-∅-pos-ile.
      PPF-8-tea all-8-all   8-REL=1SG.cook.PST 8-P1-be_cool-PST
      'All of the tea which I made is cold.'

3 *Kila* 'every'

This section presents a general overview of the universal distributive quantifier, *kila*, 'every.' *Kila* is a borrowing from Kiswahili (which borrowed it from Arabic; Zerbian & Krifka 2008). It is unknown how recently *kila* was borrowed into Kihehe, but evidence suggests that *kila* is a recent borrowing. It does not appear in Spiss's (1900) Kihehe-German dictionary, and it is not used in the Luwuko text. However, *kila* is used commonly by Kihehe speakers, except for the oldest generation.

3.1 General properties

Similar to what Zerbian & Krifka (2008) note for Kiswahili, in Kihehe *kila* must appear before the noun it modifies. It does not show agreement in noun class, and the noun modified by *kila* may not occur with the pre-prefix.[3]

(16) a. kila mw-ana
         every 1-child
         'every child'

   b. * mw-ana kila
         1-child every
         'every child'

   c. * kila u-mw-ana
         every PPF-1-child
         'every child'

Kila can modify both singular nouns, as in (16a), and plural nouns as in (17). In (17), *kila* N is interpreted as 'every group of N' (17).

(17) **Kila va-nu** v-ay-i-pig-ag-a   i-kasi   kwa u-m̩-twa.
     every 2-person 2-HAB-PRS-work-DUR-FV PPF-9.work for PPF-1-chief
     'Every group of people does work for the chief.'

Finally, note that *kila* cannot stand alone as a pronoun.

3.2 *Kila* in coordinate structures

In general, *kila* seems to resist coordination. Structures such as *every N$_1$ and N$_2$* without the repetition of *kila* were judged to be unnatural when the intended meaning was *every N$_1$ and every N$_2$*. Additionally, for several contexts created to elicit coordination with *kila*, coordination with *mbe*-AGR2-*li* was judged to be more natural (or the only coordination structure possible). However, I was able to elicit a coordinated structure in the form of *every N$_1$ and every N$_2$* which my native speaker consultant judged to be natural. This context would also permit the quantifier *mbe*-AGR2-*li*. Note that in the example (18a) with *kila*, the two coordinated nouns contain relative clauses, while in example (18b) with *mbe*-AGR2-*li*, the coordinated nouns do not.

---

[3]Steve Franks and an anonymous reviewer both point out that *kila* and the pre-prefix are in complementary distribution. This suggests that a quantified noun with *kila* is a Q + NP structure, while quantification with *mbe*-AGR2-*li* is a Q + DP structure. This is discussed with regard to crosslinguistic generalizations in §5.

(18) Context: I went to Tanzania. While I was there, I went on a safari in a *mbugayawayama* (a Kiswahili word for 'reserve' or 'park'). In the park...

a. Nd-a-tov-ige   i-picha   y-a   **kila m̩-biki**
    1SG-P3-beat-DUR.PST PPF-9.picture 9-ASSOC every 3-tree
    gw.e=nd-a-gu-won-ige   **na kila ki-koko**
    3.REL=1SG-P3-3-see-DUR.PST and every 7-animal
    ch.e=nd-a-ki-won-ige.
    7.REL=1SG-P3-7-see-DUR.PST
    'I took a picture of every plant that I saw and every animal that I saw.'

b. Nd-a-tov-ige   i-picha   y-a   **i-mi-biki**
    1S-P3-beat-DUR.PST PPF-9.picture 9-ASSOC PPF-4-tree
    mbe-ge-li n(a) i-fi-koko   mbe-fe-li
    all-4-all   and PPF-8-animal all-8-all
    fy.e=nd-a-fi-won-ige.
    8.REL=1SG-P3-8-see-DUR.PST
    'I took a picture of all the plants and animals that I saw.'

3.3 *Kila*: Like *every* or like *each*?

There is no separate lexical item in Kihehe expressing *each*. For English, linguists have investigated several differences between *each* and *every*; three of these differences are summarized in Table 1. Considering these differences, one can ask if the uses of *kila* in Kihehe correspond more to the syntax and semantics of *each*, or more to those of *every*.

Table 1: Some properties of *each* and *every* (Beghelli & Stowell 1997)

Property	*each*	*every*
Ability to float	Can float	Cannot float
Modification by 'almost'	Cannot be modified by *almost*	Can be modified by *almost*
Availability of Generic interpretation	*each* N cannot be understood as a generic	*every* N can be understood as a generic

For the properties in Table 1, *kila* patterns with *every*, rather than *each*. First, *kila* cannot float. It can appear in only one position, preceding the noun it modifies. Second, as shown in (19), *kila* can be modified by *kalibiya* 'almost,' which is a borrowing from Kiswahili.

(19) Kalibiya kila ki-nu ki-sis-ile.
      almost   every 7-thing 7-be_used_up-PST
      'Almost every thing is gone.'

Third, *kila* can be used to make generic statements, as shown in example (20).

(20) Kila senga y-ay-i-ly-(a)   a-ma-soli.
      every 9.cow 9-HAB-PRS-eat-FV PPF-6-grass
      'Every cow eats grass.'

In addition to these properties, Vendler (1962: 150) states that "'each'...directs one's attention to the individuals as they appear, in some succession or other, one by one." Consider example (21), based on a similar example in Vendler (1962: 150). The example suggests that in Kihehe, when the context establishes a one-by-one interpretation, *kila* becomes infelicitous.[4]

---

[4]An anonymous reviewer notes that this example "suggests that Kihehe employs the typologically widespread reduplication strategy for expressing 'strong distributivity' (in the sense of Beghelli & Stowell 1997)" and wonders if the reduplication method for expressing strong distributivity blocks *kila* in appearing in such contexts. The use of reduplication to indicate distributivity is also supported by the Kihehe data in (i), in which reduplication gives rise to an unambiguous distributive meaning of "2 mangos per child" (on reduplication and distributivity, see also Balusu & Jayaseelan 2013).

   (i) Ṃ-pel-e kila mw-an(a) a-ma-yembe ga-vili ga-vili.
        1-give-IMP every 1-child   PPF-6-mango 6-two 6-two
        'Give every child 2 mangos each.'

A final point of comparison between English *every* and *kila*: Beghelli & Stowell (1997: 98) note that *every* allows collective readings, as in *It took every boy to lift the piano* (their example 33a). *Kila* does not allow collective readings. This is discussed in the following section in conjunction with example (26) and footnote 6.

(21) Context: After I purchased a basket of mangos, I noticed that some of them were starting to rot. I want you to look at each one carefully so that you can sort the mangos into those that are still good to eat, and those that are spoiled. I tell you:

    a. # Li-lav-e   kila   li-yembe.
           5-see-IMP every 5-mango

           'Examine every mango.'

    b. OK li-lav-e   lí-mwí-lí-mwî.
           5-see-IMP 5-one-5-one

           'Examine (them) one after another.'

4 Collectivity and distributivity

This section discusses the properties of collective and distributive interpretations with the universal quantifiers in Kihehe. Regarding *-ote* 'all' and *kila* in Kiswahili, a reviewer of Zerbian & Krifka (2008: 396) "suggests *kila* is inherently distributive whereas *-ote* is underspecified concerning the distributive/collective distinction." This section presents data which suggest that the behavior of quantifiers in Kihehe are compatible with the hypothesis that *mbe-*AGR2*-li* is underspecified for collectivity vs. distributivity, while *kila* is distributive.

4.1 Distributive contexts

In the contexts that are distributive, *mbe-*AGR2*-li* is acceptable. For the context presented in (22), *kila* is also acceptable as shown in (22b).[5]

(22) Context: The chief was sitting in the front of the hall. Before the meeting started, the villagers went up individually to greet the chief. All of the villagers present had to greet the chief before the meeting started. Then at last, the meeting began. This evening...

    a. **a-va-nu**   mbe-va-li va-mu-∅-hunje u-mu-twa.
        PPF-2-person all-2-all   2-1-P1-greet.PST PPF-1-chief

        'all of the people greeted the chief.'

---

[5]An anyonymous reviewer asks why *kila* is felicitous here (22b), while it is not felicitous in either (21b) or (23b). One possibility is that the context in (22) does not impose that the acts of greeting were conducted in strict succession, one after another. More research is needed to clearly define the properties of the contexts which permit or require one strategy (*kila* or reduplication) versus another.

b. **Kila mu-nu** a-m̩-∅-hunje u-mu-twa.
   every 1-person 1-1-P1-greet.PST PPF-1-chief
   'every person greeted the chief.'

However, *kila* is not acceptable in all distributive contexts. In example (23), *mbe*-AGR2-*li* is possible, but *kila* is not felicitous. As with example (21), the context creates an interpretation of 'individually, one after another.'

(23) Context: The boys in the village were arguing about who was the strongest. Then one boy saw a big rock and said "Whoever throws the rock the farthest is the strongest." So one at a time, the boys threw the rock. What happened?

   a. **A-va-kwamisi mbe-va-li** v-a-hom-it(e) i-li-ganga.
      PPF-2-boy all-2-all 2-P3-throw-PST PPF-5-stone
      'All of the boys threw the rock.'

   b. # **Kila m̩-kwamisi** (a)-a-hom-it(e) i-li-ganga.
      every 1-boy 1-P3-throw-PST PPF-5-stone
      'Every boy threw the rock.'

   c. OK **U-mu-nu yu-mwi-yu-mwi** (a)-a-hom-it(e) i-li-ganga.
      PPF-1-person 1-one-1-one 1-P3-throw-PST PPF-5-stone
      'The people threw the stone one after another.'

4.2 Collective contexts

In contexts that are necessarily collective, only *mbe*-AGR2-*li* is felicitous. The use of *kila* creates distributive interpretations that are not compatible with the contexts.

(24) Context: A fire destroyed someone's house in the village. The person was elderly and could not rebuild her house, so the other villagers decided to help her. This morning...

   a. **a-va-baba mbe-va-li** v-a-senz-ile kangi i-nyumba.
      PPF-2-man all-2-all 2-P3-build-PST again PPF-9.house
      y.e=ke=yi-ka-pye
      9.REL=AUX=9-P2-burn.PST
      'all the men rebuilt the house which had burned.'

b. # **kila** ṃ-baba (a)-a-senz-ile kangi i-nyumba
every 1-man 1-P3-build-PST again PPF-9.house
y.e=ke=yi-ka-pye
9.REL=AUX=9-P2-burn.PST

'every man rebuilt the house which had burned.'

Comment from native speaker consultant: This would have to mean that there were many houses being built.

Szabolcsi (2010: 121) states that "To test collective readings it is advisable to employ punctual accomplishment verbs such as *lift up*, as opposed to *lift*, which has an activity reading." Based on this statement, the context in (25) was designed to test collective readings with the verb *kunyanyula*, 'lift up.' The consultant's judgments indicate that *mbe*-AGR2-*li* is acceptable with a collective reading, while *kila* requires a distributive reading.

(25) Context: There was a child trapped under a wagon that had fallen over in the road. The child screamed, and people rushed to the wagon. In order to rescue the child...

    a. **a-va-nu** **mbe-va-li** va-∅-nyanyuw(e) i-li-tololi.
        PPF-2-person all-2-all 2-P1-lift_up.PST PPF-5-wagon

        'all of the people lifted up the wagon.'

    b. # **kila** **mu-nu** a-∅-nyanyuw(e) i-li-tololi.
        every 1-person 1-P1-lift_up.PST PPF-5-wagon

        'every person lifted up the wagon.'

        Comment from consultant: This would mean that everyone has his/her own wagon.

However, as Robert Botne (pers. comm.) points out, we cannot be sure that *kunyanyula* is necessarily a punctual accomplishment verb (i.e., is it interpreted as 'lift up' or 'lift'?). Additional evidence that *kila* requires a distributive interpretation while *mbe*-AGR2-*li* is acceptable with a collective reading comes from the pair in (26), modeled after the data in Zerbian & Krifka (2008: 396–397). These data also show that similar to what Zerbian & Krifka (2008: 397) describe for Kiswahili, in Kihehe *kila* is not grammatical with *pamwî* 'together' as in (26b).[6]

---

[6]Note also that it is ungrammatical to add *pamwî* 'together' to the utterance in example as in (25b).

(26) a. **A-va-kwamisi mbe-va-li** v-a-lavis-igê   a-ma-shindano
          PPF-2-boy   all-2-all   2-P3-watch-DUR.PST PPF-6-competition
          pamwî.
          together
          'All of the boys watched the competition together.'

      b. * **Kila m̩-kwamisi** (a)-a-lavis-igê   a-ma-shindano   pamwî.
          every 1-boy   1-P3-watch-DUR.PST PPF-6-competition together
          'Every boy watched the competition together.'

5 Kihehe universal quantifiers and cross-linguistic generalizations

Matthewson (2013) calls for work towards a typology of quantifiers, and puts forth eight crosslinguistic generalizations based on a survey of 37 different languages. In this section, I situate the Kihehe data with respect to three of the crosslinguistics generalizations that bear on syntactic differences among the universal quantifiers.[7]

First, consider Matthewson's Generalization 6:

(27) Gen6: It is common for a word translated as 'all' to look as if it attaches to a full DP, even when other quantifiers do not. (Matthewson 2013: 35)

As described above, the Kihehe data show that *mbe-*AGR2-*li* must combine with a head noun + pre-prefix when the head noun is an argument. The data are consistent with the hypothesis that the pre-prefix on nouns is a D, and one of its functions is to combine with NPs to form DP arguments. I come to this hypothesis applying the argumentation laid out in Matthewson (2001). Gambarage (2016) arrives at a similar analysis of the pre-prefix in Nata, a Bantu language also spoken in Tanzania; see his work for a much more exhaustive investigation of this claim as well as for references of number of authors who argue that the pre-prefix is a D; see Longobardi (1994) regarding Ds forming DP arguments.

In support of this hypothesis, note that in Kihehe, the head noun of a DP argument containing the quantifier *mbe-*AGR2-*li* must appear with the pre-prefix. Main clause quantified DPs are ungrammatical without the pre-prefix (28).

---

[7]Landman has a similar goal for her (2016) study of Logoori; she finds that the generalizations from Matthewson (2013) under consideration for her study apply to the distributive quantifier *vuri* 'every,' but not to the quantifier *-oosi* 'all,' ultimately analyzing *-oosi* as a DP-internal modifier. Whether this analysis could extend to Kihehe *mbe-*AGR2-*li* is left an open question for future research.

(28) * Sénga mbé-se-li sí-fwe.
      10.cow all-10-all 10-die.PST
      'All the cows died.'

While DP arguments must contain a pre-prefix on the head noun, the pre-prefix cannot occur on a predicate noun or a predicate adjective. When the pre-prefix does occur in these contexts, it creates a relative clause (29–30).

(29) a. U-mu-nu   yu-la   **mu-twa.**
          PPF-1-person 1-DEM.DIST 1-chief

          'That person is a/the chief.'

      b. u-mu-nu   yu-la   **u-mu-twa**
          PPF-1-person 1-DEM.DIST PPF-1-chief

          'that person who is a/the chief'

(30) a. A-v-ana   **va-tali.**
          PPF-2-child 2-tall

          'The children are tall.'

      b. a-v-ana   **a-va-tali**
          PPF-2-child PPF-2-tall

          'the children who are tall'

Pre-prefixes are not needed on mass nouns when stating general information (31).

(31) **Wu-lasi** wu-nono.
      14-wulasi 14-sweet

      '*Wulasi* is sweet.'

The hypothesis that a DP noun argument must be marked with a pre-prefix when combing with the universal quantifier is strongly supported by the Kihehe data. However, one possible counterexample to this hypothesis is given in example (32). This minimal pair demonstrates the finding that the requirement of the pre-prefix on the head noun seems to be stronger for subjects and direct objects than for indirect objects. My native speaker consultant judged (32b) only marginally worse than (32a).

(32) a. Pre-prefix on indirect object head noun
Va-pel-(e) a-ma-yembe ga-vili **a-v-ana**   **mbe-va-li.**
2-give-IMP PPF-6-mango 6-two PPF-2-child all-2-all

'Give two mangos to all of the children.'

b. ? No pre-prefix on indirect object head noun
Va-pel-(e) a-ma-yembe ga-vili **v-ana mbe-va-li.**
2-give-IMP PPF-6-mango 6-two 2-child all-2-all

'Give two mangos to all of the children.'

Thus, the Kihehe evidence is consistent with Generalization 6 in that 'all' appears to combine with a full DP. The second half of Generalization 6, "even when other quantifiers do not [attach to a full DP]" will be discussed in tandem with Matthewson's Generalization 7.

(33) Gen7: In some languages, distributive universals appear to combine directly with NP, while other quantifiers do not. (Matthewson 2013: 36)

As described above, unlike *mbe-AGR2-li*, the distributive universal quantifier *kila* may not combine with a noun + pre-prefix, and in fact, *kila* and the pre-prefix are in complementary distribution (see footnote 3). If the pre-prefix is a D which attaches to NPs to form DP arguments, and *kila* may never attach to a noun with a pre-prefix, then this suggests that *kila* combines with NPs. Thus, this generalization applies to Kihehe.

Finally, consider Matthewson's Generalization 8:

(34) Gen8: A secondary pattern is to distinguish distributive universal quantifiers from other universal quantifiers, but for the former to use some other strategy such as reduplication, affixation, or adverbial quantification (Matthewson 2013: 37)

As discussed above, the data suggest that Kihehe uses reduplication to express distributivity. While the strategy of reduplication is in need of more exploration, a preliminary hypothesis is that Kihehe has one strategy of distributive quantification in which the quantifier *kila*, borrowed from Kiswahili, combines with an NP, and one strategy of distributive quantification which uses reduplication.

6 Conclusion

This paper describes general properties of the universal quantifiers *mbe-AGR2-li* 'all' and *kila* 'every' in Kihehe. It then discusses the quantifiers in light of the properties of collectivity and distributivity, and provides data that suggest that Kihehe has an additional strategy of reduplication for expressing distributive quantification. Ultimately, this paper argues that Kihehe attests patterns similar to what has been observed for other Bantu languages: *mbe-*AGR2-*li* is compatible with both collective and distributive contexts, while *kila* is distributive. Unlike English *every*, *kila* is ungrammatical with a collective reading. However, while distributive, *kila* is infelicitous in contexts in which a 'one by one' or 'one after another' reading is required, though the exact constraints on *kila*, and a more thorough investigation of the strategy of reduplication, are left for future research. Finally, this paper considers the Kihehe data in light of the typology of quantifiers crosslinguistically and demonstrates that the Kihehe data are compatible with three of Matthewson's (2013) crosslinguistic generalizations bearing on syntactic properties of universal quantifiers.

Acknowledgements

I would like to thank Richard Nyamahanga for providing the Kihehe language data and judgments presented in this paper. Data were collected by the author through elicitation sessions at Indiana University. I would like to thank Robert Botne and my fellow students in L654: Field Methods, Indiana University, Spring 2016, for their suggestions and discussion of these data. I would also like to thank Tom Grano and Steve Franks for formative comments on earlier versions of this work. Finally, I would like to thank the audience members at ACAL 48 and an anonymous reviewer for helpful feedback and suggestions.

Abbreviations

Bare numerals (e.g., 1, 2, 3) refer to noun class markers or agreement markers for that noun class.

1SG	first person singular	DUR	durative
1PL	first person plural	FV	final vowel
ADD	proximal to addressee	HAB	habitual
ADJ	adjective	IMP	imperative
AGR2	agreement marker 2	IMPF	imperfective
ASSOC	associative marker	LOC	locative
AUX	auxiliary	N	noun
DEM	demonstrative	P1	recent past

P2	hodiernal past		PRS	present
P3	remote past		PST	past
PPF	pre-prefix		REL	relative
POSS	possessive		#	infelicitous
PROX	proximal			

References

Balusu, Rahul & K. A. Jayaseelan. 2013. Distributive quantification by reduplication in Dravidian. In Kook-Hee Gil, Steve Harlow & George Tsoulas (eds.), *Strategies of quantification* (Oxford Studies in Theoretical Linguistics), 60–86. Oxford: Oxford University Press.

Beghelli, Filippo & Tim Stowell. 1997. Distributivity and negation: The syntax of *each* and *every*. In Anna Szabolcsi (ed.), *Ways of scope taking*, 71–107. Springer.

Gambarage, Joash J. 2016. *Pre-prefixes and argumenthood in Nata: An assertion-of-existence account.* Handout from the 47th Annual Conference on African Linguistics, Berkely, CA.

Gil, Kook-Hee, Steve Harlow & George Tsoulas (eds.). 2013. *Strategies of quantification* (Oxford Studies in Theoretical Linguistics). Oxford: Oxford University Press.

Jerro, Kyle. 2013. When quantifiers agree in person: Anomalous agreement in Bantu. *Studies in the Linguistic Sciences: Illinois Working Papers* 2013. 21–36.

Keenan, Edward L. & Denis Paperno. 2012. *Handbook of quantifiers in natural language* (Studies in Linguistics and Philosophy 90). Dordrecht: Springer.

Landman, Meredith. 2016. Quantification in Logoori. In Doris L. Payne, Sara Pacchiarotti & Mokaya Bosire (eds.), *Diversity in African languages: Selected papers from the 46th Annual Conference on African Linguistics*, 219–233. Berlin: Language Science Press. DOI:10.17169/langsci.b121.483

Landman, Meredith. 2019. Nominal quantification in Kipsigis. In Emily Clem, Peter Jenks & Hannah Sande (eds.), *Theory and description in African Linguistics: Selected papers from the 47th Annual Conference on African Linguistics*, 481–498. Berlin: Language Science Press. DOI:10.5281/zenodo.3367177

Longobardi, Giuseppe. 1994. Reference and proper names: A theory of N-movement in syntax and logical form. *Linguistic Inquiry* 25(4). 609–665.

Luwuko. 2011. *Ikitabu cha kavili cha Musa chekitambulwa: Luwuko (The book of Exodus in Kihehe published as LUWUKO)*. Dodoma, Tanzania: The Bible Society of Tanzania.

Maho, Jouni Filip. 2009. *NUGL online: The online version of the New Updated Guthrie List, A referential classification of the Bantu languages.* http://goto. glocalnet.net/mahopapers/nuglonline.pdf.

Matthewson, Lisa. 2001. Quantification and the nature of cross-linguistic variation. *Natural Language Semantics* 9(2). 145–189.

Matthewson, Lisa (ed.). 2008. *Quantification: A cross-linguistic perspective* (North-Holland Linguistic Series: Linguistic Variations Volume 64). Bingley, UK: Emerald.

Matthewson, Lisa. 2013. Strategies of quantification in St'át'imcets and the rest of the world. In Kook-Hee Gil, Steve Harlow & George Tsoulas (eds.), *Strategies of quantification* (Oxford Studies in Theoretical Linguistics), 15–38. Oxford: Oxford University Press.

Paperno, Denis & Edward L. Keenan. 2017. *Handbook of quantifiers in natural language.* Vol. 2 (Studies in Linguistics and Philosophy 97). Cham: Springer.

Spiss, Cassian. 1900. *Kihehe-Wörter-Sammlung: Kihehe-Deutsch und Deutsch-Kihehe.* Berlin: Reichsdruckerei.

Szabolcsi, Anna. 2010. *Quantification.* Cambridge: Cambridge University Press.

Vendler, Zeno. 1962. Each and every, any and all. *Mind* 71(282). 145–160.

Zerbian, Sabine & Manfred Krifka. 2008. Quantification across Bantu languages. In Lisa Matthewson (ed.), *Quantification: A cross-linguistic perspective* (North-Holland Linguistic Series: Linguistic Variations Volume 64), 383–414. Bingley, UK: Emerald.

Chapter 14

A closer look at the Akan determiner *bi*: An epistemic indefinite analysis

Augustina Pokua Owusu

Rutgers University

This study aims to shed light on the epistemic indefinite interpretation (EI) of the Akan (Asante Twi) determiner *bi* which hitherto had not been discussed in the Akan literature. In previous studies, Amfo (2010) and Arkoh (2011) review its referential or specific indefinite interpretation. The current study shows that in addition to the above interpretation when *bi* is used, the speaker signals that she does not have access to all the information about who or what satisfies the existential claim they are making. I employ Aloni (2001) and Aloni & Port's (2015) theory of conceptual covers and methods of identification to determine "knowledge" of a referent in a particular context. Conceptual covers are sets of individual concepts which exclusively and exhaustively covers the domain of individuals (Aloni 2001). I show that the epistemic indefinite analysis and the specificity or referential analysis are compatible. When *bi* is used, the speaker asserts she can name a noteworthy or identifying property about the referent of the NP, which is the referential or specificity interpretation. Additionally, she presupposes that she is ignorant about further characterizing information about the referent, the epistemic indefinite interpretation.

1 Introduction

The study of epistemic indefinites has become popular as the interest in non-verbal modality rises (see Aloni & Port 2015; Alonso-Ovalle & Menéndez-Benito 2003 a.o. for studies on epistemic indefinites). Epistemic determiners or pronouns, as their name suggests, signal the epistemic state of a speaker, i.e., whether the speaker knows the referent of an NP or not. The study of epistemic indefinites is usually divorced from the study of specific indefinites or the wide scope interpretation of the indefinite for two main reasons. First, in most of the well-studied

Augustina Pokua Owusu. 2019. A closer look at the Akan determiner *bi*: An epistemic indefinite analysis. In Samson Lotven, Silvina Bongiovanni, Phillip Weirich, Robert Botne & Samuel Gyasi Obeng (eds.), *African linguistics across the disciplines: Selected papers from the 48th Annual Conference on African Linguistics*, 257–280. Berlin: Language Science Press. DOI:10.5281/zenodo.3520593

languages, the specific indefinite determiner and the epistemic indefinite determiner are expressed by different morphemes. For instance, in English, specificity
is encoded by either a wide scope reading of the determiner *a* or the morpheme
certain, while epistemic indefiniteness is encoded by the quantifiers *some* or *some
or other*. In German, specificity is encoded by determiners *bestimmt* and *gewiss*
while the epistemic indefinite determiner is *irgendein*. Secondly, these markers
appear to express opposing concepts. Specificity requires that the speaker have a
particular referent in mind; these markers are often used referentially, i.e., there
is a particular referent that can be identified by the speaker or some other salient
individual. Epistemic indefinites, on the other hand, require that the speaker be
"ignorant" about the referent of the indefinite. These indefinites are, however,
not mutually exclusive. For instance, the German epistemic indefinite *irgedein*,
and specific indefinite *bestimmt*, are felicitous in the same sentence (Aloni & Port
2015).

This paper aims to show that these two types of indefinites can be encoded
in the same lexical item in a language. The Akan determiner *bi*, which has been
argued to have a specific indefinite use (Amfo 2010; Arkoh 2011) also has an epistemic indefinite interpretation. The specificity interpretation requires that the
speaker have a mental representation of a particular individual which he can
characterize by a noteworthy or identifying property. The epistemic indefinite
interpretation is a presupposition of ignorance about further characterizing information about the referent. These pieces of missing information – what the
speaker does not know – are the critical properties that determine whether the
speaker "knows" the referent. Context determines what a speaker has to know
about a referent to claim he "knows" the referent.

(1) Akan (Arkoh 2011: 37)

    a. Maame Ama yɛ-ɛ   edziban **bi**.
      woman Ama do-PAST food   IND
      'Madam Ama cooked (some specific) food.'

    b. Akan (personal knowledge)
      Maame Ama yɛ-ɛ   aduane **bi** nanso me-n-   nim aduane kro.
      woman Ama do-PAST food   IND but   1SG.-NEG- know food   one
      'Madam Ama cooked (some specific) food, but I don't know what
      food it is.'

The food in (1a) is specific; i.e., there is a particular food being cooked by
Maame Ama that the speaker has in mind. *Bi* is felicitous since the fundamen-

tal way to identify food is by its name, and the speaker does not know this. In other words, the ignorance presupposition is satisfied. The fact that the speaker does not know the name is stated explicitly in (1b). Adopting Aloni & Port (2015) methods of identification and conceptual covers, I account for what counts as "knowing" in a context.

The paper is structured as follows: In §2, I review the specific indefinite analysis of *bi*, paying attention to its scope taking properties and its felicity conditions. In §3, I discuss epistemic indefinites, their functions and the methods of identifications. §4 is the analysis and §5 the conclusion.

2 The specificity analysis

The specificity or referential interpretation of *bi* has been discussed by Amfo (2010) and Arkoh (2011). Amfo (2010) argues that *bi* is an existential quantifier that has the cognitive status of referential. The determiner *bi* is used to introduce new referents into the discourse. In the spirit of Heim's (1983) File Change semantics metaphor, when *bi* is used a new file for the NP is created. An addressee constructs a referent for the NP by identifying properties that exemplify the head noun in question. Arkoh (2011), on the other hand, argues that when *bi* is used as a determiner, it is interpreted as referential along the lines of Fodor & Sag (1982) and Kratzer (1998). She argues against Amfo's (2006) claim that it is an existential quantifier. She claims that *bi* does not have a quantificational interpretation. Amfo (2010) and Arkoh (2011) make different predictions about the scope of *bi*. A referential determiner always has wide scope while a specific existential indefinite can get an intermediate scope. For Arkoh (2011), one piece of evidence against the existential quantifier analysis is the fact that *bi*+NP can make a discourse referent that can be referred to as in (2b). The bare NP, which is interpreted as an existential quantifier does not have this property, as a result (3b) is infelicitous.

(2)   Akan (Arkoh 2011: 35)

    a. Kwame hwe-e   abɔfra (tuntum) bi.
       Kwame cane-PAST child   black   REF
       'Kwame caned a certain (dark) child.'

    b. ɔ-yɛ   bubuafɔ.
       3SG.SUBJ-be cripple
       'S/he is a cripple.'

(3)   Akan (Arkoh 2011: 35)

    a.   Kwame hwe-e   abɔfra.
          Kwame cane-PAST child

         'Kwame caned a child.'

    b. # ɔ-yɛ   bubua-fɔ.
          3SG.SUBJ-be cripple-NOM

         'S/he is a cripple.'

The English indefinite determiner *a* is ambiguous between quantificational and referential readings as shown below.

(4)   English (Abusch & Rooth 1997)
John overheard the rumor that a student of mine had been called before the dean.

    a. 'John overheard the rumor that a particular student of mine namely Bill has been called before the dean.'

    b. 'John overheard the rumor that some student of mine has been called before the dean.'

In (4a), the indefinite is interpreted as referring to a specific student, one that John is aware of. In (4b), on the other hand, John does not appear to know the referent of the indefinite. In English, the referential and quantificational interpretation results from a wide scope or narrow scope reading of the indefinite. The aim of this section is not to choose between these two analyses, but to show that a referential or specificity interpretation of *bi* has been explored. What is essential for this study is that both analyses agree that when a speaker uses N+*bi*, he intends to refer to a particular referent which he has in mind.

Even as a referential determiner, *bi* does not have the same interpretation or distribution as the referential definite determiner. Heim (1983) argues that specific indefinite, like other indefinites, can introduce a new file. A definite, on the other hand, can only be used when updating an existing file; you cannot introduce a new discourse referent with a definite marker. You can begin narratives with a specific indefinite, but not a definite determiner. Another difference is that a definite expression is used when a speaker presupposes that the referent of the expression is also accessible to the hearer. That is, the speaker assumes that there is a unique referent that the hearer can identify. Either (i) because the referent was previously mentioned in the context of discourse, or (ii) because the referent is part of the interlocutors' shared knowledge, or (iii) because there is enough descriptive content in the sentence to identify the referent. The referent becomes identifiable as the sentence is processed (Comrie 1989: 135; Givón 2001: 450; Gundel et al. 1993: 277; Hawkins 1978: 167–168; Payne 1997: 263). For specific indefinites, specificity lies in the fact that the speaker has a particular referent in mind. The addressee is just expected to be able to form a representation of this referent provided there are enough clues in the utterance itself and an accessible context. The speaker does not assume that the listener/addressee knows the referent of the NP. The difference between *bi* and the definite determiner *no* is that of assumed addressee ignorance. When a referent is familiar to both addressee and speaker, the definite determiner is used. This is the difference between (5a) and (5b).

(5) Akan (Amfo 2010)

    a. Kwame dze edziban no   maa   Ama.
           Kwame take food   Fam give-PAST Ama

       'Kwame gave the food to Ama.'

    b. Kwame dze edziban bi   maa   Ama.
           Kwame take food   IND give-PAST Ama

       'Kwame gave a certain food to Ama.'

In (5a), the food that Kwame gave to Ama is discourse old; the referent is familiar to both the speaker and the addressee. This familiarity may be due to one of the reasons mentioned above that makes a referent of NP accessible to an addressee. The referent of food in (5b) is, however, discourse new and only familiar to the speaker.

2.1 Scoping-taking properties of *bi*

One of the unique and uncontroversial characteristics of specific indefinites is their ability to escape scope islands. Scope islands are syntactic configurations which disallow wide scope for most quantifiers; these include relative clauses and antecedents of conditionals (see Fodor & Sag 1982, and much subsequent literature). In addition to taking wide scope, indefinites have been observed to take an intermediate scope, outside of the scope island but underneath a higher quantifier. In this section, I explore the scope properties of *bi* with intensional predicates, in the context of negation, with other nominal quantifiers, and in the antecedent of a conditional. We begin with intensional predicates.

When *bi* is embedded under intensional predicates, it always receives a wide scope reading. It scopes over the intensional predicate. In this way *bi* is similar to the German specificity markers *bestimmt* and *gewiss* (Ebert & Hinterwimmer 2012).

(6) Akan (Personal knowledge)

    a. Kofi re-   hwɛhwɛ CD **bi.**
        Kofi -PROG- search   CD IND
        'Kofi is looking for a certain CD.'
        $\exists y\ [CD(y) \wedge search(K,y)]]$

    b. Kofi re-   hwɛhwɛ CD.
        Kofi -PROG- search   CD
        'Kofi is looking for a CD.'

In (6a), Kofi is not going to be happy when he finds just any CD; he will only be happy if he finds his *Thriller* CD. There is no such restriction in (6b), finding any CD will make Kofi happy.

Bi is infelicitous in a negative context. Neither a wide scope nor narrow scope interpretation is available in (7a). This sentence can only be saved when the indefinite determiner is replaced by the NPI *biara* 'any' as in (7b).[1]

(7) Akan (Personal knowledge)

    a. * Kofi n-   hwɛhwɛ CD **bi.**
        Kofi NEG- search   CD IND

    b. Kofi n-   hwɛhwɛ CD biara.
        Kofi NEG- search   CD any
        'Kofi is not looking for any CD.'

Some specific indefinites like the German *bestimmt* can in principle scope under negation. When it is licensed under negation, both the wide scope and the narrow scope interpretations are technically possible, though speakers disprefer the wide scope interpretation. *Gewiss*, on the other hand, is not licensed under negation.

---

[1]The NPI is derived from a combination of the indefinite determiner *bi* and the emphatic particle *ara*. *Biara* like *any* has a free-choice interpretation that is licensed in positive sentences.

    (i) Akan (Personal knowledge)
        Kofi bɛ- gye CD biara.
        Kofi FUT- take CD any
        'Kofi will take any CD.'

The indefinite determiner also interacts with other nominal quantifiers like the universal quantifier.

(8) Akan (Personal knowledge)

    a. Obiara   hyia -a   presidential candidate **bi**.
       Everyone meet -PST presidential candidate IND

       'Everyone met a presidential candidate.'

    b. Yɛ- kɔ -e   no   obiara   tɔ   -ɔ   nwoma **bi**.
       3PL- go -PST CFM everyone buy -PST book   IND

       'When we went, everyone bought a certain book.'

(9)   a. $\exists y \forall x$[presidential candidate(x)[$\rightarrow$]met(y,x)]

      b. $\forall x \exists y$[presidential candidate(x)[$\rightarrow$]met(y,x)]

(8a) is ambiguous between a wide scope and a narrow scope reading, just like *certain* in English (see Farkas 2002: ex. 54). The wide scope interpretation is that there is a particular presidential candidate, for instance, Hillary Clinton, such that everyone met her. The narrow scope reading expresses that for everyone there is a unique presidential candidate that they met, Kofi met Trump, Ama met Hillary, and Kwame met Bernie. In this way, *bi* is similar to the German specificity marker *bestimmt*, which is also ambiguous between wide and narrow scope interpretations with nominal quantifiers. It, however, differs from the other specificity marker *gewiss* which only has a wide scope reading with nominal quantifiers.

Indefinites scope outside of conditionals despite the fact that conditionals constitute scope islands for other quantifiers (cf. Fodor & Sag 1982; Endriss 2009 and the references cited therein). The example taken from Farkas (2002) has two readings.

(10)   German (Farkas 2002)
      Wenn Ben ein Problem von der Liste löst,   wird Mr. Koens ihn loben.
      If   Ben a   problem from the list   solves will Mr. Koens him praise

      'If Ben solves a problem from the list, Mr. Koens will praise him.'

First, there is a narrow scope reading for the indefinite that says that Mr. Koens will praise Ben if he solves some problem or other from the list; any question that he answers will earn him praise. But there is also an exceptional wide-scope reading where the indefinite takes scope over the conditional, stating that there is some specific problem on the list such that Mr. Koens will praise Ben if he solves that problem.

In Akan, only the wide scope meaning is available in this context. The narrow scope interpretation is not available; it is only possible when the indefinite is replaced by the free choice item *biara*.

(11)   Akan (Suggested by reviewer)
       Sɛ Kofi tumi   bua   nsɛm   **bi** ano   wɔ   nsohwɛ no mu
       if Kofi be.able answer questions IND mouth be.located exam   DEF in
       a   mɛ-   kyɛ no   adeɛ.
       REL 1SG.FUT- give 3SG.OBJ thing

       'If Kofi answers some questions on the test/in the exam, I will give him a gift.'

(11) only has the reading that there is a particular question such that answering that question earns Kofi a gift.

2.2 Felicity conditions of indefinites

Ionin & Matushansky (2006) proposes that specific indefinites carry felicity conditions on their use: a specific indefinite can be felicitously used by the speaker only when particular pragmatic conditions have been met. She discusses two felicity conditions: *noteworthiness* and *identifiability* (cf. Abusch & Rooth 1997; Farkas 2002). Ionin (2013) argues that the indefinite *this* in English carries a condition of noteworthiness and *odin* in Russian carries a condition of identifiability. In this section, following Ionin (2013), I argue that *bi* carries both a *noteworthiness* and an *identifiability* condition. Ionin & Matushansky (2006) proposes that the use of *this* implies that the speaker knows something noteworthy about the referent of the indefinite. The condition of noteworthiness is not the same thing as speaker knowledge; the speaker can felicitously use a *this*-indefinite even if she does not know the exact identity of the individual under discussion (what counts as knowing the identity of the referent will be discussed in the next section). This is illustrated in the examples below.

(12)   English (Ionin & Matushansky 2006: 183)

       a.   # Mary wants to see this new movie; I don't know which movie it is.
       b.   Mary wants to see this new movie; I don't know which movie it is, but she's been all excited about seeing it for weeks now.

c.   I want to see this new movie – I can't remember its name and I have
no idea what it's about, but someone mentioned to me that it's
really interesting.

In all the examples above, the speaker states that she does not know the referent of the indefinite, but (12b) and (12c) are felicitous because the referent is noteworthy. (12a) is infelicitous because the condition of noteworthiness is not met. Noteworthiness must be expressed in the sentence.

Abusch & Rooth (1997) propose that the felicitous use of "a certain X" requires the speaker to be able to answer the question "which X is it?" (see also Ebert et al. (2012) for a similar proposal for *gewiss and bestimmt*). Aloni (2001) argues that in Russian when a speaker utters *odna kniga* 'one book', the speaker conveys that she can answer the question "which book is it?"; the response to this question names an identifying property that singles out a specific book, distinguishing it from all other books. The identifying property does not have to be the name of the book; it may just as easily be some other relevant property that singles out a specific book. More importantly, the identifying property must come from outside of the sentence.

The indefinite determiner *bi* has both a noteworthy and an identifiability felicity condition, but only one of these conditions needs to be satisfied for its felicitous use in a context. The difference between *bi* and the English determiner *this*, which only has a noteworthy felicity condition, is shown in (13a). In (13a), the sentence is grammatical even though the noteworthy condition is not satisfied, while in (12a), the lack of noteworthiness makes the sentence infelicitous. (13a) is felicitous in this context because there is an identifiable property 'new movie'. As stated above, identifiability does not only have to do with naming (see Aloni & Port (2015) on conceptual covers and methods of identification for epistemic indefinites) but any description that is able to set the referent of an NP apart from other NPs. Identifiability is context dependent. Context determines what counts as an identifiable property of an NP is in order to assume that the speaker "knows" it. Context and how it relates to identifiability will be discussed in detail in §4. In (13a) for instance, 'new movie' is an identifiable property that separates the movie Ama wants to watch from other movies. But there can be countless new movies at any particular time; it appears this identifying property does not qualify as enough information to say that we know the movie in question.

(13)   Akan (personal knowledge)

a. Ama pɛ   sɛ   ɔ- kɔ-hwɛ   sini   foforɔ bi a   a-   ba.
   Ama want COMP 3SG- MOT-watch movie new   IND REL PERF- come
   Me- n-   nim   sini   koro mpo.
   1SG- NEG- know movie one   even

   'Ama wants to see a certain new movie. I don't even know what movie.'

b. Ama pɛ   sɛ   ɔ- kɔ-hwɛ   sini   foforɔ bi a   a-   ba,
   Ama want COMP 3SG- MOT-watch movie new   IND REL PERF- come,
   me- n-   nim   sini   koro nanso ɔ-   a-   ka ho asɛm   saa
   1SG- NEG- know movie one   but   3SG- PERF- say self message EMP
   ara.
   EMP

   'Ama wants to see a certain new movie, I don't even know what movie but she has been talking about it for two weeks.'

c. Me- pɛ   sɛ   me- kɔ-hwɛ   sini   foforɔ bi. Me- n-
   1SG- want COMP 3SG- MOT-watch movie new   IND 1SG- NEG-
   kae   ne   din, me- n-   nim nea ɛ- fa ho mpo
   remember 3SG-POSS name 1SG- NEG- know what 3SG- take self even
   nanso obi   a-   ka a-   kyerɛ me   sɛ   ɛ- ye kama.
   but   someone PERF- say CONS- show 1SG.OBJ COMP 3SG- COP nice

   'I want to see a certain new movie – I can't remember its name and I have no idea what it's about, but someone mentioned to me that it's really interesting.'

We will now turn to the epistemic indefinite analysis of *bi*, keeping in mind the felicity conditions just discussed.

3 Epistemic indefinites (EI)

Aloni & Port (2015) distinguish between two types of indefinites: plain indefinites and epistemic indefinites. Plain indefinites like *somebody*, in addition to their conventional meaning, have an ignorance implicature.

(14)   English (Aloni & Port 2015: 117)
       Somebody arrived late.

a. Conventional meaning: Somebody arrived late.

b. Ignorance implicature: The speaker doesn't know who.

Epistemic indefinites, on the other hand, are indefinites in which this ignorance inference is conventionalized, i.e., is part of the meaning of the indefinite. Epistemic indefinites express the knowledge state of the speaker. Examples of epistemic indefinite determiners include German *irgendein* (Haspelmath 1997; Kratzer et al. 2002, cited in Aloni & Port 2015) and Italian *un qualche* (Zamparelli 2008, cited in Aloni & Port 2015). The examples below are from Aloni & Port (2015).

(15)   German (Aloni & Port 2015: 119)
       Irgendein   student hat angerufen. #Rat   mal wer?
       Irgend-one student has called   guess PRT who .
       Conventional meaning: 'Some student called' – the speaker doesn't know who.

(16)   Italian (Aloni & Port 2015: 119)
       Maria ha   sposato *un qualche* professore. #Indovina chi?
       Maria has married a   qualche professor   guess   who? .
       Conventional meaning: 'Maria married some professor' – the speaker doesn't know who.

In addition to expressing an existential proposition, these sentences have the additional claim that the speaker doesn't know who the witness to this proposition is (Aloni & Port (2015). For this reason, the continuation *guess who?* results in a contradiction. *Guess who?* presupposes that the speaker has some knowledge, which contradicts the ignorance inference of epistemic indefinites, resulting in the oddity. This assumed ignorance is not necessarily total ignorance of the referent of the NP, just the contextual relevant property to claim knowledge of the referent. Plain indefinites, on the other hand, allow for this type of continuation.

(17)   English (Aloni & Port 2015:117)
       Somebody arrived late, guess who?

As an epistemic indefinite, therefore, *bi* should behave like *irgendein* and *un qualche*. We expect that it is infelicitous with *Guess who?*, when it expresses that the speaker is ignorant about the contextually relevant property to characterize the NP that asserts knowledge.

(18)   Akan (personal knowledge)

    a. Sukuuni **bi** a-   frɛ wo.   # wo hwɛ a   ɛ-   yɛ   hwan?
       student IND PERF- call 2SG-OBJ   2SG- look REL 3SG- COP. who

       'Some student has called, guess who?'

b. Ama a-   ware professor **bi.** # wo- hwɛ a   ɛ-   yɛ hwan?
   Ama PERF- marry professor IND   2SG- look REL. 3SG- COP who

   'Ama has married some professor, guess who?'

I have to point out however that (18a) is felicitous when the speaker is sarcastic, but this context is marked. *Bi*, therefore, appears to have a conventionalized ignorance inference. In addition to *guess who*, epistemic indefinites are also infelicitous with *namely*. It becomes felicitous, however, if the speaker signals that he is reporting the name and does not know anything else about the referent.

(19)   Akan (personal knowledge)

   a. Sukuuni **bi** frɛ -ɛ   wo. # Yɛ- frɛ no   Kwadwo
      student IND call -PST 2SG   IMP- call 3SG-OBJ Kwadwo?

      'Some student called you, # he is called Kwadwo.

   b. Sukuuni **bi** frɛ -ɛ   wo. ɔ- se yɛ- frɛ no   Kwadwo.
      student IND call -PST 2SG 3SG- say IMP- call 3SG-OBJ Kwadwo

      'Some student called you, he says he is called Kwadwo.

In the subsequent sections, I will discuss *bi* in relation to the functions of epistemic indefinite discussed by Aloni & Port (2015).

3.1 Functions of epistemic indefinites

Aloni & Port (2015) discuss four functions of epistemic indefinites. These are (i) *specific unknown function* (SU), when it is used in an unembedded context, (ii) *epistemic unknown function* (epiU), when it is embedded under an epistemic modal, (iii) *negative polarity item (NPI) function*, when it gets narrow scope under negation, and (iv) *deontic free choice function* (deoFC), when it is embedded under deontic modals. They argue that for an indefinite to qualify for any of these functions, it must (a) be grammatical in the context the function specifies and (b) have the meaning that the function specifies. As I already discussed in the previous section, *bi* cannot be embedded under negation, which means that it does not have an NPI function. Also, though *bi* can be embedded under a deontic modal, it does not have a deoFc function; it only has a specific unknown interpretation under deontic modals.

(20)   Akan (personal knowledge)
       ɛ-   sɛ   sɛ   Ama ware professor **bi.**
       3SG- have COMP Ama marry professor IND

       'Ama must marry some professor.' (SU)

(20) only has the interpretation that there is a particular professor that Ama must marry. It does not have the meaning that it is necessarily the case that Ama marries some specific professor, which is the low scope reading of *bi*.

3.1.1 Specific unknown function (SU)

Syntactically, the specific unknown function is characterized by an unembedded use of the indefinite, i.e., use in matrix clause and not embedded under negation, modals or attitude verbs. Semantically, they have an obligatory ignorance effect: the speaker does not know the intended referent of the indefinite. Following Aloni & Port (2015), I will use the following continuation to distinguish between the specific and non-specific uses of the indefinite.

(21)   English (Aloni & Port 2015:118)
John wants to marry a Norwegian

    a.   She lives in Oslo and is 25 years old.

    b.   One with blond hair and blue eyes.

Bi like both *irgendein* and *un qualche* is grammatical in the specific unknown context and the interpretation specified.

(22)   Akan (personal knowledge)

    a.   Ama a- ware professor **bi**. # wo- hwɛ a   ɛ- yɛ hwan?
Ama PERF- marry professor IND   2SG- look COND. 3SG- COP who
'Ama has married some professor, #guess who?'

    b.   Sukuuni **bi** frɛ -ɛ wo.   # wo hwɛ a   ɛ- yɛ hwan?
student IND call -PST 2SG-OBJ 2SG- look COND 3SG- COP who
'Some student has called, #guess who?.'

Like *irgendein* and *un qualche*, *bi* has the weaker modal variation interpretation and not the stronger free choice interpretation. Aloni & Port (2015), following Alonso-Ovalle & Menéndez-Benito (2010), distinguish between two types of modal inference: modal variation and free choice. For the modal variation interpretation, more than one (but not necessarily all) alternatives in the relevant domain qualify as possible options. For the free choice interpretation, all the alternatives in the relevant domain qualify. In (23), the sentence is still true even if there are professors that the speaker has enough evidence to eliminate from the list of possible professors that Ama could have married.

(23) Akan (personal knowledge)

Ama a- ware professor **bi**. Me- n- nim nipa koro nanso
Ama PERF- marry professor IND 1SG- NEG- know human person but

me- yɛ sure sɛ ɛ- n- yɛ Kofi.
1SG- do sure COMP 3SG- NEG- COP. Kofi

'Ama has married some professor. I don't know who it is. I am sure it is not Kofi.'

3.1.2 Epistemic unknown function (epiU)

An ignorance effect similar to the one with specific unknowns arises when *bi* is embedded under epistemic modals.

(24) Akan (personal knowledge)

ɛ- bɛ- tumi a- ba sɛ Ama a- ware professor **bi**.
3SG- MOD- be.able CONS- come COMP Ama PERF- marry professor IND

'It could be that Ama has married some professor.'

This also has the weaker modal variation interpretation. It is compatible with the hide and seek scenario described in Aloni & Port (2015), where not all the alternatives in the relevant domain qualify.

(25) Akan (personal knowledge)

ɛ- bɛ- tumi a- ba sɛ Ama a- ware professor **bi**. ɛ-
3SG- MOD- be.able CONS- come COMP Ama PERF- marry professor IND 3SG-

te saa a me- yɛ sure sɛ ɛ- n- yɛ Kofi.
COP DEM COND 1SG- do sure COMP 3SG- NEG- COP Kofi

'It could be that Ama has married some professor. If that is true, I am sure it is not Kofi.'

Similar to *irgendein* and *un qualche*, *bi* embedded under propositional attitude verbs have agent oriented ignorance effects.

(26) Akan (personal knowledge)

Nana gye di sɛ Ama a- ware professor **bi**.
Nana collect eat COMP Ama PERF- marry professor IND

'Nana believes Ama has married some professor.'
'Nana believes that Ama married some professor, I don't know who.' (SU)
'Nana believes that Ama married some professor, Nana don't know who.' (EpiU)

Bi therefore is more similar to *un qualche* which has no NPI and deoFC functions. Table 1, taken from Aloni & Port (2015), shows some cross-linguistic comparison of epistemic indefinites; I have added *bi* to this table.

Table 1: Cross-linguistic comparison of epistemic indefinites

	SU	epiU	NPI	deoFC
irgendein	yes	yes	yes	yes
alg'un (SP)	yes	yes	yes	no
un qualche	yes	yes	yes	no
-si (Cz)	yes	no	no	no
vreun (Rom)	no	yes	yes	no
any(En)	no	no	yes	yes
qualunque (It)	no	no	no	yes
bi (Akan)	yes	yes	no	no

Akan confirms Aloni & Port's (2015) hypothesis that there should be no language where an epistemic indefinite has a deoFC function but not an NPI function.

3.2 Methods of identification and conceptual covers

There are at least two ways in which a context can determine a quantificational domain, domain widening and method of identification (conceptual covers). A conceptual cover is a set of individual concepts which exclusively and exhaustively covers the domain of individuals (Aloni 2001).

(27) [Definition of CONCEPTUAL COVERS] Given a set of possible worlds W and a domain of individuals D, a conceptual cover CC based on (W, D) is a set of individual concepts [i.e., functions $W \rightarrow D$] such that:

$$\forall w \in W : \forall d \in D : \exists! c \in CC : c(w) = d$$

She explains this with a card scenario which I repeat below. In front of you lie two face-down cards, one is the Ace of Hearts, the other is the Ace of Spades. You know that the winning card is the Ace of Hearts, but you don't know whether it's the card on the left or the one on the right. Now consider (28):

(28) English (Aloni & Port (2015))
      You know which card is the winning card.

Based on the scenario above, sentence (28) could be true or false in the described scenario. Intuitively, there are two different ways in which the cards can be identified here: by their position (the card on the left, the card on the right) or by their suit (the Ace of Hearts, the Ace of Spades). Our evaluation of (28) seems to depend on which of these identification methods is adopted. In the semantics of *knowing-wh* constructions proposed in Aloni (2001), the evaluation of (28) depends on which of these covers is adopted. She adds that this dependency is captured by letting the *wh*-phrase range over concepts in a conceptual cover instead of plain indefinites. Cover indices n are added to their logical form, and context supplies their value.

(29)   English (Aloni & Port 2015)
       You know which-n card is the winning card.
       False if $n \longrightarrow$ on-the-left, on-the-right
       True if $n \longrightarrow$ ace-of-spades, ace-of-hearts
       Trivial if $n \longrightarrow$ the-winning-card, the-losing-card

Conceptual covers and methods of identification are essential in understanding especially the specific unknown function of epistemic indefinites. When a speaker uses a specific marker, she signals that she has a particular referent in mind and that she can identify the referent of the indefinite. This appears to conflict with the ignorance inference that I have argued that epistemic indefinites have. The natural way to resolve this conflict is to assume that there are two methods of identification at play, the speaker knows one but not the other. The ignorance is not about all methods of identification for the referent, but for the essential one in that particular context.

3.2.1 Methods of identification

In this section, I explore the different methods of identification and the context of use that license *bi*. I compare *bi* to the German *irgendein* and the Italian *un qualche*. The method of identification that will be discussed are *naming, ostension* and *description.*

3.2.1.1 Description and Naming

Scenario: You are visiting a foreign university and you want to meet some professor.

(30) Akan (personal knowledge)
Me- re-   hwɛhwɛ professor **bi**,   ɔno na   ɔ- yɛ   head of
1SG- PROG- search   professor IND, 3SG FOC. 3SG- COP. head of
department, me- n-   nim   ne   din.
department, 1SG- NEG- know 3SG-POSS name.
'I am looking for some professor, he is the head of department but I don't
know his name.'
Speaker-can-identify → [Description], unknown → [Naming]

In this scenario, the method of identification contextually required for knowledge
is naming, but the referent of the epistemic definite can only be identified by
description.

3.2.1.2 Naming and Ostension

Scenario: At a conference, you have to meet a famous linguist.

(31) Akan (personal knowledge)
ɛ-   wɔ sɛ   me- hyia professor **bi**,   yɛ- frɛ no Nana Aba nanso
3SG- have COMP 1SG- meet professor IND, 3SG call her Nana Aba, but
me- n-   nim   no.
1SG- NEG- know 3SG
'I have to meet some professor, her name is Nana Aba, but I don't know
her.'
Speaker-can-identify → [Naming], unknown → [Ostension]

In this scenario, the method of identification contextually required for knowledge
is ostension, but the referent of the epistemic definite can only be identified by
naming.

3.2.1.3 Ostension and Naming

Scenario: You are watching a football match and a player gets injured, so you tell
your friends:

(32) Akan (personal knowledge)

Hwɛ player **bi** a- pira, yɛ frɛ no sɛn?
look player IND PERF- be.injured, 3PL call 3SG.OBJ what

'Look, some player is injured, what is his name?'
Speaker-can-identify → [Ostention], unknown → [Naming]

In this scenario, the method of identification contextually required for knowledge is naming, but the referent of the epistemic definite can only be identified by ostension.

Aloni (2001) ranks the method of identification as indicated in (33):

(33) Ostension > Naming > Description

Like *bi*, *irgendein* is felicitous in all the scenarios presented, *un qualche* on the other hand is infelicitous in the third scenario when the speaker could identify by ostension, but naming was unknown. *Bi* behaves like Germanic epistemic indefinites.

4 Analysis

Following Ionin (2013), I propose the following as the semantics of *bi*.

4.1 Semantics

A sentence of the form [bi α] β expresses a proposition only in those utterance contexts c where the speaker intends to refer to exactly one individual or the max of a group[2] y which is [α] in c and the relevant felicity conditions in (34a) or (34b) are fulfilled. Then [*bi* α] β is true at an index y if y is β at y and false otherwise. In addition to the felicity conditions, there is a presupposition that states the noteworthy and/or identifying property is all the information the speaker has about [bi α]. This presupposition is what differentiates *bi* and the English *some* from English the specific indefinite *a*. These sentences are only grammatical when they fulfill either of the conditions below.

(34) a. For [bi α] β, the speaker has in mind a *noteworthy property* $\varphi \in D\langle s, et \rangle$ such that $\varphi(wc)(y) = 1$.

b. The speaker is able to name *an identifying property* $\varphi \in D\langle s, et \rangle$ such that $\varphi(wc)(y) = 1$ and $\forall z[\alpha(wc)(z) = 1$ and $z \neq y] \rightarrow \varphi(wc)(z) \neq 1]$ and $\varphi \neq \alpha$ and $\varphi \neq \beta$.

---

[2] *Bi* is compatible with plural nouns.

c. Presupposition: Speaker is unable to provide any further information about who or what satisfies the existential claim s/he is making. Alonso-Ovalle & Menéndez-Benito (2003) for English *some* and Spanish *algún*. They did not, however, state it as a presupposition.

This meaning rules out a kind or generic interpretation for *bi.* (35a) can only mean that there is exactly one dog that Kofi saw, it cannot have the interpretation that Kofi saw something of the kind dog. When a plural is used with the determiner as in (35b), the determiners quantifiers over the sum or the max of the referents.

(35) Akan (personal knowledge)

    a. Kofi hu -u   kraman **bi.**
        Kofi see -PST dog   bi

        'Kofi saw a certain dog'

    b. Kofi hu -u   n- kraman **bi.**
        Kofi see -PST PL- dog   bi

        'Kofi saw some dogs.'

What is considered noteworthy is provided by the sentence, and identifiability supplied by context. For an N+*bi* to be felicitous, the noteworthy or identifying felicity condition must be satisfied, i.e., the speaker needs to be able to name at least one defining property of the referent with which an addresser can construct a referent of their own. And also the presupposition must be satisfied, i.e., whatever the noteworthy or identifying property is, its use is not sufficient to claim "knowledge" of the referent in the context. What qualifies as sufficient information to "know" the referent is regulated by the method of identification licensed by the context. In other words, in every context, there are two ways to identify the referent of an NP. One is whatever properties, descriptions or characteristics that are used in the sentence to identify it. This helps an addressee construct a referent of their own. Then, there is the way a particular context requires that the referent of an NP is identified in other to count as "knowing" the referent. For instance, if an NP is described as a "red flower" in a sentence, then the first method of identification is satisfied. But if the contexts require that someone only know what flower it is by knowing the name of the flower, then "red flower" is inadequate in this context. The use of N+*bi* signals that the second identifying property, i.e., the one required by context to "know" the referent is not satisfied. This idea of multiple methods of identification is what conceptual covers by Aloni & Port (2015) appear to capture:

Suppose *m* is the conceptual cover representing the identification method contextually required for knowledge, then EI signal an obligatory shift to a cover *n* different from *m*. That is, they existentially quantify over a cover which represents a method of identification which is not the one at play in the relevant context. (Aloni & Port 2015: 132)

If we take a look at (36), the speaker has asserted a noteworthy and identifying property about the flower. This property does not, however, show that the speaker "knows" the flower. What does it mean to know a flower? We use names to identify flowers. There are dozens of red flowers and thus knowing the color of a flower does not count as knowing it.

(36) Akan (personal knowledge)
      Me- hu -u   nhwiren kɔkɔɔ **bi.**
      1SG- see -PST flower   red   IND

      'I saw a certain red flower.'
      Speaker-can-identify → [Description], unknown → [Naming]

In this scenario, the method of identification contextually required for knowledge is naming, but the referent of the epistemic definite can only be identified by description. The ignorance component of the indefinite does not conflict with the noteworthy and identifying property requirement.

In example (37), the book is identified as the book lying on the table, as against the one on the bookshelf.

(37) Akan (personal knowledge)
      Me- hu -u   nwoma **bi** wɔ   pono no so.
      1SG- see -PST book   IND be.located table DEF top

      'There is a book on the table .'

This sentence is (in)felicitous in different contexts.

Context 1: I am sitting by the table and I can see *War and peace* on the table. Someone is looking for *War and peace*.

(38) Akan (personal knowledge)
      # Nhoma **bi** da pono no so nanso me- n-   nim   nhoma koro.
        book   IND lie table DEF top but   1SG- NEG- know book   one

      'There is some book on the table but I don't one which book it is.'

In this context, the speaker knows the name of the book and can see it. What appears to count as knowing a book is knowing its name. Thus the identification supplied by the sentence and the identification required by the sentence are the same, there is no speaker ignorance. The speaker knows what is necessary and sufficient to identify the book in this context, the ignorance component of *bi* is not fulfilled, and so the sentence is infelicitous.

Context 2: I am sitting at the table, and I can see *War and peace* on the table. Someone is looking for some book, but I do not know what book they are looking for.

(39) Akan (personal knowledge)
Nwoma **bi** da pono no so.
book IND sleep table DEF top
'There is some book book on the table.'

In this context, the speaker knows the name of the book and can see it. What s/he does not know is if the referent of the N satisfies what the addressee is looking for. So here, knowing the name of the book is not sufficient, what counts as "knowing" in this context is knowing what the speaker is looking for. The identification supplied by the sentence and the identification required by the sentence is different, speaker ignorance is satisfied, and the sentence is felicitous.

Context 3: I am cooking in the kitchen; someone is looking for *War and peace*. I remember I saw *War and peace* on the table.

(40) Akan (personal knowledge)
Me- hu -u nwoma **bi** wɔ pono no so nanso me-
1SG- see -PST book IND be.located table DEF top but 1SG-
n- nim nhoma koro.
NEG- know book one
'There is some book on the table but I don't one which book it is.'

In this context, the speaker knows the name of the book and she knows this satisfies the what the addressee is looking for. Knowing the name of the book is sufficient and counts as knowing what the speaker is looking for. The identification supplied by the sentence and the identification required by the sentence is the same. Speaker ignorance is not satisfied, so the sentence is infelicitous.

Context 4: I am cooking in the kitchen; someone is looking for *War and peace*. I remember I saw a book on the table, but I do not remember exactly what book it was.

(41) Akan (personal knowledge))
Me- hu -u   nwoma **bi**   wɔ   pono no so nanso me- n-
1SG- see -PST book   IND be.located table DEF top but   1SG- NEG-
nim   nhoma koro.
know book   one
'There is some book on the table but I don't one which book it is.'

In this context, what counts as knowing is knowing what the addressee is looking for. The speaker does not know the name of the book. Therefore the identification supplied by the sentence (description) and the identification required by the sentence (naming) are different. Speaker ignorance is consequently satisfied, and the sentence is felicitous.

5 Conclusion

I have shown how that *bi* has both a specific indefinite and an epistemic indefinite and these interpretations do not contradict each other. The identifiability felicity condition that is required for the interpretation of the specific indefinite feeds the epistemic indefinite interpretation. I have argued that when *bi* is used, the speaker signals that she does not have access to all the information that is required to "know" a referent in a particular context. She has some information about the referent to identify him, but not enough to "know" him. In so doing, I have highlighted a meaning of the indefinite determiner *bi* that has hitherto not been discussed in the Akan literature.

Acknowledgements

This paper started as a term paper for a Semantic Seminar taught by Veneeta Dayal. I will like to thank the Rutgers Semantics and Syntax Reading group, your comments and insights helped improve this paper. I am also grateful to the participants of ACAL 48, your questions and comments were beneficial. I have benefited from the comments and insights of two anonymous reviewers.

Abbreviations

CFM	Clausal Final Marker	MOT	Verb of motion
COMP	Complementizer	NEG	Negation
COP	Copular	PERF	Perfect
DEF	Definite	POSS	Possessive
DEM	Demonstrative	PROG	Progressive
EMP	Emphatic marker	PRT	Particle
Fam	Familiar	PST	Past
FUT	Fut	Ref	Referential
IND	Indefinite	REL	Relativizer

References

Abusch, Dorit & Mats Rooth. 1997. Epistemic np modifiers. In *Semantics and linguistic theory*, vol. 7, 1–18.

Aloni, Maria. 2001. *Quantification under conceptual covers*. Amsterdam: Institute for Logic, Language & Computation.

Aloni, Maria & Angelika Port. 2015. Epistemic indefinites and methods of identification. In *Epistemic indefinites: exploring modality beyond the verbal domain*. Oxford University Press, USA.

Alonso-Ovalle, Luis & Paula Menéndez-Benito. 2003. Some epistemic indefinites. In *Proceedings-nels*, vol. 33, 1–12.

Alonso-Ovalle, Luis & Paula Menéndez-Benito. 2010. Modal indefinites. *Natural Language Semantics* 18(1). 1–31.

Amfo, Nana Aba Appiah. 2006. Syntactic variation versus semantic uniqueness. In Eva Thue Vold, Gunn Inger Lyse & Anje Müller Gjesdal (eds.), *New voice in linguistics*, 211–224. Newcastle, UK: Cambridge Scholars Publishing.

Amfo, Nana Aba Appiah. 2010. Indefiniteness marking and akan bi. *Journal of Pragmatics* 42(7). 1786–1798.

Arkoh, Ruby Becky. 2011. *Semantics of Akan bi and nʊ*. University of British Columbia MA thesis.

Comrie, Bernard. 1989. *Language universals and linguistic typology: Syntax and morphology*. Chicago: University of Chicago press.

Ebert, Christian, Cornelia Ebert & Stefan Hinterwimmer. 2012. The interpretation of the German specificity markers *bestimmt* and *gewiss*. In Cornelia Ebert & Stefan Hinterwimmer (eds.), *Different kinds of specificity across languages*, 31–74. Dordrecht: Springer.

Ebert, Cornelia & Stefan Hinterwimmer. 2012. *Different kinds of specificity across languages.* Vol. 92. Springer.

Endriss, Cornelia. 2009. Exceptional wide scope. In *Quantificational topics: A scopal treatment of exceptional wide scope phenomena,* vol. 107-185, 107–185. Springer.

Farkas, Donka F. 2002. Varieties of indefinites. In *Semantics and linguistic theory,* vol. 12, 59–83.

Fodor, Janet Dean & Ivan A. Sag. 1982. Referential and quantificational indefinites. *Linguistics and Philosophy* 5(3). 355–398.

Givón, Talmy. 2001. *Syntax: An introduction.* Vol. 1. Amsterdam: John Benjamins Publishing.

Gundel, Jeanette K., Nancy Hedberg & Ron Zacharski. 1993. Cognitive status and the form of referring expressions in discourse. *Language.* 274–307.

Haspelmath, Martin. 1997. *Indefinite pronouns.* Oxford.

Hawkins, John A. 1978. Definiteness and indefiniteness: A study in reference and grammaticality prediction. *Journal of Linguistics* 11.

Heim, Irene. 1983. File change semantics and the familiarity theory of definiteness. *Semantics Critical Concepts in Linguistics.* 108–135.

Ionin, Tania. 2013. Pragmatic variation among specificity markers. In Ebert C. & Hinterwimmer S. (eds.), *Different kinds of specificity across languages,* 75–103. Dordecht: Springer.

Ionin, Tania & Ora Matushansky. 2006. The composition of complex cardinals. *Journal of Semantics* 23. 315–360.

Kratzer, Angelika. 1998. More structural analogies between pronouns and tenses. In Devron Strolovitch & Aaron Lawson (eds.), *Proceedings of Semantics and Linguistic Theory VIII,* 92–109. Cornell University: CLC Publications.

Kratzer, Angelika, Junko Shimoyama & Yukio Otsu. 2002. Proceedings of the 3rd Tokyo Conference on Psycholinguistics. In Yukio Otsu (ed.). Hituzi Syobo.

Payne, Thomas Edward. 1997. *Describing morphosyntax: A guide for field linguists.* Cambridge: Cambridge University Press.

Zamparelli, Roberto. 2008. On singular existential quantifiers in Italian. In Ileana Comorovski & Klaus von Heusinger (eds.), *Existence: semantics and syntax,* 293–328. Dordrecht, Netherlands: Springer.

Chapter 15

The interaction of *-ø-...-íle* with aspectual classes in Nyamwezi

Ponsiano Sawaka Kanijo
University of Gothenburg

This study investigates different readings of the construction *-ø-...-íle* resulting from the interaction with aspectual classes in Nyamwezi, a Bantu language spoken in Tabora, Tanzania. The study is motivated by two observations. Firstly, in previous analyses (Maganga & Schadeberg 1992), it was noted that *-ø-...-íle* in Nyamwezi selects few verbs, but the patterns governing its distribution were not identified. Secondly, not much has been done on describing the semantics of verbal roots in Nyamwezi (and many other Bantu languages), which appears to be a source of variable temporal interpretations of *-ø-...-íle*. Based on field data, I show that the first main function of *-ø-...-íle* is that of stativizer. That is, *-ø-...-íle* picks out a phase of an event or the entire event (if the event lacks phasic structure) and presents it as a stable, undifferentiated property. *-ø-...-íle* does so in three different ways, which give three different readings: (i) resultative, when it occurs with achievements, (ii) general present, which occurs with statives and (iii) a progressive-like reading, which occurs with some activity verbs classified as "directed motion verbs" in this study. The discussion of the contrast between these readings is informed by a progressive form *-lɪɪ-*. Many other activity verbs do not typically occur with *-ø-...-íle*. Those that occur with this construction either suggest the change-of-state or condition of the verb's subject (which has the semantic role of patient; patientive subject) or they are used in a special pragmatic condition where *-ø-...-íle* is coerced. Coercion of *-ø-...-íle* expresses a contradiction and/or emphasis, which can be regarded as a second main function of this construction.

1 Introduction

Sixty-six percent of Bantu languages use the verb suffix *-ile* (also *-ire*, *-ite*, *-ide* or *-i*) to refer to a variety of temporal notions, ranging from past tense, perfective

Ponsiano Sawaka Kanijo. 2019. The interaction of *-ø-...-íle* with aspectual classes in Nyamwezi. In Samson Lotven, Silvina Bongiovanni, Phillip Weirich, Robert Botne & Samuel Gyasi Obeng (eds.), *African linguistics across the disciplines: Selected papers from the 48th Annual Conference on African Linguistics*, 281–308. Berlin: Language Science Press. DOI:10.5281/zenodo.3520595

aspect to perfect/anterior (Nurse 2008; Botne 2010). In most of these languages, *-ile* occurs with the tense marker *-a-* at the pre-stem slot to refer predominantly to far or middle past. When *-ile* occurs without the tense marker *-a-*, it is used to express either past/perfective or perfect. Nyamwezi is one of these Bantu languages in which *-íle* occurs both with and without the pre-stem TAM marker *-á-*. The suffix *-íle* with *-á-* (*-á-...-íle*) indicates past perfective, as exemplified in (1). The construction *-á-...-íle* in this language occurs with all types of verbs and maintains the past perfective reading.

(1) waamálilé
    ʊ-á-mal-**íle**
    3SG-**CPL**-finish-**ile**
    'S/he finished (yesterday to infinity).'

Unlike many other Bantu languages in which the verb suffix *-ile* can occur with different types of verbs to encode different readings (see e.g. Brisard & Meeuwis 2009), in Nyamwezi the suffix *-íle*, without the tense marker *-á-* (*-ø-...-íle*) is restricted to a small set of verbs. For instance, it does not commonly occur with what is called *dynamic verbs* (those which denote a process, action or activity) such as 'plant', 'write', 'drill', etc. The same was also observed in a grammatical sketch of Nyamwezi by Maganga & Schadeberg (1992). Maganga & Schadeberg note that *-ø-...-íle* selects few verbs, mostly change-of-state verbs, to indicate the newly entered state. However, due to the restricted purpose of their study, they did not go into detail to describe all types of verbs that occur with this construction and to determine the readings when the verb occurs with *-ø-...-íle*. As they say:

> Unfortunately, we have not been able to work out the semantic subclassification of verbs which would allow us to describe the function of this tense [sic]. Maganga & Schadeberg (1992: 126)

This paper, therefore, is an attempt to provide a clearer understanding of the readings of *-ø-...-íle* in Nyamwezi when interacting with different types of verbs (which will be referred to as *aspectual classes*).

The reminder of this paper is organized as follows. §2 presents basic information about Nyamwezi, followed by a brief discussion of the relationship between *-ø-...-íle* and other tenses/aspects. The description of aspectual classes is given in §3. Following this section, §4 presents a discussion of the interaction between *-ø-...-íle* and aspectual classes. The paper closes with a brief summary of the study and some recommendations for further studies in §5.

2 Background

2.1 Nyamwezi language

Nyamwezi is a Bantu language spoken in the central western part of Tanzania, in the area called Tabora. The language is spoken by 1,320,000 people of Tanzania, where seventy-three percent of the speakers are found in the Tabora area (Lewis et al. 2013). The language is not highly endangered, despite the inevitable spread of Swahili in Tanzania. It is still spoken by people of all ages (Lewis et al. 2013).

According to Guthrie's 1967 widely acknowledged classification system, Nyamwezi is classified as F22. There are four dialects of Nyamwezi according to Masele (2001). These include Kinyanyembe, Kidakama, Sigalaganza and Kikonongo. The description in this paper is based on the Kidakama dialect, spoken in Uyui district.

2.2 -ø-...-íle and its relation to other tenses/aspects

The suffix *-íle*, apart from this basic form, can also be realized as *-íl-w-e*, *-íje* and *-iíle*. Verb stems that end with a glide create many variants. In longer stems of the form CVCW the glide /w/ is infixed within the suffix *-íle*. The form *-íje* occurs in verb stems that end in the sequence Cy, whereby the consonant /l/ of *-íle* is made palatal. Monosyllabic verb stems select a variant of *-íle* with a long vowel. All forms are exemplified in Table 1.

Table 1: Variants of *-íle*

The form of the stem	Stem	Gloss	*-íle* form
CVCw stems	*-togwá*	'love'	*-togílwe*
	-chilwa	'hate'	*-chililwe*
Stems ending in Cy	*-seßya*	'boil'	*-seßije*
	-sʊßya	'dilute'	*-sʊßije*
Monosyllabic stems	*-faá*	'die'	*-fiile*
	-pyaá	'be ripe'	*-piile*

Nyamwezi has a very complex tone system. The language is characterized by a H tone shift, where the underlying H tone of the subject/object concord and that of stem tends to shift one mora further to the right. Each type of tense and/or aspect has a distinctive tone rule. The tone of -ø-...-íle, as described in Maganga & Schadeberg (1992: 126), is shown in (2). TC/SC stands for tone copy of the subject concord. In all examples in this paper, the first sentence indicates the surface structure and the second one shows the underlying structure.

(2) The tone pattern of -ø-...-íle
     SC – (OC) – VB – íle + TC/SC

Nyamwezi has a highly agglutinative verbal structure with many possible tense, aspect and mood (TAM) prefixes and suffixes. As shown in (3), the TAM-marking morphemes in the verbal structure occupy the positions of the formative (slot 4), the post-final (slot 8) and the final (slot 9). The suffix -íle occupies the final position.

(3) Nyamwezi (Maganga & Schadeberg 1992: 97)
     The structure of verb forms

1	2	3	4	5	6	7	8	9	10
PreIn	In	PoIn	Fo	Fo2	PreR	VB		PreF	F	PoF
ASS	SC	NEG	TAM	IT	OC	Root/EXT	TAM	TAM/FV	PL

Maganga & Schadeberg (1992) note that the suffix -íle without the pre-tense marker -á (-ø-...-íle) typically indicates that a new state has been reached. This occurs most obviously in change-of-state verbs (such as -gaanda 'become thin'), as in (4), where -ø-...-íle has a resultative meaning.

(4) agaandilé
     a-ø-gaand-íle
     3SG-become_thin-íle
     'S/he is thin (because s/he has become thin)'

-ø-...-íle, while maintaining this reading, can appear in the past, present and future tenses. In the past tense, the construction occurs with an auxiliary verb -lɪ 'to be' as in (5), and in the future tense, it occurs with an auxiliary -kʊɓíí 'to be' in (6).

(5) waal'   áálaalílé   aho   tʊlɪɪɓɪtá   ŋwíípoólu
     ʊ-á-lɪ   a-ø-laal-íle   aho   tʊ-lɪɪ-ɓɪt-á   mu-ipoólú
     3SG-CPL.REC-AUX 3SG-sleep-íle when 2PL-PROG-pass-FV LOC-forest
     'S/he was sleeping when we were crossing the forest.'

(6) liindag'   hádoóo,   igolo   gakʊßii gáßoombíle
    liind-ag-a   hadoóo,   igolo   ga-kʊßií ga-ø-ßoomb-**íle**
    wait-IMP-FV short_while tomorrow cl.6-AUX cl.6-soak-**íle**
    'Wait a bit, tomorrow they will be soaked.'

In the present tense, the construction *-ø-...-íle* appears alone without *-lɪ* or *-kʊßií* as shown in (7), where the speech time is now.

(7) nalɪ́ɪ̃ßon'   áálaalíle,   kɪɪ akʊlugʊlaga   m̀lyaango!
    ná-lɪɪ-ßón-a   a-ø-laal-**íle**, kɪɪ a-kʊ-lugʊl-ag-a   m̀-lyaango!
    1SG-PROG-see-FV 3SG-sleep-**íle** why 3SG-NEG-open-REC-FV cl.3-door
    'I think (lit. see) s/he is asleep, why s/he doesn't open the door!'

Since the discussion of aspectual classes is crucial in understanding the meaning and interpretation of *-ø-...-íle*, the following section describes briefly aspectual classes in Nyamwezi. Note that aspectual classes described in this paper can be further differentiated. The discussion is limited to broad aspectual classes, but where necessary, minor classes will be highlighted. A further and detailed analysis of aspectual classes of Nyamwezi is still in progress.

3 Aspectual classes

The discussion of aspectual classes in this section pertains not only to the categorization of verbs themselves, but also to the nouns the verbs tend to associate with. Following Rothstein (2004: 1), the term *aspectual classes* (which is also referred to as *lexical aspect* or *Aktionsart*) is used in this study to refer to the event-types denoted by verbal expressions. The most widely received aspectual classes of verbal expressions are those stipulated by Vendler (1957). This includes states, activities, achievements and accomplishments. These classes are usually defined on the basis of temporal properties such as telicity and dynamicity. Telicity differentiates aspectual classes that indicate an inherent endpoint (telic) – achievements and accomplishments, and those which have the opposite pattern (atelic) – states and activities. Dynamicity differentiates aspectual classes that have complex internal structure – activities and accomplishments, and those which have homogeneous internal structure – states and achievements.

A number of diagnostic tests have been developed to determine Vendler's aspectual classes. However, as Bar-el (2015: 105) notes, many of these tests are not applicable universally. Filip (2012: 724), specifically, points out that not all the tests developed for English can be transferred to other languages, due to language-specific properties. In Bantu languages, Kershner (2002), Botne (2008) and Persohn (2017a,b), based on tenets of radical selection theories, a number of theories which classify aspectual classes with respect to the boundaries between different phases of an event, develop a number of language specific tests. These tests reveal more complex aspectual classes than those stipulated by Vendler. Before proceeding to the classification of aspectual classes in Nyamwezi using these Bantu specific tests, I will briefly outline a framework which has been used in many studies on aspectuality in Bantu languages, and also in this study, to classify aspectual classes.

3.1 Phase representation

One way in which the events named by the verbs may be differentiated is with respect to their temporal internal structures. In Bantu languages, Botne (1983), and Botne & Kershner (2000), following Freed (1979), propose a framework that takes into account three potential phases of an event, onset, nucleus and coda, to classify aspectual classes. The onset (O) phase, which may or may not be included in the event's temporal structure, constitutes the initial or preparatory phase of the event. It is a preparatory stage for the nuclear activity of the event. The coda (C) phase constitutes a final phase which brings the event to a definite end or to a state resulting from the prior event. Lastly, the nuclear (N) phase is characterized as comprising the characteristic and prominent feature of the event. All three phases are schematically represented in Figure 1.

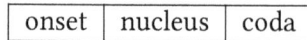

onset	nucleus	coda

Figure 1: Phase representation

In this framework, verbs are classified into different aspectual classes with respect to a number of phases they encode (only N, all three phases, N and C/O, etc.), and based on whether particular phases are punctual or durative. Botne (2010: 32–33) categorizes two major aspectual classes based on this framework, actions and achievements. The major difference between these two classes is that achievements have a punctual nuclear phase (N) that denotes a change-of-state whereas actions do not. According to Botne, actions include Vendler's (1957) activities and Smith's (1991) semelfactives. Schematic representations of these aspectual classes are shown in Figure 2.

C ⊐:   ‖
(O) N   N

Activity   Semelfactive

Figure 2: Event structures for actions (Botne 2010: 33)

Botne (2010) further classifies achievements into three subclasses which differ from one another in whether or not they incorporate an onset (O) and/or coda (C) phase. That is, inceptive achievements (such as *die* in English) encode a potential onset phase leading to the change-of-state nucleus, transitional achievements (such as *bend* in English) encode both an onset and stative coda phase, while resultatives (such as English *rupture*) encode only the point-of-transition (N phase) and the stative coda. These subclasses are schematized in Figure 3.

⊐   ⊐⊏   C
O N   O N C   N C
Inceptive   Transitional   Resultative

Figure 3: Event structures for achievements (Botne 2010: 33)

Kershner (2002: 62) based on the same framework, classifies another important aspectual class, namely statives, which is not addressed in Botne (2010). According to Kershner (2002), statives (in Chisukwa) represent an aspectual class without a phasic structure, thus she uses a dashed line to present the event structure of statives, as shown in Figure 4.

— — — — — — — —

Figure 4: Event structure for statives (Kershner 2002: 62)

3.2 Nyamwezi aspectual classes

With regard to the purpose of this study (which is not mainly about lexical aspect), Nyamwezi aspectual classes are classified into three: (i) achievements (Botne's (2010) transitional), (ii) statives, and (iii) duratives (Botne's (2010) actions). Statives fall into an independent class different from Botne (2010) who classified them under one of the achievement's subclasses called resultative. Following Botne (2010), I further classify duratives into activities and semelfactives. Semelfactives are like achievements in allowing punctual readings, but unlike canonical achievements they also allow iterative readings (cf. Kearns 2000). For this latter reason, semelfactives are classified as one of the subclasses of duratives. But, as will be further explained later, duration of semelfactives does not describe a clearly identifiable process like that of activities.

All classes are summarized in (8) and discussed in brief afterwards. I will use the framework shown in Figure 1 to show different event structures of each class, and apply at least one or two tests in each class to unveil the range and characteristics of the lexicalized temporal phases. Some of these tests were adopted from Kershner (2002), Crane & Fleisch (2016) and Persohn (2017b).

(8) Nyamwezi aspectual classes

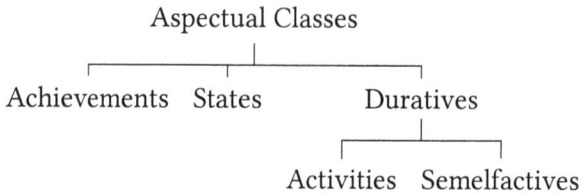

Aspectual Classes

Achievements States Duratives

Activities Semelfactives

By definition, ACHIEVEMENTS have a punctual nuclear phase, which constitutes a change (or transition) from one state (or location) to another. There are quite a number of achievements in Nyamwezi. These include *-gaasa* 'ferment slowly', *-gɪna* 'become fat', *-βola* 'become rotten', *-gwa* 'fall', *-pola* 'become cold', *-lʊla* 'become sour', *-lɪɪna* 'go up (e.g. a tree, a hill)', *-mana* 'get to know' and *-βoomba* 'soak'. As schematically represented in Figure 5, achievements encode an onset, a punctual point-of-transition and the resultant/coda phase. Achievements may be further classified based on whether an onset phase is or is not part of the event structure (see Figure 3). But, this sub-classification of achievements seems to be of minor relevance to the discussion of the readings of *-ø-...-íle*.

$$\begin{array}{|c|c|} \hline O & C \\ \hline \end{array}$$
$$N$$

Figure 5: Achievement event structure

One of the tests for achievements in Nyamwezi is their interpretation with *-andya* 'begin'. In most of these aspectual classes, *-andya* implies that the coda phase has not yet been reached, but the onset phase has started (9).

(9) gaandyága   kʊpola   ila gakapólílé
     ga-á-andy-ag-a   kʊ-pol-a   ila ga-ká-pol-íle
     cl.6-begin-CPL-start-REC-FV INF-cool_off-FV but cl.6-NEG-cool_off-íle
     kɪsoga
     kɪsoga
     good
     'It (the water) has begun to become cold, but it is not cold yet (it is warm)'

In (9), 'but it is not cold yet' gives some evidence that the onset phase has
begun, but the stative coda phase has not yet been reached.

Another test for achievements is their compatibility or incompatibility with
the persistive form -táá- 'still (being)' plus progressive form -lɪɪ-. The -táá- plus
-lɪɪ- construction, in principle, denotes a situation which is still in progress at
or around the reference time, thus usually compatible with duratives (where the
construction targets durative nucleus (see e.g. 14) and statives (where it targets
the continuing state (see e.g. 13). Since the nuclear phase of achievements is punctual, the -táá- plus -lɪɪ- construction is usually not accepted (10). However, for
those achievements which are acceptable with -táá- plus -lɪɪ- (e.g. 11), the test
selects an extended onset phase, a phase before a punctual change-of-state. So,
example (11) still emphasizes that the change-of-state nuclear phase of achievements is punctual regardless of its co-occurrence with -táá- plus -lɪɪ-.

(10) * gataálɪ   gálɪɪβólá
      ga-táá-lɪ   ga-lɪɪ-βol-a
      cl.6-still-AUX cl.6-PROG-become_rotten-FV

      Lit. 'They (e.g. mangoes) are still becoming rotten'

(11) gataálɪ   galɪɪβoómbá,   liindɪɪlagá   hadoóo
      ga-táá-lɪ   ga-lɪɪ-βoomb-a   liind-ɪɪl-ag-á   hadoóo
      cl.6-still-AUX cl.6-PROG-soak-FV wait-APPL-IMP-FV short_while
      gakʊβoomba   doó
      ga-kʊ-βoomb-a   doó
      cl.6-FUT-soak-FV few

      'They (e.g. cassava) are still soaking; wait a short while, they will be
      soaked'

STATIVES differ from achievements (and also duratives) in one aspect; they
have no phasic structure making up different phases of an event. All they do is

describe an indefinite state. Following Kershner (2002), statives are schematically represented by a dashed line, as shown in Figure 4. Examples of statives are verbs such as *-chilwa* 'dislike', *-ikólá* 'resemble', *-saata* 'be sick' and *-togwá* 'love, like'.

One way to show that statives form a separate class from achievements is their interpretation with *-andya* 'begin'. We saw that in achievements *-andya* asserts that the onset phase has started but the following coda phase has not been reached. This is not true with statives. It is impossible to specify all phases of the event in statives, thus *-andya* refers to the beginning of the stative event (not the beginning of O, N or C phase).

(12) waandyága   kʊsaata   haáŋgɪ
      ʊ-á-andy-ag-a   kʊ-saat-a   again
      3SG-begin-REC-FV INF-be_sick-FV again
      'S/he has begun to be sick again'

Another way which shows that statives and achievements fall into separate classes is their (in)compatibility with the persistive form *-táá-* 'still (being)' plus the progressive form *-lɪɪ-*. We previously saw that this test is usually incompatible with achievements (e.g. 10) or targets the extended onset phase in those achievements it co-occurs with (e.g. 11). Statives with *-táá-* + *-lɪɪ-* denote the continuation of a state, as exemplified in (13).

(13) ataálɪ   alɪɪ'saata
      a-táá-lɪ   a-lɪɪ-saat-a
      3SG-still-AUX 3SG-PROG-be_sick-FV
      'S/he is still sick'

DURATIVES, as illustrated in Figure 6, have an extended nuclear phase. There are two subclasses of durative verbs. The first subclass, called ACTIVITIES, includes verbs which indicate a clearly identifiable process of an event from moment to moment. Examples in this class are verbs such as *-lyaá* 'eat', *-lɪma* 'cultivate', *-zugá* 'cook', *-dɪtɪla* 'pour into', *-pʊʊla* 'pound', *-zeenga* 'build', *-ja* 'go', *-lila* 'cry', *-peela* 'run', *-seka* 'laugh' *-shooka* 'reverse, move backwards' and *-iza* 'come'. The second subclass of durative verbs, called SEMELFACTIVES (Seidel's (2008) "instantaneous" predicates), in principle, includes verbs whose nuclear phase is punctual, if the verb's event is viewed as a single event. But, based on the diagnostic test used in this study, semelfactives indicate an iterative series of the event, thus classified as a durative aspectual class with an extended nuclear phase. This type of aspectual class includes verbs such as *-kolola* 'cough', *-lumá* 'bite', *-boola* 'hit' and *-luusa* 'kick'.

(O)	N	(C)

Figure 6: Durative event structure

Although semelfactives (when perceived as a series) resemble activities in having an extended nuclear phase, the nuclear phase of semelfactives, as previously stated, does not encode a clearly identifiable process like that of activities. The main difference between activities and serial semelfactives can be seen in the interpretation of the persistive form *-táá-* 'still (being)' plus the progressive form *-lɪɪ-*. In activities, *-táá-* plus *-lɪɪ-* indicates a clear duration of an event. For example, in (14a), the process of lifting and setting down each foot in turn at a speed faster than a walk occupies most of the duration of the event. In semelfactives, *-táá-* plus *-lɪɪ-* does not describe a comparable process. In (14b), *-táá-* plus *-lɪɪ-* indicates serial or periodic events, i.e. the event of coughing still holds serially or periodically.

(14) a. ataálɪ́   alɪɪpeela
          a-táá-lɪ   a-lɪɪ-peel-a
          3SG-**still**-AUX 3SG-**PROG**-run-FV
          'S/he is still running'

      b. ataálɪ́   alɪɪkolola
          a-táá-lɪ   a-lɪɪ-kolol-a
          3SG-**still**-AUX 3SG-**PROG**-tremble-FV
          'S/he is still coughing (periodically)'

For the purpose of this study, it is important to note that although all activity verbs in Nyamwezi encode an extended nuclear phase, motion verbs with directional interpretation and a goal (location phrase) such as *-ja* 'go (home)', *-peela* 'run (to the shops)', *-shooka* 'reverse, move backwards' and *-iza* 'comeback towards a particular point' behave somewhat differently from other duratives and other motion verbs such as *-duumʊka* 'jump' and *-βɪtá* 'pass'. I categorize these verbs as DIRECTED MOTION VERBS (different from other duratives) because it is a category of verbs which can naturally occur with *-ø-...-íle* to encode a reading that I have referred to as "progressive-like" in this study (discussed in §4.3).

4 Interactions *-ø-...-íle* with aspectual classes

There is a correspondence relationship between lexicalized temporal phases (O, N, and C) (discussed above) and tense/aspect forms. Tense/aspect forms act as phase-selectors that "pick out" or "select" matching phases encoded in the lexical/phasal dimension (Sasse 2002: 223). In the discussion of the interactions between -ø-...-íle with aspectual classes in the following subsections, I will argue that one of the main functions of -ø-...-íle in Nyamwezi, as in Totela (Crane 2013), is that of a stativizer, i.e. it asserts a state or property of the subject, resulting from the referenced situation/event. In other words, -ø-...-íle picks out a phase of an event or the entire event (if the event lacks phasic structure) and presents it as a stable, undifferentiated property. -ø-...-íle does so in three different ways, which give three different readings. First, in achievements, -ø-...-íle selects the coda phase of the situation. In this case, -ø-...-íle denotes a state that exists as a result of the situation described by the verb constellation, hence it gives a resultative reading. Second, in statives, -ø-...-íle selects the stative phase which is part of a situation's inherent structure. In this case, -ø-...-íle asserts a state which is equivalent to the permanent state of the situation described by the verb, hence it gives a general present time reading. Lastly, in directed motion verbs, -ø-...-íle selects the nuclear phase of the situation. In this case, -ø-...-íle asserts a state of the verb's situation which is currently underway, hence it gives a reading which is translated with progressive form in English (this reading will be referred to as progressive-like). The three readings of -ø-...-íle in Nyamwezi: resultative, general present time, and progressive-like, are exemplified in Table 2.

Notice that other activity verbs, apart from directed motion verbs, are usually unacceptable with -ø-...-íle in Nyamwezi, unless the verb suggests a change-of-state or condition to the verb's subject, which has the semantic role of the patient (patientive subject), or it is used in a special pragmatic condition where -ø-...-íle is coerced. This special pragmatic condition gives a second main function of -ø-...-íle which will be discussed in §4.4. The interaction of semelfactives with -ø-...-íle, for reasons that will be provided in §4.4, is generally not acceptable in Nyamwezi.

4.1 -ø-...-íle with achievements

Achievements predominantly have a punctual nuclear phase which indicates a transition from one state to another. This is an aspectual class which typically occurs with the construction -ø-...-íle to encode a resultative reading, as exemplified in (15). As previously noted, this reading indicates that the result of a past situation holds at the moment of speech (cf. Comrie 1976; Bybee et al. 1994).

---

[1]The noun prefix *ka-* expresses a diminutive.

Table 2: Readings of *-ø-...-íle* by aspectual classes

Aspectual classes	Temporal interpretations	Examples
Achievements	Resultative	*aginíle* a-ø-gin-íle 3SG-become_fat-íle 'S/he is fat (because s/he got fat in the past)'
Statives	General present time	*kasaatíle* ka[1]-ø-saat-íle cl.12-be_sick-íle 'S/he (small child) is sick'
Activities (Directed motion verbs)	Progressive-like	*azíílé* *kʊPúgu* a-ø-z-íle kʊ-Pugu 3SG-go-íle LOC-Pugu 'S/he is going to Pugu'

(15)   a.   gʊʊfuɲág'   iisʊ   lyáa-kʊβií ɳhaná gálʊlílé
         ga-kʊ-fuɲ-ag-a   isʊʊ   lyaá-kʊβií ɳhaná ga-lʊl-íle
         cl.6-HAB-give_out-HAB-FV smell CON-to_be truth cl.6-sour-íle
         'It gives out a smell indicating that it really is sour.'

      b.   kɪβeélile   gáshy'   ʊʊɱgatɪ chʊʊβi kɪβólílé
         kɪ-ø-βeél-íle   gashí   ʊ-ɱgatɪ ch-ʊβií kɪ-ø-βol-íle
         cl.7-be_nice-íle whereas A-inside cl.7-AUX cl.7-become_rotten-íle
         nʊʊlʊ kɪβíípilé
         nʊʊlʊ kɪ-ø-βiíp-íle
         or   cl.7-become_bad-íle
         'It appears to be nice, but inside it is rotten or bad.'

      c.   ɳwaaná ɳʊnʊʊyʊ aginíle   yé
         ɳw-aaná ɳʊnʊʊyʊ a-ø-gin-íle   yé
         cl.1-child DEM   3SG-become_fat-íle very
         'The child is very fat.'

The resultative reading indicates that a causal relationship exists between the past/prior eventuality and the current state. For instance, in (16) the situation of being sour resulted from the situation of becoming sour. This relationship, as ex-emplified and illustrated in (17), can be clearly shown using the progressive form -lɪɪ-, which indicates the prior situation, and the construction -ø-...-íle, which in-dicates the current state. In (17), a horizontal dotted line indicates the flow of an event from onset phase to coda phase; the shadow marks the phase encoded by -lɪɪ- and -ø-...-íle.

(16) a. galɪɪlʊla
          ga-lɪɪ-lʊl-a
          cl.6-**PROG**-become_sour-FV
          'It is becoming sour.'

      b. galʊlilé
          ga-ø-lʊl-**íle**
          cl.6-ø-become_sour-íle
          'It is sour.'

(17) Event-structure construals of the progressive form -lɪɪ- and the construc-tion -ø-...-íle

a.

O	C
becoming sour	being sour

b.

O	C
becoming sour	being sour

All examples given in this section express a resultative reading, a reading which focuses on the present/ongoing state resulting from an event. This reading should not be confused with the perfect (of result) reading, a reading which fo-cuses on the past event which resulted in a state of affairs, which in English can be exemplified by *I have built a house next to the river*. Evidence that -ø-...-íle in Nyamwezi denotes a resultative reading (in achievements), and *not* a perfect of result, is its compatibility with -táá- 'still (being)', which indicates that the result state of the situation still holds (is extended) (18).

(18) a. ataálɪ   agɪnílé
          a-táá-lɪ   a-ø-gɪn-íle
          3SG-**still**-AUX 3SG-become_fat-íle
          's/he is still fat'

b. ataálı   amánílé   kweendéésha βasikélí
    a-táá-lı   a-ø-man-íle   kʊ-endéésh-a βasikélí
    3SG-**still**-AUX 3SG-**get_to_know**-íle INF-cycle-FV bicycle
    'S/he still knows how to ride a bicycle'

Co-occurrence of *-táá-* 'still (being)' plus *-ø-...-íle* in Nyamwezi is a good piece of evidence for the resultative reading because resultatives, unlike perfects, in principle, are incompatible with 'still' (cf. Dahl 1985:134). For example, in English **I have still built a house next to the river* is not acceptable.

4.2   *-ø-...-íle* with statives

In Figure 3, it is stated that statives denote an indefinite state. These aspectual classes have no internal change; thus I argued that they lack a phasic structure. There are very few statives in Bantu languages in general, and in Nyamwezi in particular. Non-tense-marked statives in Nyamwezi denote a general present time reading; a reading in which the state of the situation having occurred is equivalent to the prior situation. For instance, all phases of the event *asaatilé* 'S/he is suffering' in (19) are identical. Whichever point of time we choose to cut in on this event, we shall find exactly the same situation.

(19)   a.   asaatilé   kwıındgıla kʊβyaálwa   kwaákwé
          a-ø-saat-íle   kwıındgıla kʊ-βyaál-w-a   kwaákwé
          3SG-**be_sick**-íle since   INF-bear-PASS-FV POSS
          'S/he has been suffering since her birth.'

      b.   βatogilwé   kʊ́βawíılaa   βiíchaaβó   βátʊmame
          βa-ø-tog-ílwe kʊ-βa-wııl-a   a-βiíchaaβó   βá-tʊmám-eé
          3PL-**love**-íle   INF-OC-tell-FV cl.1-companions_their cl.2-work-OPT
          'They like to tell their mates that they should work (hard).'

Statives in this language do not neatly indicate a cause-result relationship between the prior eventuality and the current state, thus both the progressive form *-lıı-* and the construction *-ø-...-íle* give more or less the same interpretation, as shown in (20).

(20)   a.   kalıısaata
          ka-lıı-saat-a
          cl.12-**PROG**-be_sick-FV
          'S/he (small child) is sick.'

b. kasaatilé
ka-ø-saat-**íle**
cl.12-be_sick-**íle**
'S/he (small child) is sick.'

Although both -*lɪɪ*- and -*ø*-...-*íle* receive the same translation in English, there is a difference having to do with whether an event is bounded or unbounded. The progressive form -*lɪɪ*- suggests that the event holds at the moment of speaking but it will come to an end sometime in the future, whereas the construction -*ø*-...-*íle* does not give this implication. It just describes a (permanent) state. This distinction can be equated with Kratzer's (1995) distinction between stage-level statives which refer to temporary states and individual-level statives which refer to permanent states. Schematically, the difference between -*lɪɪ*- and -*ø*-...-*íle* is shown in Figures 7 and 8, where a bold vertical line indicates boundedness of an event in Figure 7 (stage level). The lack of this line in Figure 8 implies the event is unbounded (individual-level).

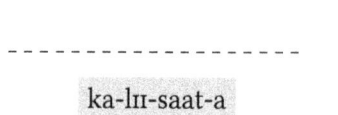

ka-lɪɪ-saat-a

Figure 7: -*lɪɪ*- event structure

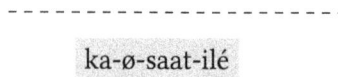

ka-ø-saat-ilé

Figure 8: -*ø*-...-*íle* event structure

It is hard to find a context where the difference between -*lɪɪ*- and -*ø*-...-*íle* occurs. One of the language consultants for this study mentioned that in many contexts he can use both ways to express the same meaning. The difficulty in finding a context where one can appreciate the difference between the two formatives lies in the fact that the situation of getting sick for instance, which for the case of achievements can be selected by the progressive, is equal to the current state (which in achievements is picked out by the -*ø*-...-*íle*). Statives do not show this type of relationship.

In order to find the difference, consultants were asked to tell which of the two forms they can use when talking about chronic diseases. They all agreed that the construction -*ø*-...-*íle* is appropriate when talking about chronic diseases (hence unacceptable in 20b), while the form -*lɪɪ*- is only used to talk about curable diseases like malaria (hence acceptable in 20a). The use of -*ø-...-íle* when referring to chronic diseases gives some evidence that this construction really describes a state, while -*lɪɪ*- denotes an event which is true for the time being, but probably it will not persist in the coming days.

(21) [Context: Someone has arrived and is looking at the children who are playing at the house compound. As she was expecting to see J, but J is not there, she then asks "where is J today?"]

a. * waaláálaga   m̀kaaya,   asaatilé   málelíyá
       ʊ-á-laál-ag-a   m̀-kaaya,   a-ø-saat-íle   maleliyá
       3SG-CPL-sleep-REC-FV LOC-homestead 3SG-be_sick-íle malaria

       'She is sleeping inside the house, suffering from malaria.'

b.   waaláálaga   m̀kaaya,   alɪɪsaata
       ʊ-á-laál-ag-a   mu-kaaya,   a-lɪɪ-saat-a
       3SG-CPL-sleep-REC-FV LOC-homestead 3SG-**PROG**-be_sick-FV
       malelíyá
       malelíyá
       malaria

       'She is sleeping inside the house, suffering from malaria.'

4.3 -ø-...-íle with activities, classified as "directed motion verbs"

As described in the previous section, duratives, in general, have an extended nuclear phase (as shown in Figure 9). Duratives are classified into two subclasses: activities (those in which the nuclear phase indicates internal change of an event from moment to moment, e.g. -*lyaá* 'eat' and -*peela* 'run') and serial semelfactives (those in which the nuclear phase constitutes multiple occurrences of a situation when perceived as series, e.g. -*kolola* 'laugh').

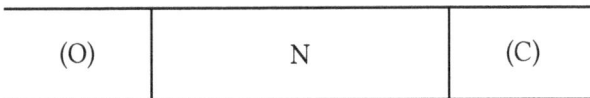

(O)	N	(C)

Figure 9: Durative event

In the discussion of activity verbs in §3.2, I stated that motion verbs with directional interpretation and a goal (called directed motion verbs), e.g. -*peela* 'run (to the store)', behave somewhat differently from other duratives. These verbs in Botne & Kershner's model do not specify the coda phase, a phase at which a result state comes about. So, they are schematically represented in Figure 10 where the last phase is nuclear phase.

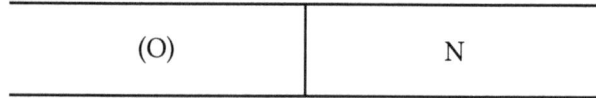

(O)	N

Figure 10: Event structure for directed motion verbs

We saw in example (16) that in aspectual classes which encode a resultant/coda phase, *-ø-...-íle* picks out this phase and gives a resultative reading. Since in directed motion verbs the coda phase is not part of the situation's event (see Figure 10), *-ø-...-íle* picks out the nuclear phase and gives a reading which can be translated with progressive form in English (progressive-like reading) (22). Ebert (1995: 194) notes a similar phenomenon in Arabic where what is called the "Active Particle" form, which usually indicates perfect/resultative meaning in other verbs, in verbs of posture, of motion and of sensory perception expresses a progressive-like reading.

It is important to state that *-ø-...-íle* in both achievements and directed motion verbs is attuned to the initial (left) edge of the nuclear phase. This means that in achievements the perspective is in the stative coda phase, but in directed motion verbs it is in the nuclear phase.

(22)   a. apeelilé   kʊjaa   kʊmadʊʊka
           a-ø-peel-íle kʊ-j-a   kʊ-madʊʊka
           3SG-run-íle INF-go-FV LOC-shops

           'S/he is/has run off to the shops.'

      b. gaángɪ   gíízilé   nágaángɪ gáshookílé
           ga-ángɪ ga-ø-iz-íle na-gaángɪ ga-shook-íle
           cl.6-other cl.6-come-íle and-other cl.6-return-íle

           'Some (e.g. lions in a narration) are coming and some are going back.'

The progressive-like reading in directed motion verbs, as exemplified above, is also a resultative in its function, just like that of achievements. The progressive reading in these verbs is a matter of the English translation (cf. Ebert 1995:189). The difference between a resultative reading of achievements and that of directed motion verbs is that, in achievements the result state is triggered by a nuclear phase which denotes the change-of-state, whereas in directed motion verbs the initial point (onset phase) is regarded as a point of change (cf. Smith 1991:70).

Since the phase following this point of transition in directed motion verbs is a nuclear phase, *-ø-...-íle* selects this ongoing/dynamic non-stative phase to encode a stative(-like) meaning along the lines of 'be directed towards a certain goal'.

One piece of evidence is present to justify the claim that directed motion verbs encode a kind of change-of-state which is similar to that of achievements. Both directed motion verbs, as shown in (23), and achievements (see e.g. 18 repeated in (24)) occur with the persistive form *-táá-* 'still (being)' plus *-ø-...-íle*. Co-occurrence of this construction with directed motion verbs indicates that a state that results from an ongoing situation still holds.

(23) ataálɪ   alɪ   m̀nzɪla azíílé   kaayá
      a-táá-lɪ   a-lɪ   mu-nzɪla a-j-íle   kaayá
      3sg-**still**-AUX 3sg-COP LOC-path 3sg-go-**íle** home

      'S/he is on the way (going) home'

(24) ataálɪ   agɪnílé
      a-táá-lɪ   a-ø-gɪn-íle
      3sg-**still**-AUX 3sg-become_fat-**íle**

      'S/he is still fat'

In directed motion verbs, English makes no distinction between the progressive form *-lɪɪ-* and *-ø-...-íle*. So, both *a-lɪɪ-peel-a* and *a-peel-ilé* are translated in English as 's/he is running'. The difference between *-lɪɪ-* and *-ø-...-íle*, however, can be settled by context. For instance, in (25), the context is such that the speaker is watching a movie but he missed a part in the movie where the actress (Kajala) saw a lion and started to run away. He then asks another person who started to watch the movie before he came "Why is Kajala running away?" (*kʊʊngʊno-kɪ ʊ-kajala a-lɪɪ-peel-a?*). A response to this question with the progressive form *-lɪɪ-* sounds fine (25a), but one with *-ø-...-íle* sounds odd (25b).

(25) a. alɪɪpeel'   iishiímbá
          a-lɪɪ-peel-a   i-shiímbá
          3sg-**PROG**-run-FV cl.5-lion

          'She is fleeing from a lion' (Lit: 'She is running away from the lion')

      b. * apeelil'   íishiímbá
          a-ø-peel-íle   i-shiímbá
          3sg-run-**íle** cl.5-lion

          'She fled from a lion' (Lit: 'She is running away from the lion')

Likewise, the progressive form *-lɪɪ-* cannot be used to refer to the continuing state of the subject, which is encoded by *-ø-...-íle*. For instance, (26) is in a context where the teacher is looking for a missing student (Anna). He then asks other students who were outside the class playing, "Have you seen Anna today?" (*w-aa-mú-βon-ág-a ʊ-ana leeloó?*). A response to this question with the progressive form *-lɪɪ-* sounds odd (26b), but one with *-ø-...-íle* sounds fine (26a).

(26) a. waaβɪtaga   apeelilé
          ʊ-á-βɪt-ag-á   a-ø-peel-íle
          3SG-CPL-pass-REC-FV 3SG-PROG-run-íle
          'She passed (here) running.'

      b. * waaβɪtaga   alɪɪpeela
          ʊ-á-βɪt-ag-á   a-lɪɪ-peel-a
          3SG-CPL-pass-REC-FV 3SG-**PROG**-run-FV
          She passed (here) running'

The co-occurrence of the *-lɪɪ-* and *-ø-...-íle* in the same construction provides further evidence that the two forms do not perform the same function. One (*-ø-...-íle*) indicates a state and the other (*-lɪɪ-*) indicates the action in progress. This distinction is illustrated in (27) where the point of speech is now, the point of reference is in the past, established by *-βɪtá* 'pass', continued by *-peela* 'run' and directed towards a location by *-ja* 'go'. The continuation of the event of running can be construed as a dynamic state (27a) or a process (27b). Similarly, *-ja* 'go' which indicates the direction of the event can be construed as a process (27a) or a dynamic state (27b). This relationship is further expressed by literal translations.

(27) a. waaβɪtaga   apeelilé,   alɪɪja   kaaya
          ʊ-á-βɪt-ag-á   a-ø-peel-íle, a-lɪɪ-j-a   kaaya
          3SG-CPL-pass-REC-FV 3SG-run-íle   3SG-**PROG**-go-FV homestead
          Lit. 'She passed (here), she was running going home'
          'She passed (here), having run, going home.'

      b. waaβɪtaga   alɪɪpeela,   azíílé   kaáya
          ʊ-á-βɪt-ag-á   a-lɪɪ-peel-a, a-z-íle   kaaya
          3SG-CPL-pass-REC-FV 3SG-**PROG**-run-FV 3SG-go-íle homestead
          Lit. 'She passed (here) running, s/he was going home'
          'She passed (here) running, gone off home.'

Another piece of evidence is that neither the progressive form *-lɪɪ-*, as in (28a), nor the construction *-ø-...-íle*, as in (28b), can be used with both *-peela* 'run' and *-ja* 'go', as each form performs a different function in Nyamwezi.

(28) a. *waaβɪtaga   alɪ̨peela,   alɪ̨ja   kaaya
        ʊ-á-βɪt-ag-á   a-lɪ̨ɪ-peel-a   a-lɪ̨ɪ-j-a   kaaya
        3SG-CPL-pass-REC-FV 3SG-**PROG**-run-FV 3SG-**PROG**-go-FV homestead

   Lit. 'She passed (here) she was running, s/he was going home'
   'She passed here, she was running towards home'

b. *waaβɪtaga   apeelilé   azíílé   kaáya
        ʊ-á-βɪt-ag-á   a-ø-peel-íle a-z-íle   kaaya
        3SG-CPL-pass-REC-FV 3SG-run-íle   3SG-go-íle   homestead

   Lit. 'She passed (here) running, going home'
   'She passed here, she was running towards home.'

4.4 -ø-...-íle with other activities and semelfactives

In the previous section, I argued that directed motion verbs in Nyamwezi behave somewhat differently from other activity verbs and (serial) semelfactives. Directed motion verbs, as we have seen, do not lexically encode the (resultant state) coda phase, they only encode an optional onset phase and a nuclear phase. In directed motion verbs, -ø-...-íle selects the nuclear phase and gives a progressive-like reading.

Another category of activity verb includes verbs such as -sha 'grind (e.g. corn)', -dɪtɪla 'pour (e.g. water) into (a receptacle)', -pʊʊla 'pound (e.g. corn)', -zeenga 'build (e.g. a house)' -lɪma 'cultivate (e.g. a farm)' and -chiβá 'block hole/way, plug', which, compared to directed motion verbs, lexically indicates a durative nucleus and an entailed resultant/coda state (cf. Persohn's (2017b) processes with a resultant state). In many of these verbs in Bantu languages, -íle tends to pick out a resultant/coda state phase to give a perfect of result reading (see e.g. Luwanga and Lusaamia in Botne (2010)) or resultative reading (see e.g. Totela in Crane (2013)). The same is also observed in Nyamwezi, verbs such as -sha 'grind' and -dɪtɪla 'pour into', as exemplified in (29a) and (29b), respectively, occur with -ø-...-íle to encode a patientive resultative reading. In this reading, the verb's subject, which has the semantic role of the patient (patientive subject), undergoes a change-of-state. Note that some verbs in this category permit the causative alternation in which the patientive resultative reading is triggered by both -ø-...-íle and the passive form -w- (29c), though some take the passive form but do not allow causative alternation (29d–e)[2]. For the purpose of this study, I will not go into detail to discuss the question why some verbs in this category permit

---

[2]For comparison, an example below indicates a sentence with agent-verb-patient S-V-O structure in Nyamwezi.

causative alternation while others do not. Further studies are required on the lexical semantics of these verbs.

(29) a. *ashiílé   vs. zishiílé
         a-ø-sh-íle   zi-ø-sh-íle
         3sG-grind-íle   cl.10-grind-íle
         'S/he has ground (the peanuts)' 'They (peanuts) are ground.'

     b. *adɪtɪlílé   vs. yɪdɪtɪlílé
         a-ø-dɪtɪl-íle   yɪ-ø-dɪtɪl-íle
         3sG-pour_into-íle cl.9-pour
         'S/he has poured (water) into a vessel.' 'It (a vessel) has been poured into'.

     c. achiβílé   vs. yɪchiβílwé   (*yɪchiβílé)
         a-ø-chiβ-íle   yɪ-ø-chiβ-íl-w-e
         3sG-block-íle   cl.9-block-PASS-íle
         'S/he has closed (a way)' 'It (the way) is closed'

     d. *apʊʊlílé   vs. gapʊʊlílwé   (*gapʊʊlílé)
         a-ø-pʊʊl-íle   ga-ø-pʊʊl-íl-w-e
         3sG-pound-íle   cl.6-pound-PASS-íle
         'S/he has pounded (the corn)' 'It (corn) is pounded'

     e. *alɪmílé   vs. lɪlɪmilwé
         a-ø-lɪm-íle   lɪ-ø-lɪm-íl-w-e
         3sG-cultivate-íle 3sG-cultivate-PASS-íle
         'She has cultivated (a farm.)' 'It (a farm) is cultivated'

Verbs shown above are subject to a second type of result state analysis which is similar to that of achievements. The resultant state in these verbs involves a "durative transition" from one state to another, whereas in achievements the change is thought of as occurring instantaneously (cf. Pustejovsky 1991).

So far, we have discussed two categories of activity verbs, i.e. those which do not lexically encode a resultant/coda phase (directed motion verbs), and those

---

    (i)   ʊkúlwá alɪnshaa   ŋhalaanga
         ʊ-kúlwá a-lɪn-sh-a   ŋhalaanga
         A-kulwa 3sG-PROG-grind-FV peanuts
         'Kulwa grinds (is grinding) peanuts'

activity verbs which typically entail a resultant/coda state and suggest a change-of-state of the verb's patientive subject. Another category of verbs includes verbs such as -*lila* 'cry' and -*seka* 'laugh', which resemble directed motion verbs in encoding an optional onset phase and a nuclear phase without a resultant/coda phase. -ø-...-*íle* in general does not occur with these verbs without additional context. The context where the interaction of -ø-...-*íle* with verbs such as -*seka* 'laugh' is accepted is when the speaker needs to show her/his ability towards what has been conceived impossible by other people. For example, in (30), the speaker may use -ø-...-*íle* to mean that s/he has the ability to make the person referred to laugh (something which no one else did).

(30) a. ʊkʊwaaneé asekíle
      ʊ-kʊ-waaneé a-ø-sek-íle
      A-LOC-POSS 3SG-laugh-íle
      'To me, s/he must laugh (just wait and see)'

In (29), we saw that -*sha* 'grind', -*dɪtɪla* 'pour into', and -*pʊʊla* 'pound' do not naturally occur with -ø-...-*íle* if the verb's subject has the semantic role of agent (agentive subject). However, the speaker can use -ø-...-*íle* if s/he wants to express a contradiction and/or emphasis in the similar way as verbs without an entailed resultant/coda phase. This is contextualized in (31) using the verb -*lɪma* 'cultivate'.

(31) [Context: It is a rainy season, Benny is uncertain whether his brother Frank has cultivated. While talking with his neighbors, he says "I wonder whether Frank has cultivated this season or whether he even has a farm" If one of the neighbors is sure that Frank has cultivated s/he can respond using -ø-...-*íle*.]
      alɪmilé
      a-ø-lɪm-íle
      3SG-cultivate-íle
      'He has cultivated (and I saw his farm.)'

In all verbs where -ø-...-*íle* is not acceptable without context, I argue that -ø-...-*íle* is coerced to occur with these verbs in order to express a contrast/contradiction and/or emphasis. Collins (1962), as cited in Crane (2012: 70), reports a similar phenomenon in Tonga, where -*ide* (another variant of -*ile*) is used to express contradiction (32). See also Woidich (1975), as cited in Ebert (1995: 194), for a marker of resultative expressing emphasis.

(32) (Collins 1962, as cited in Crane 2012:70)
      micelo ili bolede (-*bola* 'become rotten')

      'the fruits are rotten, or the fruits are *not* perfectly sound'

According to Collins (1962), the sentence in (32) would be used in argument or to express disappointment or surprise.

The use of -*ø*-...-*íle* in Nyamwezi to express contradiction/emphasis is different from that of a stativizer which gives readings such as resultative/stative and progressive-like. Contradiction and/or emphasis can be regarded as a second main function of -*ø*-...-*íle* which is enforced by context.

Let's now turn to the discussion of the interaction of semelfactives with -*ø*-...-*íle*. In all contexts attested during elicitation sessions, -*ø*-...-*íle* was not accepted with serial semelfactives. Since (serial) semelfactives resemble activities in encoding an extended nuclear phase, one of the ways to test co-occurrence of -*ø*-...-*íle* with semelfactives was to see if the interaction would lead to the progressive-like reading. To try this, the consultants were asked to say whether they would use *a-ø-kolol-ílé* (from -*kolola* 'cough') to mean that someone is coughing. The example meant to check if the sentence may get an iterative interpretation (several instances of an event within a measurable duration) (33a) or denote periodic events (33b). Both interpretations were rejected.

(33) a. * ataálɪ́   akololílé
          a-táá-lɪ   a-ø-kolol-íle
          3sg-**still**-AUX 3sg-cough-**íle**

          'S/he is still coughing (continuously)

      b. * akololílé   kʊfúma mázʊʊlí
          a-ø-kolol-íle kʊfuma mazʊʊlí
          3sg-cough-**íle** since   day before yesterday

          'S/he has been coughing since the day before yesterday'

Semelfactives cannot occur with -*ø*-...-*íle*, even though they encode a kind of extended nuclear phase which can be picked out by this construction. One of the reasons for the co-occurrence restriction is that for a verb which does not naturally occur with -*ø*-...-*íle* it needs a context where this formative can be coerced to occur with that verb. Coercion of -*ø*-...-*íle* normally suggests a contradiction/emphasis. For this reason, it is very awkward for a speaker to use -*ø*-...-*íle* with semelfactives to imply that s/he has the ability to enforce the occurrence of, let us say, 'cough' which is difficult to do to other people, in the same way it is possible with -*seka* 'laugh' in (30). So, the co-occurrence restriction is due to the inability of the speaker to enforce events denoted by semelfactives. Otherwise, if the speaker believes that s/he has the ability to enforce a semelfactive event (as in a non-literal context), then s/he may use *-ø-...-íle*.

To conclude this section, *-ø-...-íle*, in general, does not commonly occur with activity verbs. The co-occurrence is subject to two conditions (i) the verb denotes a result state that leads to the change-of-state/condition of the verb's patientive subject, and (ii) the verb is used in a special pragmatic condition where *-ø-...-íle* is coerced to express contradiction and/or emphasis.

5 Conclusion

To summarize, the paper has generally shown that the analysis of aspectual classes is crucial in understanding the functions of *-ø-...-íle* in Nyamwezi. A resultative reading occurs with achievements, a general present time reading occurs with statives, and a progressive-like reading occurs with a handful of activity verbs called directed motion verbs. It was also shown that there are some activity verbs, apart from directed motion verbs, which occur quite naturally with *-ø-...-íle*. These verbs share some commonalities with achievements, as they both lead to the change-of-state of the verb's patientive subject. More importantly, it was noted that, activity verbs which lack an entailed resultant/coda phase, in special pragmatic contexts, can be coerced to occur with *-ø-...-íle* to express contrast/contradiction and/or emphasis. It was also argued that although coercion seems to be an option in contexts where *-ø-...-íle* is not allowed with some verbs, this is not the case with semelfactives. Coercion of *-ø-...-íle* with semelfactive verbs in general is not allowed due to the inability of the speaker to enforce events denoted by semelfactives.

In short, *-ø-...-íle* in Nyamwezi has two main functions: (i) statitivizer, which leads to three readings – resultative, general present time and progressive-like – and (ii) contradiction/emphasis. These results suggest that in other Bantu languages a more detailed analysis of *-íle* can yield valuable results, which may previously have gone unnoticed.

Ponsiano Sawaka Kanijo

Abbreviations

A	Augment		NEG	Negative
APPL	Applicative		OC	Object concord
ASS	Associative		OPT	Optative
AUX	Auxiliary		PASS	Passive
CL	noun class		PL	Plural
CPL	Completive marker		POSS	Possessive
CON	Connexive		PROG	Progressive
COP	Copular		REC	Recent past
EXT	Extension		RS	Resultant state
FV	Final vowel		SC	Subject concord
HAB	Habitual		SG	singular
IMP	Imperative		TAM	Tense, Aspect and Mood
INF	Infinitive		TC/SC	Tense copy of subject concord
IT	Itive marker		VB	Verbal base
LOC	Locative			

Acknowledgements

Many thanks to the language consultants for this study, especially Margreth Nyamizi and Michael Shija, for devoting their time to feed me with data. Thanks also to Laura Downing, Malin Petzell, Elizabeth Coppock and Leora Bar-El for discussing this work with me. I thank Thera Crane and two anonymous reviewers for their insightful comments on an earlier version of this paper.

References

Bar-el, Leora. 2015. Documenting and classifying aspectual classes across languages. In M. Ryan Bochnak & Lisa Matthewson (eds.), *Methodologies in semantic fieldwork (pp.* 75–109. Oxford: Oxford University Press.

Botne, Robert D. 1983. On the notion "inchoative verb" in kinyarwanda. In Francis Jouannet (ed.), *Le Kinyarwanda: Langue Bantu du Rwanda: Études linguistiques*, 149–180. Société d'études linguistiques et anthropologiques de France (SELAF).

Botne, Robert D. 2008. *A grammatical sketch of Chindali (Malawian variety).* Philadelphia: American Philosophical Society.

Botne, Robert D. 2010. Perfectives, perfect and pasts, oh my!: On the semantics of -ILE in Bantu. *Africana Linguistica* 16. 31–63.

Botne, Robert D. & Tiffany L. Kershner. 2000. Time, tense and the perfect in Zulu. *Afrika und Übersee* 83. 161–180.

Brisard, Frank & Michael Meeuwis. 2009. Present and perfect in Bantu: The case of lingála. *Journal of African languages and linguistics* 30(1). 21–43.

Bybee, Joan, Revere Perkins & William Pagliuca. 1994. *The evolution of grammar: Tense, aspect and modality in the languages of the world.* Chicago: The University of Chicago Press.

Collins, B. 1962. *Tonga grammar.* London: Longmans.

Comrie, Bernard. 1976. *Aspect: An introduction to the study of verbal aspect and related problems.* Cambridge, UK: Cambridge University Press.

Crane, Thera M. 2012. -ile and the pragmatic pathways of the resultative in Bantu Botatwe. *Africana Linguistica* 18. 41–96.

Crane, Thera M. 2013. Resultatives, progressives, statives, and relevance: The temporal pragmatics of the -ite suffix in Totela. *Lingua* 133. 164–188. DOI:10.1016/j.lingua.2013.04.006

Crane, Thera M. & Axel Fleisch. 2016. Event type lexicalization across language boundaries: Verbs in South African Ndebele varieties. In. http://blogs.helsinki.fi/bantu-6/files/2016/09/Bantu6-CraneFleisch-Event-Type-Lexicalization-Across-Language-Boundaries.pdf. Paper presented at the Bantu 6 Conference.

Dahl, Östen. 1985. *Tense and aspect systems.* Oxford, UK: Blackwell.

Ebert, Karen H. 1995. Ambiguous perfect-progressive forms across languages. In Pier Marco Bertinetto (ed.), *Temporal reference, aspect and actionality*, vol. 2, 185–202. Torino: Rosenberg & Sellier.

Filip, Hana. 2012. Lexical aspect. In Robert. I Binnick (ed.), *The Oxford handbook of tense and aspect*, 721–751. Oxford: Oxford University Press.

Freed, Alice F. 1979. *The semantics of English aspectual complementation.* London: D. Reidel Publishing Company.

Guthrie, Malcolm. 1967. *Comparative Bantu: An introduction to the comparative linguistics and prehistory of the Bantu languages.* Vol. 1-4. Upper Saddle River: Gregg.

Kearns, Kate. 2000. *Semantics.* New York: Palgrave Macmillan.

Kershner, Tiffany L. 2002. *The verb in Chisukwa: Aspect, tense, and time.* Indiana University dissertation.

Kratzer, Angelika. 1995. Stage-level and individual-level predicates. In Gregory N. Carlson & Francis Jeffry Pelletier (eds.), *The generic book*, 125–175. Chicago: University of Chicago Press.

Lewis, Paul M., Gary F. Simons, Charles D. Fennig, et al. 2013. *Ethnologue: Languages of the world.* SIL International. https://ethnologue.com/language/nym. https://ethnologue.com/language/nym.

Maganga, Clement & Thilo Schadeberg. 1992. *Kinyamwezi: Grammar, texts, vocabulary.* Köln: Rüdiger Köppe.

Masele, Balla F. Y. P. 2001. *The linguistic history of Sisuumbwa, Kisukuma and Kinyamweezi in Bantu zone F.* Memorial University of Newfoundland dissertation.

Nurse, Derek. 2008. *Tense and aspect in Bantu languages.* Oxford: Oxford University Press.

Persohn, Bastian. 2017a. Aspectuality in Bantu: On the limits of Vendler's categories. *Linguistic Discovery.*

Persohn, Bastian. 2017b. *The verb in Nyakyusa: A focus on tense, aspect and modality.* Berlin: Language Science Press. DOI:10.5281/zenodo.926408

Pustejovsky, James. 1991. The syntax of event structure. *Cognition* 41. 47–81.

Rothstein, Susan. 2004. *Structuring events: A study in the semantics of lexical aspect.* Oxford: Blackwell Publishing.

Sasse, Hans-Jürgen. 2002. Recent activity in the theory of aspect: Accomplishments, achievements, or just non-progressive state? *Linguistic Typology* 2(6). 199–271.

Seidel, Frank. 2008. *A grammar of Yeyi: A Bantu language of Southern Africa.* Cologne: Rüdiger-Köppe Verlag.

Smith, Carlota S. 1991. *The parameter of aspect.* Dordrecht: Kluwer Academic Publishers.

Vendler, Zeno. 1957. Verbs and times. *The Philosophical Review* 66. 143–160.

Woidich, Manfred. 1975. Zur Funktion des aktiven Partizips im Kairenisch-Arabischen. *Zeitschrift der Deutschen Morgenländischen Gesellschaft* 125(2). 273–293.

Chapter 16

Logophoricity in Ibibio

Lydia Newkirk

Rutgers University

This paper presents a description and analysis of logophoric pronouns in Ibibio. I show that Ibibio logophors, although they behave in most respects like typical logophoric pronouns in West African languages, obey Shift Together like shifted indexicals. In order to explain this data I propose that Ibibio logophors are sensitive to two operators in the left periphery of the embedded CP: a shifting operator and a logophoric binding operator. Ibibio indexicals (which do not shift) differ in that they are defined to be insensitive to shifting operators. Thus indexical shift requires cooperation between the semantics of the indexical and of the shifting operator. This proposal in turn expands the predicted typology of possible *de se* pronouns cross-linguistically.

1 Ibibio logophors

Ibibio (Cross-River, Nigeria) logophors are distinct from both ordinary pronouns and reflexives (1), and can only occur in embedded clauses (2).[1]

(1) a. Ekpe$_i$ a-bo   ke (imọ)$_i$ ì-ma   í-to   Udo   logophor
         Ekpe 3SG-say C LOG   LOG-PST LOG-hit Udo
         'Ekpe$_i$ says that he$_i$ hit Udo.'

    b. Ekpe$_i$ a-bo   ke **anye**$_{i/k}$ a-diyọnọ ikwo ikwo mfọnmfọn   pronoun
         Ekpe 3SG-say C 3SG   3SG-know sing song well
         'Ekpe$_i$ says that he$_{i/k}$ sings well.'

    c. Ekpe$_i$ a-bo   ke ì-ma   í-tọ   **idem**$_i$ reflexive
         Ekpe 3SG-say C LOG-PST LOG-hit self
         'Ekpe$_i$ says that he$_i$ hit himself$_i$.'

---

[1]With the exception of the logophoric markers, on which I annotated the tone for clarity, I use the Ibibio orthography developed in Essien (1990), which does not mark tone.

Lydia Newkirk. 2019. Logophoricity in Ibibio. In Samson Lotven, Silvina Bongiovanni, Phillip Weirich, Robert Botne & Samuel Gyasi Obeng (eds.), *African linguistics across the disciplines: Selected papers from the 48th Annual Conference on African Linguistics*, 309–323. Berlin: Language Science Press. DOI:10.5281/zenodo.3520597

(2) a. * Ekpe$_i$ a-ma   a-diya adesi **imọ**$_i$ logophor
          Ekpe 3SG-PST 3SG-eat rice LOG.POSS

          Intended: 'Ekpe$_i$ ate his$_i$ rice'

    b. Ekpe$_i$ a-ma   a-diya adesi **amọ**$_{i/k}$ pronoun
          Ekpe 3SG-PST 3SG-eat rice 3SG.POSS

          'Ekpe$_i$ ate his$_{i/k}$ rice'

Logophoric pronouns differ in both agreement and morphology from the other pronominals in Ibibio (both the pronominals and logophors are listed in Table 1). However, like all of the other pronouns in the language, their independent forms are optional except in cases of emphasis or disambiguation. In (2a), the logophor cannot occur as a possessive in an unembedded clause, even though in the same context a regular third person pronoun is acceptable as corefering to the local subject.

Table 1: Ibibio pronouns and agreement markers

	Pronouns		Agreement	
	Subject	Object	Subject	Object
1SG	ami	mien	n-	n-
2SG	afo	fien	a-	u-
3SG	anye	anye	a-	a-
1PL	nnyin		i-	i-
2PL	ndufo		e-	e-
3PL	ọmmọ		e-	e-
LOG.SG	imọ		i-	i-
LOG.PL	mmimọ		i-	i-

Note from (1b) that Ibibio patterns like Yoruba (Adesola 2005: (3)), which has a strong pronoun *oun* that must refer to the attitude holder, and a weak pronoun *o* that is ambiguous between referring to the matrix attitude holder and taking some other third person referent. By that same token, Ibibio's pattern is distinct from Abe's (Koopman & Sportiche 1989: (4)), in that regular Ibibio pronouns do not show anti-logophoricity; a regular pronoun can still corefer with the matrix subject.[2]

---

[2]In these and other examples from the literature, I preserve the glossing and capitalization from the cited work.

(3) (Adesola 2005: 34)

Olú$_i$ ti kéde NO$_{\{i\}[+LOG]}$ pé oun$_i$/o$_{i/k}$ ǹ bsò Isóla
Olu ASP announce   that he   PROG come tomorrow

'Olu$_i$ has announced that he$_i$/he$_{i/k}$ is coming tomorrow.'

(4) (Koopman & Sportiche 1989: 64a)

yapi$_i$ hE kO O$_k$/n$_{i,(k)}$ ye sE
Yapi said kO he   is handsome

'Yapi$_i$ said that he$_{i/*k}$ is handsome'

Assuming the facts from Abe are robust, this points to one potential variance in how logophors and regular pronouns tend to get their antecedents.

There are also separate plural logophoric pronouns in Ibibio:

(5) ọmmọ$_i$ e-ke e-bo ke mmimọ$_{i/*k}$ ì-ma í-kot n̄wet
3PL   3PL-PST 3PL-say C LOG.PL   LOG-PST LOG-read book

'They$_i$ said that they$_{i/*k}$ read a book.'

Split antecedence is possible with a plural logophor (see also Yoruba; Adesola 2005), so long as the closest potential logophoric antecedent is included in the group taken to be the antecedent for the logophor.

(6) Ekpe$_i$ a-bo ke mmimọ$_{\{i,k\}}$ í-diya afìt adesi adọ
Ekpe 3SG-say C LOG.PL   LOG-eat all rice DEM

'Ekpe$_i$ says that they$_{\{i,k\}}$ ate all of the rice'

(7) Ekpe$_i$ a-bo ke Udo$_j$ a-kere ke ete mmimọ$_{\{i,j\}/\{j,k\}}$ a-ya
Ekpe 3SG-say C Udo 3SG-think C father LOG.PL   3SG-FUT

ì-di í-wọ
LOG-come LOG-visit

'Ekpe$_i$ says that Udo$_j$ thinks that their$_{\{i,j\}/\{j,k\}}$ father will come visit.'

The inverse relation, where a singular logophor has a plural antecedent, is impossible:

(8) *[Akpan ye Udo]$_i$ e-ma e-bo ke imọ$_i$ ì-ma í-diya sokoro
Akpan CONJ Udo 3PL-PST 3PL-say C LOG LOG-PST LOG-eat orange

Intended: '[Akpan and Udo]$_i$ said that he$_i$ ate the orange.'

This all is analogous to the facts of Yoruba as reported by Adesola (2005).

Logophors in Ibibio are subject-oriented, established in (9a–10):

(9) a. Ekpe$_i$ a-ma   a-kop   ke Udo$_k$ a-ma   í-kịt
       Ekpe 3SG-PST 3SG-hear C Udo 3SG-PST LOG-see

       'Ekpe$_i$ heard that Udo$_k$ saw him$_i$.'

    b. Ekpe$_i$ a-ma   a-kop   a-to   Akpan$_j$ ke Udo$_k$ a-ma   í$_{i/*j}$-kịt
       Ekpe 3SG-PST 3SG-hear 3SG-from Akpan C Udo 3SG-PST LOG-see

       'Ekpe$_i$ heard from Akpan$_j$ that Udo$_k$ saw him$_{i/*j}$'

(10) Akpan$_i$ a-ma   a-dọkkọ Ekpe$_k$ ke a-kpe   a-na   nte (imọ$_{i/*k}$)
    Akpan 3SG-PST 3SG-tell Ekpe C 3SG-COND 3SG-MOD C LOG

    í-dep   adesi mfịn
    LOG-buy rice today

    'Akpan$_i$ told Ekpe$_k$ that he$_{i/*k}$ should buy rice today.'

Rather than being tuned to the source in (9b), the embedded logophor can only refer to the syntactic subject, which 'hear' licenses as a logophoric antecedent independently (9a). Similarly, in (10), a logophor cannot refer to the addressee introduced in the matrix clause, but must refer to the subject.

Like what has been reported for Yoruba (Adesola 2005; Anand 2006), but unlike what has been reported for Ewe (Pearson 2015), Ibibio logophors are obligatorily interpreted *de se*:[3]

Context: Ekpe sings on occasion, but will never admit that he is any good. So one time, during one of his performances, you record him without his knowledge. Some time later, you play back the recording to him without telling him who is singing. Ekpe doesn't recognize himself in the recording, and comments "he sings well."

(11) a.   Ekpe$_i$ a-bo   ke **anye**$_{i/k}$ a-diyọñọ ikwo ikwo mfọnmfọn
        Ekpe 3SG-say C 3SG   3SG-know sing song well

        'Ekpe$_i$ said that he$_{i/k}$ sings well.'

    b. # Ekpe$_i$ a-bo   ke **imọ**$_i$ ì-me   í-diyọñọ ikwo ikwo mfọnmfọn
        Ekpe 3SG-say C LOG LOG-PRES LOG-know sing song well

        Intended: 'Ekpe$_i$ says that he$_i$ sings well.'

---

[3] *De se* in this case refers to knowing self ascription of a property. For example, the *de se* reading for "John believes that he wrote the best paper" is the reading where John has the belief "I (John) wrote the best paper." This differs from a *de re* reading, where John may have read his paper without remembering that he wrote it, although he still comes to the conclusion that the paper that he wrote (but does not remember) is the best paper. Because in this case John does not identify himself as the writer of the best paper, this latter interpretation is *de re*.

In the above context, Ekpe does not knowingly attribute singing well to himself, but instead does so accidentally. That is, he only ascribes singing well to himself *de re*, but not *de se*. In such a context, only a regular Ibibio third person pronoun can be used, and the logophor is illicit.

When multiply embedded, Ibibio logophors can take antecedents more than one clause away:

(12) Ekpe$_i$ a-bo   ke Udo$_k$ a-ke   a-kere   ke (imo$_{i/k}$) ì-ke   í-kịt
      Ekpe 3SG-say C Udo 3SG-PST 3SG-think C LOG   LOG-PST LOG-see
      Ima
      Ima
      'Ekpe$_i$ says that Udo$_k$ thinks that he$_{i/k}$ saw Ima.'

But when there is more than one logophor in the same clause, the coreference options are more limited:

(13)   Ekpe$_i$ a-ma   a-kop   ke Udo$_k$ a-ke   a-bo   ke ayin-eka imo$_{k/*i}$
        Ekpe 3SG-PST 3SG-hear C Udo 3SG-PST 3SG-say C brother LOG.POSS
        a-ma   a-kịt   imo$_{k/*i}$ ke udua
        3SG-PST 3SG-see LOG   at market
        'Ekpe$_i$ heard that Udo$_k$ said that his$_{k/*i}$ brother saw him$_{k/*i}$ at the market.'

(14) * Ekpe$_i$ a-ma   a-kop   ke Udo$_k$ a-ke   a-bo   ke imo$_{i/k}$ ì-ma
        Ekpe 3SG-PST 3SG-hear C Udo 3SG-PST 3SG-say C LOG   LOG-PST
        í-tọ   imo$_{i/k}$
        LOG-hit LOG
        Intended: 'Ekpe$_i$ heard that Udo$_k$ said that he$_{i/k}$ hit him$_{i/k}$'

While (13) is grammatical, the only available interpretation is the one where both logophors take the same antecedent.[4] More striking is that in (14) this effect is

---

[4] An anonymous reviewer asked whether multiple multiply-embedded logophors must also take the closest antecedent. Unfortunately I do not have data to confirm whether this is in fact the case. However, if Ibibio logophors indeed behave like shifted indexicals (as I will claim), then it should be possible for the two logophors to take a more distant antecedent, as in Zazaki (Anand & Nevins 2004):

(i) (Andrew): Ali$_A$ mɨ$_U$-ra va   kɛ   Hɛseni$_H$ to$_U$-ra va   ɛz$_{\{H,A,*U\}}$ braye   Rojda-o
              Ali me-to said that Hesen   you-to said I   brother Rojda-GEN
     'Ali said to Andrew that Hesen said to Andrew that { Hesen, Ali, *Andrew } is Rojda's brother.'

not ameliorated even to avoid a Condition B violation.[5] Instead, the sentence is simply ungrammatical. Similarly the context in (15) fails to license two embedded logophors:

Context: Udo and Akpan are two young schoolchildren, and are brothers. Ekpe is their friend, and is the same age as they are. One day, Udo and Akpan's father comes home and says that he saw Ekpe at the market when Ekpe was supposed to be in school. Word that he has been spotted skipping class gets back to Ekpe.

(15) # Ekpe$_i$ a-ma   a-kop   ke [Akpan ye Udo]$_k$ e-ke   e-bo   ke
      Ekpe 3SG-PST 3SG-hear C Udo   CONJ Akpan 3PL-PST 3PL-say C
      ete   mmimo$_k$ a-ma   í-kịt   imo$_i$ ke   udua
      father LOG.PL.POSS 3SG-PST LOG-see LOG PREP market

      Intended: 'Ekpe$_i$ heard that [Akpan and Udo]$_k$ said that their$_k$ father saw him$_i$ at the market.'

The context in (15) does not support partial/split antecedence for the plural logophor, and so the plural embedded logophor has to take a different antecedent than the singular logophor. But (15) is completely infelicitous in this context. In sum: Clausemate logophors (in Ibibio at least) have to refer together.

This particular restriction on logophors is (to my knowledge) unattested in the *de se* literature. Abe, Yoruba, and Ewe are all reported to allow multiple embedded logophors to take separate antecedents:

(16) Abe (Koopman & Sportiche 1989: 41, 44a)

      a. n$_i$ ceewu n   kolo n$_{i/*k}$
          n friend Det likes n

          'his$_i$ friend likes him$_{i/*k}$'

This example is unfortunately complex, because there is potentially multiple shifting acts happening. But most importantly, although Hesen **can** be the antecedent for the deeply embedded first person pronoun, that is not the only reading of the sentence. Ali, the more distant attitude holder, is also eligible to antecede the shifted first person pronoun. I have no reason to expect Ibibio logophors to behave otherwise.

The reviewer also asked whether reflexives have any impact on multiple logophors or long-distance antecedents. Logophoric reflexives are not themselves long-distance reflexives, but only local anaphors, and as such would have to have a logophor as a local antecedent, as in (1c)

[5] A Condition B violation occurs when a (non-reflexive) pronoun is bound locally. For example, *John$_i$ likes him$_{k/*i}$* is unacceptable on an interpretation where *John* and *him* refer to the same person (that is, *John likes him* cannot mean *John likes himself*), because the pronoun would be bound locally, which violates Condition B of the Binding Theory, which states that a pronominal must be free within its clause. Note that if the pronoun is not in the same clause as its antecedent, binding is possible (e.g., *John$_i$ said that he$_i$ is a genius*), because this does not violate Condition B.

b. Api$_i$ bO wu ye **n**$_{i/k}$ kolo **n**$_{i/k}$
Api believe *ye n* likes *n*

'Api$_i$ believes that he$_{i/k}$ likes him$_{i/k}$'

(17) Yoruba (Anand 2006: 177)
Olu$_i$ so pé Ade$_k$ ro pé bàbá **oun**$_{i/k}$ ti rììyá òun$_{i/k}$
Olu say that Ade think that father oun.gen PERF see mother oun.gen

'Olu$_i$ said that Ade$_k$ thought that his$_{i/k}$ father had seen his$_{i/k}$ mother.'

(18) Ewe (Clements 1975: 73)
Kofi$_i$ xɔ-e se be Ama$_k$ gblɔ be **yè**$_{i/k}$-ʄu **yè**$_{i/k}$
Kofi receive-PRO hear that Ama say that LOG-beat LOG

'Kofi$_i$ believed that Ama$_k$ said that he$_i$ beat her$_k$.' or
'Kofi$_i$ believed that Ama$_k$ said that she$_k$ beat him$_i$.'

The Abe data requires a bit of explanation: Koopman & Sportiche (1989) report that *n*-series pronouns (logophors) are licit in matrix clauses, but if two of them occur they must have the same antecedent (16a). When embedded, however, they are able to receive disjoint interpretations. This puts (16b) in the same general pattern with the Yoruba (17) and Ewe (18) examples, and all of them in contrast with Ibibio.

In order to explain this unusual property of Ibibio logophors, I must take a brief detour into the shifted indexicals literature, which will shed light on the difference between Ibibio and other logophoric languages.

2 Ibibio logophors as shifted indexicals

2.1 Indexical shift cross-linguistically

The leading analysis of shifted indexicals in the literature is that proposed by Anand (2006), and essentially followed by Sudo (2012); Shklovsky & Sudo (2014); Deal (2017), inter alia. Descriptively speaking, shifted indexicals are cases of person, locative, or temporal indexicals (such as *I, here*, or *yesterday*) which, when embedded under an attitude verb or verb of saying, do not refer to the utterance context, but instead refer to the context established by the embedding verb (in these examples, AUTH(c) denotes the speaker of the entire utterance, and ADDR(c) denotes the addressee of that utterance. That is, they are used for the English non-quotative senses of *I* and *you*).

(19)   Zazaki (Indo-Iranian, Turkey), (Anand & Nevins 2004: 13)
       vɨzeri   Rojda Bill-ra va   kɛ   **ɜz to**-ra   miradiša
       yesterday Rojda Bill-to said that **I   you**-to angry.be-PRES

       'Yesterday Rojda said to Bill, "I am angry at you."'
       'Yesterday Rojda said to Bill, "AUTH(c) is angry at ADDR(c)."'
       *'Yesterday Rojda said to Bill, "AUTH(c) is angry at you."'
       *'Yesterday Rojda said to Bill, "I am angry at ADDR(c)."'

One property of shifted indexicals cross-linguistically is that they obey Shift To-gether: Two indexicals embedded under the same attitude verb must either both shift or neither shift, as demonstrated by the possible interpretations of (19), and illustrated schematically below.

(20)   SHIFT TOGETHER Constraint (Anand 2006: 297)
       All shiftable indexicals within an *attitude-context domain* must pick up ref-erence from the same context.

       a. C_A [...*modal* C_B ...[ind$_1^A$ ...ind$_2^A$]]
       b. C_A [...*modal* C_B ...[ind$_1^B$ ...ind$_2^B$]]
       c.   * C_A [...*modal* C_B ...[ind$_1^A$ ...ind$_2^B$]]
       d.   * C_A [...*modal* C_B ...[ind$_1^B$ ...ind$_2^A$]]

Anand (2006) derives Shift Together by defining shifting operators that over-ride the context values under attitude verbs. Where context parameters typically refer directly to the utterance context, these operators modify the context so that indexicals in their scope refer to the context set by the attitude verb, rather than the context set by the utterance.

(21) $[\![\text{OP}_{auth}\ \alpha]\!]^{c,i} = [\![\alpha]\!]^{j,i}$, where $j = \langle \text{AUTH}(i), \text{ADDR}(c), \text{TIME}(c), \text{WORLD}(c) \rangle$

(22) $[\![\text{OP}_{per}\ \alpha]\!]^{c,i} = [\![\alpha]\!]^{j,i}$, where $j = \langle \text{AUTH}(i), \text{ADDR}(i), \text{TIME}(c), \text{WORLD}(c) \rangle$

Because the operators overwrite the contextual information rather than simply adding to it, any indexical dependent on an overwritten value is forced to shift, and can never "un-shift".

Another analysis present in the literature is that of Schlenker (2003). He pro-poses in indexical shift languages, the shiftable indexicals are lexically defined to optionally shift under the right sort of attitude verb. Non-shiftable indexicals, on the other hand, are defined to always take the utterance context, rather than any embedded context variable. In this sense, they act very much like bindees under an attitude verb (c^* refers to the utterance context).

(23)   a. English 'I': +indexical, +c*

      b. Amharic 'I': +indexical, [underspecified]

There is one main objection to Schlenker's proposal: If shiftable indexicals are underspecified for a context variable, two embedded indexicals are expected to be able to take different context variables; Shift Together is left unexplained. As a result, the theory by Anand (2006) summarized above is the analysis more commonly used in the literature. However, Schlenker's theory will come into play for my analysis of Ibibio logophors, which I now turn to.

2.2 Logophors as shifted indexicals

A tempting solution to the problem of Ibibio logophors is to propose that they are actually first-person indexicals, and that Ibibio has a shifting operator that shifts those indexicals like in Zazaki and Amharic. This is unfeasible however, because true Ibibio indexicals never shift, even if they occur clausemate with a logophor:

(24)   Ekpe$_i$ a-kere   ke (imǫ$_i$) i-ma   i-n-kịt   **mien**

      Ekpe 3SG-think C LOG   LOG-PST LOG-1SG-see 1SG.OBJ

      'Ekpe$_i$ thinks that he$_i$ saw me.'

If there is a shifting operator present in (24) that overwrites the AUTH value in the context (as would be expected for a pronoun that refers to the attitude-holder), then the first person indexical should also shift. But the true indexical stays constant to the utterance context.

    In light of this, I claim that although an operator-based approach is essentially correct for shifted indexicals, the behavior of Ibibio logophors indicates that operators alone are not sufficient to account for indexical shift. I propose to integrate Schlenker's insight that the pronominals should be defined as shiftable, but with the adjustment that a pronominal's sensitivity to shifting is defined lexically, and no pronominal is underspecified for what context variable it takes. Either a pronominal will always shift in the presence of an operator, or it never will. For Ibibio, this means that its logophors are defined to shift, so that they take a shiftable context variable, while true Ibibio indexicals are defined as unshiftable: they take only the matrix context directly.

(25)   a. $[\![\, imǫ \,]\!]^{g,c} = $ AUTH(c) SHIFTABLE

      b. $[\![\, \text{1SG} \,]\!]^{g,c} = $ AUTH(c^*) NOT SHIFTABLE

The actual shifting for the logophor cases is accomplished by the author shifter in (21) above. Shiftable logophors will otherwise receive the same interpretation as unshiftable logophors; the distinction between the two will emerge only in deeply embedded clauses where multiple logophors appear; that is, in precisely the complex cases I discuss in this paper. In these examples, shifting logophors will obligatorily take the same antecedent (as is the case in Ibibio), while non-shifting logophors will not be obligated to take the same antecedent (as in Yoruba, Able, and other languages).

A relevant question at this point is whether Ibibio logophors are merely shifted indexicals, or whether there is also logophoric binding. A brief consideration of the *De Re* Blocking Effect indicates that Ibibio logophors are also true logophors, involving binding by a logophoric operator.

The *De Re* Blocking Effect (Anand 2006) states that a *de se* pronominal (such as a logophor) cannot be c-commanded by a *de re* pronominal. I illustrate this with the following examples from Yoruba (Adesola 2005):

(26)   Yoruba (Adesola 2005)

    a. Adé$_i$ so pé **oun**$_i$ ti   rì ìwé **rè**$_{i,j}$
       Ade say that oun PERF see book o-gen

       'Ade$_i$ said that he$_i$ has seen his$_{i,j}$ book.'

    b. Olu$_i$ so pé o$_{*i/j}$ rì bàbá **òun**$_i$
       Olu say that o   see father oun-gen

       'Olu$_i$ said that he$_{*i/j}$ has seen his$_i$ father.'

    c. Olu$_i$ so pé bàbá **rè**$_{i/j}$ rì ìyá   **òun**$_i$
       Olu say that father o-gen see mother oun-gen

       'Olu$_i$ said that his$_{i/j}$ father has seen his$_i$ mother.'

In Anand's theory of logophoricity, (26b) does not allow the weak pronoun to refer to the logophoric center because in cases where it is co-indexed with the logophor, it is a competing binder for the more deeply embedded logophor, causing a condition B effect. This is ameliorated by interrupting c-command between the two pronouns, as in (26c).

Crucially for determining the status of Ibibio logophors, shifted indexicals do not show *De Re* Blocking Effects, demonstrated in Zazaki by (27).

Context: At a friend's party, Hesen is shocked to see Ali, the boyfriend of his good friend Rojda, flirting with a woman in a big red dress and hat that obscures her face. After seeing her kiss Ali, Hesen rushes off to find Rojda. When he finds her, he tells her, "The woman in the big red dress kissed your man." Of course, it was Rojda all along, only hidden under a costume!

(27) (Anand 2006: 333)

Heseni va kɜ **Rojdaa** layik **tɨya** pach kerd
Hesen.OBL said that Rojda.OBL boy your kiss did

'Hesen said (to Rojda$_i$) that Rojda$_i$ kissed her$_i$ man.'

In the context, Hesen identifies Rojda only with the *de re* relation "the woman in the big red dress", making the occurance of *Rojda* in the embedded clause *de re*, while the embedded second person indexical is shifted to refer to Rojda. Despite the fact that the *de se* indexical is c-commanded by the *de re* name, the sentence is felicitous in the context. Anand takes this as evidence that shifted indexicals are not operator-bound in the same way that logophors are.

Therefore, if Ibibio logophors are in fact merely shifted indexicals that happen to look like logophoric pronouns, we can expect them to show no *De Re* Blocking Effect, parallel to typical shifted indexicals. However, Ibibio logophors behave parallel to Yoruba logophors:

(28) Ekpe$_i$ a-ma a-bo ke imọ$_i$ ì-ma í-kịt ete amọ$_{i/k}$
Ekpe 3SG-PST 3SG-say C LOG LOG-PST LOG-see father 3SG.POSS

'Ekpe$_i$ said that he$_i$ saw his$_{i/k}$ father.'

(29) Ekpe$_i$ a-ma a-bo ke anye$_{*i/k}$ a-ma a-kịt ete imọ$_i$
Ekpe 3SG-PST 3SG-say C 3SG 3SG-PST 3SG-see father LOG.POSS

'Ekpe$_i$ said that he$_{*i/k}$ saw his$_i$ father.'

(30) Ekpe$_i$ a-ma a-bo ke ete amọ$_{*i/k}$ a-ma a-kịt eka
Ekpe 3SG-PST 3SG-say C father 3SG.POSS 3SG-PST 3SG-see mother

imọ$_i$
LOG.POSS

'Ekpe$_i$ said that his$_{*i/k}$ father saw his$_i$ mother.'[6]

According to Anand (2006), the *De Re* Blocking Effect is due to binding competition between the *de re* pronoun and the logophoric operator in the embedded left periphery. Given that Ibibio shows this effect, this is evidence that Ibibio logophors are not only shifted, but also logophorically bound. (Along with the fact that Ibibio logophors cannot appear in matrix clauses, cf. (2b).)

This means that Ibibio logophors are sensitive to both a shifting operator and a logophoric binding operator, a combination otherwise unattested in the *de se* literature. Moreover, the fact that Ibibio logophors shift while Ibibio indexicals

---

[6]Interestingly, interrupting the c-command relation in Ibibio does not seem to improve this case in Ibibio as it does in Yoruba. While this is an interesting distinction between Yoruba and Ibibio logophors that bears further investigation, it is orthogonal to the point that Ibibio logophors also show the *De Re* Blocking Effect.

do not indicates that there is a conspiracy of factors required for indexical shift: Not only is there a shifting operator in the left periphery, but the indexicals of the language also have to be lexically sensitive to that shifting operator. This creates a new source of typological variance, which I elaborate on in the next section.

3 Typological implications

The above discussion of Ibibio logophoricity and its insight into indexical shift brings to light additional typological considerations; namely, it is now clear that languages can vary with regard to what pronominals are defined as shiftable, independent of what shifting operators (if any) are defined for the language.

This additional parameter only introduces minimal extra typological variance however, because for indexical shift to actually occur a language must have both shifting operators in its lexicon as well as some pronominal that is defined to shift under that operator. Similarly for logophors (as has been implicity assumed throughout the literature), a logophoric pronoun by itself is not sufficient for logophoric reference; it also must be bound by a logophoric operator and appropriately related to the attitude holder. Given this conspiracy of factors, the actual typology predicted is in Table 2, filled in with languages that (potentially) exemplify each typological option.

Table 2: Typology of logophors and shifted indexicals

| | No Logophors | Logophors | |
		Shiftable	Unshiftable
No Shifted Indexicals	English	Ibibio	Ewe,[a] Yoruba[b]
Shifted Indexicals	Zazaki[c] Amharic[d] Uyghur[e]		Aghem?[f]

[a]Clements (1975); Pearson (2015)
[b]Adesola (2005)
[c]Anand & Nevins (2004); Anand (2006)
[d]Schlenker (2003)
[e]Sudo (2012); Shklovsky & Sudo (2014)
[f]Hyman (1979)

I have already given examples of most of the languages types predicted, but Aghem requires some further comment. As described in Hyman (1979), Aghem might be an example of a language with both logophoric pronouns and shifted indexicals:

(31)   Aghem (Hyman 1979: 14)

a. ? wìzɨ́n   'vʉ́ ndzɛ̀ à wɨ́n ñɨ́'á **é**   ŋgé   'lɨ́ghá **wò**
     woman that said to him that **she/LOG** much like   **you**

'The woman said to him that she liked him a lot.'
'The woman said to him "I like you a lot."'

b. sǒogɔ̀? 'vʉ́ mé   ñɨ́'á **wò** lɨ̀ghá **mùɔ**, mɔ̀ **wò** mbaàŋ lɔ́ wì
     soldier that (said) that **you** like   **me**   and **you** yet   are wife (of)
     bà?tòm˚...
     chief

'The soldier said, "you like me, and yet you are the wife of the chief."'

These two examples are the only examples in Hyman (1979) containing both logophors and embedded indexicals, or even potentially shifted indexicals at all. But to my knowledge Aghem indexicals have not been put through any tests to show that they are not quotation or partial quotation, nor are there are sentences with multiple embedded logophors, so there is no way to tell whether the logophoric pronouns behave like shifted indexicals either. Aghem's status as a indexical shift and logophoric language is therefore uncertain, but I mention is as an area of further investigation.

4 Conclusion

In this paper I have described Ibibio logophors and situated them in the typology of *de se* pronominals cross-linguistically. I have shown that they differ from other logophoric pronouns in that two clausemate logophors cannot take separate antecedents, but instead must refer together. This behavior, while unlike other logophoric languages, is reminiscent of a widely-attested restriction on shifted indexicals, which must Shift Together. I account for the Ibibio logophor behavior by proposing that they are sensitive to the same indexical shifting operator that is commonly proposed to account for indexical shift. True indexicals in Ibibio, which do not shift, are lexically defined as insensitive to this operator.

The introduction of lexical sensitivity to shifting operators expands the typology of *de se* pronominals in a restricted way, allowing for the existence of languages like Ibibio, where logophors shift but regular indexicals do not, and potentially languages where both logophors and indexicals shift, as well as languages that have (unshiftable, but bound) logophors and shifted indexicals.

Lydia Newkirk

Abbreviations

This paper follows the Leipzig Glossing Rules. Additional abbreviations are:

AUTH	author (or speaker)		LOG	logophoric pronoun/marker
ADDR	addressee		PERF	perfect
ASP	aspect		PREP	preposition
C	complementizer		PRES	present
CONJ	conjunction		PST	past

Acknowledgements

Special thanks to Mfon Udoinyang, Harold Torrence, the students of the Spring 2014 Field Methods class at the University of Kansas, Andrew McKenzie, and all the attendees of Syntactic Theory @ Rutgers (ST@R). This research was partially supported by NSF BCS-1324404.

References

Adesola, Oluseye. 2005. *Pronouns and null operators – A-bar dependencies and relations in Yoruba*. Rutgers dissertation.

Anand, Pranav. 2006. De de Se. MIT dissertation.

Anand, Pranav & Andrew Nevins. 2004. Shifty operators in changing contexts. In Robert B. Young (ed.), *Proceedings of SALT 14*, 20–37. Ithaca, NY: Cornell University.

Clements, George N. 1975. The logophoric pronoun in Ewe: Its role in discourse. *Journal of West African Languages* 10. 141–177.

Deal, Amy Rose. 2017. Shifty asymmetries: Universals and variation in shifty indexicality. UC Berkeley.

Essien, Okon. 1990. *A Grammar of the Ibibio language*. Ibadan: University Press Limited.

Hyman, Larry M. 1979. Aghem grammatical structure. *Southern California Occasional Papers in Linguistics* 7.

Koopman, Hilda & Dominique Sportiche. 1989. Pronouns, logical variables, and logophoricity in Abe. *Linguistic Inquiry* 20(4). 555–588.

Pearson, Hazel. 2015. The interpretation of the logophoric pronoun in Ewe. *Natural Language Semantics* 23. 77–118.

Schlenker, Philippe. 2003. A plea for monsters. *Linguistics and Philosophy* 26. 29–120.

Shklovsky, Kirill & Yasutada Sudo. 2014. The syntax of monsters. *Linguistic Inquiry* 45. 381–402.

Sudo, Yasutada. 2012. *On the semantics of phi features on pronouns.* Massachusetts Institute of Technology dissertation.

Chapter 17

Control of logophoric pronouns in Gengbe

Thomas Grano

Indiana University

Samson Lotven

Indiana University

Control is a phenomenon in which the subject of an embedded clause (the "controlled argument") is obligatorily bound by an argument of the immediately embedding predicate (the "controller"). Cross-linguistic research has revealed variation in how control sentences are syntactically instantiated, though no studies to date have documented cases where the controlled argument is realized by an overt logophoric pronoun. Based on novel field data, we argue that precisely this happens in Gengbe (Gbe, Niger-Congo), though only with some embedding verbs (such as *dʒí* 'want') and only when the embedded clause has potential (as opposed to jussive) mood marking. We propose an account of the facts whereby control complements are property-denoting and whereby logophoricity and jussive mood are two independent routes for creating property-denoting clauses. The upshot is a view of control as an emergent phenomenon; there is no "control construction" or "control pronoun" (PRO) but rather several independent components of the grammar that interact to give rise to control under certain conditions for principled type-theoretic reasons.

1 Introduction

Control is a phenomenon in which the subject of an embedded clause (the "controlled argument") is obligatorily bound by an argument of the immediately higher embedding predicate (the "controller"). In (1), for example, the unexpressed subject of *leave* (represented here as PRO) can only be understood as coreferential with *Bill*; it cannot be coreferential with *John* nor can it take an antecedent

Thomas Grano & Samson Lotven. 2019. Control of logophoric pronouns in Gengbe. In Samson Lotven, Silvina Bongiovanni, Phillip Weirich, Robert Botne & Samuel Gyasi Obeng (eds.), *African linguistics across the disciplines: Selected papers from the 48th Annual Conference on African Linguistics*, 325–337. Berlin: Language Science Press. DOI:10.5281/zenodo.3520599

outside the sentence. (See e.g. Landau 2013 for a recent survey of the vast theoretical literature on control.)

(1)   (John$_1$ said that) **Bill$_2$** wants [PRO$_{*1/2/*3}$ to leave].

Cross-linguistic research has revealed a fair amount of variation in the syntax of control. Diverging from the pattern instantiated by English, some languages like Tsez (a Nakh-Daghestanian language spoken in northeast Caucasus) evidence BACKWARD CONTROL, wherein the controlled argument is overt and the controller is covert, as in (2).

(2)   Tsez (Nakh-Daghestanian; Polinsky & Potsdam 2002: 248)
      ∅   [**kid-bā**   ziya   b-išr-a]   y-oq-si.
      II.ABS girl.II-ERG COW.ABS III-feed-INF II-begin-PST.EVID
      'The girl began to feed the cow.'

Still other languages exhibit COPY CONTROL, wherein both the controller and the controlled argument are overtly represented, as in San Luis Quiaviní Zapotec, illustrated in (3).

(3)   San Luis Quiaviní Zapotec (Lee 2003: 102)
      R-càà'z   **Gye'eihlly** [g-auh **Gye'eihlly** bxaady].
      HAB-want Mike   IRR-eat Mike   grasshopper
      'Mike wants to eat grasshopper.'

Another pattern involves control of an overt anaphor, as found for example in Korean and illustrated in (4).

(4)   Korean (Madigan 2008: 237)
      Inho-ka   Jwuhi-eykey [**caki-ka** cip-ey   ka-keyss-ko]
      Inho-NOM Jwuhi-DAT   self-NOM home-LOC go-VOL-COMP
      yaksok-ha-yess-ta.
      promise-do-PST-COMP
      'Inho promised Jwuhi to go home.'

Finally, yet another pattern involves control of an overt nominative expression, which Szabolcsi (2009) has shown obtains in Hungarian under some conditions, as in (5).

(5) Hungarian (Szabolcsi 2009: 8)
Szeretnék   [csak **én** magas lenni].
would.like.1SG only I   tall   be.INF
'I want it to be the case that only I am tall.'

The focus of this paper is yet another pattern which is to our knowledge unattested in the control literature: control of an overt logophoric pronoun.[1] We argue that this happens in Gengbe, in sentences like (6).

(6) Gengbe (Elicitation)
(Kòfí₁ bé) **Ámá̃**₂ dʒí [bé **jè**_{*1/2/*3} lá dù nú].
Kofi   say Ama   want COMP LOG   POT eat thing
'(Kofi said that) Ama wants to eat.'

In what follows, after providing more background on Gengbe and our data collection (§2), we will show that control of logophors in Gengbe obtains only with some embedding predicates, and only with potential (as opposed to jussive) mood marking (§3). Then, in §4, drawing on relevant theoretical literature, we will sketch a formal semantic account of the observed facts wherein control complements denote properties (Chierchia 1984, Dowty 1985) and wherein there are two routes to propertyhood: (i) a logophoric subject (Pearson 2015) or (ii) jussive mood marking (Zanuttini et al. 2012). The upshot is a view of control as an emergent phenomenon; there is no "control construction" or "control pronoun" but rather several independent components of the grammar that interact to produce control under certain conditions for principled type-theoretic reasons. We conclude in §5.[2]

2 Background on Gengbe and our data collection

Gengbe (also known as *Gen* or *Mina*) is a Niger-Congo (Kwa) language closely related to Ewe and spoken in southern Togo and Benin. According to Ethnologue, it has 278,900 speakers worldwide. All Gengbe data reported in this paper were collected via elicitation sessions at Indiana University during 2014–2016 with Gabriel Mawusi, a native Gengbe speaker from Batonou, Togo. These sessions were conducted by Samson Lotven and supported by Professor Samuel Obeng.

---

[1]Landau (2015), for example, citing Culy (1994), says that overt logophoric pronouns are never found in control complements.
[2]The core data and analysis presented in this paper are reported also in Grano & Lotven (2018), where we focus on the implications of the Gengbe data for theories of mood.

3 Core data and puzzles

We begin with the observation that Gengbe has mood markers that are used to express future possibility and deontic necessity, respectively, as illustrated in (7) and (8). Following Essegbey (2008) on the cognate Ewe particle *a*, we label the former POT(ENTIAL), and following Ameka (2008) on cognate Ewe particle *ne*, we label the latter JUSS(IVE).

(7) Akú **lá** ḍù nǘ.
     Aku POT eat thing
     'Aku will/might eat.'

(8) Akú **nɛ́** ḍù nǘ.
     Aku JUSS eat thing
     'Aku should eat.'/'I want Aku to eat.'

Against this backdrop, the first puzzle we want to consider is that when embedded under *dʒí* 'want', (9) (with potential marking) results in an unacceptable sentence whereas (10) (with jussive marking) results in an acceptable sentence:

(9) * Ámǎ **dʒí** [bé Àkú **lá** ḍù nǘ].
     Ama want COMP Aku POT eat thing
     Intended: 'Ama wants Aku to eat.'

(10) Ámǎ **dʒí** [bé Àkú **nɛ́** ḍù nǘ].
     Ama want COMP Aku JUSS eat thing
     'Ama wants Aku to eat.'

At first glance, the puzzle in (9–10) seems familiar enough: in many languages, verbs that embed clausal complements can only combine with clauses that bear a particular mood. In Romance languages, for example, 'want' requires the subjunctive mood (see e.g. Palmer (2001) for an overview). Hence we might hypothesize that in Gengbe, *dʒí* 'want' requires jussive mood.

But additional data reveal that this cannot be the whole story. Gengbe has a logophoric pronoun *jè* which in sentences like (11–12) behaves like other logophoric pronouns reported in the literature: it must be anteceded by an attitude holder, and multiple embedding gives rise to an ambiguity in antecedent choice whereby any c-commanding attitude holder can serve as the antecedent (see e.g. Clements 1975; Pearson 2015).[3]

(11) **Ámǎ₁** kǎ_ḍó_é_dʒí [bé **jè₁/*₂** dù nǔ].
  Ama be.certain COMP LOG eat thing
  'Ama is certain that she (= Ama) ate.'

(12) **Kòfí₁** bé **Ámǎ₂** kǎ_ḍó_é_dʒí [bé **jè₁/₂/*₃** dù nǔ].
  Kofi say Ama be.certain COMP LOG eat thing
  'Kofi said Ama is certain that he/she (= Kofi/Ama) ate.'

This leads us to our second puzzle. When *jè* is embedded under *dʒí* 'want', both potential and jussive mood become acceptable in the embedded clause, but with consequences for antecedent choice. When the potential marker is used, the logophor can only be anteceded by the immediately higher subject, instantiating a control relation as illustrated in (13), whereas when the jussive marker is used, the logophor is obligatorily obviative with respect to the immediately higher subject and instead must be bound remotely, as illustrated in (14).

(13) **Kòfí₁** bé **Ámǎ₂ dʒí** [bé **jè*₁/₂/*₃ lá** dù nǔ].
  Kofi say Ama want COMP LOG POT eat thing
  'Kofi said Ama wants to eat.'   CONTROL

(14) **Kòfí₁** bé Ámǎ₂ **dʒí** [bé **jè₁/*₂/*₃ nɛ́** dù nǔ].
  Kofi say Ama want COMP LOG JUSS eat thing
  'Kofi said Ama wants him (= Kofi) to eat.'   OBVIATION

As expected given this second puzzle, if the desire reports in (13–14) appear unembedded, the former is grammatical and has an obligatory control interpretation (15), whereas the latter is simply ungrammatical (16): the logophor demands an antecedent, but the jussive marker forces obviation with respect to the only potential antecedent, leading to an irreconcilable conflict.

(15) **Ámǎ₁** dʒí [bé **jè₁/*₂ lá** dù nǔ].
  Ama want COMP LOG POT eat thing
  'Ama wants to eat.'

---

[3]We use underscores in *kǎ_ḍó_é_dʒí* 'be certain' to signal that it is morphologically complex, consisting of a verb *kǎ* 'cut' and a third-person singular pronoun *é* flanked by two adpositions *ḍó* 'at' and *dʒí* 'top'. An English gloss more faithful to this underlying structure would be 'count on it that ...'. We nonetheless gloss *kǎ_ḍó_é_dʒí* as 'be.certain' in the interest of perspicuity.

(16) *Ámɛ̃́ dʒí [bé jè **nɛ̃́** dù nṹ].
Ama want COMP LOG JUSS eat thing
Intended: 'Ama wants to eat.'

Other attitude predicates that pattern like *dʒí* 'want' with respect to this puzzle include *wɔ̀_súsú* 'intend' (*lit.:* 'do thought'), *dʒɛ̀_àgbàgbá* 'try' (*lit.:* 'do ability'), *lɔ̃* 'agree', and *fjɛ̂_dʒɔ̀gbè* 'pledge'.

In contrast with 'want' and the other attitude predicates just mentioned, the majority of attitude predicates do not behave likewise with respect to these puzzles; these predicates include *kɛ̃́_ɖó_é_dʒí* 'be certain', *ɲɛ̃́* 'know', *gblɔ̂* 'say', and *kúù_dɾĩ̌* 'dream' (*lit.:* 'die dream'). With these attitude predicates, complement clauses do not have to contain an overt mood marker (as already illustrated for 'be certain' in (11–12) above). And when they do contain an overt mood marker, both potential and jussive mood are compatible with a full-NP subject, as seen in (17–18). Furthermore, with a logophoric subject, potential marking gives rise to ambiguity in antecedent choice (19) whereas jussive marking patterns like it does for 'want' in forcing obviation (20).

(17) Kòfí bé Ámɛ̃́ **kɛ̃́_ɖó_é_dʒí** [bé Àkú lá dù nṹ].
Kofi say Ama be.certain COMP Aku POT eat thing
'Kofi said Ama is certain that Aku will eat.'

(18) Kòfí bé Ámɛ̃́ **kɛ̃́_ɖó_é_dʒí** [bé Àkú nɛ̃́ dù nṹ].
Kofi say Ama be.certain COMP Aku JUSS eat thing
'Kofi said Ama is certain that Aku should eat.'

(19) **Kòfí**₁ bé **Ámɛ̃́**₂ **kɛ̃́_ɖó_é_dʒí** [bé jè₁/₂ lá dù nṹ].
Kofi say Ama be.certain COMP LOG POT eat thing
'Kofi said Ama is certain that he/she (= Kofi/Ama) will eat.'

(20) **Kòfí**₁ bé Ámɛ̃́₂ **kɛ̃́_ɖó_é_dʒí** [bé jè₁/*₂ nɛ̃́ dù nṹ].
Kofi say Ama be.certain COMP LOG JUSS eat thing
'Kofi said Ama is certain that he (= Kofi) should eat.'

See Grano & Lotven (2018) for further discussion and analysis of this class of predicates. In what follows, we focus on the class exemplified by 'want'.

4 Toward an account

In (21), we illustrate a run-of-the-mill modal semantics for *want*-sentences modeled after Hintikka's (1969) influential approach to attitude reports, achieved compositionally via the denotation for *want* supplied in (22) and revised in (25) below. Here, WANT(x,w) denotes the set of worlds compatible with x's desires in w. This is no doubt an oversimplified view of the semantics of desire reports for reasons discussed in such works as Heim (1992), but it is sufficient for our purposes, where all that is crucial is that *want* denotes some kind of relation between individuals and propositions.

(21) [[John wants Bill to eat]]^w
    = $\forall w'[w' \in \text{WANT}(j,w) \rightarrow \text{EAT}(b) \text{ in } w']$
    ≈ 'All those worlds compatible with what John wants in w are worlds in which Bill eats.'

(22) [[want]]$^w = \lambda p_{\langle st \rangle} \lambda x. \forall w'[w' \in \text{WANT}(x,w) \rightarrow p(w')]$ Version 1/2

When we turn to control sentences like (23), on the other hand, we observe that the matrix subject *John* appears to play two roles semantically, naming both the attitude holder and the individual who eats in those worlds compatible with the attitude holder's desires. In other words, it has a denotation like (24).[4]

(23) John wants to eat.

(24) [[John wants to eat]]^w
    = $\forall w'[w' \in \text{WANT}(j,w) \rightarrow \text{EAT}(j) \text{ in } w']$
    ≈ 'All those worlds compatible with what John wants in w are worlds in which John eats.'

Borrowing an insight from Chierchia (1984) and Dowty (1985), we can achieve this compositionally with a revised semantics for *want* as in (25). Here, *want* denotes a relation between individuals and properties. When the individual x is plugged in, it values both the attitude holder and the unsaturated argument associated with the property.

(25) [[want]]$^w = \lambda P_{\langle e,st \rangle} \lambda x. \forall w'[w' \in \text{WANT}(x,w) \rightarrow P(x)(w')]$ Version 2/2

---

[4]Something not captured by the denotation in (24) and that we abstract away from since it is orthogonal to our purposes is that attitude reports expressed by control sentences have an obligatory *de se* semantics. See Stephenson 2010; Pearson 2015, 2016 for recent approaches.

Turning our attention back to Gengbe, we propose that *nɛ̃* 'juss' contributes an individual argument whereas *lá* 'pot' does not. As schematized in (26), this means that if the semantic type of an unmarked clause in Genge is proposition-denoting (type $\langle st \rangle$), a jussive-marked clause is property-denoting (type $\langle e, st \rangle$). Potential marking, by contrast, has no type-theoretic effect; a potential-marked clause is proposition-denoting.

(26) a. [Kofi eat]$_{\langle st \rangle}$ → [λx . Kofi JUSS eat]$_{\langle e,st \rangle}$

  b. [Kofi eat]$_{\langle st \rangle}$ → [Kofi POT eat]$_{\langle st \rangle}$

This is a natural extension of ideas developed by Portner (2004; 2007); Zanuttini et al. (2012) that imperative clauses (and jussive clauses more generally) are property-denoting rather than proposition-denoting. Intuitively, the individual argument introduced by the jussive marker can be thought of as the individual who bears the responsibility for bringing about the action named by the clause. See Grano & Lotven (2018) for further discussion.

With these proposals in place, the first part of the puzzle is now solved, provided Gengbe *dʒí* 'want' has the property-theoretic denotation in (25). As schematized in (27), when 'want' combines with a potential-marked clause, the result is a type mismatch, because 'want' needs to combine with a property-denoting complement and yet its complement is propositional. When 'want' combines with a jussive-marked clause, on the other hand, there is no problem, since jussive clauses are property-denoting.

(27) a. Ama want$_{\langle\langle e,st \rangle,\langle e,st \rangle\rangle}$ [Aku POT eat]$_{\langle st \rangle}$ ← *!

  b. Ama want$_{\langle\langle e,st \rangle,\langle e,st \rangle\rangle}$ [λx.Aku JUSS eat]$_{\langle e,st \rangle}$ ← ok!

In order to solve the second part of the puzzle, we need to say something about the semantic analysis of logophors. Following Heim (2002), von Stechow (2009; 2003), and Pearson (2015), we adopt the proposal that what distinguishes logophoric pronouns from ordinary pronouns is that logophors are obligatorily bound by an attitude predicate, thereby creating a derived property for the binding attitude predicate to combine with. As schematized in (28), this means that if a logophor is embedded under two attitude predicates, it can in principle be bound either by the immediately embedding attitude predicate or by the more distant one, but if it is not bound by either, the result is ungrammatical.[5]

---

[5] According to an anonymous reviewer, a logophor can be embedded under a non-attitude verb

(28) a. Kofi say [Ama **be.certain** [λx. [LOG$_x$ eat]]]   ← *ok!*

     b. Kofi **say** [λx. [Ama be.certain [LOG$_x$ eat]]]   ← *ok!*

     c. Kofi say [Ama be.certain [LOG$_x$ eat]]   ← **!*

This approach to logophors, together with the other proposals already introduced, are sufficient for solving the second part of the puzzle. To see this, consider (29–30). In (29), where the complement to 'want' has potential marking, local binding of the logophor is licit since this will yield the needed property-theoretic denotation for the complement to 'want', but remote binding is ruled out since it results in a proposition-denoting complement to 'want'. In (30) with jussive marking, by contrast, the opposite obtains: local binding of the logophor results in a type $\langle e, \langle e, st \rangle \rangle$ denotation for the complement to 'want', yielding a type mismatch, whereas remote binding of the logophor preserves the property-denoting status of the complement clause and is hence licit.

(29) a. Kofi say Ama [want$_{\langle\langle e,st\rangle,\langle e,st\rangle\rangle}$ [λx. LOG$_x$ POT eat]$_{\langle e,st\rangle}$]   ← *ok!*

     b. Kofi say [λx.Ama want$_{\langle\langle e,st\rangle,\langle e,st\rangle\rangle}$ [LOG$_x$ POT eat]$_{\langle st\rangle}$]   ← **!*

(30) a. Kofi say Ama [want$_{\langle\langle e,st\rangle,\langle e,st\rangle\rangle}$ [$\lambda x\lambda y$. LOG$_x$ JUSSNNN eat]$_{\langle e,\langle e,st\rangle\rangle}$] ←
         *!

     b. Kofi say [λx.Ama want$_{\langle\langle e,st\rangle,\langle e,st\rangle\rangle}$ [λy. LOG$_x$ JUSSNNN eat]$_{\langle e,st\rangle}$] ← *ok!*

---

as long as it appears in a clause introduced by the complementizer *be*, as in the following example supplied by the reviewer (using Ewe orthography but holding for Gengbe as well, according to the reviewer).

(i) Kofi yi Lome be   ye-a-*fle*   avɔ.
     Kofi go Lome COMP LOG-SUBJ-buy cloth

     'Kofi went to Lome to buy cloth.'

We note, however, the following example due to Pearson (2015) showing that logophors in Ewe cannot be embedded under a causative predicate even in the presence of the complementizer *be*.

(ii) Kofi wɔ be   e/*ye   dzo.
      Kofi do COMP 3SG/LOG leave

      'Kofi caused himself to leave.' (Pearson 2015:96)

In light of the asymmetry between (i) and (ii), we hypothesize that (i) may contain a silent attitude predicate that licenses the logophor; plausibly it has a meaning like 'intend' given that the rationale clause in (i) is paraphrasable as 'with the intention of buying cloth'.

Finally, consider what happens when the desire reports in (29–30) are unembedded. When potential marking is used as in (31), local binding of the logophor leads to type-theoretic well-formedness. The only other option is to leave the logophor unbound, which leads both to a type mismatch as well as to a violation of the constraint that logophors must be bound. When jussive marking is used as in (32), on the other hand, local binding of the logophor leads to a type mismatch and non-binding of the logophor violates the constraint that logophors must be bound. Thus we accurately predict ungrammaticality for such cases.[6]

(31) a. Ama [want$_{\langle\langle e,st\rangle,\langle e,st\rangle\rangle}$ [$\lambda x.$ LOG$_x$ POT eat]$_{\langle e,st\rangle}$] ← ok!

  b. Ama want$_{\langle\langle e,st\rangle,\langle e,st\rangle\rangle}$ [LOG$_x$ POT eat]$_{\langle st\rangle}$ ← *!

(32) a. Ama [want$_{\langle\langle e,st\rangle,\langle e,st\rangle\rangle}$ [$\lambda x\lambda y.$ LOG$_x$ JUSSNNN eat]$_{\langle e,\langle e,st\rangle\rangle}$] ← *!

  b. Ama want$_{\langle\langle e,st\rangle,\langle e,st\rangle\rangle}$ [$\lambda y.$ LOG$_x$ JUSSNNN eat]$_{\langle e,st\rangle}$ ← *!

In a nutshell, the observed interaction between mood choice and logophoric antecedent choice falls out automatically from familiar, previously proposed ideas about the type-theoretic effects of mood markers, logophors, and embedding verbs.[7]

5 Conclusions

Our central conclusions are twofold. First, on the empirical end, we have argued that Gengbe exhibits control of logophors under particular syntactic conditions in a way that depends on the choice of the embedding verb and on the mood

---

[6] An anonymous reviewer asks what happens when a non-logophoric pronoun is used in place of a logophoric pronoun in configurations in cases like (31–32). Unfortunately, we do not have data on this, but we can say a few words about what our theory predicts. Insofar as non-logophoric pronouns are distinct from logophoric pronouns in that they are *optionally* (as opposed to obligatorily) bound by attitude predicates, the prediction of our theory is that they should be grammatical both with potential marking (since they can be bound) and with jussive marking (since they need not be bound). That being said, Pearson (2015: 97) reports variation among Ewe speakers in whether they accept bound construals of non-logophoric pronouns. Possibly, rejection of a bound construal could be due to a kind of pragmatic blocking effect whereby the failure to use a logophor biases an interpreter toward a non-bound interpretation. If logophors force a *de se* construal then such a blocking effect would be nullified by setting up a non-*de se* context so that the logophor would not be a viable alternative; however, a central claim of Pearson (2015) is that logophors (at least in Ewe) need not be construed *de se*, *contra* the received wisdom.

[7] Another consequence of this approach is that 'be certain' and other predicates that pattern like it need to be type-theoretically flexible in being able to take either a property or a proposition as their first argument. See Grano & Lotven (2018) for illustration and further discussion.

marking in the clause containing the logophor. On the theoretical end, we have shown how to account for the relevant facts in a system whereby independently acting parts (verbs, logophors, and mood markers) interact with each other to give rise to control in certain combinations for principled type-theoretic reasons. As already alluded to in the introduction, one consequence of this system is a view of control as an "emergent" phenomenon: no single element in the structure of the sentence is responsible for control, it is only their interaction that ends up mattering.

If the type-theoretic principles that form the backbone of our proposal have wide cross-linguistic currency, why is control of logophors seemingly so rare? We suggest that this is because it depends on the convergence of two features that vary independently. First, not all languages have logophors to begin with, so for obvious reasons, only those languages that have logophors have the potential for control of logophors. Second, in many languages, verbs like 'want' that typically take control complements also typically tend to take structurally impoverished complements that preclude an overt subject. Gengbe, on the other hand, has both logophors and the syntax to support a logophor under a verb like 'want', thereby giving rise to the right conditions for the phenomenon to emerge.

Abbreviations

ABS	Absolutive	JUSS	Jussive
COMP	Complementizer	LOC	Locative
DAT	Dative	LOG	Logophor
ERG	Ergative	NOM	Nominative
EVID	Evidential	POT	Potential
HAB	Habitual	PST	Past
INF	Infinitive	VOL	Volitional
IRR	Irrealis	1/3SG	1st/3rd-person singular

Acknowledgements

Thanks first and foremost go to our Gengbe linguistic consultant Gabriel Mawusi. We also thank Samuel Obeng for supporting this research, and we thank audiences at the Indiana University Semantics Reading Group (August 2016), *Sinn und Bedeutung* 21 in Edinburgh (September 2016), and ACAL 48 at Indiana University (March 2017) for their feedback on the work presented here. Finally, thanks are due to two anonymous reviewers for helpful suggestions on an earlier version of this paper.

References

Ameka, Felix K. 2008. Aspect and modality in Ewe: A survey. In F. K. Ameka & M. E. Kropp Dakubu (eds.), *Aspect and modality in Kwa languages*, 135–194. Amsterdam: Benjamins.

Chierchia, Gennaro. 1984. *Topics in the syntax and semantics of infinitives and gerunds*. University of Massachusetts dissertation.

Clements, George N. 1975. The logophoric pronoun in Ewe: Its role in discourse. *Journal of West African Languages* 10. 141–177.

Culy, Christopher. 1994. Aspects of logophoric marking. *Linguistics* 32. 1055–1094.

Dowty, David R. 1985. On recent analyses of the semantics of control. *Linguistics and Philosophy* 8. 291–331.

Essegbey, James. 2008. The potential morpheme in Ewe. In F. K. Ameka & M. E. Kropp Dakubu (eds.), *Aspect and modality in Kwa languages*, 195–214. Amsterdam: Benjamins.

Grano, Thomas & Samson Lotven. 2018. Control, logophoricity, and harmonic modality in Gengbe desire reports. In Robert Truswell, Chris Cummins, Caroline Heycock, Brian Rabern & Hannah Rohde (eds.), *Proceedings of Sinn und Bedeutung 21*, 481–498.

Heim, Irene. 1992. Presupposition projection and the semantics of attitude verbs. *Journal of Semantics* 9. 183–221.

Heim, Irene. 2002. Features of pronouns in semantics and morphology. Handout of talk given at USC.

Hintikka, Jakko. 1969. Semantics for propositional attitudes. In J. W. Davis, D. J. Hockney & W. K. Wilson (eds.), *Philosophical logic*, 21–45. Dordrecht: Reidel.

Landau, Idan. 2013. *Control in generative grammar: A research companion*. Cambridge: Cambridge University Press.

Landau, Idan. 2015. Direct variable binding and agreement in obligatory control. ms., Ben Gurion University.

Lee, Felicia. 2003. Anaphoric R-expressions as bound variables. *Syntax* 6. 84–114.

Madigan, Sean William. 2008. *Control constructions in Korean*. University of Delaware dissertation.

Palmer, F. R. 2001. *Mood and modality*. 2nd edn. New York: Free Press.

Pearson, Hazel. 2015. The interpretation of the logophoric pronoun in Ewe. *Natural Language Semantics* 23. 77–118.

Pearson, Hazel. 2016. The semantics of partial control. *Natural Language & Linguistic Theory* 34. 691–738.

Polinsky, Maria & Eric Potsdam. 2002. Backward control. *Linguistic Inquiry* 33. 245–282.

Portner, Paul. 2004. The semantics of imperatives within a theory of clause types. In Robert B. Young (ed.), *Proceedings of SALT 14*, 235–252. Ithaca, NY: Cornell University.

Portner, Paul. 2007. Imperatives and modals. *Natural Language Semantics* 15. 351–383.

Stephenson, Tamina. 2010. Control in centred worlds. *Journal of Semantics* 27. 409–436.

Szabolcsi, Anna. 2009. Overt nominative subjects in infinitival complements: Data, diagnostics, and preliminary analyses. In Patricia Irwin & Violeta Vásquez Rojas Maldonado (eds.), *NYU working papers in linguistics: Papers in syntax*, vol. 2, 1–55. New York: NYU.

von Stechow, Arnim. 2003. Feature deletion under semantic binding. In M. Kadowaki & S. Kawahara (eds.), *Proceedings of NELS 33*, 133–157. Amherst, MA: GLSA Publications.

von Stechow, Arnim. 2009. Tenses in compositional semantics. ms.

Zanuttini, Raffaella, Miok Pak & Paul Portner. 2012. A syntactic analysis of interpretive restrictions on imperative, promissive, and exhortative subjects. *Natural Language & Linguistic Theory* 30. 1231–1274.

Name index

www.ingramcontent.com/pod-product-compliance
Lightning Source LLC
Chambersburg PA
CBHW050737110426
42814CB00006B/287